YEARS

SIMON &
SCHUSTER

ALSO BY STEPHEN BREYER

The Authority of the Court and the Peril of Politics

The Court and the World: American Law and the New Global Realities

Making Our Democracy Work: A Judge's View

Active Liberty: Interpreting Our Democratic Constitution

Breaking the Vicious Circle: Toward Effective Risk Regulation

Regulation and Its Reform

Judges in Contemporary Democracy (edited with Robert Badinter)

Administrative Law and Regulatory Policy (with Richard B. Stewart)

Energy Regulation by the Federal Power Commission (with Paul W. MacAvoy)

Reading the Constitution

Why I Chose Pragmatism, *Not* Textualism

STEPHEN BREYER

SIMON & SCHUSTER

New York   London   Toronto   Sydney   New Delhi

100 YEARS
SIMON &
SCHUSTER

1230 Avenue of the Americas
New York, NY 10020

First Simon & Schuster hardcover edition March 2024

SIMON & SCHUSTER and colophon are registered trademarks of Simon & Schuster, LLC

Simon & Schuster: Celebrating 100 Years of Publishing in 2024

For information about special discounts for bulk purchases, please contact Simon & Schuster Special Sales at 1-866-506-1949 or business@simonandschuster.com.

The Simon & Schuster Speakers Bureau can bring authors to your live event. For more information or to book an event, contact the Simon & Schuster Speakers Bureau at 1-866-248-3049 or visit our website at www.simonspeakers.com.

Interior design by Wendy Blum

Manufactured in the United States of America

1   3   5   7   9   10   8   6   4   2

Library of Congress Cataloging-in-Publication Data is available.

ISBN 978-1-6680-2153-8
ISBN 978-1-6680-2155-2 (ebook)

This book is dedicated to my colleagues on the Court: CJ Rehnquist, John, Sandra, Nino, Tony, David, Clarence, Ruth, CJ Roberts, Sam, Sonia, Elena, Neil, Brett, and Amy

Do not explain your philosophy. Embody it.

—Epictetus

CONTENTS

Preface: My Way   xv

PART I:
Purpose vs. Textualism

1. Purpose-Based Approaches   5
2. The Textualist Approach   16

PART II:
Interpreting Statutory Law

3. The Traditional Use of Text and Purpose   37
4. The Text/Purpose Divide   42
5. Static or Dynamic?   51
6. Consequences   63
7. Legislative History   68
8. Constitutional Values   89
9. Resolving the Text/Purpose Tension   94
10. Why Judges Should Consider Purposes: A Summary   104

PART III:
Interpreting the Constitution

11. The Constitution   114
12. The Traditional Approach to Constitutional Interpretation   117
13. Constitutional Textualism   124
14. When the Text Runs Out: The Limits of Constitutional Textualism   160
15. Legal Stability: *Stare Decisis*   181

PART IV:
Why Values, Purposes, and Workability Provide a Better Way to Interpret the Constitution

16. Workability: History and Practical Experience   197
17. Workability: Deciding Where Values Conflict   209
18. Workability: Direct Application of Basic Values   219

PART V:
Paradigm Shifts on the Court

19. Three Paradigm Shifts   231
20. Are We Undergoing the Next Paradigm Shift?   246

Conclusion   261
Acknowledgments   265
Author's Note   267
Notes   269
Index   323

Reading the Constitution

PREFACE

My Way

For forty-one years I have worked (for thirteen years) as a federal court of appeals judge and (for twenty-eight years) as a Justice of the United States Supreme Court. My job was interpreting statutes—that is, laws—and the Constitution. On the court of appeals, I reviewed the decisions of trial courts, and on the Supreme Court I reviewed the decisions of courts of appeals and state supreme courts. My work, like that of almost all federal appellate judges, has consisted primarily of reading documents and helping to decide what they mean and how they apply to facts before the Court in a particular case. Unlike trial court judges, who hear cases for the first time, appellate judges do not try cases and rarely review new evidence. Appellate judges are most often concerned with making sure that trial courts correctly interpreted and applied the law to the facts of the cases in front of them.

When I explain to a class of middle school students the nature of an appellate judge's job, I use an example drawn from a story I read in a French newspaper. A high school biology teacher was traveling on a train from Nantes to Paris. She had with her, in a wicker basket, twenty live snails. The train conductor asked her what was in the basket; she told him; and the conductor then said, "You must buy a ticket for the snails." "That's ridiculous," the teacher replied. "Well," said the conductor, "read the fare rules. They say, 'Passengers cannot bring animals on the train except in a basket, in which case they must buy a ticket for the animals.'" "But," protested the teacher, "it means dogs or cats or perhaps rabbits, not snails." "Doesn't it say 'animals,'" said the conductor, "and isn't a snail an animal?"

At this point I ask the class: Who is right? The class breaks up into fierce argument. "What about mosquitoes?" says one. "Why would they want you to pay for snails?" asks another. "But isn't a snail an animal?" says a third. I add, "There you have the interpretive job of an appellate judge. How do we find the 'right' answer?"

An appellate judge is unlikely to have to decide a case about train fares and snails. But the judge will often have to answer questions that take the same general form as the snail example. Do the words "endangered species" in a law apply to species of birds not known when Congress enacted the law? Does the Second Amendment's phrase "keep and bear arms" protect the right of individual citizens to keep a firearm in the home to protect against robbery? Questions of that form will often lead a judge to ask what, in general, is the best way to go about finding an answer.

In recent years, many scholars who write about judging and many judges themselves have emphasized the role of text in answering this kind of question. Many now say that judges should put primary weight, perhaps exclusive weight, on the text of the statute, as understood by an ordinary person. Indeed, one of my Supreme Court colleagues recently said (perhaps tongue in cheek) "We're all textualists now."[1]

But I am not.

Without ignoring the text, I normally put more weight on the statute's purposes and the consequences to which a particular interpretation will likely lead. I will sometimes ask how a (hypothetical) "reasonable legislator" would have interpreted the statute in light of its purposes. And I will sometimes examine the legislative history of a statute in order to answer these questions. I will approach and understand broad statutory or constitutional phrases in light of the values that underlie them—including notions of due process of law. I have, for example, argued that the Constitution in certain circumstances permits those who wish to exhibit monuments of the Ten Commandments to do so. The State of Texas exhibited a Ten Commandments monument on its state capitol grounds; the monument was attacked on the ground that it violated the Constitution's Establishment Clause, which forbids government from favoring or to some degree supporting religion. I thought that the clause did not forbid maintaining that particular monument, largely because it had been there for a long time without controversy. Given the monument's longevity, I feared that a contrary interpretation that required it to be taken down would produce friction and hostility among different religious groups—the kind of conflict that the Constitution seeks to prevent.[2] And I have argued in favor of a flexible interpretation of certain procedural statutes, for example, a statute that limited the time a state prisoner could ask a federal judge to review his conviction. I thought the courts should have the power to extend that limited time so that the law would ensure—consistent with Congress's intent—that those convicted of state crimes will have an opportunity to obtain a federal judge's review of their state conviction.[3]

That is not to say my purpose-oriented approach is merely a matter of choosing which outcome I believe to be best in any given case. I have, for instance, sided with a majority of the Court in affirming a death penalty sentence I believed undesirable and in denying the ability of an incarcerated person to bring a claim in federal court.[4] I did so not because I believed those outcomes best as a matter of policy. I did so because, in both instances, Congress had established legislation whose aims demanded that outcome. (It told the federal judge, for example, to leave in place a state court decision unless the state decision was "contrary to or involved an unreasonable application of, clearly established federal law, as determined by the Supreme Court").[5]

But by considering purposes, consequences, and values, I place less weight on the so-called plain meaning of a statute or the Constitution than do many of my textualist colleagues. And I do so to arrive at an interpretation that is more faithful to the desire of the Constitution's Framers to establish a workable framework for long-lasting government. The Constitution sets forth a structure and principles that aim to create and hold us together as a single nation for hundreds of years or more. I have approached the interpretive task with that fundamental objective in mind.

How have I come to my views? Like most of us, I am in part a product of my family background. I grew up in San Francisco in the late 1940s and 1950s. My father was the legal advisor to the San Francisco Board of Education for forty years. (I wear his retirement watch.) He was wise, kind, and always interested in the life of the city. He used to say that, to work for the school board, you had to know the answer to a question about geography: "Where is City Hall?" He also taught me a few basic lessons, including to "stay on the payroll," "do your job well and you will benefit (from satisfaction) even if you aren't promoted," and to "listen to others." And he loved working with others from the city's many different neighborhoods and communities to produce, in his words, a "better education for *all* the children."

My mother participated in various civic associations, such as the League of Women Voters, the United Nations Association, and several political campaigns. It is not surprising that words such as "community," "organization," "cooperation," and "civic life" have a positive association in my mind and in that of my brother (who is a federal trial court judge in San Francisco). Nor is it surprising that we would see law as an institution that, in part, seeks to make it easier for people to live together productively and freely in their communities.

My legal career reinforced these views. I was lucky. My first job after graduating from law school was working as a law clerk for Supreme Court Justice Arthur Goldberg. He was a practical man, and he saw law as a practical enterprise. His favorite quotation was from Shakespeare: "The time of life is short! / To spend that shortness basely were too long / If life did ride upon a dial's point, / Still ending at the arrival of an hour."[6] I worked too for Archibald Cox when he ran the Watergate Special Prosecution Force. He was an intelligent, competent, and above all, completely honest civil servant. And I twice worked in the Senate for Senator Ted Kennedy. The first time, I organized and ran a set of subcommittee hearings on airline regulation. The second time, I served as chief counsel of the Senate Committee on the Judiciary (Senator Kennedy was the chairman). The senator firmly believed that most senators, including senators of different parties, had in common the fact that they hoped to achieve a better America—though they often had different ideas of just what that "better America" might be. His object: work together with those who agree and those who disagree to produce a result that will benefit Americans. These jobs helped me associate "law" with honesty and with working together toward practical and beneficial goals.

The views I take about interpreting law also reflect those of my law school professors, for example, Henry Hart, Albert Sacks, and Lon Fuller. Each of these professors was an expert on interpreting the law. Lon Fuller taught and wrote about jurisprudence, the philosophy of law. Henry Hart taught about federal courts and wrote a famous book on that subject. Albert Sacks was his collaborator and later dean of Harvard Law School. Each of them viewed interpretation as a search for an outcome that was faithful to the objectives of the legislators who enacted it, and would rely on a wide range of interpretive tools to get there. Their approaches, in turn, reflect those that Chief Justice John Marshall set forth in *McCulloch v. Maryland*. In that case, the Chief Justice explains that "it is a *Constitution*" that we are interpreting and that Constitution is designed to create a workable system of government that is to last for decades, perhaps centuries. I shall discuss the case later at some length.[7] They are traditional views in that many eighteenth- and nineteenth-century judges used those approaches when interpreting difficult statutory (or constitutional) phrases.

Twentieth-century judges used them, too. Those judges include such luminaries as Justices Oliver Wendell Holmes, Louis Brandeis, Benjamin Cardozo, and Felix Frankfurter. Justice Cardozo's book *The Nature of the Judicial Process* instructs a judge first to look to see whether a definite rule or precedent requires a particular decision in the case at issue.[8] If not, the judge will look to the history of that case, asking precisely why the issue it presents has come before the court, and consider traditional ways of handling that issue. And the judge will want to know if a contemplated decision will conform to prevailing notions of fairness and sound public policy.[9] Similarly, Justice Frankfurter wrote that legislation (and I would add the Constitution, too) has an aim: "[I]t seeks to obviate some mischief, to supply an inadequacy, to effect a change of policy."[10] And Justice Holmes made clear that a law's "general purpose is a more important aid" to judicial reasoning "than any rule which grammar or formal logic may lay down."[11] Each of these judges approached statutory interpretation with purposes, consequences, and values front of mind.

If my approach to interpreting the law is traditional, as I think it is, then why am I writing this book? The reason lies in the growth and popularity among many judges, lawyers, and others in the legal community of an approach to interpretation that is, or may become, very different. When interpreting a text, every judge will read that text and will recognize that, at the least, its words limit the scope of a proper interpretation. The word "fish" in a statute does not mean "fowl." But some judges adopt a form of interpretation, sometimes called "textualism," which in many difficult cases places more interpretive weight upon the text (or in some circumstances, other linguistic considerations that supplement the text) than I believe, and others have long believed, is appropriate.[12] Those following textualism will often prioritize the so-called original public meaning of words, which is the meaning that an ordinary speaker of English would attribute to those words at the time they were written. In constitutional cases, this approach leads to the interpretive method called "originalism," which will try to put determinative weight upon the meaning given a constitutional text by the Constitution's Founders or by their contemporaries.[13]

Those following a textualist or originalist view of interpretation may ask only a handful of closely related questions, including, for example: What do the words of the statute or the Constitution literally mean?[14] What did their authors linguistically mean or what did the public take the words to mean at the time Congress enacted the statute or the states adopted the Constitution?[15]

Of course, a judge must consult the text and understand the text as limiting or helping to explain the scope of the statutory phrase. But I have learned over and over again that *text is but one interpretive tool among many.* And I fear the current enthusiasm for widespread adoption of more purely textual or linguistic approaches to interpretation means that other equally or more important tools will be set aside. It is as if an artist were to try to paint with only half a palette.

As the examples I provide in Parts II and III will show, this trend in statutory and constitutional interpretation may make more difficult (or may seriously undercut) the law's ability to achieve its basic objectives. It underestimates the difficulty of writing legal phrases with more than proximate precision.[16] It wrongly treats many of those phrases as statements describing the world rather than as words that perform (often technical) legal functions.[17] It may make it more difficult for the legislator to perform a constitutionally delegated legislative function.[18] It may increase the difficulty for the public to hold legislators democratically responsible.[19] Purely textual interpretations of statutes may produce undesirable consequences at the expense of more desirable consequences that the statutes' authors intended. Purely originalist interpretations of the Constitution may create a less workable Constitution, diminishing its ability to hold together over time a nation now of 332 million people seeking to put into practice the Constitution's democratic, humane values. In addition to these costs, I do not believe that textualism or originalism will achieve their own often articulated objectives: making law more definite and simpler to understand, while avoiding a judge's temptation to substitute the judge's own ideas about what is "good" for what the law in fact demands. I shall explain through examples why I fear these consequences. And I shall illustrate the virtues of what I believe is a more traditional method of interpretation, as well as the pitfalls that lurk beneath a more strictly textualist or originalist method.

In explaining how I interpret statutory and constitutional language, I shall minimize the extent to which I make theoretical arguments. I shall mention, but not dwell upon, the theoretical problems I see, for example, in "textualism" or the theoretical virtues I find in what some scholars call "purposivism" (a word that simply describes a purpose-oriented approach to interpretation[20]) or legal "pragmatism." Many scholars have written at length about these subjects in terms of their academic drawbacks or virtues.[21] Rather, I shall mostly describe cases in which I have participated—cases that illustrate why, and how, I have used what one might call "purpose-oriented" or "pragmatic" approaches. And I shall explain why, in those cases, I have rejected the more "textual-based" approaches that several of my colleagues have embraced.

I should like to remind the reader that I am, and have been, a working judge. And, I should like the reader to keep in mind how that fact influences the interpretive approach that I have taken.

A judge must make decisions, often fairly quickly, always within a limited time. A judge has no room to dither or try to determine what approach to take where. The matter is to some degree inevitably instinctive. Moreover, an appellate court judge works with colleagues. The judge must take account of their views. And the judge must remember that those whom the decision has affected or will affect are normally far more interested in what a *court* says than in what an individual member of that court says, no matter how well written (or reasoned) that member's separate (dissenting or concurring) opinion may be.

Further, a Supreme Court Justice will normally keep in mind the fact that the Supreme Court itself is a special legal institution, not only in that it typically speaks the last word as to the meaning of the Constitution, but also in that it must consider how Americans will understand what the Court is saying and how they will act in response. How far should a Court's determination extend? What can the Court decide in *this* case that will help implement the holding (say the unlawfulness of segregation) that it has set forth in earlier cases? To what extent should a judge write an opinion in language that to the reader will seem technical? To what extent can a judge write an opinion that will deliver a "message" that stretches beyond the law?

In a recent case, for example, the Court had to decide whether a school could suspend an angry cheerleader from a sports team because, *outside school hours*, she had sent messages from a coffee shop to school classmates with vulgar expressions, such as "f**k school."[22] The Court held that the First Amendment protected even the student's vulgar speech uttered outside class hours. But, in explaining that result, the Court also had to explain why the First Amendment allowed a school to regulate student speech, even some after-school speech, in other circumstances. How did the Court justify its conclusion that the school had gone too far in this particular case? The Court used (among other things) a metaphor and general language to convey a message about the school's duties as an institution in a democratic society:

The school itself has an interest in protecting a student's unpopular expression, especially when the expression takes place off campus. America's public schools are the nurseries of democracy. Our representative democracy only works if we protect the "marketplace of ideas." This free exchange facilitates an informed public opinion, which, when transmitted to lawmakers, helps produce laws that reflect the People's will. That protection must include the protection of unpopular ideas, for popular ideas have less need for protection. Thus, schools have a strong interest in ensuring that future generations understand the workings in practice of the well-known aphorism "I disapprove of what you say, but I will defend to the death your right to say it."[23]

Was this the right language, the right style, the right quotation, the right tone to express the "message" the Court intended the paragraph to carry?[24] No treatise answers questions like these. The language in part reflects the values that a judge holds.

The nature of the Court's "institutional" role and just how individual opinions should reflect that role are matters that vary from time to time, from issue to issue, from judge to judge. My Supreme Court predecessor Harry Blackmun told me many years ago, "You will find this an unusual assignment." And when, on occasion, he would come by my office (formerly his) for a cup of coffee, he made clear that the practical nature of the job, the openness of the questions, the different views held firmly by different members of the Court, the need to try for compromise, the importance of writing in a way that the general public can understand, all made the job "unusual." He was right.

Three more general descriptions of law and judging have influenced the way I approach interpretive questions. The oldest of these comes from Montaigne, written in 1584. In his essay "On Experience," he points out that human life itself is far more capacious, filled with far more incidents, subject to more vicissitudes, unexpected and unforeseeable events and consequences, than human beings writing a set of laws could possibly cover. Centuries ago, he warned us against trying to capture the infinite varieties of human experience within the confines of any single set of laws. Referring to the detailed Code of the Roman emperor Justinian, he argued that an effort to do so will lead to a lengthy, complex set of codes, filled with words. And nearly every word will prove to be a potential subject for legal dispute. He argued in favor of lawmakers' use of standards, approaches, norms, rather than highly detailed codified provisions. He added that he would prefer to live in a country with no laws at all than in France, which, he thought, had far too many.[25]

Montaigne believed that a legal system had to account for the fact that while the human experience changes, the text of the law does not. One of the great pleasures, and challenges, of being a judge is the task of applying old laws to new circumstances. Who could have imagined, for example, that a man attempting to block the City of Riviera Beach from demolishing its port to make way for a housing development would become part of a dispute in which the city contended that his stationary houseboat, with French doors and flowers decorating the windows, was a "vessel" subject to admiralty jurisdiction? (He won.)[26] And who could have predicted that the ancient writ of *habeas corpus* would be invoked by military prisoners detained as "enemy combatants" at a naval base on the tip of Cuba? (They won too.)[27] Or that the Privileges and Immunities Clause of the Constitution, which was designed to "serve the essential role of fusing the several states into one nation," would two centuries later form the basis of a suit by a Vermont attorney who alleged that New Hampshire's residency requirements for bar admission discriminated against nonresidents? (She lost.)[28]

Cases like these are the norm, not the exception. Consequently, judges should heed Montaigne's wisdom and beware of creating too many detailed black-and-white, clear-cut rules that are broad in application. Such rules give an impression of certainty; one either follows the rule or one does not. But too many general rules set forth in judicial opinions can, when applied throughout a nation, run up against obstacles, cause problems, generate unforeseen consequences, and lead the law away from the basic objective of a statute or constitutional provision. That fact does not mean opinions should not embody broad rules; they will sometimes prove necessary and helpful. But it does mean that judges, through interpretation without adequate thought, can too often go too far too fast. Of course, judges typically must resolve the dispute before them; resolving disputes is one of law's basic purposes. Regardless, it is experience, not a treatise, that is more likely to help a judge determine whether a decision that resolves a dispute should be written in a broad or narrow way.

Along with experience comes a quality I would call "judicial instinct." I would not go as far as the so-called legal realists, who believed that judgments were irreducibly tethered to subjective policymaking. Emblematic of this view is Judge Jerome Frank, who wrote, "Judging begins . . . with a conclusion . . . and afterwards tries to find premises which will substantiate it."[29] It is romance, not practice, to believe that judicial decisions are based "on a perspicacious flash termed the 'judicial hunch,'"[30] and that "whatever produces the judge's hunches makes the law."[31] Lord Coke's phrase is closer to the truth when he says that "[r]eason is the life of the law."[32] But Holmes is yet closer to what I have found when he writes that it is a "fallacy" to believe that "the *only* force at work in the development of the law is logic. . . . Behind the logical form lies a judgment as to the relative worth and importance of competing legislative grounds, often an inarticulate and unconscious judgment."[33]

Law is not science. And high praise for a judge is not praise along the lines of "intelligent," "hardworking," "energetic," or "good stylist." It is often a greater compliment to say that a judge's opinions are "sound." And what is a sound opinion? What is a sound judge? One experienced judge writes that the term encompasses certain qualities of mind, such as "a sense of proportion,"[34] an understanding of "fit," including the ability to understand the relation between wrong and remedy, a tendency to ask what will happen next, and a gift for finding creative solutions.[35] It includes certain qualities of character, namely an ability to gauge in advance the reactions of others, a sense of calm or self-discipline allowing the judge to emphasize reason over emotion, a willingness to make decisions perhaps on incomplete information, an instinct for order, and a seriousness of purpose. These qualities have long been valued in our society. The preface of the Book of Common

Prayer "speaks of that happy mean between too much stiffness in refusing and too much easiness in admitting variation in things once advisedly established."[36] And Thomas Jefferson said of George Washington, "His mind was great and powerful, without being of the very first order; his penetration strong, tho' not so acute as that of a Newton, Bacon or Locke; [but] as far as he saw, no judgment was ever sounder. It was slow in operation, being little aided by invention or imagination, but sure in conclusion."[37]

Judges aspire to these virtues. They can employ legal approaches that, they hope, will help them along the way. But there is no single approach that sets forth an all-purpose solution. Judge Learned Hand analogized a judge's work interpreting statutes to that of a musician playing a musical score. He wrote, "[T]he meaning of a sentence may be more than that of the separate words, as a melody is more than the notes."[38] The musician must remain true to the composer's creation. Certain approaches will help, but ultimately one must combine them with the performer's own talents, abilities, and creativity. Approaches, not outcome-determining theories, are, I believe, what we search for when judges perform their judicial interpretive tasks. As Justice Frankfurter once advised, interpreting a statute is not "a ritual to be observed by unimaginative adherence to well-worn professional phrases." Instead, "[t]he purpose" of interpretation "being the ascertainment of meaning, every consideration brought to bear for the solution of that problem must be devoted to that end alone."[39]

The approaches that I believe are traditional will help us when we interpret statutes and constitutional phrases. They fall within a tradition that the Constitution's Framers saw as highly practical. That tradition sees legal interpretation as an activity that is basically pragmatic, undogmatic, and adaptive. It sees law, including constitutional law, as an untidy body of understandings among groups and institutions, inherited from the past and open to changes, mostly at the edges. It is a tradition that communicates its vision, not through the application of any single theory but through detailed study of cases, institutions, history, and the human needs that underlie them. Its practice requires learning, sensitivity, and dedication.[40] The opinions I describe in this book will help overall to communicate this vision of the law through thought and analysis, through a degree of aesthetic coherence, and by reflecting an awareness of the variety of the human needs and relationships that have called forth our American institutions.

The approaches that I have just described are often more complex to apply than textualism and originalism. Perhaps what appears to be simpler, what holds out the promise of a single "right" interpretive answer, what is touted as a way to prevent a judge from substituting what the judge believes is "good" for the "correct" legal interpretation—perhaps all this helps account for the fact that textualism and originalism have gained considerable favor among many judges, many legal scholars, and lawyers as well. Sometimes I fear that a tidal wave of nearly pure textualism is just offshore. But experience suggests that interpreting legal phrases must often be more complex than Justice Owen Roberts once suggested, namely that the "judicial branch of the government has only one duty; to lay the article of the Constitution which is invoked beside the statute which is challenged and to decide whether the latter squares with the former."[41] I have written this book in large part to show the reader why that is not so, and why the many promises of textualism and originalism often are not, or cannot be, realized. I do so desiring that the next generation or two of law students will learn about and understand the more traditional approaches to interpretation. In that way, I hope to contribute to the effort to slow the tidal wave.

A word as to style: Judge John Wisdom was one of the great judges of the federal Fifth Circuit, which helped to desegregate the South. When I first became a judge, he told me that when I, as an appellate court judge, received and strongly disagreed with a draft from one of my colleagues, I should sit down and write a strong dissent, not sparing emotion, perhaps containing subtle insults, and certainly complaining fiercely (in language that the reader would notice) about how wrong that decision was. "Then," he added, "read it, tear it up, throw it in the waste basket, and start again, this time to write a judicial, i.e., a judge's, dissent." I have tried to follow that stylistic advice generally, and I shall try to do so here.

Much of this book will focus on my experience as a judge interpreting statutes and the Constitution. Because statutory phrases are typically less abstract and more detailed than constitutional phrases, it is more tempting to believe that focusing upon text alone in the statutory context will produce precise answers, permitting less subjective judicial leeway. I intend to show that, in fact, reliance upon textualism will not achieve the advantages for which its users hope and that such reliance instead threatens to produce a less workable legal system. As to the Constitution, I intend to show that similar disadvantages flow from originalism and an approach that often accompanies originalism: a strong preference for creating broad, black-and-white, clear-cut rules. These methods will not help achieve the goals of those who write statutes or those who wrote and adopted the Constitution: to create laws that work well—workable laws—that will in practice help those communities that the laws affect live together peacefully and productively.[42]

This book's organization in a general sense mirrors what I often tell students about a career in the law: that career asks you to exercise both your head and your heart. Everyone has a heart; but not everyone has a good head. The first half of the book focuses on statutes and is often technical. It asks the lawyer or judge to use his or her head, i.e., logic and thought, though heart is present too. The second part of the book focuses on the Constitution, and, because values predominate here, one's heart plays a bigger role (though of course, one's head matters as well). Metaphorically speaking, the book puts intellectually difficult statutory questions first. What the reader learns there should help the reader understand and evaluate the more value-laden constitutional questions that follow.

The book will proceed in five parts. In Part I, I briefly describe textualism, on the one hand, and the traditional approach of emphasizing purpose (which scholars of the subject almost uniformly call "purposivism"[43]), on the other. I will additionally describe a few reasons why I find textualism and its cousin originalism not very helpful. Part I also briefly summarizes, to a greater extent than the rest of the book, some of the theoretical reasons that scholars have advanced in favor or against particular methods of interpreting statutes and the Constitution.

In Part II, I provide examples of cases requiring judicial interpretation of statutes. I emphasize cases in which I have participated. They will show the reader just how some Justices have followed a textual approach while others have followed a more traditional, purpose-oriented approach. The examples will help the reader understand why, in general, I find the latter approach more likely to help produce a system of workable laws that better achieves the laws' objectives.

In Part III, I refer to cases that require judges to interpret the Constitution. Again, the cases provide examples in which some Justices have followed a textualist or originalist path; others have emphasized purposes and values. The cases will illustrate why I do not believe that textualism and originalism are desirable methods for interpreting the Constitution. And I shall illustrate and explain why I believe purpose-oriented or value-oriented methods are preferable.

In Part IV, I illustrate the importance and usefulness of recalling that the Founders meant the Constitution to work well perhaps for centuries to come. Chief Justice John Marshall explained that clearly two centuries ago in *McCulloch v. Maryland*. I shall use examples to show how his notion of constitutional "workability" can help contemporary judges reach sound decisions in constitutional cases.

Finally, in Part V, I speculate about what will happen next. Have textual methods become too deeply embedded in the judicial enterprise for the more traditional interpretive methods that I describe to win the day? I cannot be certain. But, perhaps this book's description of other nonexclusive tools of interpretation will help to convince some that they point the way to a better interpretive path.

And, if that better-taken path is ignored? In the ninth century, a group of monks on the Island of Iona, led by Saint Columba, produced the Book of Kells, a beautifully illustrated volume, which one can see to this day at Trinity University in Dublin. There are those who believe that the monks produced this book because they thought a great darkness had fallen over Europe and the Book of Kells could preserve a ray of light. This book is not the Book of Kells, but, in my more pessimistic moments as I write, I think of those monks.[44]

Reading the Constitution

I

PURPOSE VS. TEXTUALISM

Judges have traditionally used a variety of tools to help them determine the proper interpretation of the language of statutes and of the Constitution. These have included text, history, precedent, tradition, purposes, values, and consequences relevant to those purposes.[1] These are not all the interpretive tools a judge might use, and I discuss other related tools below. For now, I repeat the words of Chief Justice Marshall, that "[w]here the mind labours to discover the design of the legislature, it seizes every thing from which aid can be derived."[2] Aside from first reading the text itself, there is no specified rank order among these tools. Which of these many tools proves more helpful depends upon the particular case.

Thus the train conductor in our earlier example (were he a judge interpreting a statute) might ask whether railroad officials, when writing the fare book, really meant the word "animals" to include all animals, even a chameleon? If not chameleons, why snails? What is the provision's objective or purpose? What is the mischief it seeks to avoid? To keep larger animals off the train? And, what are the consequences of applying the word to small animals such as hamsters or snails?

Judges have long differed in the importance they tend to attach to some of these tools compared with others. Some judges, when they interpret statutes or the Constitution, place greater weight on the text and related linguistic features.[3] Other judges place greater weight on a statutory or constitutional phrase's purposes.[4]

But experience tells me that all judges will use most of these different tools at one time or another. Which they use and how much weight they place upon them depends upon the particular statutory or constitutional phrase at issue and the words that make up the statutory context surrounding the phrase.

Recently, the differences between "textualist" judges and "purpose-oriented" judges have become more pronounced. Many judges, legal scholars, and practicing lawyers will say that they are textualists and mean by that that they look primarily, perhaps exclusively, to a phrase's text to find its proper interpretation or application.[5] Other judges will maintain that they are more "traditionalist," meaning they are "purpose-oriented" and will use some or all of the tools to which I have referred.[6]

Throughout the book I consider the merits of these different approaches by examining them from the perspective of my many years as a practicing judge. I use cases as examples. And those case examples will help explain why I believe that the textualist approach, particularly in its more text-exclusive versions, is an undesirable way to interpret legal text. Still, in laying out these case examples, I have endeavored also to present the textualist perspective, and I hope thereby to allow the reader ultimately to make up his or her own mind.

But before I turn to case examples, I examine some basic tenets of the traditionalist and textualist approaches, to help us start on common ground.

1.

Purpose-Based Approaches

The basic purpose-related tool is the question "why?" Why did Congress or the Constitution's Framers choose these words? What purposes do they serve in this statute or constitutional provision? What purposes does this legal provision serve in our nation? How will my interpretation further (or create an obstacle to achieving) those purposes? By "purposes," I call to mind Justice Frankfurter's observation that "laws are not abstract propositions. They are expressions of policy arising out of specific situations and addressed to the attainment of particular ends."[1] They have "an aim." They seek "to obviate some mischief, to supply an inadequacy, to effect a change of policy, to formulate a plan of government."[2] A purpose-oriented judge will ask: What does this phrase seek to do? And how? And to quote Justice Holmes again, a law's "general purpose is a more important aid to the meaning than any rule which grammar or formal logic may lay down."[3]

I should like the reader to keep in mind three highly general features of these approaches. First, purpose-based approaches are often closely entwined with the "common law" mode of judging, which proceeds case by case, often resolving new questions based upon the particular facts of new cases. In addition, purpose-based approaches are firmly rooted in judicial pragmatism, which accounts for how a particular legal decision will affect other legal rules and principles as well as the lives of those who fall within their scope. And finally, a judge focused on purpose will often consult a hypothetical "reasonable legislator" to determine how a statute serves broader democratic ends.

Purpose-based approaches will sometimes, but not always, make it easier for judges to benefit from what some have called the "experimental" methods of the common law.[4] In principle, the "common law" refers to that body of law that has developed through judicial decisions rather than through statutes. There are not many judges today who work directly with the common law. In many states, subjects such as contracts, property, and torts, once the common law's domain, take the form of rules contained in statute books.[5] Almost every state, for example, has adopted the Uniform Commercial Code, a statutory code that governs commercial transactions.[6]

Common law methods, however, remain with us, particularly when judges approach a difficult problem of statutory interpretation.[7] The common law often proceeded example by example. It focused heavily upon the facts of the particular case before the court; and it left for later legal development or articulation the precise characteristics of the legal rule that might grow out of the case. Justice Cardozo described the common law as working "inductive[ly]," drawing "its generalizations from particulars." He quoted others as pointing out that the "rules and principles" of common law cases are not "final truths" but are "working hypotheses."[8] By way of contrast, statutes, because they set forth rules, encourage judges to state their interpretation of a statutory phrase in the form of a broader, black-and-white, clear-cut rule. And the resulting rule may well go beyond the facts of the particular case before the judge.

That is not always so. A judge, interpreting a statute, can write an opinion that decides the case narrowly, not broadly. The breadth of the holding, i.e., the breadth of the rule of law it sets forth, is itself a matter for judicial decision. And there is no treatise that tells the judge when to express a holding narrowly, rather than broadly. Suppose that we know the purpose of the statutory words "prison officials" is to achieve a fairer system of punishment within a prison. We might then apply the statute to the "official" before us, say a prison guard, without deciding who the other officials are to whom it applies. If so, we will decide the case narrowly or by using the facts of the case as an example. We can tailor the holding to the statute's purpose, while leaving the full scope of the language to be fleshed out or decided in future cases. Common law decisions often exhibited similar, incremental characteristics.[9]

Here is another example to illustrate the common law's incremental approach. In the 2020 case of *County of Maui v. Hawaii Wildlife Fund*,[10] which involved the Clean Water Act, the Supreme Court divided on a similar question (6–3; I authored the majority opinion for six Justices, including Chief Justice John Roberts, and Justices Ruth Bader Ginsburg, Sonia Sotomayor, Elena Kagan, and Brett Kavanaugh): To what extent should the Court have left aspects of the problem before it to be decided in future cases?

County of Maui focuses upon a federal environmental statute. The relevant part of that statute is clear as to its basic purpose. It says that the act seeks "to restore and maintain the integrity of . . . the Nation's waters."[11] The act then uses statutory definitions designed to help achieve this objective. First, the act defines a "pollutant." And it does so broadly. A "pollutant" is, among many other things, "discarded equipment," "sand," "solid waste," "incinerator residue," and even "heat."[12] It then defines "discharge of a pollutant." That "discharge" includes "any addition of any pollutant," "from any *point source*," "to navigable waters,"[13] such as streams, rivers, even the ocean. But what is a "point source"? A "point source" is "any discernible, confined and discrete conveyance . . . from which pollutants are or may be discharged," such as a "container," a "pipe," a "ditch," a "tunnel," a "conduit," even a "well."[14] The act then says that it is illegal to "discharge" any "pollutant" without a federal government permit.[15] So, you need a permit to "discharge" just about anything bad (for the water) from a "point source" (which is just about anything) into navigable waters.

But what happens if a prospector in Colorado throws his shaving water (containing whiskers and bits of soap) on the ground where it mixes with groundwater (which is, essentially, nonnavigable, underground water), travels some distance as part of an underground stream, and eventually reaches the ocean? Has the prospector discharged shaving cream (a "pollutant") from a "point source" into navigable waters? Does he need a federal permit? Or what happens, and this is what the actual Supreme Court case was about, if a sewage treatment plant in Hawaii discharges some sewage into the ground, where it mixes with groundwater, and the entire mixture after traveling through the ground eventually reaches the Pacific Ocean? Does the sewage plant need an EPA "permit" in order to discharge the sewage into the ocean, a "navigable water"?[16]

The Court held that the plant may need a federal permit.[17] But why would it need this permit? After all, the sewage mixed with lots of groundwater and traveled underground a considerable distance before it arrived at the navigable water.

The Court said that the simple fact that the sewage mixed with groundwater could not, by itself, make a difference under the statute. Otherwise a polluter could send the pollution through a pipe that ended, say fifty feet in the air above, or fifty feet on the sand next to, a navigable stream. The pollution would mix with the air or sand before ending up in the stream. Surely that fact—that the pollutant enters the water in the form of a mixture—does not suddenly mean "no permit needed."[18] But if that is right, then what about the prospector whose shaving cream or whiskers mix with groundwater and travel, not fifty feet, but hundreds of miles before entering the sea? Must he get a permit? Does the distance the mixture travels make all the difference?

In this context, a broad and rigid rule could lead to extreme consequences. On the one hand, to hold that distance *does not matter* would require nearly everyone (even the Colorado prospector) to obtain a federal permit. On the other hand, to hold that distance *does matter* means that the Court must decide how much distance makes a difference.

What to do? The Court reached a compromise that drew heavily from the common law method. Rather than adopt either extreme, the Court decided that a permit was needed if the addition of the pollutants through groundwater "is the *functional equivalent* of a *direct discharge* from the point source into navigable waters."[19] The Court added some considerations that would help lower courts determine when the "functional equivalent" standard applied. They included, for example, the length of underground travel, its duration, and its having mixed with other nonpolluted water.[20] And the Court offered a few examples to guide future cases: discharges (say of tons of incinerator residue) that fall five feet through the air between pipe and sea would still need a permit; discharges that travel underground for fifty miles over the course of several years would not.[21] But the Court did not say much more than that. Rather, it set forth the "functional equivalent" standard, and it left the application of that general standard to the lower courts and to the federal environmental agencies to develop and to apply in the future. In leaving room for future development, the Court recognized the usefulness of the "traditional common-law method"—even in "an era of statutes." That method encourages "making decisions that provide examples" over time, which in turn can "lead to ever more refined principles."[22]

Not surprisingly, three Justices, including some who favored a textualist approach, dissented. The standard is far too vague, said one. What does "functional equivalent" mean? The environmental agencies and the lower courts will not be able to figure that out. The result will be uncertainty. Sometimes a sewage plant with a discharge pipe that terminates just before the water's edge will fall within the statute's scope; sometimes it will not.[23]

One Justice who often favors textualism, Clarence Thomas, thought that the majority had not tried hard enough to find a more precise meaning in the words of the statute. His opinion pointed to the word "addition."[24] (Recall that a "discharge" is "any addition of any pollutant" to navigable waters from a "point source."[25]) He wrote that the word "addition" means that "the statute" does not apply to "anything other than a direct discharge."[26] When a pollutant drops into groundwater from, say a pipe, it has been *added to* the groundwater *from* the pipe (a "point source"[27]); but when the pollutant travels with the groundwater to the sea, it has been *added to* the sea *from* the *groundwater*, not *from* the pipe. And groundwater is not a point source.[28]

The basic problem with this approach, the majority thought, was that it created too broad and precise a rule to govern future cases. What if a polluter terminates its pipes fairly close to a river (or any other navigable water), allowing the pollutant to flow into the river along with groundwater, thereby obviating the need for a permit? That result would obviously undercut the basic purpose of the statute.[29] And that is the general point I wish to make here. The Court's decision basically shows a division between those who put greater weight on purposes (and are willing to tolerate greater openness and uncertainty lest an interpretation seriously undercut an important statutory purpose) and those who fear that openness. The latter group would embrace complex interpretations of language in order to avoid openness and uncertainty.

The first group—those who put significantly more weight upon purpose—will inevitably place greater power in the hands of the agency or perhaps the lower courts. At the least, they will postpone important decision-making to a later date, when the Court has more information about how the statute operates in practice. Their method here resembles the methods that common law courts used for centuries.[30] Why did they decide the case in that way? First, because to interpret the statute literally, as the dissenting judges would have done, would have interfered with its purpose; it would have allowed potential polluters to avoid the federal permitting requirement. Second, because to have adopted a rigid rule applying the requirement wholesale to groundwater mixtures would have produced other undesirable (and unforeseen) consequences. Adopting a flexible rule and leaving the area for future legal development provided a better way (the majority thought) to implement the statute in accordance with its purposes.

Another general feature of purpose-based approaches that the reader should keep in mind is the relationship between those approaches and "pragmatism." Critics sometimes refer to judges who emphasize purposes as "pragmatic" judges.[31] They use the word to suggest, I think, that judges act in a manner better reserved for legislators. That is to say "pragmatic" often refers to doing whatever one thinks is good as a policy matter. Used in that way, I disagree that purpose-oriented judges are or should be "pragmatic" judges. Purpose-based approaches advance constitutional and congressional purposes, not the judge's own agenda.

In the context of judging, however, the word "pragmatic" has a special meaning. "Pragmatic" in this context does not refer simply to the choice of a result that will do "good" for the greatest number of people or that will do "good" for those who work with, or are affected by, the statute.[32] A good pragmatic decision must take account, to the extent practical, of the way in which a proposed decision will affect a host of related legal rules, practices, habits, institutions, as well as certain moral principles and practices, including the practical consequences of the decision, such as how those affected by the decision will react.[33] For example, a "pragmatic judge" who would overrule an earlier decision will have to take account of the new decision's consistency with, and its effects upon, legal notions of *stare decisis* (the rule requiring courts to follow prior decisions), particularly the effects of the new decision (including its discussion of precedent) upon the law's stability.[34] And purpose-oriented judges, when choosing, for example, not just the result of a case but also what to say about it, may have to take account of the statute's language, precedent, the role of courts, the constitutional role of the Supreme Court, the ability of lawyers to follow, and to apply, the decision, and so forth. A purpose-oriented judge can define a "positive effect" in terms of the statute's purpose. But that judge is also pragmatic when he or she knows that (or shrewdly guesses that) overall the decision will have a positive effect upon those to whom it applies (or to Americans in general), taking account of the institutions, practices, and beliefs that make up our legal web of beliefs.[35] Only then can we say with at least some degree of confidence that we have written a decision that works "better" or that will help society function "better." Considering "good" or "better" in that light, a judge might then choose to be "pragmatic."

Finally, the reader should keep in mind the fact that a purpose-oriented judge will sometimes ask, "what would a reasonable (or idealized) legislator have thought about a statutory phrase's purpose?"[36] In asking this question I believe the judge is using a legal fiction in order to determine the purpose of statutory language. That, in part, is because members of Congress often fail to consider (and they often cannot consider) the scope or reach (now or later) of every word in a statute. Indeed, the scope of a single phrase can differ over time because new situations arise that Congress simply did not think about or could not have thought about at the time of enactment.[37]

Moreover, Congress will sometimes deliberately use abstract or vague language, allowing interpretive uncertainty, in order to obtain a majority of members who will vote for the statute.[38] Different members, if they have formed any opinion at all on the subject, may well believe the same phrase differs as to its scope. Taking the objective perspective of a hypothetical reasonable legislator may very well be the best way fairly to resolve disputes among members as to the meaning of such deliberately abstract or vague language, thus recognizing the compromises inherent to the legislative process.

When faced with interpreting a phrase, judges will therefore ask themselves what a hypothetical but *reasonable legislator would have thought* about the matter had the legislator known about and considered the matter at the time of enactment. The judge will assume that the legislator would have taken account of the statute's purposes and chosen, in light of those purposes, the "scope" that best fits them.[39] At the time of the founding of the Republic, many judges referred to this way to determine the scope of an ambiguous statutory phrase as an "idealized" legislative reading.[40]

Why is this fiction helpful? For one thing, using it increases the likelihood that the statute will work better in light of Congress's basic purposes. If those purposes include efforts, for example, to provide medical care for those who are ill or education for those who are disabled, the fiction will at least sometimes help the statute's beneficiaries obtain the benefits Congress may well have intended.[41] One statute, for example, allows a parent with a disabled child the right to obtain a court order that will give the child a better public education. The statute gives that parent the right to recover court-related "costs." Do those costs include the costs of hiring an educational expert who testifies in favor of the child?[42] As I shall discuss, an "idealized" legislative reading will help the statute's beneficiaries receive benefits that Congress likely intended.

For another thing, use of the fiction helps the voters. Members of Congress do not always try to achieve reasonable objectives; but much of the time they do so. And, they will explain to their voters just why and how a bill they voted for did, or tried to do, just that. If a court interprets an ambiguity in a way that makes it more difficult for the statute to achieve a reasonable objective, the legislator can blame the court, not his own bill, for any unfortunate consequences, leaving the voter uncertain whom to blame. The legislator voting for the bill that allowed the parents of a disabled child to recover "costs," for example, can argue to those who thought that the word should cover the costs of experts that the legislator agreed and intended that but the courts did not properly interpret the word "costs." Insofar as judges interpreting uncertainties use the "reasonable legislator" fiction, the statute is more likely to achieve the basic purposes the members of Congress intended. It is more likely that those judges will interpret the word "costs" to include expert fees, thereby helping parents who win their legal cases recover the costs of bringing the cases (including the experts' fees). The members can then take credit with the voters for what they have done; or, if the statute has not worked well, the voters will know whom to blame. The members of Congress cannot shift the blame for the statute's failure to mechanical interpretations that judges have given to the written words.[43] Voters' ability properly to place praise or blame for what takes place is a virtue in a democratic society.

Of course, those opposed to these methods of interpretation argue that the use of this fiction allows judges greater ability to replace their own view of what constitutes a desirable statute for the statute that Congress actually enacted, i.e., the judges just believe it is "better" to allow the parents to recover the experts' costs.[44] But is that so? The judge normally uses the fiction when the language of the statute, together with other commonly used tools of interpretation, yields no definite result. Thus, the judge's choice is between ignoring the fiction and thereby achieving (in respect to the will of Congress) a random result, or using the fiction and thereby achieving (in respect to the will of Congress) a reasonable result more consistent with Congress's basic purposes. It is not surprising that many judges have used the fiction for decades, perhaps centuries.[45]

Critics also maintain that what a "reasonable" or "idealized" member of Congress would wish to achieve with a particular bill or statutory phrase is often too difficult for judges to discern.[46] That observation may more often prove true of Supreme Court cases where, typically, lower court judges have reached different conclusions as to the application of the same statutory phrase.[47] But where that is so, the judge need not use the fiction. That is not a reason to forgo its use in the many cases where a "reasonable" interpretation is easy, not difficult, to determine. When my wife says,

"There isn't any butter," I have no trouble understanding she means "in the refrigerator," not "in the city."

Finally, some critics agree with a key premise of the "reasonable legislator" fiction—namely, that statutory enactments can reflect the differing intentions of multiple legislators and are often deliberately vague or ambiguous as a result of those differing intentions. Yet these critics maintain that the best way to resolve questions of vagueness or ambiguity is to ask how a hypothetical ordinary *reader* would interpret a statute rather than how a hypothetical *legislator* intended the statute to be interpreted.[48] They therefore turn to tools like dictionaries or canons of interpretation (general rules for interpreting statutory language) to approximate the understandings of ordinary readers.[49] But ordinary readers don't always adopt interpretations that align with dictionary definitions.[50] In fact, empirical evidence suggests that ordinary readers often interpret statutory meaning in light of statutory *purpose*. Three legal scholars, Kevin Tobia, Brian Slocum, and Victoria Nourse, surveyed a random sample of ordinary people, asking them to interpret a hypothetical statute prohibiting vehicles in the park. They found that, in interpreting the words of the hypothetical statute, people often rejected literal dictionary definitions in favor of readings that comported with the statute's context and likely purpose.[51] Asking about the purposes of a "reasonable legislator" can therefore be a useful tool in determining how a reasonable reader would understand a particular statute. Not to mention the various other benefits that come with the "reasonable legislator" tool, including its usefulness in helping statutes achieve their purposes and in helping voters hold Congress accountable.

In sum, I should like the reader to keep in mind: 1) that a purpose-oriented judge, not surprisingly, will first and foremost put considerable weight upon the purposes that a statutory phrase seeks to achieve and, drawing on the traditional common law method, will interpret the statutory phrase narrowly or flexibly; 2) that the purpose-oriented judge is a "pragmatic judge," not in the sense that he or she decides a case to achieve what he or she believes is "good" but rather in the special sense that the judge works within a framework of rules, approaches, standards, presumptions, legal institutions, and a host of other doctrines that inevitably shape which is the "better" view of a case; and 3) that one legal tool that often helps that judge understand and interpret statutory silence or ambiguity is a fiction: the hypothetical reasonable legislator, a fiction useful in some, but not all, cases.

The three considerations I have mentioned are not the only tools or considerations that a purpose-oriented judge will use. I will discuss others when I consider examples. My object is not exhaustively to list or discuss theoretical virtues and vices of "purpose-oriented" compared with "textualist" systems of interpretation. It is to describe examples that will show how I, and others, look to purposes, or alternatively look almost exclusively to texts, when we interpret statutes and the Constitution. My object is to help the reader better understand how I have found these two different approaches to work in practice.

2.

The Textualist Approach

Textualism and originalism, while coming in different varieties, are relatively easy to define. They ask the judge to look, almost exclusively, to language. And their main point is that statutory (or constitutional) words mean what a reasonable person would have taken them to mean at the time they were written.

My late colleague and friend Justice Antonin Scalia wrote that "textualism" refers to an approach toward interpretation that emphasizes that words in a statutory phrase, "[i]n their full context . . . mean what they conveyed to reasonable people at the time they were written—with the understanding that legal terms may embrace later technological innovations."[1] Justice Samuel Alito has said that statutory words "mean what they conveyed to reasonable people at the time they were written."[2] Justice Neil Gorsuch has added that in a statute, or in the Constitution, the text maintains its "original public meaning."[3] Sometimes textualist judges will refer to dictionaries to find this "original meaning." But reference to a dictionary is not always necessary.[4] With or without that dictionary, a judge will understand that the word "nail" in a building code means something different than the word "nail" in a beauty salon ordinance, because context matters.[5]

Where the Constitution's broad language is at issue, the textualist (perhaps then referred to as an "originalist") may emphasize the need to understand the word or phrase as it was used in the late eighteenth century or the mid-nineteenth century when the Constitution or an amendment was adopted. And some textualists, such as Justice Scalia, whether considering a statute or the Constitution, add that the judge should try to express a decision's holding in the form of a broad black-and-white rule. They believe that this kind of rule (like a First Amendment rule forbidding "content discrimination") will diminish the judge's power to substitute the judge's view of "what is good" for "the law."[6]

Most judges will accept some of what the textualist says, at least as a starting point applicable to many, but not to all, legal issues. Recall the earlier train fare example where we puzzled over the scope of the fare guide's word "animal." But the textualist often goes well beyond that starting point. The major debate that arises concerns the textualist's refusal to use, or at least his tendency to downplay, the importance of other judicial tools that might point the way toward a proper interpretation.

Justice Scalia, writing with Bryan Garner, says, for example,

> Both your authors are textualists: We look for meaning in the governing text, ascribe to that text the meaning it has borne from its inception, and *reject judicial speculation about both the drafters' extratextually derived purposes and the desirability of the fair reading's anticipated consequences.*[7]

Some of these words provide wiggle room (e.g., "speculation," "extratextually," "desirability," "fair"). But the basic idea is nonetheless clear: "Judge, beware the search for (or the interpretive use of) legislative intent, purposes, and consequences. You are safest when you stick to the text alone."

I, like all judges, believe text is important. But why go so far as to rule out other useful tools? The textualist replies in two ways:

The first consists of *criticism.*

The textualist criticizes the use of other tools of interpretation upon the grounds that those other tools suffer from worse problems. Looking to a provision's purposes, for example, offers promises that cannot be kept. To search for *legislative intent* is like hunting the snark. It encourages the search for the nonexistent. Legislators, like parties to a contract, may agree upon the words of a statute without agreeing about just what they mean. Their presence may reflect agreement among different congressional factions, with each side accepting a particular word while (perhaps hopefully) ascribing to that word a different meaning.[8]

Moreover, the statute's words may reflect the views of congressional staffers, interested parties who write or review the statutory words, without the elected individual, the member of Congress, paying particular attention to those words, perhaps not even reading them. Or, interested groups of outsiders, lobbyists or others, may have written the words with the hope that staffers or members of one congressional faction would insert them into the statute while giving them a specific (though controverted) meaning.[9] Why, the textualist asks, should unelected judges try to find a legislative intent in respect to a matter that the elected legislators themselves may not even have thought about or come to agreement about? There is too great a risk that the judge, if doing so, will substitute what the judge believes desirable for the words that the elected representatives actually chose.[10] As one textualist, Judge Frank Easterbrook, put it, "a method that sees legislative history as a *friend* rather than as merely inevitable leads to a jurisprudence in which statutory words become devalued."[11]

The textualist adds that, even if one is able to find a general statutory purpose, it is difficult to go farther. Take, for example, the Freedom of Information Act. The general purpose of the statute is to allow the public to obtain information, for instance, about how the government or a particular government agency is working, what it has done, what possible alternatives it has considered, and what information it has had available.[12]

But the act contains exceptions. Those exceptions, for example, allow the government to withhold information about, say, potential criminal indictments or certain confidential advice that government decision-makers received.[13]

When interpreting the statute in light of its purposes, which purposes should the government consider: the general purpose to make information available to the public or the more specific purpose to withhold certain information from the public? To which purpose should the judge give more weight?

To ask a judge to try to answer this question, the textualist believes, is to invite the judge to engage in a freewheeling policy exercise. There is likely no right answer. After all, the Freedom of Information Act seeks to provide the interested public with information of what takes place in the executive branch; but it also seeks to keep from the public certain information contained in exceptions (say, related to criminal matters).[14] When a judge considers the meaning of words in an exception, which are the predominant purposes? The judge may well use the purpose that will lead to the case outcome that he or she finds preferable in terms of policy. Policy, however, is the legislator's job, not the judge's. Unless the statute directly authorizes the judge to make policy, it is better to do away with (or at least minimize) the search for policy.[15] The search for the policy aims of a hypothetical or fictive "reasonable" legislator, in the textualist's view, embodies the same problems but even more so.[16] Similarly, the textualist will say that, in asking questions such as, "will this interpretation allow the government to administer the program effectively," or "will this interpretation make it more difficult for injured parties to pursue their claims," the judge goes beyond the bounds of the judicial office. It is for elected legislators, not unelected judges, to decide what policies to embody in statutes.[17]

The textualist, recognizing that a text can lend itself to different interpretations, says that *linguistic* (sometimes called *semantic*) tools of interpretation can often help resolve textual ambiguities and uncertainties—without permitting the judge to substitute what the judge believes is good for the law itself. John Manning, the dean of Harvard Law School, has written a book about textualism in which he calls these clues as to the proper meaning of an unclear text "semantic" clues, for they have to do with language. He describes them as "contextual evidence that goes to customary usage and habits of speech."[18]

One such tool, to which textualists often refer, is what judges call "canons," or "canons of interpretation." Common law judges often used canons of interpretation as descriptions of how judges had interpreted particular sets of words frequently and over time. They are typically rules of thumb, applying to similar words appearing in different statutes. In principle, they reflect how ordinary readers would understand a text[19] or reinforce particular constitutional values.[20] One canon, for instance, tells judges to avoid reading statutory language in a way that simply duplicates other language in the same provision.[21] Another tells judges not to interpret words in a way that will make them ineffective.[22] Another assumes that a word bears the same meaning when it is used throughout a text and, by the same token, that a variation in terms suggests a variation in meaning.[23] Yet another assumes that "words are known by their associates" (Latin: *noscitur a sociis*), meaning that the statutory words "other animals," used in the phrase "cows, pigs, horses, or other animals" does not include crickets (or mosquitoes, and perhaps not snails).[24] And yet others promote legal values, such as a canon that promotes federalism by directing judges to avoid reading statutory language in a way that abrogates the traditional powers of the states.[25]

There are both theoretical and practical reasons for rejecting the textualists' two replies to using other judicial tools. As to their criticism of purpose-oriented approaches, I would say that sometimes it is difficult to determine a statute's basic nonlinguistic purpose or to separate major from minor purposes. But sometimes it is not difficult. And why should judges at least not look to purposes then? We shall examine these matters more closely in Part II, in light of actual cases.

As to their efforts to find linguistic ways to interpret linguistically ambiguous or unclear statutory language, I would point to studies such as that of Professors Lisa Schultz Bressman and Abbe Gluck. They have demonstrated, through a survey of 137 congressional staffers from both parties and chambers of Congress, that while the people who draft our laws know and employ a few of the basic linguistic rules of thumb (including canons of interpretation, like the presumption that a term tends to associate with other terms of the same kind), there are many more linguistic rules that those who actually draft legislation either reject outright or of which they are simply unaware.[26] This empirical fact strongly suggests that linguistic rules alone do not, in fact, provide a good method for understanding what our laws are meant to do and how they should be interpreted. After all, if legislators do not understand those linguistic rules, it is unlikely that ordinary citizens or even the average lawyer will know and understand them, especially the older ones, like a canon that the eighteenth-century legal commentator, William Blackstone, says is based upon an eighteenth-century monarchical system of government.[27] Legislative history, however, is a more accessible tool. The people who draft our laws are able to look up legislative history produced, as it is, by near contemporaries working for, or with, interest groups, executive departments, experts, legislators, staff members, and others interested in the legislation and the legislative process.[28]

That is not normally said of legal or judicial work.

For another thing, the natures of the legislative job and the judicial job are different. The decision-making time frame differs. A judge may take weeks or months to write an opinion. But the legislators' job is political. And, as Harold Wilson, former prime minister of Great Britain, once said, "A day is a long time in politics."

Moreover, the legislator's job (compared to the appellate judge's job) is more often likely to involve wholesale (as compared to retail) work. A vote for a bill about the use of chemical weapons, for example, is likely to be characterized broadly, say in the press, as, for example, showing that a legislator favors (or disfavors) a ban on the use of chemical weapons; the legislator's constituents will react accordingly; and legislators can, and do, pay close attention to the reactions of their constituents. If the judge considers the same subject matter, the judge is more likely to consider, say, a chemical weapons ban as embodied in a statute and applied in specific circumstances.

To illustrate: Congress enacted legislation that copied portions of an international chemical weapons treaty. Congress made those portions of the treaty a part of domestic criminal law. Congress's statute subjected to seven years imprisonment any person who "use[d]" a "chemical weapon."[29] The statute defined a "chemical weapon" as "any chemical which . . . can cause . . . temporary incapacitation . . . to humans or animals" unless the chemical is being used for "peaceful purposes."[30]

The Court considered the ban, not as if it were a general problem of banning chemical weapons but rather as the ban applied to an individual, Carol Anne Bond, whom the federal government had prosecuted for violating the statute. Bond, the federal government claimed, had violated the statute by ordering a chemical used to print photographs and then spreading it on a car door, mailbox, and doorknob of a neighbor's home. Bond believed that the neighbor was having an affair with Bond's husband, and she hoped that touching the chemical on, say the doorknob, would make the neighbor's fingers itch and temporarily incapacitate her. The Court decided that the statute did not turn this minor form of misbehavior into a serious infraction of federal criminal law.[31] The Court held that Congress would have believed that the states, not the federal government, would decide whether the type of behavior at issue should constitute a serious crime.[32] Note the Court's focus on the facts of the particular case and note that the statute's text said nothing about state authority.

I do not mean to suggest that the subject of the Court's work is always case specific or highly detailed. Nor is Congress's work always highly general. But, considered as a whole, the legislators will more often, and sometimes more quickly, have to make decisions at what I call a wholesale level, leaving retail application of its more wholesale decisions to the other branches of government.

The legislative process works in ways that make legislators more likely than a judge to understand certain features of a piece of enacted legislation. If the law passed through ordinary legislative procedures, the legislator or at least the staff will know who is most likely to be affected by it, where problems might lie, which language might cause particular problems (and why), and what alternative language had been suggested. The legislator, or at least the staff, would more likely know where and how the bill would fit within a nest of laws related to the same subject. The legislator, or at least the staff, would more likely know how the bill fit within a set of laws or potential laws that, when taken together, could make up, in part or in whole, a coherent political program. And all these aspects where the legislator, compared to the judge, will often have a superior understanding mean that the legislator and the appellate judge are often ships that pass in the night.

At a personal level these differences struck me when, as chief counsel of the Senate Judiciary Committee, I once received a call from Chief Justice Warren Burger, who wished to discuss a piece of legislation. Why, I immediately thought, is he calling me, a staffer? He should be talking to a senator. Then I realized that no senator was available to talk to him. All were working with constituents. No one intended to be rude; the difference was in the jobs. Judges and judicial work only on occasion played a significant role in the working life of a legislator. That fact makes it less likely that Congress will focus directly on the many linguistic rules of thumb or understandings that the textualist believes will determine the meaning of obscure phrases in a bill.

In addition to criticizing the use of purposes and the failure to rely upon, for example, linguistic rules of thumb, the textualist makes four important promises.

First, the textualist believes that, comparatively speaking, textualism will suggest that there is a *single right answer* to interpretive problems. It is the answer to which the text, as properly interpreted, points. The existence of a single right answer, to which text and linguistic methods lead us, means fewer disagreements among judges and greater public faith in the courts.[33]

But the law is not mathematics, and the search for the "correct" or "right" answer is often misguided. As a theoretical matter I believe that textualists too often use the word "meaning." I would beware of that word, for it often fails to describe in sufficient detail what a case is about. If the textualist wishes to use linguistic jargon, instead of talking about meaning, we should often talk about the "scope" of a statutory phrase. A statute that uses the word "costs," for example, is less likely to lead to a question about the meaning of the word "costs" than to create an argument about the scope of that word as used in that particular statutory phrase. Does the word, as set forth in the phrase, include the "costs" of hiring experts?

Consider Title VII of the Civil Rights Act of 1964. That statute imposes liability upon an "employer" who "fail[s] or refuse[s] to hire" or "discharge[s]" or otherwise "discriminate[s] against" an "individual . . . because of such individual's race, color, religion, sex, or national origin."[34] In *Bostock v. Clayton County*,[35] the Court had to decide whether the statute forbids discrimination on the basis of a person's sexual orientation or transgender status.[36] Textually speaking, the question concerns not so much the *meaning* of the word "sex," but rather the *scope* of that word as used in the statute. Does it include discrimination against the latter persons within its scope?

In *Bostock*, the Court decided 6–3 that the scope of the word "sex" does include discrimination on the basis of sexual orientation or the fact that a person is transgender.[37] If the scope of a statute's words is at issue, one can find more linguistic indeterminacy, vagueness, or ambiguity than one might think. When deciding questions of scope, one is more tempted to look for the statute's, or the legislators', purpose or intent.

How can the textualist keep his "single answer" promise?

Second, the textualist promises that textualism means (in part because it produces single answers) that judges will become less likely to overstep the bounds of their constitutionally specified task. As discussed above, a purpose-oriented judge is concerned with the social forces that led to the enactment of the particular statutory phrase at issue. In addition to legislative history, a purpose-oriented judge is likely to look to factors such as the social conflicts that led to enactment of the statute in order to decide the same question.[38]

This willingness by some judges to look beyond text and semantic context underscores a major reason why many judges and commentators embrace textualism. They fear that, without textualism, judges will overstep the bounds of their job, namely to *interpret* statutes. The Constitution's insistence upon a separation of powers means in their view that the job of an unelected federal judge does not extend to the making of policy. That job belongs to an elected legislator or perhaps to an executive branch agency implementing a legislature's broader enactment. A theory that permits the judge to reach beyond the linguistically determined meaning of the text will, textualists believe, almost inevitably and systematically encourage judges to decide cases according to what they believe is desirable.[39] Textualism keeps at bay the judicial mindset that asks "[w]hat is the most desirable resolution of this case, and how can any impediments to the achievement of that result be evaded?"[40]

Adhering to the text, the textualist believes, will lead judges away from consideration of materials such as legislative testimony, events taking place outside the legislative chamber, even newspaper articles, and other materials that lobbyists, interest groups, and others can shape to secure what they believe is a more favorable policy interpretation. It will minimize judges' consideration of that which the Constitution does not (at least, does not explicitly) include as part of the legislative process. Justice Scalia argued that it will tend to limit consideration to that which is voted by elected representatives, signed by the president, or possibly vetoed and then overridden in Congress.[41] Exceptions, where they exist, can be well defined and restricted. Again, we shall look into this promise further in Parts II and III's discussions of examples.

Third, the textualist promises that sticking to the text will help the legislator as well as the judge. It provides hope for the development of a fairly definite system for reaching compromises within the legislature, i.e., deciding just how far Congress can reach compromises with dissenting groups. It makes it easier for Congress to incorporate competing purposes. Dean Manning writes:

> Giving precedence to semantic context [i.e., looking almost exclusively to the words of the statute, perhaps modified by, e.g., canons of interpretation] (when clear) is necessary to enable legislators to set the level of generality at which they wish to express their policies. In turn, this ability alone permits them to strike compromises that go so far and no farther. Ultimately, then, the affirmative justification for textualism lies in the idea that semantic meaning is the currency of legislative compromise.[42]

A Congress (the promise runs) that knows the courts will take the words of the statute for what they say and no more will be able more effectively to compromise and to shape the resulting policy responses. The constitutional three-branch compromise will become easier to work in practice.[43]

Justice Scalia wrote that the need for a "science of statutory interpretation" (a set of clear rules that would inform those charged with the drafting of statutes just how they should do so) was a major causal factor leading to the development of a theory of textualism.[44] "What is of paramount importance is that Congress be able to legislate against a background of clear interpretive rules, so that it may know the effect of the language it adopts."[45]

Thus, in principle, textualism could help develop a kind of feedback loop between lawmakers and judges that could lead to a set of interpretive rules or principles, operating nearly irrespective of legislative subject matter. And their existence would help legislators give judges the rulebook they need to make sure that legislative policies are properly implemented.

What is wrong with that? For one thing, as Professors Bressman and Gluck have demonstrated empirically, this feedback loop does not exist.[46] And, for reasons I set forth above, it is unlikely to come into existence in part because the legislative and judicial jobs are different. I have little reason to believe that legislators, or their staffs, will become convinced that a feedback loop is desirable, read the textualist's semantic rules, and conclude that they offer just the ticket to legislative precision. And, please, do not forget Montaigne: technology changes, society changes, life changes. The scope of words that encapsulate important values may themselves have to change, in part or in whole, if we are to maintain those values. Again, examples (in Part II and Part III) will help the reader understand the importance of this point.

Fourth, the textualist promises that the textualist system is a fairer system. Those who must follow the law will find it easier to understand what the law means. It will mean the same thing in the hands of every judge. The result will be increased fairness. "[I]t is simply incompatible with democratic government, or indeed, even with fair government," the textualist may add, "to have the meaning of a law determined by what the lawgiver meant, rather than by what the lawgiver promulgated."[47] The latter is public, available to all; the former may be hidden deep in the recesses of the lawmaker's mind.[48] It is "words," wrote Justice Gorsuch, not abstract concepts such as deep intentions, that allow the "law" to "constrain[] power."[49] Again, examples will help the reader determine the extent to which this is so.

My discussion so far focuses upon general claims and criticisms, along with general answers and responses. But I have not, nor have I tried to, set forth a complete set of propositions that, as a matter of logic, will disprove the textualist's position. Summarizing my criticism in a single sentence, however, I have found the legal world too complex, too different from the world the textualist assumes, to believe that the theoretical virtues the textualists mention can justify the textualist approach.

I will provide in the next two parts examples based upon cases that I have participated in deciding. For the most part these cases involve questions of interpretation, of statutory language, or language of the Constitution. The questions are complicated. A description of the questions along with the judicial answers judges have provided will ultimately show why I find textualism, particularly in its more extreme forms, if not wrong-headed, at least not useful. They will also show why and how textualism can lead the law in an undesirable direction.

In an effort to be clear, I shall repeat what I take to be the essence of textualism considered as a kind of legal construct rather like the "reasonable legislator." So considered, I believe *textualism* itself normally has three, perhaps four, essential parts.

First, there is a heavy reliance upon the statute's text, along with general linguistic or semantic tools and rules, such as canons, to help interpret that text.[50] And there is a simultaneous downplaying of the use of purposes, and purpose-related considerations, as part of the interpretive effort. I have described this aspect earlier.

Second, *originalism* constitutes an essential part of textualism, particularly when the Constitution is at issue.[51] That is because many words in the Constitution are abstract and highly general. Consider "liberty," "due process of law," or "the freedom of speech." The textualist believes that interpretation of these constitutional words requires the judge to consider (often as determinative) how they would have been understood by the ordinary person, or their original public meaning, at the time they were written, 1787, 1789, or in the case of the Thirteenth, Fourteenth, and Fifteenth Amendments, just after the Civil War.[52]

There are instances, however, where text-oriented judges have found support in originalism even though their interpretation is not tethered to the original public meaning of a constitutional text. And in Part III, I will describe how judges have sometimes used originalism as an interpretive tool to resolve questions about the structure of the Constitution, even when there is no clear textual answer.[53] Thus normally, when I refer to originalism, I refer to the practice of looking to a text's original public meaning. I address originalism's role in resolving structural constitutional questions later on, in Part III.[54]

Third, those who favor textualism, such as Justice Scalia, often argue that judges in their opinions should try to create or follow broadly applicable, black-and-white rules.[55] Rules are easier to follow than precedents standing alone. They can more easily be explained to a client. And their use can, like textualism and originalism, reinforce the idea that legal questions have a *single best answer*: You either follow the rule or you don't.

Fourth, and here I am uncertain, I believe textualists should normally emphasize and follow previously decided cases. That is to say, they should strongly favor rules of *stare decisis*.[56] Courts, including the Supreme Court, did not often use textualist methods in the past. Thus *stare decisis* is needed to avoid the legal chaos that would arise were judges to consider nontextualist cases not to be good law. I discuss this in relation to the *Dobbs*[57] case in Part III.[58]

In Part II, I draw on my experience on the Court to illustrate what I believe to be serious shortcomings in a purely textualist approach to interpreting statutes. Those shortcomings include textualism's inability to answer whether statutory phrases should be interpreted statically or dynamically,[59] its unwillingness to take into account the consequences of a particular interpretation,[60] and its skepticism about the use of legislative history.[61] I also address the importance of purpose-oriented interpretive tools such as looking to underlying constitutional values.[62]

Then, in Part III, I shall discuss originalism and explain why I believe its approach, including its emphasis upon the use of broad, clear-cut rules, has had a negative impact upon the interpretation of the Constitution. Part III will also point out that Chief Justice John Marshall, along with other Founders, emphasized the need to maintain a workable Constitution, a Constitution that will work well as the nation grows and changes, transmitting its basic values across the centuries. I fear that originalism will make this objective harder to achieve.

Examination of actual cases will show that neither textualism nor originalism will produce the single clear answers to legal questions for which they strive. They will not prevent judges from substituting what they believe is "good" for the "law." They will not help to create a "science" of law through feedback loops to Congress. They will, however, make a workable Constitution more difficult to maintain. And they will undercut many of the values that a more traditional purpose-based system supports—values that, through law, help members of our society live together more productively and in peace.

I now turn to examples that illustrate why I believe it is unlikely that textualism in practice will achieve the virtues that its supporters claim.

II

INTERPRETING STATUTORY LAW

Both a textualist judge and one who is purpose-oriented will normally start to interpret a statute by reading its text. No one wants an interpretation that is inconsistent with the statute's clear meaning: "Vegetable" does not mean "animal" or "mineral." That is why Portalis, an early-nineteenth-century author of the French Civil Code, said "when the law is clear, it must be heeded."[1] But, as Portalis recognized, the texts that are the subject of serious legal disputes are rarely clear.[2] That is particularly true of statutory phrases at issue in Supreme Court cases. The Supreme Court, after all, normally need not take a case for consideration; if it does so, it is often because lower court judges have come to different conclusions about the meaning or application of the same statutory phrase.

That lack of clarity is often true for another reason. There are many ways in which, or reasons why, a word or phrase might seem unclear. The word or phrase may be indeterminate. The ancient Greeks found it paradoxical that the normally clear word for "heap" is in fact not clear as to how many grains of sand are needed to make a "heap."[3] One grain will not do; add another, another, another, etc., and eventually we have a heap, but we cannot say just when our small pile of sand became a "heap." So, if we need to know the meaning of the word (say, because the word is in a statute), we had better look beyond the word itself.

Moreover, outside the law, people ordinarily look well beyond a written text or a spoken utterance to discover the meaning or the application of the words used. When my wife says, "fish for dinner," I need not ask anyone if she means raw fish, nor need I ask whether the fish might be Chilean sea bass. I know her too well; she likes neither. I know just what her statement means and how it applies, but I know these things through context and not through her spoken word alone. Consulting a dictionary for what she meant by "fish" would not do me—or her—any good in trying to decipher what she meant.

There are cases where, behind a written text or a spoken utterance, there is no meaningful intention to discover. For example, I gather that the newest artificial intelligence— ChatGPT—can write essays; were we to find in the midst of one of its essays the words "hip wedding on Mount Tam," there would be no point in asking ChatGPT what it means. There is no human being hiding behind the curtain to ask, and ChatGPT likely cannot answer the question: The algorithm has spoken, but without any meaning beyond mere mimicry of human speech patterns. But, uttered or written words do more than simply make statements, whether about the dinner table or any other part of the world. They perform tasks ("I do" said at the wedding ceremony). They express emotions ("Hooray!"). They pre-scribe or proscribe activities ("Don't you dare touch your brother's soccer gear."). Importantly for our purposes, some words make statements (like "I do") that are true simply by virtue of the fact that the right person uttered them in the right way at the right time.

Statutes often make performative statements. They can tell people what to do or what not to do. Consider, for example, "taking money from a fed-erally insured bank through the use of force or threat of force is a crime."[4] Moreover, the utterance of this statement (in the right way) is what makes it true. The statement was uttered by human beings—not ChatGPT—and when a person utters a performative statement that we find unclear or oth-erwise indeterminate, it is natural (within as well as outside the law) to ask, "Well, what exactly did you want us to do?"

We do not automatically turn to dictionaries alone to resolve uncer-tainties about just what, for instance, the televangelist Kenneth Copeland meant when he uttered his sermon about how to behave during a global pandemic.[5] When we learn from the minister that he is dispelling corona-virus by "blow[ing] the wind of God," we do better to uncover his meaning by looking at his reasons for articulating his sermon in the way that he did than by consulting dictionaries for definitions of "blow" and "wind."

When the text is not clear, a purpose-oriented judge will typically look beyond the text to determine the relevant purpose of the statutory phrase; and the judge will then interpret the language (if possible) in light of that purpose. For example, the Court once had to determine whether the Food and Drug Administration had the legal authority to regulate tobacco products.[6] The majority thought that it did not, but I thought the contrary. In dissent, I emphasized that the statute gave the FDA the authority to regulate "articles (other than food) intended to affect the structure or the function of the body."[7] In my view, tobacco fell within the scope of this statutory phrase in part because the statute's basic purpose was *"to protect the public health."*[8] I found this purpose by examining not only earlier court cases but also the social context in which Congress had enacted the statute and the executive branch had applied it. My textualist colleagues might fear that an approach to interpretation that allows me to give significant weight to considerations of this kind would allow me to substitute my own subjective desires or beliefs about what is good for those that Congress intended to write into this statute. Is that so? Or, to put the matter more precisely, is it *more* so than any other method of interpretation? After all, a judge who uses textual analysis exclusively might do so in ways that favor his or her basic beliefs about what is "good."

Justice Scalia and I would often debate this question before law school audiences.[9] The audience would likely come away believing that we were good friends, but we did not agree about the answer to this question.

Why exactly should judges work so hard to find statutory purposes beyond the text? For one thing, we live in a constitutional democracy. We elect legislators. And those legislators will normally try to achieve the objectives that those who elected them desire. When a court interprets statutory language in a way that is consistent with its basic objectives, that court is more likely to implement what the legislator believes his or her constituents desire, which is a worthy goal in a constitutional democracy.

For another thing, ordinary citizens are more likely to be able to determine (by looking to consequences) whether the legislator has or has not taken a step in the "right direction." In essence, when a judge interprets a statute in light of its general purposes, the ordinary citizen is more likely to be able to hold the legislator accountable for what that legislation does. That citizen cannot as easily know what to say to the legislator when the consequences of the legislation reflect application of highly complex, judicially imposed canons of linguistic interpretation.

Finally, the search for purposes means that the statute will likely work better for those whom it affects. After all, that is the crux of the legislator's purpose. The legislator has typically spent hours, directly or through staff, learning about a complex bill. Therefore, the legislator will often understand, better than does the judge, the empirical context, practical problems that have led to the legislation, its aims, its drawbacks, the significance of the legislation (whether enacted or proposed), how the new law fits into a party's overall approach to solving the nation's problems, and the public's feelings about the matter.

To find the purposes that will guide an interpretation, the judge can look in many different places. The diligent judge must be flexible and open-minded in looking to those sources.

Sometimes, *statutory context* will help. That context often includes other words, phrases, provisions, and sometimes other statutes as well. Textualist judges, too, will look here, though they may just be looking for "semantic" help.

So, too, *precedent* may help the judge: Did the Court previously decide this issue or related issues in a way that Congress might have known about and relied on?

Additionally, judges will (and should) often look to *common experience.* Even the most ardent textualist will avoid interpreting a statute in a way that "no reasonable person could approve."[10] As we shall see, an interpretation of a Medicare statute that makes it difficult, perhaps next-to-impossible, for the Department of Health and Human Services to reimburse hospitals for certain costs (within, say, a year or two years or more) is unlikely to reflect a proper interpretation of the statute's language, even if that is what the statute seems to say.[11]

Sometimes, *nonstatutory* context is helpful. In particular, the substantive

- 34 -

problems and issues that legislators were considering at the time are often highly relevant. In other words, the *policy context* in which Congress enacted the statute may be important. Federal financial legislation enacted soon after the 2008 financial crisis, for example, is likely designed to achieve certain related ends, such as, say, stabilizing the market for residential mortgages, increasing the ability of lenders to understand the precise nature of collateral, or modifying or forbidding particularly risky lending practices. Legislation, of course, rarely pursues a primary end to the nth degree.[12] Congress would not want to end all lending or overwhelmingly raise the costs of those in the lending business. Similarly, a Congress interested in increasing the safety of drinking water is unlikely to insist that all water be 100 percent pure. But the difficulty of determining where Congress drew the line does not obviate the need for judges to try to find relevant information and to use that knowledge in deciding cases where that knowledge may, in fact, help.

Legislative history also can prove a useful source. That history includes congressional committee hearings, committee reports, legislative statements on the House or Senate floor, and statements made there by a law's primary sponsors.

Judicial use of this kind of source is highly controversial, so I will discuss it in greater detail. Justice Scalia thought that courts should not consider these sources at all.[13] After all, the elected members of Congress did not write the reports themselves. Staff wrote the reports, and staff may well have prepared questions and statements for the members, both in committee and on the floor. This objection is less weighty in my opinion than Justice Scalia thought. And, even though legislative history is sometimes inaccurate, and sometimes contradictory, as it reflects the potentially different views of different members, it nonetheless will often suffer few of these defects. More importantly, it will sometimes provide a reliable source for a judge searching for purposes.

Sometimes *consequences* are important: Does interpretation yield consequences inconsistent with the likely purpose? Legislative history can shed light on the possible relevant purposes and consequences. Interpretations by the executive branch, including executive agencies, can also shed light on the subject. Sometimes, it is particularly important to try to determine whether the Congress that (perhaps long ago) enacted a statute expected the scope of the statute to change over time. Sometimes, it is important to examine what a hypothetical "reasonable legislator" would have intended, even if actual legislators did not consider the particular interpretive question before the Court.

Finally, there is the Constitution itself. It sets forth certain basic values and principles. Judges will not interpret statutes in ways that they believe directly conflict with the Constitution. And most judges will try to interpret a statute in a way that is consistent with, and indeed furthers, constitutional values and principles.

Which of these "tools," or others, that are useful for interpretation should the judge use, and when, and where? It depends. No treatise provides clear answers, and there is no list of "tool-related canons." Which tools we use depends upon the legal issue; it depends upon the case; it depends upon what is accessible; it depends upon the extent to which a judge believes that further examination will shed useful light upon the legal question.

I turn now to a set of examples that I hope will illustrate the general points I have just set forth by showing how a purpose-oriented judge can use these tools to help answer interpretive questions about the meaning and application of even highly complex statutory language and phrases. The examples will also compare the answers that a purpose-oriented judge would reach with the answers that a text-oriented judge would likely provide.

3.

The Traditional Use of Text and Purpose

FDA v. Brown & Williamson Tobacco Corp. (2000)[1]

I begin with what I consider a traditional example of the use of text and purpose. Traditionally, judges would use both approaches: They would consider, and make, arguments based on text, as well as arguments related to the text's purposes. It is the effort to shift the judge's attention away from purposes and toward the use of text alone that has made textualism controversial. I begin with this kind of example because I believe that most difficult court cases are of this kind.

My example elaborates a case I mentioned briefly a few pages earlier, a case that concerns tobacco. The relevant statute, the Federal Food, Drug, and Cosmetic Act (FDCA),[2] grants a federal agency, the Food and Drug Administration (FDA), the authority to regulate "drugs" and "devices." The statute defines "drugs" to include "articles (other than food) intended to affect the structure or any function of the body."[3]

For decades, the FDA had not regulated cigarettes or other forms of tobacco. Then, in the early 1990s, the FDA changed its mind. By that time, scientists had basically agreed that cigarettes delivered nicotine to the lungs; that nicotine altered moods in ways that both stimulated and calmed the smoker; and that nicotine was highly addictive.[4] Moreover, nicotine had harmful health effects and facilitated the bodily transmission of carcinogens. Nicotine was also related to heart disease and respiratory diseases, and the FDA found that one of the best ways to stop the use of nicotine was to make it more difficult for children to begin smoking.

Consequently, the FDA promulgated a set of anti-tobacco rules aimed primarily at sales to children.[5] The rules forbade most nicotine sales to children; they specified permitted methods of advertising; and they limited methods of marketing cigarettes. The FDA said that a cigarette was a "device" that delivered a "drug" to the body.[6] It said that the manufacturers knew that smoking brought about this delivery. The FDA added that the statute allowed it to "restrict[] . . . the sale, distribution, or the use" of a device "if because of its potentiality for harmful effect" the FDA "determines that there cannot otherwise be reasonable assurance of its safety."[7] Tobacco companies, and others, challenged the lawfulness of the FDA's rules. Did the statute authorize the FDA to promulgate these regulations?

Five members of the Court, a majority, took the side of the tobacco companies.[8] Why? Did the statute not say that the FDA could regulate devices that deliver unsafe drugs? Yes, it did. But the statute said more. It said, in the majority's words, that a core objective was to ensure that any product that the FDA regulates was "'safe' . . . for its intended use," and at the least, that the therapeutic benefits of the FDA's regulated products outweighed its safety risks.[9] More than that, explained the majority: The FDA could not allow a drug to be distributed unless it was "safe" for "its intended purpose"[10]; it had to withdraw a drug from the market if it discovered the drug was unsafe"[11]; and it could only "place conditions upon the sale or distribution of a device" if there was a "reasonable assurance of the safety and effectiveness of the device."[12] So, if the FDA believed cigarettes to be dangerous and misbranded devices, then the statute seemed to say that the FDA *had to* withdraw them from the market.

But, the Court continued, the FDA had not withdrawn, and did not propose to withdraw, cigarettes from the market.[13] Indeed, a different statutory provision required the FDA to approve (for marketing) only those devices where there is a "reasonable assurance that such device is safe under the conditions of use" set forth in the labeling.[14] Furthermore, in a different statute, Congress had forbidden the FDA from removing cigarettes from the market.[15] These statutes nowhere gave the FDA the power to regulate cigarettes in other ways. The purpose of the original statute was to allow the FDA to require manufacturers to make drugs safe; if they were not safe, they could not be sold, and that was the end of the matter. The upshot, said the majority, was that the literal statutory language, coupled with the FDA's findings, meant that the FDA lacked the statutory power to do what it has tried to do, namely regulate sales to children, regulate labeling, regulate promotion or marketing, but not withdraw cigarettes (which remain unsafe) entirely from the market.[16]

The majority referred to several other acts of Congress, which, for example: removed from other agencies the authority to ban cigarette sales; limited the extent to which agencies can regulate cigarette advertising; encouraged states, not the federal government, to regulate cigarettes; and much else besides.[17] The majority also referred to the many instances in which the FDA itself denied it had the legal authority to regulate cigarettes.[18] Taken together, the majority said, "these actions by Congress over the past 35 years preclude an interpretation" of the FDA statute that would permit the FDA to "regulate tobacco products."[19]

Is all of the preceding analysis textualist? Probably. But I cannot be certain, for the majority depended heavily on Congress's expressed purposes in enacting the FDA statutes. The majority used the text to show that Congress's statutes lacked a certain purpose, namely, that of delegating to the FDA the authority to regulate (without removing from sale) tobacco products. But it also explicitly referenced congressional purpose—manifested in a Senate report—to reaffirm that "any further regulation in this sensitive and complex area [of tobacco regulation] must be reserved for specific Congressional action."[20] It looked to Congress's "consistently evidenced . . . intent to preclude any federal agency from exercising significant policymaking authority in the area."[21] These statements were not grounded specifically in statutory text, but generally in congressional purpose.

The dissent (which I wrote) also used a combination of text and purpose, though it put greater emphasis upon the statute's broadly defined purpose. It began by pointing to the statutory language giving the FDA authority to regulate "articles (other than food) intended to affect the structure or any function of the body,"[22] and noting that tobacco products fall within this definition. Then, it said that "the statute's basic purpose—the protection of public health—supports the inclusion of cigarettes within its scope."[23] And it cited precedent, saying that the statute "[wa]s to be given a liberal construction with [its] overriding purpose to protect the public health."[24]

But what about the statutory language upon which the majority seemed to rely? That language appeared to say that the FDA *had to* withdraw an unsafe drug or device from the market. But, the dissent said that the language was not so clear. Other statutory language provided that the FDA "may" ban a device where there was "an unreasonable risk of substantial harm to the public health."[25] By using the word "may," that statute "permit[ted] the FDA to conclude that a drug or device was *not* "dangerous to health" when regulated if the regulation rendered it "as harmless as possible."[26] The FDA might conclude that a total ban would lead smokers to use more dangerous products, leaving *regulated cigarettes* the safest alternative. Congress could not have intended that the FDA have authority only to prescribe a more dangerous, more draconian, remedy.

The dissent also said that the remaining statutes and administrative views to which the majority referred meant only that Congress intended to leave what was a controversial debate about the FDA's authority just where Congress found it, with some members believing the FDA had the requisite authority and some believing it did not.[27] The dissenters believed that Congress initially thought that habit-forming nicotine consequences reflected the smoker's own psychology, not the nicotine. But later scientific development showed that nicotine, the drug, was responsible for the habit.[28] And, whatever Congress thought when it first enacted the FDA, Congress did not originally, nor through amendment, express a view about that authority should science develop as it did.

This case, I believe, is typical of the way in which the Court reached its statutory conclusions during most of the time I was a member. Five Justices, writing in the year 2000, focused upon the fact that cigarettes and other tobacco products were major consumer products that had been enjoyed by millions of Americans and others throughout the world for at least two centuries. Congress simply could not have intended an administrative agency to possess the authority to regulate those products, at least not without having said more about it, and certainly not without enacting language that provides a stronger basis for that conclusion. Four Justices, looking at the basic purpose of the statute, believed that Congress *could* well have intended it to cover cigarettes, once science showed the danger that was present; and that neither the language in the FDCA, nor in other statutes, demanded that the Court decide to the contrary.

How did the two sides approach the legal problem? Did one side emphasize only text, while the other side emphasized only purposes? No. Both sides used both kinds of arguments. At the same time, intuition undeniably played a role. Some Justices may have thought that "tobacco products are simply too important, used by too many people, for Congress to have authorized FDA regulation without saying more about it." The other side may have thought that "changes in scientific analysis bring tobacco within the scope of the statute's regulation-authorizing language; and the purposes of the statute (public health) warranted interpreting the statute to authorize regulation." Both sides used both textual and purpose-related arguments.

4.

The Text/Purpose Divide

Now let us consider two more recent cases in which there are clearer, more marked differences between text-based and purpose-based approaches. In these cases, it is fair to say that methodological differences are primarily responsible for different members of the Court reaching different results. In reading the examples, consider whether the majority relied too heavily upon text, or whether the dissenters relied too heavily upon purposes.

Return Mail, Inc. v. United States Postal Service (2019)[1]

The first case is a patent case. The Court decided the case in 2019 by a vote of 6–3. I wrote the dissent. Though the case is technical, many Supreme Court statutory cases are technical. The case also, like many statutory cases, involves complex text. That complexity may tempt an interpreter to rely only upon text without fully answering the "why" question: Why did Congress enact this statute in this way?

As you consider the case, keep in mind the fact that you, or anyone else with an invention, can apply to the United States Patent and Trademark Office (PTO) for a patent. That patent will protect you from others using your invention without your permission for twenty years.[2] To obtain the patent, you must convince the PTO that you have invented something that is useful, that is novel, and which meets certain other conditions.[3] After obtaining a patent, you can sue someone who uses your patent without your permission for patent infringement.[4] But that person, the defendant in your lawsuit, can successfully defend against your suit by showing that the PTO should not have awarded you a patent in the first place.[5] That defendant would have to show that your patent is invalid by clear and convincing evidence.[6]

Ordinarily, A, who holds a patent, will sue B for patent infringement in a federal court. B can make his "A's patent is invalid" defense right then and there. But Congress has provided other, administrative ways that B can invalidate A's patent even before A goes to court. Among those other ways, "a person" (as the statute says) can ask the agency that granted the patent (namely, the PTO) to conduct a post-grant review.[7] If the office grants the motion for a post-grant review, the office will set up a special board to conduct that review. That board will have three members drawn from the PTO's Patent Trial and Appeal Board,[8] who will then hold a hearing. That hearing may be elaborate, involving discovery, affidavits, written memoranda, and even oral testimony.[9] The board can then affirm the PTO's issuance of the patent, or it can cancel some or all of the patent's claims.[10] If either party is dissatisfied with the board's result, that party can ask for review in a specialized federal appeals court.[11]

Now, here is the legal question in the case: Remember that I first put the words "a person" in quotation marks. That is because those words come from the statute, and the statute specifies who may ask the PTO to set up a review board.[12] The question before the Court in *Return Mail* was whether the United States Postal Service, which asked the PTO for a post-grant review, could do so.[13] Could a government agency, in other words, use the patent agency's administrative procedure to try to invalidate another person's patent? Did the statutory words "a person" include a government agency, such as the Postal Service?

A divided Court, using textual reasoning, concluded (6–3) that the word "person" did not include a government agency.[14] Why not? First, there were earlier cases in which the Court said that there was a "presumption" that the word "person" in a statute does not include the "sovereign" (i.e., a nation).[15] And the very first part of the United States Code, originally called the Dictionary Act, says that (unless context indicates the contrary) a "person" includes "corporations, associations, firms, partnerships, societies, and joint stock companies, as well as individuals."[16] It says nothing about federal government agencies. Thus, there was a "presumption" that the word "person" in the patent statute did not include the federal government, and there was no "affirmative showing of statutory intent to the contrary."[17]

Second, while the Postal Service said that the word "person" elsewhere in the Patent Act clearly included the government, the Court found that these other provisions contained linguistic clues that they required inclusion of the government; they were all necessary parts of a statutory system designed to allow the government to obtain patents.[18] That was not so in the case of the use of "person" in the provision allowing administrative challenges to a patent's validity.[19] Thus, the statute used the word "person" in "multiple conflicting ways."[20] (This is to say, "so what" to the argument that, elsewhere in the statute, "person" includes government persons.)

Third, though it was true, as the Postal Service pointed out, that the government had long participated rather like private persons in patent proceedings, the administrative provisions at issue in *Return Mail* (i.e., the administrative review provisions) were new—only eight years old.[21] The relevant question, to the majority, was whether the *new* 2011 statutory revision displaced the presumptive meaning of the word "person" in the administrative provisions at issue. And the majority thought it did not.[22]

Fourth, even though the Postal Service, like private parties, was subject to damages suits for patent infringement, the majority noted that the procedures and remedies a private person might obtain in a court proceeding and those a government entity might there obtain were not symmetrical. A private patent holder's court suit against others allows the private patent holder to obtain a jury trial, an injunction, and punitive damages. None of these procedures or remedies is available when the patent holder is a government agency.[23] It did not follow, in other words, that just because the Postal Service was liable for damages in infringement claims, it was entitled to the same rights as others to claim in administrative proceedings that the patent was invalid, nor did it follow that the Postal Service should be able to obtain the same administrative reexamination that those others might obtain.[24]

Finally, the majority made one argument that was not purely textual. It said that to allow one government agency (the Postal Service) to attack the validity of a private party's patent before another government agency (the PTO) would produce an "awkward situation."[25]

My point in listing all these arguments is to show the reader what a text-based argument is often like. I am tempted to say it consists of next to nothing but "text, text, text" in various forms, along with a host of different arguments as to why a particular reading of the text is the "best" reading.

Now consider the dissenters' arguments. Though they began with text, they were primarily purpose-oriented. The dissenters agreed that there was a statutory "presumption" that the word "person" did not include the government.[26] But they pointed to case law that said that "there [wa]s no hard and fast rule of exclusion."[27] Rather the "purpose, the subject matter, the context, the legislative history, [or] the executive interpretation" all may "'indicate an intent' to include the government."[28]

The dissenters then said that most of the statutory provisions that used the word "person" but might be read as excluding a government agency concerned matters that could not possibly *include* a government agency (for example, travel arrangements or personal qualifications).[29] But other provisions that used the word "person" concerned such matters as how to obtain patents, and the dissenters believed that those provisions clearly *did* include government agencies.[30] For those reasons, the dissenters said, the text of the statute supported the claim that the word "person" at issue also included government agencies.

The dissent's main argument, however, was not textual. It instead focused upon purposes. Referring to congressional reports and PTO manuals, it said that Congress enacted the statute in order to "make the patent system more efficient" by making it easier to challenge "questionable patents" in somewhat simpler administrative proceedings.[31] This purpose was satisfied whether government parties or private parties used the statute's administrative-based patent-validity challenge procedures. Congress also sought to allow a patent holder (say "B"), when sued for infringing a different but related patent (owned by, say "A"), to protect his own patent by more easily proving that A's different patent is invalid.[32] Again, this rationale applied precisely to the same extent whether B was a private person or a government agency.

Government defendants in patent infringement suits, the dissent explained, risk serious liability, sometimes ranging in the billions of dollars.[33] Hence, there was good reason to permit government agencies accused of infringement to invoke the administrative procedures. Allowing the Postal Service to do so could lead to its victory in the court suit against it by invalidating the allegedly infringed patent that it was using. This was the same kind of reason that led Congress to enact the statute that allowed private persons to invoke the administrative proceedings. And, as for the "awkwardness" of one government agency initiating an administrative procedure before another government agency: Well, the dissent did not see any such awkwardness.[34]

The basic question, asked the dissent, was, "Why?"[35] Government agencies can "apply for and obtain patents," "maintain patents," "sue other parties for infringing their patents," "be sued for infringing patents by private parties," and "be forced to defend their own patents when a private party" invokes PTO administrative invalidation procedures.[36] Why, then, would Congress have declined to give federal agencies the power to invoke those same administrative procedures? The dissenters could find no good answer to the "why" question.

That "why" question is one of purpose. What is the purpose of the statutory provision? To believe, as the dissenters believe, that the "why" question is the main question leads to one answer: Namely, that the government is a "person" within the meaning of the statute in *Return Mail*. To look at text-related considerations alone led the majority to a different answer.

Duncan v. Walker (2001)[37]

A second case, decided in 2001 by a vote of 7–2, is also highly technical. But I wrote a dissent in which I tried to illustrate the text-oriented/purpose-oriented difference. To understand this case, you must know something about *habeas corpus*. Among other things, a prisoner convicted of a state crime (say robbery) can eventually ask a federal court to issue a writ of *habeas corpus* setting aside his state conviction.[38] This may be done on the ground that the state courts committed a serious legal error (say, they failed to provide the prisoner with an adequate lawyer at his criminal trial).

You must also keep in mind three procedural rules related to a federal *habeas corpus* proceeding. First, the state prisoner cannot present a particular claim or issue (such as what, he says, went seriously wrong at his state trial) to the federal judge unless he has first presented the claim to state judges in a state proceeding.[39] Second, a federal statute, the Antiterrorism and Effective Death Penalty Act, sets forth a statute of limitations that applies to a petition for *habeas corpus*. The state prisoner must file his federal petition for *habeas corpus* in federal court *within one year after his state conviction becomes final.*[40] Third, there is an exception to the one-year statute of limitations. The federal statute says that, for purposes of calculating the one year, the federal court shall not count the "time during which a properly filed application for *State post-conviction or other collateral review with respect to the pertinent judgment or claim is pending.*"[41]

Duncan v. Walker focused upon this last requirement. A state prisoner named Sherman Walker was convicted of robbery, had pursued state appeals and other state remedies, and had lost them all.[42] He then filed a petition asking a federal court to issue a writ of *habeas corpus* on the ground that his trial counsel at his state trial was inadequate.[43] Unfortunately for Walker, he had never raised this *particular* claim in a state court, i.e., he violated the first rule I just mentioned. So, the federal judge dismissed his claim so that he could go back to state court and raise the claim in a state proceeding.[44] He did so, but he lost in that state proceeding, too, so he then filed a second *habeas corpus* petition in federal court.

Now we come to the issue. Imagine (for ease of numbers) that Walker had filed his first *habeas corpus* petition four months after the conclusion of state post-conviction proceedings. Then suppose that the federal judge took *seven months* to decide to send Walker back to state court. And, then suppose another *two months* passed before Walker filed his state petition in an available state proceeding. The clock is paused during any time Walker spends in that state post-conviction proceeding. But when Walker wants to come back to federal court to file his second *habeas corpus* petition, it looks like he may have a problem: four plus seven plus two is 13, which is more than the year allotted to him to file his claim by the federal statute.

But the statute also says we should not count the time in a "state post-conviction or other collateral review" proceeding.[45] Do the words "other collateral review" include federal *habeas* proceedings (which are "collateral")? If so, we can subtract seven months, the months during which Walker's first *habeas corpus* petition was pending in federal court and the judge was deciding what to do. Walker can then bring his second *habeas corpus* petition. Or do those words ("other collateral review") refer only to "other" collateral *state* proceedings, in which case Walker is out of luck? That was the question before the Supreme Court.[46]

The Court agreed with the state, by a vote of 7–2, that the words "other collateral review" did not include federal *habeas* proceedings. Textually speaking, argued the majority, it seemed as if the relevant statutory provision applied only to applications for *state* post-conviction review or applications for other *state* collateral review. The words referring to applications for "*other collateral review*" followed the words "state post-conviction or."[47] Though a federal *habeas corpus* proceeding is a "collateral proceeding," the words of the statutory phrase say nothing about *federal* collateral review. Moreover, in other roughly similar provisions, Congress used both words; it referred to both "State or Federal postconviction proceedings."[48] Further, had Congress wanted to include federal proceedings, it could simply have omitted the word "state," for doing so would have strongly suggested that the statutory phrase included both kinds of (state and federal) proceedings.[49] Finally, no word in a statute (here "state") should be treated as unnecessary surplus.[50] The majority relied upon these textual arguments to show that the statutory provision did not suspend the running of the statute of limitations during periods where petitions for federal writs of *habeas corpus* were pending.

By contrast, the dissent relied primarily upon purpose-based arguments. It did not find the textual arguments totally convincing. The statute does not explicitly say "federal" but it does say "other."[51] Why doesn't "other" include "federal"? Rather than debating the text, the dissent first asked *why* Congress would have subtracted from the one-year limitations period the time that the prisoner spent in *state* post-conviction proceedings.[52] The answer must be that collateral proceedings, whether state or federal, take time. To count all that time as part of the one-year limitations period would simply mean that state prisoners would almost always use up their year.[53]

Then the dissent asked the key purpose-related question: *Why* would Congress not have wanted time spent in federal collateral proceedings to be deducted from the one-year limitations period? Doesn't the same time problem arise for the state prisoner who files a federal collateral proceeding, as for the state prisoner who files a state collateral proceeding? Why would Congress not have wanted to help the first prisoner in the same way that it wanted to help the second? The question, in other words, was why not interpret the word "other" as applying to other federal, as well as other state, proceedings.[54] Why not?

The statutory language did not answer the "why" question, nor did it place the dissent's position out of bounds. The statute simply uses the term "other." That "other" is indeterminate: It could refer exclusively to some "other" kind of state collateral review proceedings, or it could also refer to federal collateral review proceedings, which are, after all, "other" proceedings. The words of the statutory phrase, standing alone, do not provide an answer.

For the dissent, the "why" question *did* help determine what the word "other" meant.[55] The dissent argued that it could find *no good reason* for giving the prisoner this time-related break where state proceedings were involved but not where federal proceedings were involved. Prisoners are often not well represented, or represented at all, when they first file a federal *habeas corpus* petition.[56] They may go first to the wrong court.[57] And a petition for *habeas corpus*, filed, for example, too soon in federal court, can take time for the judge to resolve. An eventual decision that the prisoner has filed his petition in federal court too soon (as Walker did) may well have eaten up quite a lot of time. A broader interpretation of the word "other" to include federal proceedings, as well as state proceedings, helps prevent a prisoner from losing his federal *habeas* case without its ever having been heard. It prevents the case from being lost forever simply because the prisoner failed to understand a complex area of federal law.[58]

The majority provided some possible answers to the question of why Congress might have wanted to treat federal and state failures differently. Perhaps Congress wanted to encourage a state prisoner to exhaust his claim in state court first.[59] But the dissent did not find the majority's efforts to explain "why" particularly convincing.[60] It noted that many prisoners knew little about the law governing *habeas* petitions. It added that federal judges dismissed close to half of all *habeas* petitions, and that close to 40 percent were dismissed for failure to exhaust state remedies. Moreover, at the time, more than half of all *habeas* petitions were pending in federal court for more than six months, and 10 percent were pending for over two years.[61] It is also difficult to imagine the statute, read as the majority read it, leading any prisoner (not expert in law) to act more speedily.[62]

More to the present point, the majority concluded with these words:

[Walker] contends that [the State's] construction of the statute creates the potential for unfairness to litigants who file timely federal habeas petitions that are dismissed without prejudice after the limitation period has expired. *But our sole task in this case is one of statutory construction*, and upon examining the language and purpose of the statute, we are convinced that [it] does not toll the limitation period during the pendency of a federal habeas petition.[63]

Does this say more than: "Well, that is what the statute says." Does it? This case, I believe, provides a good example of what happens when one looks to language, virtually alone, in an effort to resolve statutory ambiguity. Here, the dissent argued that the result was unfair in a way that Congress would not have intended.[64] It found little, if anything, to be said in favor of reading the statutory language to bring about that unfairness; and it implied that the majority's emphasis upon text along with its failure to explore the "why" question more thoroughly was responsible for that unfairness.

5.

Static or Dynamic?

Whether to interpret a statutory phrase statically or dynamically is often a particularly difficult decision for a judge using a purely textual approach. The issue arises when relevant facts or law change during the time that the statute is in effect. Do those changes affect the statute the judge is interpreting? Should the judge take them into account?

Suppose, for example, that Congress in 1985 enacted a statute requiring owners of property that creates a "habitat" for "endangered species" to take certain actions.[1] Suppose further that in 1985, no one considers the Siberian mink an "endangered species." But, by 2005, it is clear that the Siberian mink *is* an endangered species. Does the 1985 statute apply to the Siberian mink? If the statutory phrase is "static," it will apply only to those species that were endangered in 1985; if the phrase is "dynamic," then it will apply to species that have become endangered after 1985. So, which is it? Should judges treat the statute as "static" or as "dynamic"?

The reason that this kind of interpretive question often proves particularly difficult for a textualist judge to answer is that Congress often does not say. The text says nothing about the matter. In fact, legislators may not even have thought about it. Here are two examples of the difficulty.

Wisconsin Central Ltd. v. United States (2018)[2]

Many years ago, the federal government created a special retirement scheme by statute (the Railroad Retirement Tax Act) that was akin to

Social Security for certain railroad workers.[3] While they were actively employed, the workers and their employers had to pay a tax to the federal government.[4] Then, when the workers retired, they would receive payments from the government. The payments varied depending upon how much the workers had earned during their working years, and the tax the workers paid during those years also varied in amount depending upon the amount of what the statute called the workers' "money remuneration."[5] The question before the Court focused on those last two words, "money remuneration."

Everyone agreed that those two words did not include the value of non-monetary compensation such as food, lodging, railroad tickets, and the like, even though the railroads frequently gave those items to their employees at the time the statute was enacted.[6] But what about *stock options*? When Congress initially enacted the statute, railroads did not normally provide stock options to employees as compensation. But, as time passed, more and more railroads directly included stock options in employee compensation. Railroads also gave employees stock options indirectly: The employee could check a box; the employer would tell the employee how much he had received in the form of stock options; and an agent of the employer would sell the options immediately and include the proceeds in the employee's pay packet.[7]

Were stock options a form of "money remuneration"? In 2018, by a 5–4 vote, the Court held that the stock options were not.[8] Thus, their receipt did not count as part of the worker's taxable pay. In essence, unlike the Siberian minks (if we treat the words "endangered species" as dynamic), payment of the stock options—which were a fairly recent development—did not fall within the scope of an old statutory phrase.

The majority reached this conclusion primarily through textual methods applied to the words "money remuneration." Relying upon dictionaries in circulation in 1937 when Congress enacted the law, it said that "money" meant currency "issued by [a] recognized authority as a medium of exchange."[9] At least, the majority considered that to be the ordinary meaning of the term. The majority then wrote that the Court's "job is to interpret the words consistent with their 'ordinary meaning . . . at the time Congress enacted the statute.'"[10]

Why, according to the majority, did stock options not fall within the scope of that old definition? Well, because we cannot buy groceries with a stock option. The word "remuneration," of course, can include all kinds of compensation, but Congress modified that word with the word "money," which, at least, meant that Congress did not want to tax things that are not money.[11]

Indeed, on the majority's telling, when Congress enacted the 1939 version of the Internal Revenue Code two years later, it treated "money" and "stock options" as two different things.[12] When Congress later enacted a pension law applicable to other workers, that law taxed "*all* remuneration," including remuneration "paid in any medium other than cash."[13] "We usually 'presume,'" said the majority, that "differences in language like this convey differences in meaning."[14]

The dissenters, however, took a different approach. (I wrote the dissent.) They first argued that the statutory language was ambiguous.[15] They pointed out that half or more of the railroad's employees who received stock options asked the railroad immediately to exercise the option, thereby buying the stock to which the option referred and then selling the stock "with the proceeds deposited into the employee's bank account—just like a deposited paycheck."[16] Moreover, a stock option, unlike say, free railroad tickets or free food, had a "readily discernible value: namely, the difference between the option price and the market price when the employee exercises the option."[17] Further, other dictionary definitions of "money," even some available in 1937, said that "money" includes "property considered with reference to its pecuniary value," and "property or possessions of any kind viewed as convertible into money."[18] These definitions at least loosely fit not just a stock option (which must first be sold to become a "medium of exchange"), but also a paycheck, which normally cannot be used as a "medium of exchange" unless it is first deposited into a bank account.[19]

The dissent, having found linguistic ambiguity, asked, "What could

Congress' purpose have been when it used the word 'money'?"[20] The most obvious purpose would have been to exclude certain nonmonetary in-kind benefits, either because they are nontransferable or otherwise difficult to value. In 1937, "it was common for railroad workers to receive free transportation for life."[21] That benefit was particularly difficult to value. So were other in-kind benefits those workers often received, such as "board, rents, housing," and "lodging"—benefits once included in an early version of the bill but later dropped as "superfluous."[22] To read the statute's language as excluding stock options was not consistent with this basic purpose, argued the dissent, for "stock options are financial instruments. They could readily be bought and sold, they were not benefits in kind (i.e., they had no value to employees other than their financial value) and—compared to, say meals or spontaneous train trips, they were not particularly difficult to value."[23] Thus, they were very much like other forms of "money remuneration" and very much unlike those items that Congress, in using the word "money," intended to exclude.

The dissent also thought that including stock options within the term "money remuneration" would produce consistency between the statute at issue and other federal pension-like schemes. That consistency was especially important in respect to a matter where the dissent could find no purpose-related reason for treating the railroad statute differently.[24] Finally, the government had treated Railroad Act stock options in the same manner that these other acts treated stock options, i.e., as a form of remuneration, for many years after initial enactment of the law.[25] Long-standing practice, in the dissent's view, should not be loosely tossed aside if the statutory text is ambiguous.

The upshot: To look at text alone does not answer the question. To look at purpose and history as well breaks what seems to be a linguistic tie. A purpose-based approach suggests that, even if Congress never thought about stock options in 1937, a legislator who voted for the bill then would likely have wanted its "money remuneration" phrase to include stock options should they become a way to compensate workers in the future. So, why refuse to look at purpose? What is gained by limiting the universe of interpretive tools to text alone?

Jam v. International Finance Corp. (2019)[26]

Let us look at another case (decided in 2019) that presents the same kind of problem. Is the relevant statutory phrase "dynamic" or "static"? To answer the question, the judge should at least examine the statute's history and ask why Congress enacted it. To look at the text alone will shed no light on the answer.

In 1945, Congress enacted a statute called the International Organizations Immunities Act.[27] The relevant statutory language focuses upon lawsuits that private persons might try to bring against international organizations in the United States. It says that international organizations, such as the World Health Organization, the United Nations, the Food and Agriculture Organization, and so forth, will enjoy "the *same immunity* from suit . . . as is enjoyed by *foreign governments*."[28]

The static/dynamic problem arose out of the fact that, when Congress enacted this statute in 1945, foreign governments enjoyed broad sovereign immunity.[29] Private persons normally could not sue foreign governments without their permission, even when those governments had engaged in commercial activities (such as buying or selling goods in America, or borrowing or lending Americans money). By the late 1970s, however, Congress had changed immunity law in the Foreign Sovereign Immunities Act, at least as it applied to foreign *governments*.[30] By that time, the United States would not allow foreign governments to claim sovereign immunity (preventing lawsuits) when those governments engaged in commercial activities in the United States.[31] To be more specific, Congress had carved out an exception (appropriately termed the "commercial exception") from that earlier grant of sovereign immunity provided to foreign nations, thereby allowing lawsuits against the foreign nation based upon commercial activities that the foreign nation had engaged in in the United States.

Now you can see the question. Foreign *governments* engaged in commercial activities are no longer immune, but are *international organizations* still immune from suit when they do the same? The answer depends upon how the Court interprets the two statutory words "same immunity." Are those words "static"? Do they mean that international organizations shall enjoy the "same immunity as foreign governments enjoy when this statute became law in 1945"? Or are they "dynamic"? Do they mean that international organizations will enjoy the "same immunity" as foreign nations at the time of the lawsuit, including a lawsuit brought decades later? If the former, an international organization engaged in commercial activity in the United States can assert sovereign immunity and prevent a private person from bringing a lawsuit. If the latter, the organization cannot assert sovereign immunity and prevent the bringing of a lawsuit.

Jam involved citizens of India who brought a suit for damages against the International Finance Corporation (IFC), an international development bank with offices in Washington, D.C.[32] The IFC lends money to foreign enterprises helping to develop foreign economies. The IFC had loaned money to a corporation that then built a power plant in India. Local fishermen and farmers sued the IFC in the United States arguing that it was responsible for harmful pollution. The IFC argued in the federal courts that it was absolutely immune from the lawsuit.

The Court by a vote of 8–1 concluded that the language was dynamic,[33] and that neither the IFC nor other international organizations could assert sovereign immunity in federal courts. The Indian citizens could therefore proceed with their lawsuit. I was the sole dissenter. I believed that the Court, at the least, should not have based its conclusion upon textual considerations alone.

How did the Court's text-based reasoning work? First, the majority said that the statute's language "more naturally len[t] itself" to a dynamic reading.[34] Why? The words "same immunity" did not specify whether they meant "same as in 1945" or "same as at the time of the lawsuit." Nevertheless, the majority concluded that the statute's continued textual linkages between international organizations and foreign governments demonstrated Congress's desire to "ensure ongoing parity between the two."[35]

Second, the majority pointed to a canon of interpretation called the "reference canon."[36] Some textbooks and cases referred to that canon in the nineteenth century, and in 1945 as well.[37] The canon says that "when a statute refers to a general subject, the statute adopts the law as it exists whenever a question under the statute arises."[38] When a statute applies statically (i.e., only to law as it then stands), it normally will refer to existing law by its name, title, or code reference. A statute, for example, that says a certain kind of bridge-building company can "collect the same tolls" as other bridge-building companies means to refer to the tolls that other companies are allowed to collect at the time of a lawsuit, perhaps many years after the statute was enacted. But a statute that says that a certain kind of bridge-building company can "collect the same tolls" as are listed in "the Golden Gate Bridge Manual" means that it can collect only the tolls listed there at the time the statute was passed. I think it is fair to say that this canon—the reference canon—is obscure; I doubt many judges or legislators have ever heard of it, and many court cases ignore it. Nevertheless, the majority found it meaningful.

Third, the Court rejected the IFC's contrary arguments. The IFC said that absolute immunity was needed to protect it from lawsuits that would make it difficult for it to carry out its basic mission of helping poor countries develop. The Court said this claim was unproven.[39] The IFC also pointed out that other language in the statute, which gave the U.S. president authority to remove immunity when the president thought a suit should go forward, could prevent unfair results.[40] The Court thought the "most natural[]" reading of the language allowed the president to exercise this authority on a case-by-case basis, taking "retail" rather than "wholesale" action.[41]

Finally, the IFC claimed that international organization immunity served a different purpose than foreign nation immunity. Foreign nations engage in many different activities, and commercial activity is but one of those many. An international organization, however, is more likely to pursue a single goal, such as economic development. The purpose of giving that kind of organization immunity, according to the IFC, was "to allow such organizations to freely pursue the collective goals of member countries without undue interference from the courts of any one member country."[42] Limiting foreign nation immunity provided no good reason for removing virtually all immunity from international organizations. The Court responded that the IFC's argument based upon purposes and consequences "gets the inquiry backward." It said:

> We ordinarily assume "absent a clearly expressed legislative intention to the contrary," that "the legislative purpose is expressed by the ordinary meaning of the words used." . . . Whatever the ultimate purpose of international organization immunity may be . . . , the immediate purpose of the immunity provision is expressed in language that Congress typically uses to make one thing continuously equivalent to another.[43]

The majority's arguments show textualism in action.

My dissent did not deny that the legal question before the Court was a close one. But it tried to show how a purpose-oriented approach would work better where the Court was tasked with deciding whether statutory language is "static" or "dynamic." Using a purpose-oriented approach, the Court would have reached a different result.

The dissent said that the language of the statute was ambiguous.[44] Linguistically speaking, one can read the words "same immunity . . . as *is* enjoyed by" to refer to "as of 1945" or "as of the time of the lawsuit." "Language alone cannot resolve the statute's linguistic ambiguity."[45] In the dissent's view, "judges . . . have long resolved ambiguity not by looking to the words alone, but by examining the statute's purpose as well."[46] And here, the dissent felt that we could more easily reach the best conclusion by weighing the statute's history, context, purposes, and consequences.

At the outset, the dissent pointed to cases in which courts had interpreted the words "same . . . as" by looking at the statute's purposes as well as its words.[47] The dissent also recognized that a textualist judge can consider more than the language of the particular statutory phrase at issue, and that here, the majority had placed considerable weight upon the reference canon of interpretation.[48] The dissent did not think the canons provided much help because treatises describing the "reference canon" upon its emergence had "long explained that whether a reference statute adopts the law as it stands on the date of enactment or includes subsequent changes in the law . . . [was] 'fundamentally a question of legislative intent and purpose.'"[49]

In *Jam*, the dissent contended that we could learn much by looking directly to the statute's basic purposes. The history of the statute, as set forth in congressional reports written just after World War II, showed two such purposes.[50] First, the statute would "enabl[e] this country to fulfill its commitments in connection with its membership in international organizations."[51] Second, it would "facilitate fully the functioning of international organizations in this country."[52]

In 1945, the major multilateral international organizations that Congress would have considered included the United Nations, the World Bank, the International Monetary Fund, the Food and Agriculture Organization, and post–World War II refugee relief organizations (e.g., the United Nations Relief and Rehabilitation Administration).[53] The founding documents of those organizations called upon members to grant them broad immunity from suit.[54] In 1945, that meant immunity when those international organizations engaged in commercial, as well as in noncommercial, activities.

Consider the United Nations Relief and Rehabilitation Administration (UNRRA). The United States and Allied nations created UNRRA as World War II was ending.[55] Its objective, as described by President Franklin Roosevelt, was to "assure a fair distribution of available supplies among" those nations liberated in World War II and to "*ward off death by starvation or exposure among those peoples.*"[56] By 1945, when Congress passed the Immunities Act, UNRRA had obtained and shipped billions of pounds of food, clothing, and other relief supplies to children freed from Nazi concentration camps and others in serious need.[57] This work involved contracts. UNRRA spent two-thirds of its budget buying goods and services in the United States.[58] UNRRA trained foreign doctors in the United States, likely under contracts. In essence, UNRRA's mission *was* unavoidably commercial. "Would Congress, believing that it had provided the absolute immunity that UNRRA sought and expected, also have intended courts to interpret the statute 'dynamically,'" thereby removing most of the immunity that it had provided in 1945?[59] That removal would implicate not just UNRRA's immunity but also other, future international organizations with similar commercial objectives.

That, of course, was just what happened to foreign nations.[60] But as the dissent noted, unlike foreign governments, most international organizations were *not* sovereign entities engaged in a host of different activities, but rather organizations with specific missions. The missions of most of those international organizations at issue in 1945 required them to engage in activities that the United States might well have considered to be "commercial." Further, Congress may well have hoped that many of those international organizations—often buying goods or making contracts within the United States—would also locate their headquarters within the United States.[61] Congress, by contrast, did not hope that nations such as Britain or France would relocate and end up in New York.

To the dissent, the act's purposes suggested a static interpretation. That interpretation was consistent with the statutory language: One could read the statute's reference to the immunities of "foreign governments" as a shorthand for the immunities those foreign governments enjoyed in 1945, the time the act was passed.[62]

The dissent then considered consequences. In other cases, the Court had interpreted the "commercial exception" broadly.[63] International organizations such as the World Bank, the Inter-American Development Bank, the Multilateral Investment Guarantee Agency, and others, promote development by guaranteeing investments (or by themselves investing) in foreign projects throughout the world. Under the Court's "dynamic" interpretation, they might well find that their core functions fall within the American statute's commercial exception. Suddenly, they would become subject to American law and lawsuits in respect to many of their activities.[64]

Furthermore, the dissent continued, international organizations, unlike sovereign nations, were multilateral, with members from many different nations. For one nation—the United States—to remove immunity from commercial activities meant that one nation could, through its liability rules, shape the policies of the international organization through lawsuits attacking its actions, rules, and regulations.[65]

Of course, a static interpretation means that certain meritorious lawsuits in the commercial area will not be able to proceed. I was not unsympathetic to those concerns, but a static interpretation does not leave those injured by the international organization without remedy. As the dissent explained, many international organizations have narrowed their own immunity, thereby permitting lawsuits.[66] But they have done so carefully in areas they have defined, and under conditions they have set forth. They have sought to maintain limitations upon categories of suits where total removal of immunity would interfere with their ability to carry out their core functions. The United Nations, for example, has agreed to "make provisions for appropriate modes of settlement of . . . [d]isputes arising out of contracts or other disputes of a private law character."[67] (The U.N. normally does so by agreeing to submit commercial disputes to arbitration.[68])

The dissent acknowledged that these alternatives might sometimes prove inadequate but noted that the act itself provided a way to set aside immunity. As I wrote, the Immunities Act grants to the president the authority to "withhold," to "condition," or to "limit" any of the act's immunities in "light of the functions performed by any such international organization."[69] So, the president could "withhold" the immunity from suit that the act granted to an international organization. Were the Court to interpret the statute statically, "the default rule would be immunity in suits arising from an organization's commercial activities," but with the executive branch having the power to withdraw immunity.[70] In making that determination, the executive branch could consider whether allowing the lawsuit would "jeopardize the organization's ability to carry out its public interest tasks."[71] Thus, the executive branch would "have the authority it need[s] to separate" the weak-lawsuit sheep from the strong-lawsuit goats.[72]

Under the majority's interpretation, however, there was "no such flexibility."[73] The majority's interpretation removed an international organization's commercially related immunity across the board, and neither the executive branch, nor the courts, nor the organization itself could restore it. Consequently, international organizations could no longer address "any resulting potential liability, where a lawsuit seriously threatens interference with an organization's legitimate needs and goals."[74] The upshot, I wrote, is that "a static interpretation" of the statute results in the statute itself "com[ing] equipped with flexibility."[75] The static interpretation provides a way to "withdraw immunity where justified"; the majority's dynamic interpretation "fr[oze] potential liability into law."[76]

I do not claim that a judge looking at purposes, history, and consequences would automatically interpret the statute as I would interpret it. The question presented is difficult, regardless of whether the judge uses a textual or a purpose-oriented approach. I claim only that asking a specific kind of question is useful to the judicial inquiry: What does history, tested by recognition of related consequences, tell us about the mischief that Congress intended statutory language to address? To determine those purposes is often necessary, or at least very helpful, in understanding something that text alone cannot easily tell us (namely, whether courts should read a statutory phrase statically or dynamically). And purpose will more often than not lead us to legally sound, workable interpretations than will purely textual methods. In my view, this immunity case provides a good illustration of what it means for the judge—here our statutory painter—to proceed with key colors missing from the palette.

6.

Consequences

Complex cases provide a fertile field for disagreement between text-oriented and purpose-oriented judges. In their line of work, judges have to determine the meaning or the application of seemingly indeterminate phrases serving obscure purposes, embedded in technical statutes that themselves require expert knowledge to understand their objectives. Textualist judges may suffer from having to interpret language that is not at all clear.

Purpose-oriented judges may also find it difficult to determine the objective of an obscure phrase. In these circumstances, a purpose-oriented judge may find help by looking to the consequences of interpretation. They will assume that Congress did not intend—and thus the language does not mean to produce—consequences that cause obvious practical problems or otherwise do not make sense. I shall provide, and simplify, a highly technical example to help show what I mean.

Azar v. Allina Health Services (2019)[1]

To understand the legal question in this case, one must know something about the Administrative Procedure Act (APA), a key federal administrative law statute.[2] The APA applies to most federal agencies. It explains how judges will often review the legality of an agency's actions. For example, the agency cannot act unreasonably, i.e., it cannot be arbitrary, capricious, or abuse its discretion. The APA also describes ways in which agencies can make rules or take other actions that implement policy.

In the sections that concern the agency's making of rules, the APA distinguishes between different types of rules. One kind of rule—often called a "legislative rule"—the courts treat gingerly. These rules often create substantive policies to implement a statutory objective. For instance, the Federal Aviation Administration might be tasked by statute with ensuring the safety of commercial flights—a very broad goal. The agency might, in turn, create detailed legislative rules to implement that statutory goal, like a rule that prohibits takeoffs in bad weather or a rule that prohibits the carrying of firearms on board. Courts typically give agencies broad leeway to write different, often detailed, legislative rules. Contrast this with an "interpretive rule." When an agency writes an "interpretive rule," it is simply interpreting the words of a statute; and courts are less likely to give as much legal leeway to the agency's conclusion. After all, courts know how to interpret statutes, too.

Go back to our snail example. Imagine the fare book is a statute, and that it uses the word "animal." If the agency (say the railroad) writes a legislative rule saying that a mouse is an "animal," courts may well treat a mouse as if it were part of the statutory word "animal." But if the agency writes an interpretive rule that says a mouse is an animal, the courts may think that the agency is doing no more than a court usually does, i.e., interpreting the words of a statute (here "animal"), and thus the court may prove more willing to second-guess the agency's interpretation.

The APA makes a distinction that concerns *how* the agency should set about creating these different kinds of rules. Normally, the agency must create *legislative* rules through a complex process called "notice and comment rulemaking." The agency writes a notice to the public setting forth the rule it is thinking of creating; the public sends the agency comments; and the agency then adopts a rule and it often explains its result primarily by discussing the public's comments.[3] When the agency wants to create an *interpretive* rule, it normally need not go through this complex procedure.[4]

For many years, the Department of Health and Human Services (DHHS) often did not have to go through these procedures at all because much of the Medicare program was exempt from this part of the APA. But, in the late 1980s, Congress changed the law. It said that the Medicare administering departments, such as **DHHS**, *did* have to use notice and comment rulemaking. But *when*? When, the statute said, the agency made any "rule, requirement or other statement of policy . . . that establishes or changes *a substantive legal standard* governing the scope of benefits . . . or the eligibility of individuals, entities or organizations to receive [Medicare benefits]."[5]

Now we can understand the issue in the case. Just what rules or other agency actions establish or change a "substantive legal standard," thereby triggering the complex notice-and-comment rulemaking procedure? Unfortunately, the phrase "substantive legal standard" was basically unknown to man, woman, or beast, nor to administrative lawyers before this particular enactment.[6]

The textualists on the Court, who were in the (7–1) majority in 2019 when the Court decided the case, used a host of text-based arguments to determine just where this phrase applied. Other parts of the statute, for example, seemed to use words such as "substantive" to include something like interpretive rules.[7] Moreover, the APA did *not* require the use of notice-and-comment procedures when the agency created "general statements of policy"; but the recent statute did require the agency to use notice-and-comment procedures if it created any "other statement of policy."[8] This textual difference, the majority thought, showed that the new statute required much more use of notice-and-comment procedures than prior law, and that fact supported the use of notice-and-comment procedures when the agency set forth interpretive rules.[9] That was the issue in the case: Could the agency write interpretive rules without going through notice-and-comment procedures?

Writing the dissent, I believed I had satisfactory answers to these textual matters (which I shall spare the reader here).[10] But most important for me was a nontextual matter, namely the *consequences* of the majority's approach. What would happen if the agency had to use notice-and-comment procedures when it set forth a rule—including an "interpretive rule" that simply interpreted the statute without itself having the force of law? The majority scarcely considered these consequences.

Why are consequences important? The strongest reason for believing that Congress meant the Medicare Act's notice-and-comment require-ment to apply to "legislative rules" but not to "interpretive" rules, argued the dissent, was a practical one. Medicare is a vast federal program that is "embodied in hundreds of pages of statutes and thousands of pages of often interrelated regulations," many of which have been subject to notice-and-comment rulemaking under the Administrative Procedure Act.[11] To help participants navigate the statutory and regulatory scheme, the agency has long issued "tens of thousands of pages of manual instructions, interpretive rules, and other guidance documents" that have not ordinarily been sub-ject to notice and comment under the APA.[12] DHHS followed this practice since well before Congress enacted the notice-and-comment provisions at issue in *Allina Health*. The result was a "sensible structure" for the complex Medicare reimbursement process.

Notice-and-comment procedures are elaborate and take time to com-plete. The government referred to a study that estimated that notice-and-comment procedures took four years on average to complete.[13] As the dissent put it, "[t]o imagine that Congress wanted the agency to use [notice-and-comment] procedures in respect to a large percentage of its Medicare guidance manuals is to believe that Congress intended to enact what could become a major roadblock to the implementation of the Medi-care program."[14] Yet, there is nothing in the statute's history that suggests that this was its purpose.

Why would Congress have wanted to require lengthy notice-and-comment proceedings before the agency could enact provisions of the kind that courts had held were interpretive (i.e., did not have the force of statutory law)? Courts, for example, had long held that rules in Medi-care's Provider Reimbursement Manual were interpretive rules exempt from the notice-and-comment requirement.[15] The manual, which is thousands of pages long, contains rules interpreting a provision of the Social Security Act that authorizes reimbursement to health care provid-ers for "reasonable costs" related to the treatment of patients on Medi-care.[16] The rules are rather minor and technical. One, for instance, deals with whether health care facilities can be reimbursed for certain kinds of retirement benefits that they provide to employees.[17] Another rule declines to reimburse corporate hospitals for the costs of complying with securities regulations.[18] There are many, many more rules like these in the Reimbursement Manual. The agency also publishes dozens more manuals governing "the scope of benefits, payments for services, [and] eligibility for benefits or services."[19] These manuals are the bread and butter of Medicare administration.

In dissent, I asked whether it was "reasonable to believe that Congress intended to impose notice-and-comment requirements upon" substantive agency rules and practices that were often of a minor technical kind.[20] Was it reasonable, moreover, to believe that Congress did so without saying a word about the significant effects this change would have on Medicare administration? Or that Congress did so without any evidence that others, outside of Congress, wanted this requirement? Perhaps because the matters I have just discussed are not textual, our Court did not consider them in any depth. And there is the problem. I do not believe it desirable or reasonable to interpret the statute's words in a way that would potentially have far-reaching negative consequences of the kind I have mentioned, absent evidence that that was Congress's intent. Those consequences would, at least potentially, "impose [a] . . . severe burden on the administration of the Medicare scheme."[21]

The words of the statute themselves are far from clear. That is why this case ended up in the Supreme Court. But the Court's method of clarifying the language—relying upon text and only upon text—draws aside the curtain in the darkened room to reveal nothing beyond but pitch-black night.

Now it should be apparent why I have discussed this technical example at some length. To look for legal enlightenment in text and text alone simply does not work. To fail to consider practical, purpose-based arguments means (here and elsewhere) a governmental system that will work less well and risk confusion, burden, delay, and perhaps incoherence for those who must administer complex governmental programs such as Medicare. Consideration of the practical consequences, as well as the need for simplicity and coherence in the law, in conjunction with the text, would have likely led to an interpretation of the statute that worked better, not just for administrators but for hospitals, patients, and also for the general public.

7.

Legislative History

If judges are to look to purposes, should they, in doing so, examine the legislative history of the statute? In particular, should they examine the congressional history of the bill or bills that eventually became the statute that the judge must interpret? Forty years ago or more, the answer to this question would have been easy.[1] Many, perhaps most, judges interpreting ambiguous words in a statute would likely have examined the legislative history of the statute in order better to understand its purposes. That history could include congressional floor debates, committee reports, hearing testimony, presidential messages, and sometimes more.[2] Those judges would have tried to learn from this material the nature of the problems that concerned Congress and how Congress intended the new law to deal with those problems. Before the 1980s, opinions in nearly every statutory case in the Supreme Court would refer to what the judges might have learned from relevant legislative history.[3]

Interpretive practice, however, has changed. Today, few judges refer to legislative history. Some, such as Justice Scalia, strongly oppose its use.[4] Why? Some say that its use tempts judges to treat this history as if they were looking over a crowd at a cocktail party in order to find their friends.[5] Others believe that searching legislative history as part of a search for a statute's purposes is a fruitless task or, perhaps, a mystical exercise like that hunt for the snark.[6] Still others believe it is constitutionally improper.[7] Regardless, aware that few of my colleagues believe legislative history an important interpretive tool, when I discuss that history in an opinion I often preface my discussion with words such as: "And, for those who believe legislative history helps determine the statute's meaning, I have found . . ."[8]

Are the critics right? If they are not, then judges diminish the effectiveness and vibrancy of their interpretive palette. They deprive themselves of a useful tool for determining a statute's purpose. And by doing so, they diminish the usefulness of looking for a statute's purpose as compared with, say, examining the text alone. In my view, the critics are wrong; and I shall use examples to help show why.[9]

All judges recognize that context can help resolve linguistic ambiguity. I once tried to bring up this fact during an oral argument at the Court. I recalled Professor Lon Fuller's example: Does a sign saying "No vehicles in the park?" apply to a jeep used as a war memorial?[10] Unfortunately, I could not recall the exact words, so I began by noting: "I learned the second year of law school that when you have a text which says 'all,' that there are often implied (not-written) exceptions." Then I was stuck. I could not think what came next. I ended up saying, "All animals in the park. No animals in the park doesn't necessarily apply to a pet oyster. . . ." The lawyer just looked puzzled. Chief Justice William Rehnquist looked over and said what I later thought was "Did you have a pet oyster?" But the transcript says he limited himself to saying, "Well, it's not an animal."[11]

Here, however, "no animals in the park" will do. Using ordinary speech, we know that a sign that says "no animals in the park" does not include squirrels, snails, or insects—once we know that the sign is placed at the entrance to a city park. But we are less certain about whether a K-9 unit meant to fight crime in the park should be considered an animal for the purposes of the sign.[12] If a statute's history comprises part of its context, then why not look to that context? Why not look to the background of the statute, the terms of the debate over its enactment, the factual assumptions the legislators made, the interpretive conventions the legislators thought applicable, and their expressed objectives, all in an effort to understand the statute's relevant purposes?

For one thing, the use of legislative history has not totally disappeared.[13] Many judges, including many textualist judges, continue to use legislative history in certain narrow statutory contexts.[14] They will examine legislative history, for example, in order to *avoid an absurd interpretive result*.[15] Blackstone, the eighteenth-century legal writer who compiled the law, roughly as it was, at that time, himself pointed out that if "collaterally . . . absurd consequences, manifestly contrary to common reason," arise out of statutes, those statutes "are, with regard to those collateral consequences, void."[16] He added that, when an interpretation leads to an "unreasonable" collateral result, "the judges are in decency to conclude that this consequence was not foreseen by the parliament, and therefore they are at liberty" to modify the legislation parliament enacted by principles of "equity."[17]

The best-known example of reading a text to eliminate words that would undercut its purpose is probably that attributed to the seventeenth-century legal philosopher Samuel von Pufendorf: A law in Bologna said that "whoever drew blood in the streets should be punished with the utmost severity."[18] The law contained no exceptions, but judges, said Pufendorf, must not interpret the law to apply to a surgeon who opens the vein of a person who fell down in the street in a fit. One can understand this example as reflecting the need to avoid an absurd result.

Take yet another example.[19] A procedural rule limited the use of prior criminal convictions where doing so would hurt "defendants" by suggesting a defendant's bad character.[20] Did this rule apply to defendants in civil, as well as in criminal, cases?[21] Justice Scalia, a strong textualist, thought the rule applied only in criminal cases and that it would be absurd to apply the rule in civil cases.[22] He added that he thought "it entirely appropriate to consult all public materials, including the background of [the rule] and the legislative history of its adoption, to verify . . . what seems to us an unthinkable disposition."[23]

Moreover, nearly all judges will look to legislative history *to verify that odd language in a statute results simply from a drafting error and nothing more.*[24] A federal criminal statute, for example, forbids the "possess[ion]" of any "false, forged, or counterfeit coin" with intent to defraud.[25] Does this statute apply only to American coins, or to South African coins as well?[26] On the one hand, the words *"any* coin" suggest foreign, as well as domestic coins. But the statute's history showed that it was the result of Congress in 1965 rewriting a similar older statute that clearly applied only to Ameri-

can coins.[27] To examine the 1965 law's legislative history helped answer the question.

Indeed, the 1965 House and Senate Reports on the bill make the answer clear. They specify that Congress in 1965 reorganized the law in this area, rewrote the statutes, and did so for purely organizational reasons. The staff members who wrote the law's language would have "thought that the legislators wanted them to accomplish a purely technical, nonsubstantive drafting objective."[28] Given these congressional reports, it is fair to say that any member of Congress interested in the 1965 statute would have thought its redrafting furthered a technical, not a substantive, objective. Hence, a judge wishing to interpret the statute in a manner consistent with Congress's objective would have limited the scope of the words "any coin" to "any American coin."

Nor should it be controversial for judges to look at a law's history *to determine whether a word bears a special technical meaning.*[29] Consider a Supreme Court case in which the Court held that the words "substantially justified" (in a statute that required the government to pay the other side's attorney's fees when the government's position was not "substantially justified") in effect meant "reasonable."[30] Justice Scalia, writing for the Court, drew this conclusion in large part from the way in which a different act, the Administrative Procedure Act, used the word "substantial" to mean "reasonable."[31] Justice Scalia knew that the APA meant "reasonable" (when it said "substantial") because a Supreme Court case decided eight years *before the APA became law* said that the word "substantial" meant "reasonable."[32]

Here is the point: The APA's legislative history said that the APA's language was taken (eight years later) from that case.[33] Complicated, but if one focuses (in Justice Scalia's opinion) on his important citation of a case called *Consolidated Edison Co. v. NLRB*,[34] one realizes that the only way Justice Scalia could have thought that case relevant is that he noticed (many years later) that the APA (enacted eight years after *Consolidated*) referred to *Consolidated*. The upshot is that Justice Scalia, a textualist, looked here to what others might have called a form of legislative history to determine whether the words "substantially justified" in context carried a specialized meaning. And he concluded that they did.

The more important question, however, is not about absurdity, mis-drafting, or specialized meanings. It is about purposes. That question lies at the heart of the dispute over the use of legislative history. Should a judge look to legislative history to determine which of several possible reasonable purposes Congress's law embodies? More difficult yet, suppose that the statute is politically controversial. Suppose that different members of Congress held different views about what the statute sought to achieve.[35] In that circumstance, may the judge look to legislative history in order to determine the statute's purpose (which will then help the judge interpret an ambiguous statutory phrase)?

Describing how Congress works helps answer this question. In doing so, I draw upon my own experience working for Senator Ted Kennedy. When, from 1974 to 1975, I was a staff member of the Administrative Practices Subcommittee of the Senate Committee on the Judiciary, I helped run hearings, draft legislation, and attempt to get legislation enacted into law. When, from 1979 to 1980, I was chief counsel of the Senate Committee on the Judiciary (of which Senator Kennedy was the chairman), I worked with both Democratic and Republican staff for the senators who were members of the committee. I would meet and discuss bills with those staff members as well as with the senators. I would discuss—at some length—plans for enacting legislation (and confirming presidentially nominated federal judges) with my Republican counterpart, who worked for Senator Strom Thurmond, the ranking Republican member. I would help write or edit Senate Reports on legislation that passed the committee. I would write or review dissenting report opinions. I would work with others to revise statutory language to improve a bill's chances of enactment. I would draft some parts of some laws, while sending bills to the Senate's Legislative Counsel's office for revision or for drafting of other parts.

I mention all this to suggest that I was reasonably familiar with Congress's law-drafting process as it existed at that time. Because I doubt that the aspects of the work I describe have changed radically, I believe I can describe roughly how Congress did, and likely still does, work. And I can also describe how it does not work.

Congress today is not made up of part-time citizen-legislators who burn

the midnight oil as they themselves draft the laws needed to resolve the social and political problems revealed during the day's spontaneous debate interchange. Rather, Congress is a more bureaucratic organization: its more than twenty thousand employees work full-time to generate legislation through complicated, but organized, processes of interaction with other institutions and groups. Those other institutions and groups include executive branch departments, labor unions, business organizations, and public interest groups, as well as their representatives (including lobbyists), who often initially draft legislation. Members of Congress typically make clear to congressional staff just what they are trying to achieve, and why; they may suggest content and text, not only for statutes, but also for reports or floor statements; they review proposed changes; and they negotiate and compromise with staff, with legislators, and with each other. The congressional staff works with these groups, the legislators, and other staff members to do the same.

When this process works well, staff members for each legislator will carefully review statutory language, report language, and significant proposed language for floor statements (modified and uttered by the staff member's own senator or other legislators). These words are checked for consistency with the legislator's own objectives and positions. Staff members, reflecting their legislator's point of view, will suggest changes in language, and they will negotiate compromises. The staff member will flag matters of significant substantive or political controversy, bring them to the legislator's attention, discuss them with the legislator, and obtain instructions from the legislator about how to proceed. On important matters, staff members for legislators who are directly involved will examine with care each word and proposed change, often with representatives of affected interest groups or institutions, not only in the language of the statute but also in each committee report and in many floor statements. Significant matters will again be brought to the attention of legislators for development of their individual positions, and for them to discuss and resolve with other legislators.

The process involves continuous interaction among legislators, staff members, and representatives of various institutions, as well as with groups that the proposed legislation is most likely to affect. This process requires each legislator to rely upon staff in the first instance to separate the matters that are significant from those that are not; it requires each legislator to make decisions about, and to resolve with other legislators, each significant matter; and it requires each legislator further to rely upon drafters and negotiators to carry out the legislator's decisions.

The process I have just described in a somewhat idealized form is an institutional one, in which the legislator relies in part upon the work of staff. In this process, no legislator reads every word of every report or floor statement or proposed statute, which may consist of hundreds of pages of text. However, through this process, those words are carefully reviewed by at least some of the people whom they will likely affect, as well as by the legislator's own employees. Moreover, in this process, the legislator makes the significant decisions and takes responsibility for the outcome.

This process, which the legislator manages, is similar to the processes through which managers of businesses, labor unions, government departments, and numerous other organizations reach decisions. No one expects top officials of large organizations to have read every word of every document they generate (or, for that matter, to have personally put together every part of every automobile or computer they manufacture). Most institutions work through downward delegation, with responsibility flowing upward to the ultimate decision-maker. The judiciary, with its smaller staff and decentralized decision-making, does not. But why should we expect, or want, Congress to resemble the judiciary? Why should the comparatively public legislative process not involve legislators checking, often through staff, with those whom proposed legislation will likely affect, and then, perhaps publicly adopting and explaining their differing points of view? Nothing in the Constitution forbids Congress's working in this way. Why should doing so diminish the legitimacy of the result? If it should not, then why should courts not take account of the way in which Congress works, when doing so will help the courts determine the purposes of legislative phrases that require judicial interpretation?

Now let me describe one important way in which Congress does not work. In the United Kingdom and in many other countries, judges have developed linguistic conventions, or a canon-like system of statutory interpretation that depends upon a broad understanding of just how statutes are written in order to interpret the scope of, the meaning of, or the objectives of, statutory language.[36] Judges, legislators, and statutory drafters do not need to consider legislative history in similar detail because, given the conventions and even cooperation in the drafting process, the relevant interpretive actors are more likely to know what the statutory language means and the purposes it seeks to serve.

But the United Kingdom's political and judicial systems differ from ours.[37] The British executive introduces nearly all important legislation through a minister who is both head of a department and a member of Parliament.[38] The executive controls the initial draft of the language. And the executive department's civil servants' knowledge of technical difficulties will often influence particular statutory language. A small, highly professional group of drafters will likely help write the legislation, and the party in power almost always has enough votes to secure passage of the bill without major changes.

At the same time, the relatively small group of British judges are drawn from only a slightly larger group of barristers. Few are appointed who have not been barristers for more than twenty years. The professional legislative drafters study the opinions of these judges, determine their relatively uniform interpretive practices, and draft language accordingly.[39] The drafters believe that those practices are likely to change only slowly over long periods of time.

Whatever the future in the United Kingdom, the American judiciary here is not likely to be homogeneous enough to keep the "interpretive conventions" as stable as they are in that country. The American system has never had an agreed-upon theory of statutory interpretation, and commentators across the interpretive spectrum have agreed on this as a matter of historical fact.[40] Despite the oft-repeated, perhaps ironic, suggestion that "we're all textualists now,"[41] there is not even agreement among textualists regarding how that methodology should be employed.[42] Farther apart still are congressional views on a unified set of British-like interpretive assumptions.[43] As I have said, Professors Lisa Schultz Bressman and Abbe Gluck have exhaustively demonstrated that our American interpretive conventions are inconsistently applied and understood by Congress.[44] There is no evidence that these conventions are likely to stabilize soon, and without those conventions, I believe that it is eminently reasonable for American judges to "seiz[e] everything from which aid can be derived" in interpreting statutes.[45]

Three examples will help show why I believe that legislative history can often help a judge understand the purposes that drive a statute. Legislative history can thereby help that judge reach a more faithful, purpose-oriented interpretation. And a purpose-based interpretation, as I have tried to show, is often a better interpretation than an interpretation based upon text alone.

Ali v. Federal Bureau of Prisons (2008)[46]

The Federal Tort Claims Act waives the federal government's sovereign immunity, thereby allowing victims to sue federal employees for damages.[47] That waiver of sovereign immunity, however, does not apply where "any officer of customs or excise or *any other law enforcement officer*" is sued for damages for wrongfully destroying the victim's property.[48] The case before our Court, decided in 2008 (by a 5–4 vote) involved a federal prisoner who brought a lawsuit against federal prison officers for having lost the prisoner's property.[49] The question in the case was whether the words "any other law enforcement officer" included prison officers.[50] Did those words apply only to officers acting in a customs or excise capacity, or did those words apply broadly to *any* law enforcement officer (including, say, prison and other law enforcement officials)?

The Court read the statutory words broadly and held that the words applied to all law enforcement officers, including prison officials.[51] Why? The reasons were primarily textual. First, the Court emphasized the word "any."[52] It pointed to earlier cases that interpreted the word "any" broadly.[53] One of them, referring to a dictionary, said, for example, that "read naturally, the word 'any' has an expansive meaning, that is 'one or some indiscriminately of whatever kind.'"[54] The Court therefore said that the word "any" is "most naturally read to mean law enforcement officers of whatever kind." And it noted that "the word 'any' is repeated four times in the relevant portion" of the section.[55]

Second, the majority pointed to a different Federal Tort Claims Act section that restored the government's waiver of immunity in instances where property was subject to forfeiture (e.g., a car used to transport illegal drugs).[56] It noted that the section had an exception to its exception (i.e., it restored the ability to sue the government) where the property was "in the possession of any officer of customs or excise or *any other law enforcement officer*," and the property was not seriously involved with forfeiture.[57] The phrase "any other law enforcement officer" here, said the Court, could not be limited to customs and excise officials, for they had nothing to do with forfeiture in the first place.[58] And if the phrase in the forfeiture section applied more broadly, it should also apply more broadly in the section before the Court, for the Court should interpret similar language in related statutes similarly.

Third, the Court refuted several of the losing side's textual arguments related to the canons of interpretation.[59] For example, the losing side argued that courts should interpret general words following specific words as limited to the same kinds of subjects.[60] But, responded the Court, the words "customs or excise" were not very specific, and reading of the phrase more broadly made the words "customs or excise" superfluous.[61]

Justice Anthony Kennedy wrote a dissent for himself, Justice John Paul Stevens, Justice David Souter, and me. I also wrote a separate dissent, which Justice Stevens joined. It said that we also dissented for different and nontextual reasons.[62] For one thing, we believed the basic question concerned

> the statute's *scope*. What boundaries did Congress intend to set? To what circumstances did Congress intend [its waiver of immunity] to apply? . . . [Reference to] the word "any" is no help because all speakers . . . who use general words such as "all," "any," "never," and "none" normally rely upon context to indicate the limits of time and place within which they intend those words to do their linguistic work.[63]

As I wrote, when my wife tells me "there isn't any butter," she does not mean there isn't any butter in town. Context makes clear that she is speaking of the refrigerator, not the supermarket.[64] It is context, and not the dictionary, that sets the boundaries of time, place, and circumstance within which words such as "any" will apply. The canons will sometimes help identify context, but normally a judge can find many other clues.[65]

In this case, drafting history helped determine Congress's purpose, which, in turn, helped determine the scope of the relevant statutory phrase. The relevant statute originally concerned only customs and excise officials.[66] Who wrote the language? A special assistant to the attorney general, Alexander Holtzoff (a well-known expert in legal procedure), wrote the additional words "any other law enforcement officer" and sent them to Congress with a report that said that the additional language of the bill was suggested by a similar British bill that referred only to customs and excise officials.[67] Holtzoff's draft replaced the phrase Congress had initially come up with,[68] and was intended to more clearly encompass customs and excise *officials*, rather than simply any individual connected with the assessment or collection of a tax or customs duty.[69] The report added that the suggested language intended to maintain immunity "from liability in respect of loss in connection with the detention of goods or merchandise by any officer of customs or excise."[70] In enacting the statutory phrase, members of Congress referred repeatedly to customs or excise officials and not to anyone else.[71]

Further, the Court's reading of the words considerably expanded government immunity. Granted, even a limited interpretation of the words would have included some additional individuals, such as those law enforcement officers working at borders and helping to enforce customs and excise laws. The majority's broad interpretation, however, which extended the statute to all federal "law enforcement officers," meant that it covered what the Justice Department estimated were an additional 100,000 law enforcement officers who did not work with or for customs and excise.[72] One would have thought that someone in Congress would have mentioned an expansion of this magnitude, but no one at all said anything about it.[73]

Indeed, all references in Congress were to customs and excise officials. As Justice Scalia once pointed out, Congress does not "hide elephants in mouseholes."[74]

Does reference to the legislative history not help us here? We know who drafted the bill, the bill's purpose, what members of Congress likely knew and thought about it, and all with no evidence that Congress was trying to compromise or otherwise achieve something different. So, then, why not look at the legislative history as a clue to the statute's meaning? The majority had no response.

Bruesewitz v. Wyeth LLC (2011)[75]

A second case focuses upon the National Childhood Vaccine Injury Act of 1986.[76] In the years leading up to the act's passage, the families of children who had taken vaccines (particularly diphtheria, tetanus, and pertussis vaccines) had brought product liability tort suits against vaccine manufacturers.[77] These lawsuits claimed that the children had suffered side effects and that the manufacturers were strictly liable under state tort law. The costs associated with these lawsuits had led several manufacturers to withdraw from the market.[78]

The federal act created a federal, no-fault compensation system for those suffering side effects.[79] A family could nevertheless turn down the system's compensation offer and bring an ordinary tort lawsuit, but the act limited the company's tort liability. The statutory language that did so (the language at issue in the case) said:

> No vaccine manufacturer shall be liable in a civil action for damages arising from a vaccine-related injury or death . . . if the injury or death resulted from *side effects that were unavoidable even though the vaccine [1] was properly prepared and [2] was accompanied by proper directions and warnings.*[80]

The plaintiffs in the case before the Court had rejected the compensation system's monetary offer, brought an ordinary tort suit, and had claimed that the vaccine was *not* "properly prepared" because the company might have *designed* it differently.[81] For that reason, they said, the company was strictly liable for the child's resulting injury.

In 2011 the Court (by a vote of 6–2) held against the plaintiffs, and it relied heavily upon textual arguments.[82] Look, the Court said, at the words "properly prepared and [labeled]."[83] The statute did not refer to "design," and in fact said nothing about design. Indeed, the manufacturer could not sell the vaccine unless the federal government (the Food and Drug Administration) had approved the design.[84] Thus, the statute required the manufacturer properly to prepare the specific dose according to the approved design. The manufacturer also had to label the vaccine properly with "proper directions and warnings."[85] If those two conditions were met, then the "injury or death resulted from side effects that were unavoidable."[86] State law design-defect claims were therefore preempted (i.e., nullified by federal law),[87] and victims had to instead rely upon the federal no-fault scheme for compensation.

The majority added a "further textual indication."[88] "Products-liability law establishes a classic and well known triumvirate of grounds for liability: defective manufacture, inadequate directions or warnings, and defective design."[89] "If all three [traditional grounds for liability] were intended to be preserved," said the majority, "it would be strange to mention specifically only two, and leave the third to implication."[90]

A concurrence (which I wrote) agreed with the majority's result, but argued that the majority's lengthy textual analysis did not convincingly lead to that result.[91] It argued for looking at the statute's legislative history. That history, had the majority referred to it, would have provided a far simpler way to reach the majority's conclusion.[92]

The House committee report said about the statutory clause that "if" vaccine-injured persons:

> cannot demonstrate under applicable law either that a vaccine was improperly prepared or that it was accompanied by improper directions or inadequate warnings, [they] should pursue recompense in the compensation system, not the tort system.[93]

As I explained, "the Report list[ed] two specific kinds of tort suits that the clause does not pre-empt."[94] These were ordinary lawsuits based upon improper manufacturing, and ordinary lawsuits based upon improper labeling. The report went on to say that compensation for other tort claims (e.g., design-defect claims) lay "in the Act's no-fault compensation system, not the tort system."[95]

What could be more direct? The House report said that an injured person could bring an ordinary lawsuit in court if that person wished to claim improper manufacturing or labeling. It directly added that the person could not bring other tort claims in court but instead had to accept the act's compensation award. No legislator dissented from this statement. It is consistent with the act's language. It comes from a kind of legislative history (namely, a House committee report) that the Court has called "authoritative" in determining legislative intent.[96] What else is there to say?

The concurring opinion did concede that the House report once referred to a comment in the Restatement of Torts, and that comment did refer to design-defect lawsuits.[97] But both the majority and the concurrence thought this fact unconvincing because the House report did not say to which part of the restatement's long multipart comment (which discussed many different kinds of strict-liability lawsuits) the House report was referring.[98] (The report spoke only generally of the "principle" of the comment.) In sum, the House report indicates that the legislators agreed upon the fact that the statutory words "even though the vaccine was properly prepared" refer to proper manufacture and labeling, and not to faulty design.

The concurrence quoted other parts of the House report.[99] Those parts stated that an increase in tort lawsuits had led some manufacturers to find they were unable to obtain product liability insurance, that it had led some manufacturers to withdraw from the market, that the Food and Drug Administration decided when a vaccine is safe enough to be licensed, and that the new federal act sought to create a simpler system for compensation.[100] Given these "broad general purposes," the concurrence added, "to read the pre-emption clause as preserving design-defect [tort] suits [in courts] seems anomalous."[101] The concurrence added that the department and the government had argued in favor of the ultimate result that both the majority and the concurrence reached.[102]

For present purposes, I want this case to suggest that there is often nothing wrong with textual analysis, and that it can help judges reach a sound interpretive result. But it also suggests there is nothing wrong with the judge's examining a statute's history. That, too, can help. And sometimes, legislative history can provide a simpler and clearer way to understand what a highly compact statutory phrase is all about.

Arlington Central School District Board of Education v. Murphy (2006)[103]

In this third case, the text and the legislative history pointed in different directions. Which direction should the Court have taken?

Murphy arose out of a federal statute, the Individuals with Disabilities Education Act, that gives disabled children the right to a "free appropriate public education."[104] The statute also says that parents who disagree with a school district's plan for educating their disabled child can contest the plan before state administrative officials, and that the parents may be able to bring a lawsuit in federal court.[105]

The plaintiffs in this case, Mr. and Mrs. Murphy, had a child with severe learning disabilities.[106] They disagreed with the school district's education plan. They brought a lawsuit in federal court and they won, but the proceedings were expensive: The Murphy family had hired an educational expert who charged them over $29,000 for her help. The federal statute said that the federal court may "award" a winning party, like the Murphy family, "reasonable attorney's fees as part of [their] costs."[107] The Murphy family argued that the word "costs" included the cost of the expert, and the lower courts agreed.[108]

Does the word "costs" include expert fees? One can read that word as limited to attorney's fees plus a few extras, such as court filing fees.[109] Courts have often interpreted the word "costs" as used in other statutes as restricted in this way.[110] But one might also read that word as including the fees of educational experts. Their fees do not differ radically in kind from attorney's fees, and indeed, attorneys themselves often hire experts and pass an expert's charges on to the client as part of the attorney's bill. In addition, an expert's fee is a "cost" as the word "cost" is often used in everyday affairs.[111]

Now consider the statute's purposes. The statute seeks to make available to disabled children the kind of education that few parents can afford.[112] It more specially creates procedures (including court procedures) that will allow parents to dispute a school district's claim that it is already doing so.[113] To challenge the school district's plan successfully, parents often must turn to experts, who are expensive. Thus, a reading of "costs" that *excludes* expert fees will place education to which a child is entitled beyond the reach of a typical family. That doesn't seem consistent with the statute's basic purpose.[114]

Congress, however, may have had a subsidiary purpose, namely saving public money. That possible purpose suggests that it intended to exclude expert fees from the term "costs." Which purpose controls? Here is where an examination of legislative history can help. A House Senate Conference Committee's report (the report of the committee that tries to reconcile the Senate's and the House's differing versions of a bill and produce an agreed-upon text) said that the statutory language includes reasonable "expenses and *fees of expert witnesses*"[115] (emphasis mine). Both houses of Congress adopted this report, and did so *unanimously*.[116] Thus, the legislative history of the act showed an intent that is both consistent with the basic purpose of the statute and fits within the language of the text, at least as ordinarily used. But, I'm sorry to say, the majority of the Court saw the matter differently.[117] In 2007, by a vote of 6–3, it adopted a reading of "costs" that followed its narrow reading of "costs" in other statutes.[118] (I dissented.) Perhaps more common use of legislative history would have produced a better legal outcome.[119]

Criticisms

Many judges and scholars have criticized the use of legislative history.[120] They often quote Judge Harold Leventhal's statement, the one I alluded to earlier, that searching congressional documents for a statute's legislative history is like "looking over a crowd and picking out your friends."[121] But this statement criticizes the *mis*use of congressional history, not its use. Judges do not look for "friends": They look at what the documents say and then determine which reading (if any) of ambiguous language that legislative history supports. The words "expert fees" in a joint House-Senate report, unanimously adopted by both houses of Congress, offer support for a reading of the statutory word "costs" that includes those fees.[122] The legislative history in my other two examples also *helps* the judge decide the scope of ambiguous language. Legislative history will not always help, and when it does not help, it should not be used. Where it does help in clarifying ambiguous language, however, judges do themselves and the law a disservice by ignoring it.

Of course, judges can misuse legislative history. But the same is true of any other interpretive tool, including canons of interpretation, context, and text itself. And, often, when a case is difficult, it is only the judge (and not the readers or scholars) who will know whether the judge has fairly and honestly used an interpretive tool. That is the nature of the judicial job. No one believes, or should believe, that legislative history provides a magic key that will unlock the meaning of an obscure set of statutory words. I have tried to show only that it will sometimes help.

Some critics of the use of legislative history point to the Constitution.[123] They argue that the Constitution sets forth certain requirements for enacting a law. A bill must pass both houses of Congress and obtain the president's signature (or a veto override). The result is a statute. A floor speech, testimony at a hearing, a committee report, and a presidential message do not go through that process. The use of legislative history, these critics complain, tends to make these other matters the "law" even though they did not normally receive a majority vote or a presidential signature.[124]

The argument, however, misses the point. No one claims that a committee report is "the law." The claim is that reading it helps a judge understand the circumstances in which a bill has become law; what the bill's drafters had in mind; what mischief Congress sought to ameliorate; and what purposes it sought to further when it enacted the bill into law. Legislative history is one tool among others. And, like other interpretive tools (e.g., dictionaries, long-standing agency practices, and related historical contro- versies), it is not itself enacted into law. The answer to the argument that Congress did not enact a statute's history into law is a polite "true, but so?"

Critics also point out that the Constitution vested legislative power in members of the House and Senate, and did not vest legislative power in staff members or in lobbyists. Yet, goes the criticism, these unelected in- dividuals typically write the testimony, reports, and floor statements that make up legislative history. Indeed, many members may not even read what staff members write. Thus, using legislative history to interpret stat- utes permits the exercise of legislative power by those to whom the Consti- tution did not grant it.[125]

There is nothing in the Constitution, however, that forbids members of Congress from hiring employees to help them accomplish their legislative tasks. Nor does the Constitution forbid legislators from relying upon out- side groups and institutions in the ways I have described. Any unfairness in relying upon lobbyists (or, say, constituents), for example, lies in a failure to consult different lobbyists holding different views about the merits of a particular bill or statutory language. It does not lie in the simple fact of consultation itself. Thus, it is not surprising that the Constitution nowhere forbids that consultation.

Moreover, constituents are likely to hold a legislator responsible for the statute that emerges from this "institutional" process, not for having listened to floor statements or read committee reports. Indeed, a legisla- tor's personal involvement with a statute's text may or may not be greater than the legislator's personal involvement with report language or a floor statement. Involvement is a function of the importance of the substantive, procedural, or political *issue* facing the legislator, not of the "category" of the text that happens to involve that particular issue. Perhaps there is a better way to organize Congress, but I am not aware of it. And, regard- less, the Constitution, I repeat, nowhere forbids use of a staff-oriented, consultation-related process.

Critics also argue that the use of legislative history depends upon a "the- ory of language" mistake, and that legislative history rests upon a false be- lief that behind every statute lies a congressional "intent."[126] Congressional "intent," they say, is a myth.[127] We do not know what was in the mind of the legislator who voted for the bill on the basis of a staff member recommendation. How can a document written by a committee staffer indicate the inner workings of the mind of one legislator, let alone the several hundred who voted for the law, perhaps for different (sometimes purely selfish) reasons?

This argument, however, misunderstands the workings of words such as "intent" and "purpose" in statutory interpretation.[128] One can easily ascribe an "intent" to Congress if one means the word to stand for "purpose" rather than "motive." One often ascribes group *purposes* to group actions.[129] A law school raises tuition to obtain funds for a new library. A basketball team stalls to run out the clock. A tank corps feints to draw the enemy's troops away from the main front. One way to find out the purpose of these actions is to ask members of the group that took the action, but that is not the only way. Nor does it mean that the group member's *motives* and the group's *purposes* must be identical.

The participating members of the group, including those whose participation is necessary for the group action's success, may have different private *motives* behind their participation. But that fact does not necessarily change the proper characterization of the group's purpose. Perhaps several members of the faculty voted for the tuition increase just to please the dean. A better library is nonetheless the object of the *law school's* action. Perhaps the basketball team is just reacting instinctively, following preplanned plays. Nonetheless, the purpose of the team's action is to *stall*. Perhaps the members of the tank corps do not understand why they head in the direction they take. Do those added facts make any difference in respect to the purpose of the individual troop movements? No, just as they do not affect our intuitive assessments of the law school and basketball team examples.

It is true that ascribing purposes to institutions is a complex enterprise. Sometimes, but certainly not always, it is difficult to describe that enterprise abstractly. But that fact does not make those ascriptions improper. In practice, we make those ascriptions (of purposes to institutions or groups) without difficulty, and we do so all the time.[130]

The relationship between individual members' purposes and a group's purposes may be complex (depending on the type of group). It may depend upon the group's internal rules and practices, upon background under-standings of the group's role in its social context, and upon the kind of individual purposes or motives at issue, along with the individual state-ments and actions that reveal those individual purposes. But those who understand the group do not ordinarily have trouble ascribing purposes to the group's activities.[131]

A legislator, for example, may vote for language that she believes will extend a statute of limitations. And she may do so solely in order to obtain campaign contributions, to gain political support, or to defeat the bill on the floor. Those personal motives, however, do not change the purpose of the bill's language (namely, to extend the limitations period).

A legislator may vote for technical language that the legislator does not understand, knowing that committee members believe (perhaps because of their faith in the drafting process) that it has a proper function. That fact does not necessarily *change* its function or its purpose. If I am correct in believing that the ascription of a purpose to an institution is an activity related to, but different from, ascribing a purpose to an individual, then I do not see how one can criticize *on conceptual grounds* judges who sometimes use legislative history as an interpretive tool. To refuse to ascribe a purpose to Congress when it enacts statutory language (simply because one cannot find many legislators who claim that that purpose was their *personal* pur-pose) is rather like, as Oxford philosophy professor Gilbert Ryle explained, refusing to believe in the existence of Oxford University because one can find only its constituent colleges.[132]

Some critics also point out that the legislative process I have described relies heavily upon interactions of legislators, staff, and interest groups to create, review, criticize, and amend legislative language, reports, and floor statements. The process is a fair one as long as those whom the laws will affect have roughly equal access to the legislating process. But do they? Executive branch departments, trade associations, many businesses, labor unions, and some public interest groups may well have access to most parts of this process, but are there not many persons who do not? What about disadvantaged groups? What about average or "typical" citizens?[133]

In my own view, the answer to these questions too often is, "yes, unfortunately, they do not." But the relevant question here is whether judicial abandonment of the use of legislative history would make matters any better. I think it would not.[134] To some degree, judicial use of that history encourages legislators themselves to favor public hearings, public reports vetted by staff, and fairly detailed floor debates. To some extent, judicial failure to examine legislative history encourages the practice of amending a bill on the floor of the House or the Senate. And floor amendments often have escaped the public scrutiny that committee hearings and consideration would have given them.

That fact, in turn, can produce laws that suffer a variety of flaws. Congress, for example, enacted into law an amendment introduced during a floor debate that dramatically increased the prison term mandatorily imposed upon persons convicted of possessing crack cocaine.[135] The law, however, used the term "under this subsection" to describe the offense of conviction.[136] And the subsection concerned the simple possession of cocaine, not possession of cocaine with intent to distribute it. The result was that the law punished a person convicted of the first, less serious, crime far more severely than it punished a person convicted of the second, far more serious, crime.[137] Had the amendment gone through the committee process, legislators would have heard from experts who would have explained the anomaly and how it might have been avoided. I do not claim that the committee system always produces better legislative results; nor would I claim that the judicial use of legislative history matters significantly in this respect. I claim only that abandonment of judicial use of legislative history is not likely to make the legislative process significantly better.

Finally, it is important to remember that our discussion of legislative history in this context is as a *judicial* tool used to resolve difficult problems of judicial interpretation. That tool can be justified in part by its ability to help judges interpret statutes in a way that makes sense, and that will produce a workable set of laws.[138] If it produces this kind of result, courts can use it as part of their overarching interpretive task of producing a coherent and relatively consistent body of statutory law. This would remain the case even if the "rational member of Congress" were to be a pure fiction, created out of whole cloth by the judges, which I should add it is not.

8.

Constitutional Values

I now turn to a final purpose-related tool. Judges have long agreed that they can interpret ambiguous statutory language in a way that permits them not to decide a constitutional question, typically whether the statute, as interpreted, would violate the federal Constitution.[1] Textualists, like purpose-oriented judges, will accept a reading of the text that avoids the constitutional question even if that reading is not its most natural reading.[2] But still there is room for argument in a particular case: Is there really a constitutional problem? How serious a problem? Will a proposed reading avoid the problem? And, most difficult, does the language of the text in fact permit the reading that might avoid the constitutional problem? The following related cases illustrate these difficulties.

Zadvydas v. Davis (2001)[3]

The government can order an alien removed from the United States if that alien is unlawfully present here.[4] An immigration statute applicable to certain removable aliens defines the period in which the removal might take place, called the "removal period," as ninety days after the entry of a final order of removal.[5] The removable aliens include persons whom the government has ordered removed because they violated various entry conditions, because they violated the criminal law, or because their removal is required for reasons of security or foreign policy.[6] The statute then says that those persons who have been ordered removed *"may be detained beyond the* [ninety-day] *removal period* and, if released, shall be subject to . . . terms of supervision."[7]

The question in *Zadvydas* was how long "beyond" the ninety-day "removal period" could the government detain them. The case involved two persons with no right to remain in the United States.[8] One of them, Kestutis Zadvydas, had entered the United States when he was eight years old. He had a long criminal record. Once he finished serving his prison terms, the government tried to deport him, initially to Germany and then to Lithuania. Neither country would accept him. The second, Kim Ho Ma, born in Cambodia, came to the United States with his family when he was seven. After his prison term expired, the government sought to deport him to Cambodia. But Cambodia would not accept him. Hence the government kept both these men in detention long after the ninety-day removal period had expired. The government had sought to keep both Zadvydas and Ma in indefinite custody, at least until they found countries that would take them. The Court was asked whether the statute permitted the attorney general "to detain a removable alien *indefinitely* beyond the removal period, or only for a period *reasonably necessary* to secure the alien's removal."[9]

In 2001, a majority of the Court, in a 5–4 decision, construed the "statute to contain an implicit 'reasonable time' limitation."[10] (I wrote the majority opinion.) It did so because it believed that the "indefinite detention of aliens" (who had been admitted to the United States but subsequently ordered removed) "would raise serious constitutional concerns."[11] Both Zadvydas and Ma were released in subsequent proceedings.

The Constitution's Due Process Clause, history, purpose, and precedent were all relevant. The clause itself protects "those settled usages and modes of proceedings existing in the common and statute law of England, before the emigration of our ancestors."[12] Blackstone wrote in 1769 that every prisoner in England (except for a convict serving his sentence) was entitled to seek release on bail.[13] In the United States, the Judiciary Act of 1789[14] said that for a noncapital defendant, "bail shall be admitted," and for a capital defendant that bail may be admitted in the discretion of the judge.[15] Similar laws remained on the books throughout the following centuries. Standards for granting bail have changed today; judges will take account of flight risks and dangers to the community.[16] But the right to seek bail has not changed. Thus, in order to avoid the due process problems that would be raised if the statute permitted indefinite detention, the Court concluded that the statute only allowed for detention for a finite, reasonable period of time.

Jennings v. Rodriguez (2018)[17]

In 2018, by a vote of 5–3 the Court decided a second case, *Jennings* (Justice Amy Coney Barrett joined the Court too late to participate). I asked in dissent why the Constitution, which typically insists upon the right to seek bail in a criminal case, would not also insist upon the same right in a civil case, where an alien seeks asylum.[18] After all, the Court in *Zadvydas* had limited the government's right to hold in confinement an alien who had committed a crime. In this second case the alien had committed no crime; he sought asylum. This immigration case was a civil case, not a criminal case. And we sometimes detain an individual for civil reasons. (Consider dangerously mentally ill persons who pose dangers to themselves or to others.) The government in *Jennings* was detaining the alien, not because it believed he had committed a crime but simply because it had not yet determined whether he was entitled to asylum in the United States.[19] Does that fact—that the proceeding was civil and not criminal—make a difference and allow the government greater power to hold an individual without bail?

Precedent suggested it should not make a difference.[20] And why should it? The reasons for confining an individual without bail are not *stronger* when the individual seeks asylum than when the individual has been charged with having committed a crime. Ask yourself: Which class of persons, criminal defendants or asylum-seekers, seems more likely to have acted in a manner that typically warrants confinement? Is there any evidence that noncitizens seeking asylum in the United States are more likely than criminal defendants to threaten the safety of the community if released on bail? Which group is more likely to present a flight risk? What basis is there, founded in fact or evidence, to treat confined noncitizens worse than ordinary defendants charged with a crime; worse than convicted criminals appealing their sentences; worse than civilly committed citizens?[21]

Confining noncitizens *after* they have completed criminal sentences, the issue in *Zadvydas*, raised these same questions. Because the statutory answers were at best unclear, the statute suffered from a serious constitutional problem. And the Court in *Zadvydas* noted that citizens convicted of a crime could if confined seek bail once they had completed their sentences.[22] Why should noncitizens not be able to do the same? The upshot is that—in the Court's view in *Zadvydas* and in my dissenting view in *Jennings*—to read the statute as giving the government the power to confine an individual without bail would raise a serious constitutional problem.[23]

Despite the constitutional problem, however, if "Congress has made its intent in the statute clear," the Court "must give effect to that intent" or invalidate the statute on constitutional grounds.[24] The statute says that the government "*may*"[25] detain an alien after the ninety-day removal period has expired. But the word "may" does not "suggest unlimited discretion."[26] It does not suggest that the government may detain the aliens at issue *indefinitely*, perhaps *permanently*. And so, the Court in *Zadvydas* interpreted the language of the statute so as to effectuate (or at least not undermine) the value that the Constitution (in its Due Process Clause) attaches to the right to seek bail.[27]

The Court recognized that, in some instances, the ninety-day removal period might prove too short to find a foreign country willing to take the alien who had completed a criminal sentence.[28] But Congress might have considered detention greater than six months (beyond the removal period) too long.[29] Hence, "for the sake of uniform administration," the Court recognized six months as a reasonable detention period.[30] After six months, if the alien "provides good reason to believe that there is no significant likelihood of removal in the reasonably foreseeable future," then, unless the government rebuts the showing, the alien's detention is no longer presumptively reasonable. The basic rule of law in *Zadvydas*, interpreting the word "may" in the statute, is that the "alien may be held in confinement until it has been determined that there is no significant likelihood of removal in the reasonably foreseeable future."[31]

What about the asylum-seekers in *Jennings*? The majority there held that the government could confine them (within the United States) while Immigration and Customs Enforcement determined whether they were eligible for asylum.[32] And it held that they *could not* seek bail.[33] Why not? One might have thought the asylum-seekers' constitutional claim to seek bail was, if anything, stronger than that of a convicted criminal who had spent time behind bars.[34]

The problem for the majority was the statute. This statutory provision did not use the word "may." Rather, it said that the aliens who tried to enter the United States and who had a credible fear of persecution abroad "*shall* be detained" for further consideration of their applications for asylum.[35] My dissent in *Jennings* conceded that although it may be highly desirable to interpret a statute in a way that would avoid deciding a difficult constitutional question, we cannot read the statute to mean the opposite of what it says. Where Congress has made its intent clear in the statute, we must give effect to that intent.

But did the words "shall detain" at issue in *Jennings* make that intent clear? Long ago, English dictionaries provided definitions for the word "detain" that apparently included detention but *with a right to seek bail*.[36] American precedent also used that word to include detention that provided for bail.[37] The Board of Immigration Appeals, in its regulations, did the same.[38] Nor did the statutory language refer to detention "without bail," as did other nearby statutory provisions, one of which says that certain aliens "shall be detained . . . *until removed*."[39] The statute at issue in *Jennings* seemed sufficiently unclear—as to whether it permitted, rather than forbade, bail applications—that it did not forbid a reading that allowed bail applications. That being so, the constitutional values at issue strongly argued in favor of a statutory interpretation that permitted them.[40] The majority did not believe that the statute allowed bail applications. It said so, and it postponed deciding the constitutional question that arose on that interpretation.[41]

9.

Resolving the Text/Purpose Tension

The examples set forth above show that looking to the purpose of the words of a statute can prove a valuable interpretive tool. But they do not show that, when text and purpose point in different directions, the judge should always follow statutory purpose. To the contrary, purpose is merely one tool among several that a judge may use. The judge will certainly examine the text, the statute's history, legal tradition, and precedent, as well as purposes and purpose-related consequences. But what happens when these different tools suggest different answers? The judge can take account of the different related considerations in deciding the case.

I can describe the making of the decision itself, in a difficult case, as an exercise of judicial instinct, likely informed by experience.[1] And it is that instinct, informed by the result of text-oriented purpose-oriented inquiries, and other examinations, that will lead to a decision that the judge, as well as the affected public, hopes is sound. Knowledge of purposes will help the judge reach a sound decision, but it will not necessarily dictate that decision. My examples show why a judge should often emphasize purposes; why purposes will help the judge decide whether the statute calls for a "static" or a "dynamic" interpretation; how consequences can help the judge determine purposes and their importance; why reading legislative history can help the judge determine purposes; and why constitutional values often count heavily when determining purposes.

But I began this discussion of examples by describing the traditional use of text and purpose in *Brown & Williamson*—the case in which the Court, by a 5–4 vote, thought that the Food and Drug Administration lacked the power to regulate tobacco.[2] That case shows how, where the arguments are closely balanced, the judge is left to his own common sense, based upon his judicial experience (or what I sometimes would refer to as his judicial instinct). *Brown & Williamson* asked whether the FDA's effort to regulate tobacco was a bridge too far, or was well within the statute's scope. Here are two other cases that similarly illustrate the need for sound decision-making judgment, *informed by* knowledge of purposes and other considerations.

Church of the Holy Trinity v. United States (1892)[3]

In the late nineteenth century, Congress passed a statute that made it:

> unlawful for any person . . . in any manner whatsoever, to . . . assist or encourage the importation . . . of any alien . . . into the United States . . . under contract or agreement . . . made previous to the importation . . . to perform labor or service of any kind in the United States.[4]

The statute made exceptions for "professional actors, artists, lecturers, singers and domestic servants."[5]

In 1877, the Church of the Holy Trinity in New York City entered into a contract with E. Walpole Warren, an alien, to come to New York City from England and to serve as its rector and pastor.[6] The United States attempted to prosecute the church under the statute. The legal question for the Court was whether those who made this contract had violated the statute. In 1892, the Court unanimously decided that they had not.[7]

Why not? The Court conceded that the language of the statute seemed to make what they did unlawful.[8] After all, they did make a "contract" with a person the statute calls an "alien" (prior to the alien's coming to the United States). That contract did "assist" the alien to come to New York. The contract was for the purpose of performing "labor or service" of some kind. And service as a pastor did not seem to fall within any of the exceptions. So how could the Court escape the statute's language?

The Court wrote that it "is a familiar rule that a thing may be within the letter of the statute and yet not within the statute, because not within its spirit nor within the intention of its makers."[9] The Court quoted precedent stating that:

> All laws should receive a sensible construction. General terms should be so limited in their application as not to lead to injustice, oppression, or an absurd consequence. It will always, therefore, be presumed that the legislature intended exceptions to its language which would avoid results of this character. . . . The common sense of man approves the judgment mentioned by Pufendorf, that the Bolognian law which enacted "that whoever drew blood in the streets should be punished with the utmost severity" did not extend to the surgeon who opened the vein of a person that fell down in the street in a fit.[10]

Similarly, a prisoner did not violate a law forbidding prison breakouts when the prison caught on fire.[11]

The Court added that the act's title was: "An act to prohibit the importation and migration of foreigners and aliens under contract or agreement to perform labor."[12] And that title, the Court believed, showed that the act reached only to the work of the "manual laborer."[13]

Another guide to the meaning, the Court thought, was purpose. It said that meaning, i.e., purpose, "is found in the evil which" the Act was "designed to remedy."[14] To find that evil, "the court properly look[ed] at contemporaneous events, the situation as it existed, and as it was pressed upon the attention of the legislative body."[15] Here, other contemporaneous courts and "testimony presented before the committees of Congress" showed that the evil Congress had in mind was "cheap, unskilled labor."[16] Committee reports showed that Congress meant the phrase "labor and service" to mean "manual labor" and "manual service."[17] Therefore, the Court viewed Congress as intending the law to "stay the influx of this cheap, unskilled labor."[18]

The Court then spent the latter half of its opinion explaining that America was, and long had been, a religious nation.[19] It wrote that "beyond all these matters, no purpose of action against religion can be imputed to any legislation, state or national, because this is a religious people."[20] It provided examples suggesting that a reading of the statute as applying to religious ministers would be close to absurd.[21] Or, in light of the religious freedom that the First Amendment guarantees, unconstitutional.

Would today's textualist, even a mild textualist, agree with the Court's unanimous result? Likely not.[22] The statutory language here is strong, and the list of exceptions does not include religious pastors or any similar occupations. Indeed, that list suggests that the scope of the rest of the statute would extend (but for the exceptions) to others who are not manual laborers. Go back to *Jam* and its discussion of whether international organizations possess sovereign immunity.[23] It is easy to imagine today's Court writing, "If the statute's scope is too broad, go to Congress (and not to the courts) in search of a remedy." Justice Scalia vocally argued that *Holy Trinity* represented little more than "judicial lawmaking."[24]

Had I been on the Court in 1892, would I have agreed with the majority's judge-created exception for religious ministers? I would have asked the following questions: Who else besides ministers falls within the judge-created "ministerial" statutory exception?[25] Actors do not, singers do not (because they have their own statutory exceptions), but who else falls in this category? What about geographers, teachers, writers, scientists, and others? Is an interpretation that puts these and others outside the statute a workable one? Is there a way to interpret the statute so that it becomes workable—say, by excluding those professions the inclusion of which would create chaos or would have nothing to do with the harms that importing large numbers of uneducated workers might bring, but including others? I do not know. But on the facts before the Court, it seemed as if the Justices' choice was 1) to confine the text to *manual laborers*, or 2) to read the text as including *all* the professions I have just mentioned, and others. If that were the Court's choice, I would consider the majority's choice the better choice. Then, though the case remains difficult, I would have joined the *Holy Trinity* majority and read the words "labor" or "service of any kind" to mean *manual* labor or manual service of any kind, as the title of the statute, and the legislative history, suggest.[26]

Barnhart v. Sigmon Coal Co. (2002)[27]

Now consider a more recent case, decided in 2002 by a vote of 6–3, that pitted text-oriented and purpose-oriented approaches directly against each other. This case focused upon a complex system for financing health care benefits given to individual retired coal miners.[28] Between 1950 and 1990, many coal companies had signed collective bargaining agreements that created retirement plans (including health insurance benefits) for retiring coal workers.[29] By the 1990s, however, Congress feared that many of these retirement plans would become insolvent.[30] In 1992, Congress enacted a new law, the Coal Industry Retiree Health Benefit Act,[31] designed to help the retired workers. The act requires coal companies that had signed relevant collective bargaining agreements to contribute funds to the plans.[32] The act calls coal companies that had signed those agreements "signatory operators."[33] And it requires each of those companies to contribute amounts related to the number of retired workers that the act assigns to them.[34] Certain other companies, called "related persons," must also contribute funds to the plans.[35] But remember the key language as to amounts: The *amount* the company must pay depends upon how many retired workers the commissioner of Social Security *assigns* to that company.[36] Remember also the key language as to *which* companies must pay: "signatory operators" and "related persons."[37] The text/purpose problem in *Barnhart* arose out of these definitions of the companies that must contribute and how much they must contribute.

Let us look at what the 1992 act says about this. It says that the "Commissioner of Social Security shall . . . assign each coal industry retiree" who is a beneficiary of the industry health care plan "to *a signatory operator* which (or to any *related person* with respect to which) remains in business."[38] Reread the last sentence, for it is critical; that is what the case was about.

The act then sets forth the order in which a retired miner will be assigned. That order of assignment is to: (1) the "signatory operator" for whom the retired miner had most recently worked for at least two years;[39] 2) if the miner had not worked for any signatory operator for at least two years, then to the "signatory operator" for whom the miner had most recently worked;[40] and 3) if the miner still is not assigned, then to the "signatory operator" who is not quite a signatory operator (because it did not sign a specific 1978 agreement) for which the miner had worked the longest.[41]

Suppose the commissioner cannot find a "signatory operator" that meets any of these three criteria. Then the commissioner might try to assign a retired miner to a "related person." The statute says that "a person shall be considered to be a related person to a signatory operator if that person" falls within one of three categories:

- Both that company and the signatory company are members of a specially defined "controlled group of corporations"; or

- That person conducts a trade or business and that trade or business, along with the signatory operator, is "under common control"; or

- That person is any other person who has "a partnership interest or joint venture with a signatory operator in a business in the coal industry."[42]

The statute then adds that a "related person shall also include *a successor in interest of any person described in clause (i), (ii), or (iii)*."[43]

Now, let us go back to the question in this case. Suppose the commissioner cannot find a "signatory operator" to which he can assign a retired miner. How could that be? Because the signatory company for which the now retired miner once worked *has gone out of business*. Indeed, that is just what happened in the case. The original "signatory company," the Shackleford Coal Company, had gone out of business.[44] But there was a successor company to Shackleford, called Irdell Mining, to which Shackleford had sold all its assets.[45] Is Irdell a "signatory operator"? No, answered the Court majority.[46] That is because Irdell had signed *nothing*. It had not signed any of the collective bargaining agreements.

Well, is Irdell then a "related person"? The majority said no.[47] Why not?

Because (i) Irdell was not, and never had been, a member of a "controlled group of corporations" that included Shackleford; (ii) Irdell was not, and never had been, a part of a commonly controlled "trade or business" along with Shackleford; and (iii) Irdell had not, and never had had, any partnership or joint venture interest with the signatory operator Shackleford.[48] Thus, for the textualist, the legal issue was not very difficult to decide. The statute nowhere includes words that allow the commissioner to assign the retired miner in the case to Irdell, the successor in interest of the signatory operator, Shackleford. End of the matter.

In fact, the majority contended precisely this: "There is no contention that [Irdell] was ever a member of a controlled group of corporations including Shackleford, that it was ever a business under common control with Shackleford, or that it ever had a partnership interest or engaged in a joint venture with Shackleford."[49] The majority acknowledged that Irdell was a "successor in interest" to Shackleford, a "signatory operator." But Irdell was not itself a "signatory operator," and the three categories describing "related persons" did not "include[] the signatory operator itself."[50] Hence, Irdell was not a "person" who was "related" to a signatory operator.

Furthermore, the majority continued, "because the statute is explicit as to who may be assigned liability,"[51] and no "provision" says that "successors in interest to signatory operators may be assigned liability, the plain language of the statute necessarily precludes the Commissioner from" assigning liability to Irdell.[52] On the majority's view, the Court's role was

> to interpret the language of the statute enacted by Congress. . . . [C]ourts must presume that a legislature says in a statute what it means and means in a statute what it says there. When the words in a statute are unambiguous, then, this first canon is also the last: "judicial inquiry is complete.". . . We will not alter the text in order to satisfy the policy preferences of the Commissioner. These are battles that should be fought among the political branches and the industry. Th[e] parties should not seek to amend the statute by appeal to the Judicial Branch.[53]

I joined Justice Stevens's dissent. What could the dissent say in reply? First, it pointed out a peculiar result of the majority's more literal interpretation: put simply, the result made no sense.[54] Imagine a group of companies under a single corporation's control. The companies include a biscuit-maker, a lawn mower manufacturer, and a coal company named Shackleford. Because we have three companies under common control, they fall within the definition of "related person" as set out in (i) and (ii) of the statute. The commissioner can assign a retired miner to any one of these companies, including the biscuit-maker, for they are "related persons" under (i) or (ii). That being so, if the biscuit-maker or the lawn mower manufacturer goes out of business and has a "successor in interest," the commissioner can assign the retired miner to either of their successors in interest. (Remember that a "related person shall also include a successor in interest of any person described in (i), (ii), or (iii).")[55]

But the *Barnhart* majority concluded that the commissioner could *not* assign a retired miner to Irdell, the successor in interest of Shackleford, because Shackleford did not fall within (i), (ii), or (iii). Irdell was not part of a partnership or joint venture; it was not a "trade or business . . . under common control . . . with such signatory operator" (i.e., itself); and it was not a member of a specially defined "controlled group" of corporations that includes itself. The dissenting Justices pointed out the incoherence of such an outcome.[56] An ice cream parlor successor to a grocery store would (assuming partnerships or control of certain kinds) have to pay for a retired coal miner's health care, but a coal mining company, successor to the coal mining company that once employed the miner, would not have to do so. Why? There was no reason that the majority or the dissent could imagine.

The dissent also found evidence that the majority's result did not reflect any kind of compromise among members of Congress. Senator Jay Rockefeller of West Virginia, the original author of the bill, said on the floor of the Senate that the term "'signatory operator' includes a successor in interest of such operator."[57] Senator Malcolm Wallop of Wyoming, the drafter of the "related person" language, said that the term included "successors to the collective bargaining agreement obligations of a signatory operator."[58] No one said anything to the contrary. Indeed, nothing in the bill's legislative history suggested the contrary.[59] Had there been opposition to this aspect of the bill, it is likely someone would have mentioned it.[60]

Finally, the dissent referred to the Dictionary Act, an early part of the United States Code that, as I mentioned previously, suggests how general terms in the statute books should often be interpreted.[61] That act says that the word "person" in a statute can include "corporations, companies, associations, firms, partnerships, societies, and joint stock companies, as well as individuals."[62] It adds that the words "corporation" or "association," when used in reference to a corporation, shall be deemed to embrace the words "'successors and assigns of such company or association' in like manner as if these last-named words, or words of similar import, were expressed."[63] These Dictionary Act instructions are permissive and not mandatory. But they *permit* a court to read the statute as if it applies to coal-mining "successors" of "signatory" coal mine "operators," as well as to "successors" of ice cream parlors.

I agreed with the dissent that the majority wrongly interpreted the statute. Why? Because the majority looked to text—immediately adjacent text at that—and not to purposes, consequences, nor possible (even if less natural) readings of text when doing so is necessary to avoid consequences inconsistent with the statute's basic objectives.

Compare this statute with the one implicated in *Holy Trinity*. In that earlier case, it was difficult to find an interpretation that, even if consistent with the purposes of the legislators who enacted it, was consistent with the language. And where the text is clear, most (perhaps nearly all) judges will follow the text. But *Barnhart* is different. The text *permits* an interpretation that will avoid consequences that are seriously inconsistent with the statute's basic objectives.[64] A reading of the legislative history, as well as common sense, makes that clear.[65] Since one can accept the latter reading (via the Dictionary Act) without simply ignoring the text, I would have (and did) follow it. I was, however, in a three-Justice minority in the case.

These last two cases show how judges may emphasize purposes when purpose and text conflict. But they also show that a judge might emphasize text more than I would. It is informed judicial instinct that reaches a decision. I have emphasized here the need to *inform* that instinct with a consideration of purposes. How deeply one investigates purposes, how extensive an effort one makes to find textual analogies, how broad the search for consequences, how much legislative history one needs—like the emphasis placed upon text or purpose itself—depends upon the circumstance. Like most judicial matters, it is influenced by, or determined by, the judge's experience and judicial instinct.

10.

Why Judges Should Consider Purposes: A Summary

Because my examples are often technical, it may be helpful, at the price of repetition, to summarize several of the major points about purpose and text that I have made. I have provided examples intended to show that, when judges interpret statutes, they may and sometimes must look beyond the text. We have seen examples showing how looking to text alone or primarily to text, rather than looking to statutory purpose, can make a major difference in interpretive outcome. We have also seen examples of interpretive tools that can help the judge determine purpose. They include the statute's or phrase's history, its context, the consequences (viewed in terms of the statute's purposes) of choosing one interpretation over another, its legislative history, and the nation's basic values, as revealed both by our history and our Constitution. All these factors can help a judge interpret a statutory phrase, both because they reveal the mischief that Congress intended the phrase to combat, and because they can help the judge determine how much weight to give purpose, or purpose-related factors, when faced with text that might be interpreted in a contrary way.

Why should a judge ever look beyond the text? Why ever place weight upon these purpose-related factors? Why not just stop at the textual place where the judge began? Why not look to text alone, or to text and other semantic factors, such as other words in the statute, other words in related statutes, or linguistic canons of interpretation? Many who emphasize text believe that doing so will produce more uniform interpretations of statutes;

that those interpretations will in the long run prove more consistent with what legislators actually wanted or expected; and that interpreting statutes in this way is more consistent with our democratic form of government. Those textualists believe that their practices will diminish the likelihood of a judge substituting what that judge believes is good for what the legislature actually enacted (or intended to enact).

How would I answer a person who wholeheartedly believes this? The examples I have provided will, I hope, illustrate some of my answers. But I can also summarize what I perceive as the major advantages of not simply stopping at the text but also looking beyond the text to purposes and purpose-related factors as well. In brief, for several reasons I discuss below, the use of purposes and purpose-related tools makes our democracy more *workable*.

First, a purpose-oriented approach to statutory interpretation is more consistent with the democratic values upon which legislation rests. A member of Congress is likely familiar with the basic purposes motivating a statute; and a staff member, accountable to that member, will likely know the reasons why each particular phrase was inserted in a bill. Those actors, working in tandem, will often have a better idea than a judge regarding the issue-related background, other related statutes, and the political program into which the statute (given its purpose) will fit. The public, which elects the member, will sometimes have at least a general idea of whether the bills for which the member voted worked well or worked badly (from that citizen's point of view). Insofar as subsequent judicial interpretation of the law is consistent with a bill's or a phrase's basic purposes, that member of the public knows whom to praise or to blame. And in the latter case, the elected member, during an election, cannot easily blame the judges for having interpreted the law in a manner inconsistent with that member's basic purposes.

If I am right about the purposes underlying the word "costs" in the Individuals with Disabilities Education Act, for example, or about the phrase "money remuneration" in the Railroad Retirement Tax Act, legislators who voted for those laws would not have approved of the Court's textual results. Those members of the public who voted for those legislators (in part because of the legislators' views on those issues) may notice that the members did not completely get their way. But many voters in that group will not know whom to blame. The legislature? The courts? All those voters will know is that the results of the statute are somewhat less favorable to their point of view than they might have hoped.

That is a problem if we understand legislation in a delegated democracy to reflect the people's will, either directly, insofar as legislators translate how their constituents feel about each proposed law, or indirectly, insofar as legislators exercise delegated authority to vote in accordance with what they see as the public interest.[1] Either way, an interpretation of a statute that tends to implement the legislature's will helps implement the public's will, thereby furthering the Constitution's democratic purpose. For similar reasons, any interpretation that undercuts the statute's objectives tends to undercut that constitutional objective as well.

Ordinary citizens think in terms of general purposes. They readily understand their elected legislators' thinking. It is entirely possible to ask an ordinary citizen to determine whether a particular law is consistent with a general purpose the ordinary citizen might support. And it is entirely possible to ask an ordinary citizen to determine what general purpose a legislator sought to achieve in enacting a particular statute. But it is impossible to ask an ordinary citizen or an ordinary legislator to understand the operation and interoperation of the many linguistic canons of interpretation that the textualist has collected. And it is impossible to ask an ordinary citizen to draw any relevant electoral conclusion when courts reach a purpose-thwarting interpretation of a statute based upon their near-exclusive use of text and interpretive canons. If a segment of the public was unhappy with the Court's application of the Individuals with Disabilities Education Act, the Antiterrorism and Effective Death Penalty Act, the Railroad Retirement Tax Act, or the Medicare Act, whom should it blame? Not the purpose-oriented judge. Purpose-oriented judging will often provide a better answer than will textualism. And a better answer will better promote political accountability.

Second, a purpose-oriented approach makes Congress more workable in that it helps Congress do its job better. Congress cannot write statutes that precisely address every possible application of each phrase in all circumstances. Life is too unpredictable. Congress will almost inevitably write words that overshoot or undershoot their mark. Congress can often ameliorate this human circumstance by writing more abstract, general words instead of detailed, precise phrases. But it can do this if, and only if, courts cooperate by considering legislative purposes when the courts interpret statutes. *Ali*—the "other law enforcement official" case[2]—provides a perfect example: The statutory language therein overshoots the mark. The Court's acceptance of that statutory overshoot decreased prison officer liability in a way that neither the executive nor the legislative branches were likely to have intended. Only by examining the phrase's history and understanding the detailed intentions of those who wrote the statute can its scope be squared with Congress's purposes in imposing liability.

Third, textualist efforts to interpret statutes in light of what an "ordinary person" would have thought they meant at the time they were written[3] will not provide a key to the meaning or scope of statutory phrases (at least, not in many difficult cases). What kind of "ordinary person" is the textualist talking about? A journalist? A railroad worker? A lawyer? A prisoner? A foreign policy expert? A hospital's financial officer? The good lawyer's answer is, as always: It depends. It depends on the subject matter, on the statute, on the particular problem Congress sought to address.[4] So, if the judge must determine what Congress had in mind when it enacted this statute or this statutory phrase, why not look at that question directly: What purpose does the statute or the phrase seek to serve?

One might, of course, develop a technical vocabulary or a linguistically uniform way of dealing with particular recurring drafting problems. As I described earlier, the United Kingdom has developed such a drafting system that produces greater linguistic uniformity. But, as I said, that is likely because the executive branch there, i.e., the cabinet offices, have staff who draft bills that Parliament (where the prime minister's party often controls a majority) will simply enact without much change. Uniform interpretations are more readily achieved, and Parliament, knowing that fact, is more likely to draft with accepted drafting conventions in mind. The United States, with its more complete separation of powers, is less likely to be able to do so.

Fourth, a purpose-oriented approach means that laws are more likely to work better for the people they affect. Law is tied to life,[5] and a failure to understand how a statute is so tied can undermine the human activity that the law seeks to benefit. We have seen how a more literal, text-based, canon-based interpretation of the Foreign Sovereign Immunities Act as applied to international organizations, for example, risks undermining the work of those organizations.[6] Similarly, we have seen how a textual approach to the federal *habeas corpus* statute randomly closed courthouse doors in a way that runs contrary to our commitment to basic human liberty.[7] Both cases came out the way they did because the Court failed to ask the key purpose-based question: Why would Congress have wanted a statute that produced those consequences?

The purpose-based question, quite simply, is "why?" Why did Congress put those words in that statute? If no one in Congress seems to have thought about the particular matter before the court, then a judge might still ask what a reasonable legislature faced with these circumstances would have wanted those words to do. Putting the question in that way generates a better body of laws under which society can develop and community life can flourish. Judges ought not to shy away from such considerations.

Fifth, and finally, courts have asked purpose-oriented questions like this for hundreds, if not thousands of years. Saint Thomas Aquinas, embodying medieval Christian perspectives, elaborated upon this. Antiquity understood the letter of the law to yield to "natural right" and "equity" where an overly wooden interpretation would frustrate the aims of the law.[8] Blackstone, summarizing English practice, considered it unproblematic for judges to "expound the statute by equity" when its general words appear to the judge to be unreasonable.[9] A modern student of history, in summarizing founding-era practices of statutory interpretation, concluded that its function "was to help the legislature govern in the public welfare" by acting as "part of the work of governance."[10]

Many great twentieth-century American jurists felt similarly. Oliver Wendell Holmes rejected the notion that "a given collocation of words has one meaning and no other. . . . You have to consider the sentence in which it stands to decide which of those meanings it bears in the particular case, and very likely will see that it there has a shade of significance more refined than any given in the word-book."[11] Benjamin Cardozo noted that judicial gap-filling in the face of incomplete laws was "nothing revolutionary or even novel in this view of the judicial function."[12] Cardozo's words ring out strongly today: "The difference from age to age is not so much in the recognition of the need that law shall conform itself to an end. It is rather in the nature of the end to which there has been need to conform."[13] Learned Hand decried the "dictionary school" of interpretation and its associated canons of interpretation as "likely to lead us astray."[14] Instead, Hand favored "imaginative reconstruction," or the judges' active role in putting themselves in the shoes of the legislator and imagining how they would have answered the question at hand.[15] These judges and Justices represented the apotheosis of a school of American judging that began with Chief Justice John Marshall, who advised that "[w]here the mind labours to discover the design of the legislature, it seizes every thing from which aid can be derived."[16]

Throughout my career as a judge and a Justice, I have endeavored to preserve that tradition of pragmatic, purpose-oriented judging in matters of statutory interpretation. I have fought stridently to preserve the tradition as both normatively desirable and practically useful, and I shall be heartened if, as I hope, its use continues on the Court for years to come after my departure.[17] I close this part with an elaboration on words I first wrote over thirty years ago: "[I]n light of the judiciary's important objective of helping to maintain coherent, workable statutory law, the case for abandoning the use of" purpose-oriented approaches to statutory interpretation "has not yet been made."[18] For the reasons I have articulated here, I do not believe that case can ever be made—at least not without fundamental changes to our system of democratic government.

III

INTERPRETING THE CONSTITUTION

We shall now turn to interpreting the Constitution. Again, my basic objective is twofold. I want to suggest, by way of examples, that there is no single "way" to interpret all phrases of the Constitution. And I also want to suggest, by way of examples, that a solitary focus on textualism—perhaps aided by some related methods that textualists tend to use in constitutional interpretation (more on that below)—will not achieve the goals that textualists seek and will often make the Constitution less workable.

The language of the Constitution will sometimes help, say by setting boundaries for the interpreter. So will history and practice. Precedent may prove useful, but that depends on the phrase, the case, and the question at issue. Values (or purposes) matter; and so do consequences, including the interpretation's workability. Which of the relevant matters—e.g., text, values, consequences—the judge should emphasize will vary depending on the circumstances. It is, as Oliver Wendell Holmes and others have pointed out, judicial instinct, informed by experience and focused upon the particular case, that normally tells the judge which of these judicial tools to emphasize.

It is important to remember that the Constitution is not a statute. It delegates broad authority to the federal government; it protects value-laden personal rights, often through open-ended or highly general terms; some central principles are implicit in its structure and purpose, rather than spelled out in explicit text; and as Chief Justice John Marshall long ago pointed out, it is meant to last and work well for the ages.[1] These unique features of the Constitution's structure and purpose often bear on the interpretive analysis.

I shall first describe the Constitution itself. By doing so, I hope to show why I believe that judges must be prepared to use many different interpretive tools, not a single, say text-based, tool, when interpreting different constitutional phrases. Then, I shall describe Chief Justice Marshall's opinion in *McCulloch v. Maryland*.[2] Written in 1819, that opinion reaches its constitutional conclusion through the use of several different interpretive tools. And, as importantly, it emphasizes the need to maintain a *workable* Constitution—a Constitution that provides a pragmatic, democratic framework for a society that Chief Justice Marshall knew would change dramatically over time.

Then I shall discuss efforts to achieve, in the constitutional context, the purported benefits of textualism. Recall that textualism is justified, at least in part, as an interpretive method that provides one best answer to every interpretive question, and that consequently prevents judges from substituting their views of what is good for the law.[3]

In the constitutional context, textualists often turn to originalism. That term might simply suggest looking to history in order to help determine how a constitutional phrase applies today. And so limited, the suggestion is often perfectly appropriate and helpful. But the term originalism is also used to describe an interpretive system that focuses on history alone. Today, most originalists contend that constitutional meaning is fixed at the time of its enactment by its "original public meaning," or how ordinary members of the public would have understood the particular words in that period.[4]

This overly rigid reliance upon history is, I believe, harmful. Like textualism in respect to statutes, it misunderstands the normal use of language. Contrary to what the originalist hopes, it will not deter judges from substituting their own views of what is good for the law. And it will make of the Constitution a document that is too rigid, that will not pass the test of time, and that will not serve its basic value-laden objectives.

Some of the judges who believe strongly in textualism and originalism, such as Justice Scalia, also believe that judges should try to decide cases according to clear-cut rules that are broad in application, derived from past cases, or created when a judge disposes of the case before him or her.[5] Again, cases decided through application of that kind of rule suggest that there is one correct interpretive answer: You either follow the rule or you do not. I shall try, again through examples, to show why overemphasis upon rule creation dangerously discourages judges from using standards, purposes, approaches, and flexible, rather than determinative, rules instead. Some constitutional clauses, those protecting free speech, for example, demand the use of greater flexibility if they are to continue to work well, protecting the human rights values that underlie them.

I shall go on to explain why considerations of "workability," not the use of these textualist methods, normally provide a better way to answer questions concerning the federal government's structure. And I shall consider the instability that the use of textualist methods can bring to the legal system.

11.

The Constitution

The Constitution of the United States is the shortest governing document of any major nation. It has seven articles and twenty-seven amendments. The articles contain 4,543 words (about 16 ordinary book pages); together with amendments, the Constitution contains 7,591 words (about 27 pages).[1] In 1803, the Supreme Court made clear that the Court has the power of judicial review, that is, the authority to determine whether laws are consistent with the Constitution.[2] Since then, that Court, with a few exceptions (involving, for example, military and foreign affairs), has had the last word as to just what most of the words in the Constitution mean and how they are applied.

From a legal perspective, the document is highly complex. A brief review of the structure and content of the Constitution will help the reader understand the different ways in which I and other Supreme Court Justices have approached the interpretation of different parts of that document.

The body of the Constitution, specifically its original seven articles, creates the structure of the federal government. The first three articles describe the three branches of the federal government—the legislative, the executive, and the judicial branches, respectively. The legislative branch (Article I) consists of a Senate and a House of Representatives.[3] The Constitution vests in that branch "all legislative Powers herein granted."[4] Article II "vest[s]" the "executive Power" in "a President of the United States of America."[5] And Article III provides that the "judicial Power of the United

States, shall be vested in one supreme Court, and in such inferior courts as the Congress may from time to time ordain and establish."[6]

Article IV imposes several specific obligations upon the states (e.g., each must give "Full Faith and Credit . . . to the public Acts, Records, and judicial Proceedings" of the others[7]), and it describes how new states shall be admitted to the Union.[8] Article V primarily describes the amendment process.[9] Article VI, among other things, says that the Constitution (and the laws and treaties of the United States) "shall be the supreme Law of the Land."[10] And, Article VII provides for the "Establishment" of the Constitution once nine states ratify it.[11]

The first ten amendments to the Constitution set forth a "Bill of Rights."[12] It contains many of the most well-known constitutional rights, for example, freedom of speech and religion,[13] the right against unreasonable searches and seizures,[14] and the right to a jury trial in criminal cases.[15]

After the Bill of Rights, the next two amendments concern federal court jurisdiction[16] and the presidential election process.[17] The Thirteenth, Fourteenth, and Fifteenth Amendments, arising out of the Civil War, seek to assure an end to slavery,[18] equal and fair treatment of all citizens,[19] and no race-based discrimination in voting.[20] Of the next twelve amendments, three guarantee voting rights: to women,[21] to those eighteen and older,[22] and by forbidding any poll tax.[23] Almost all of the remaining nine are comparatively speaking more technical. Five concern the election or terms of office of federal officials (e.g., popular vote to elect senators;[24] two terms for the president;[25] dates of beginning service;[26] incapacitation of the president;[27] District of Columbia presidential voting[28]); two concern prohibition of "intoxicating liquors" (enacting,[29] then repealing, Prohibition[30]); one concerns compensation of members of Congress;[31] and one permits the government to impose an income tax.[32]

Despite its brevity, the Constitution, as I have said, is complex. Some of its phrases are highly general. Neither the states (nor the federal government), for example, can "deprive any person of . . . liberty . . . without due process of law."[33] Congress can enact "no law . . . abridging the freedom of speech."[34] Congress has the power to "regulate Commerce . . . among the several states,"[35] and to "make all Laws which shall be necessary and proper" for carrying this and other powers "into Execution."[36]

Some of its phrases are specific. "The Senate of the United States shall be composed of two Senators from each State";[37] "The terms of the President and Vice President shall end at noon on the 20th day of January";[38] "No State shall . . . coin Money."[39]

Some of its language, though specific on its face, can still raise difficult interpretive problems, such as Congress's power to make uniform bankruptcy law,[40] its power to give "Inventors" the "exclusive Right" to their "Discoveries,"[41] and the powers belonging to the president as "Commander in Chief" of the armed forces.[42]

Some of its language seems to refer to mostly out-of-date problems. "No state shall, without the consent of Congress, lay any Duty of Tonnage";[43] "No Soldier shall, in time of peace be quartered in any house"[44] without the owner's consent.

And some language seems to call out for unsaid limitations or qualifications. The First Amendment, for example, provides that "Congress shall make no law . . . abridging the freedom of speech."[45] But it has long been recognized that even "[t]he most stringent protection of free speech would not protect a man in falsely shouting *fire* in a theatre and causing a panic."[46]

The nature of the document, its abstract phrases, its underlying values, its different phrases' different objectives, taken together, all suggest that there will not be any single tool that, when applied to all its provisions, can produce satisfactory answers to a myriad of different interpretive questions.

12.

The Traditional Approach to Constitutional Interpretation

McCulloch v. Maryland (1819)[1]

When, soon after the founding, Chief Justice John Marshall interpreted the Constitution, he took account of the features I have just described. They include 1) the complexity of the document; 2) the many different subjects to which it directly or indirectly refers; 3) the varying degrees of treatment of those subjects; and 4) the different levels of abstraction and detail in constitutional phrases. How then did he proceed? His early, but still authoritative, interpretation of the Constitution in *McCulloch v. Maryland* provides the foundational and traditional approach to constitutional interpretation.

In 1816, Congress established a national bank. Many states (which had their own banks) opposed the national bank and were of the view that Congress lacked the constitutional power to create such a bank. Maryland was one of those states, and it decided that it would levy a tax on the national bank.[2] This laid the groundwork for Chief Justice Marshall's opinion in *McCulloch*: The Court had to decide whether the Constitution granted to Congress the power to establish a Bank of the United States.[3] If so, the Court also had to decide whether the Constitution forbade Maryland's efforts to tax that bank.[4]

Chief Justice Marshall initially stated the interpretive problem in general terms: Can a state deny the obligation of a law that Congress has enacted? May it do so here, where the federal law establishes a Bank of the

United States? He pointed out that questions of this type—concerning the relative powers of the Union and its members—"must be decided peacefully, or remain a source of hostile legislation, perhaps, of hostility of a still more serious nature." He added, "if it is to be so decided [peacefully] [, then], by this tribunal alone can the decision be made." Marshall then turned to the more specific initial question: "[H]as Congress power to incorporate a bank?"[5]

For present purposes, I emphasize that the Chief Justice brought to bear several different tools to help the Court answer this constitutional interpretive question. First, he turned to past practice, what American governments have thought of this question over the preceding thirty years. He pointed out that many state legislatures, the judicial department of the federal government, and by that time the federal legislature, Congress, have thought and did think that Congress had the power to do as it did. And, he said, where "the great principles of liberty are not concerned," a question "ought to receive a considered impression from" that past "practice."[6]

Second, he pointed out that the states could not avoid following the Constitution as interpreted. Marshall turned to a general question important at the time: Who were the parties to the Constitution—the states or the people? If the former, the Constitution was more like a treaty among nations;[7] and treaties delegating powers were interpreted narrowly at that time.[8] Marshall answered by saying that document "proceeds directly from the people"[9] (its first words, after all, are "We the People"[10]). Though the Constitution was ratified by conventions in each state, the members of those conventions were chosen by the people. And the people, when they act, often act through the states, but "the measures they adopt do not, on that account, cease to be the measures of the people."[11] "The Government of the Union . . . is emphatically and truly, a Government of the people. . . . Its powers are granted by them, and are to be exercised directly on them, and for their benefit."[12] Because the Constitution was not like a treaty among nations, then, the powers it delegated ought not be interpreted narrowly.[13]

Third, Marshall conceded that the powers of the federal government were limited in that it was a government of "enumerated powers." But he specified that the federal government, "though limited in its powers, is supreme within its sphere of action."[14] The Constitution states that the "Constitution, and the laws of the United States, which shall be made in pursuance thereof . . . shall be the supreme law of the land, . . . anything in the Constitution or any laws of any State to the contrary notwithstanding." State, as well as federal, officials must take an oath of fidelity to the federal Constitution.[15]

Fourth, Marshall explained why reading the text of the Constitution alone could not provide the answer to this interpretive question. He conceded that the Constitution did not expressly grant to the federal government the power to create a bank. But, he added, in a statement that was highly important then and remains highly important now:

> A constitution [that] . . . would partake of the prolixity of a legal code . . . could scarcely be embraced by the human mind. . . . [O]nly its great outlines should be marked, its important objects designated, and the minor ingredients which compose those objects be deduced from the nature of the objects themselves. . . . In considering this question, then, we must never forget that it is *a constitution* we are expounding.[16]

Consequently, the Constitution must implicitly or explicitly delegate to Congress the power to determine the means within "the dictates of reason" for carrying out the powers explicitly granted.[17] The nature and scope of these authorized means must be "deduced from the nature of the objects" delegated—here, the power to create a national bank was implied by the explicitly granted powers to lay and collect taxes, to borrow money, to regulate commerce, to declare and conduct war, and to raise and support armies and navies.[18]

Regardless, Marshall continued, the Constitution itself made the existence of this authority clear when it explicitly delegated to Congress the power to make "all laws which shall be necessary and proper for carrying into execution the foregoing powers, and all other powers vested by this Constitution."[19]

The word "necessary" here, the Chief Justice emphasized, did not mean that one thing could not exist without another. It "frequently import[ed] no more than that one thing is convenient, or useful, or essential to another." It referred to a means being "calculated to produce the end." "Such is the character of human language, that no word conveys to the mind in all situations one single definite idea," and "nothing is more common than to use words in a figurative sense." The word "necessary" "has not a fixed character peculiar to itself." Like many other words, though it may "import something excessive" (such as "absolutely necessary"), it should be "understood in a more mitigated sense," a sense that "common usage justifie[d]."[20] The word, he said (and I highlight this especially for the textualist reader), "is used in various senses, and, in its construction, the subject, the context, the intention of the person using them, are all to be taken into view."[21]

Fifth, and perhaps most importantly, the nature of the Constitution, as a basic document intended to endure for ages to come, demands that its interpretation prove workable. We are interpreting, the Chief Justice pointed out, "great powers" upon which the "welfare of a nation essentially depends." Further:

> [T]hose who gave these powers [sought] to insure, so far as human prudence could insure, their beneficial execution. This could not be done . . . [without] leav[ing] it in the power of Congress to adopt any [means] which might be appropriate, and which were conducive to the end. [For] [t]his provision is made in a Constitution intended to endure for ages to come, and consequently to be adapted to the various crises of human affairs. . . . It would have been . . . unwise . . . to provide by immutable rules, for exigencies which, if foreseen at all, must have been foreseen dimly, and which can be best provided for as they occur. To have declared that the best means shall not be used . . . would have been to deprive the legislature of the capacity to avail itself of experience, to exercise its reason, and to accommodate its legislation to circumstances.[22]

It would be absolutely "impracticabl[e]" to maintain the narrow construction Maryland advocated without "rendering the Government incompetent to its great objects."[23] It could not have been intended, Marshall added, "almost" to "annihilate, this useful and necessary right of the legislature to select its means."[24]

Sixth, the Chief Justice drew added textual support for his argument. The "necessary and proper" clause is "placed among the powers of Congress, not among the limitations on those powers." Moreover, its "terms purport to enlarge, not to diminish, the powers vested in the Government."[25]

Seventh, the Chief Justice emphasized the document's purpose. He said that the Constitution must not become a "splendid bauble." It "must allow to the national legislature that discretion, with respect to the means by which the powers it confers are to be carried into execution, which will enable that body to perform the high duties assigned to it in the manner most beneficial to the people."[26]

Conclusion: "Let the end be legitimate, let it be within the scope of the Constitution, and all means which are appropriate, which are plainly adapted to that end, which are not prohibited, but consist with the letter and the spirit of the constitution, are constitutional."[27] The national bank was constitutional.[28]

One final point: The Court also held that the State of Maryland could not tax the national bank. In doing so, the Court made a purely practical argument. The states' voters held the state back from taxing state objects that the people of the state did not want taxed. They had no such incentive when the state sought to impose a tax upon a federal, not a state, object.[29]

Now let us review the tools or the legal instruments that the Court used in its efforts to interpret the language of the Constitution. The Court did not rely upon originalism or textualism. Many of its tools were purpose-oriented. They included: 1) history; 2) why the Constitution is unlike a treaty; 3) the nature of the document; 4) text understood in light of purposes; 5) workability; 6) text again; 7) purpose; and, 8) at the end, a purely practical argument based on the nature of the document and the need for flexibility.

As far as *McCulloch* reveals the interpretive methods likely needed to interpret the constitutional document, it does not exclude much. The opinion uses text, purposes, workability, history, and others I have just mentioned. All seem helpful.

McCulloch's Guiding Principles: Workability

Few would deny that the values that the Constitution embodies include a democratic form of government characterized by the separation of powers both vertical (state and federal) and horizontal (legislative, executive, and judicial branches) so that no small group of people becomes too powerful. The Constitution also protects basic human rights, including, for example, free speech, religious liberty, and freedom from unreasonable searches and seizures. It seeks to assure equality before the law. And it insists upon application of the rule of law itself.

Underlying these principles, however, is another, an implied principle, which judges only on occasion discuss explicitly, but which a judge must keep in mind when interpreting the Constitution. The Constitution is a practical document. It must hold together a nation, which has grown from four million people at the time it was written to 332 million people today.[30] I would use words such as "viable," "workable," "practical," and "feasible" to reflect the basic need to interpret the Constitution so that it works well, maintaining the basic democratic, human, and legal values that underlie it.

John Marshall's statements to this effect in *McCulloch* are worth repeating. The Constitution's provisions that grant power to the federal government were intended to "insure, so far as human prudence could insure, their beneficial execution" for "ages to come, and consequently to be adapted to the various crises of human affairs."[31] "[W]e must never forget that it is *a constitution* we are expounding."[32] Those final words are engraved across the wall in the lower Great Hall of the Supreme Court building, directly behind a statue of Chief Justice Marshall himself.

And indeed, the sentiment has not been forgotten. Justice Robert Jackson, writing along these same lines, pointed out that the Constitution's separation of powers, while "diffus[ing] power the better to secure liberty," also intends an "integrat[ion]" of those "dispersed powers into a *workable* government."[33] Other Justices, such as Chief Justice Rehnquist, have noted that the Supreme Court has often referred to a "constitutional plan" designed "to make the Constitution a workable governing charter."[34] Historians have praised the document's workability, noting that without its "open texture . . . Americans would have needed either to formally amend the Constitution much more frequently than they have done, or else to scrap it as of merely antiquarian interest."[35] That open texture is by design: "'We the People,' who 'ordain[ed] and establish[ed]' the American Constitution, sought to create and to protect a workable form of government that is in its 'principles, structure, and whole mass,' basically democratic."[36] Madison himself thought that interpretation of the Constitution's language would prove necessary to adapt the Constitution to changing times, and that a just construction of that language would allow it to do so.[37] Jefferson also advocated an adaptive approach to constitutional interpretation, on the ground that "[t]he earth belongs always to the living generation"[38] and that our ancestors should not have the power to permanently bind their successors.[39] Interpreting the Constitution in the present day, judges normally should (and do) keep in mind that the "Founders meant the Constitution as a practical document that would transmit its basic values to future generations through principles that remained workable over time."[40] In a word, the Constitution must remain workable.

13.

Constitutional Textualism

A rigid or narrow textualism, as I have previously described it, could not achieve certain of its basic goals were it to be transposed without change to the task of interpreting the Constitution. It could not brake a judge's tendency to write into law what that judge believes is "good," nor could it suggest that every interpretive problem has a clear textual answer. The Constitution's text may well say nothing about either the scope of, or the restrictions that Congress might impose upon, a set of constitutional words.

Consider Congress's spending power. After mentioning the taxing power, the relevant language simply says that "Congress shall have the Power To . . . provide for the common Defence and general Welfare of the United States."[1] Does this mean Congress can authorize the spending of federal funds for any purpose at all unless expressly forbidden?[2] Also, Congress often imposes restrictions upon a state's expenditures of federal money. Where does the Constitution say Congress can do this? What restrictions can it impose? The Constitution (with a few explicit but general exceptions) does not say.[3] Consider, too, the variety of different kinds of constitutional provisions, some narrow, some broad. Is there a single textual theory that can usefully tell a judge how to approach their interpretation?

Textualist judges might, as some have suggested, simply recognize that many constitutional phrases are textually abstract using language that admits of several, perhaps many, different interpretations.[4] But many have, instead, developed a theory of originalism, looking back to the founding (or post–Civil War) to discover what the text meant at that time.[5] They have also stressed the need for interpreting the Constitution's phrases in terms of general rules.[6]

Both originalism and the emphasis (in my view, overemphasis) upon the creation of broad, clear-cut rules are spinoffs of textualism as used to interpret statutes. But the use of originalism and clear-cut rules in the constitutional area cannot achieve textualism's basic objective of finding a singular "best" answer. There are many reasons. The originalist approach, at least in its more rigid forms, does not produce definite answers. It will not necessarily act to restrain judges from substituting their own views for "the law." The constitutional text is often too abstract or too limited to help resolve the constitutional dispute. Nor have originalists made clear whether they would, or would not, overrule many of the earlier constitutional cases where judges reached their conclusions without using originalist methods. If they feel free to overrule precedents that do not rely upon originalist methods, originalism poses a threat to the law's need for stability. For these and other reasons, *McCulloch*'s workability principle—not originalism, nor emphasizing rules, nor textualism itself—represents a far more satisfactory approach to interpreting the Constitution.

Originalism

Originalism can be defined as a form of textualism that takes account of the fact that a long time has passed since the relevant text first appeared. It consists of the principle or belief that a text should be interpreted in a way consistent with how it would have been understood or was intended to be understood at the time it was written.[7] Justice Scalia and Professor Garner define "originalism" as

> The doctrine that words are to be given the meaning they had when they were adopted; specif., the canon that a legal text should be interpreted through the historical ascertainment of the meaning that it would have conveyed to a fully informed observer at the time when the text first took effect.[8]

A recent press article described "originalism" as "the belief that the meaning of the Constitution was fixed at the time it was adopted."[9] In its 2022 decision in *New York State Rifle & Pistol Association v. Bruen*,[10] the Court majority spoke of "examination of a variety of legal and other sources to determine *the public understanding* of a legal text in the period after its enactment or ratification."[11] In a word, the originalist, instead of looking to the text and asking what the words mean now, may well ask what they would have meant to an ordinary eighteenth-century person in order to then apply the words to a contemporary issue.

As applied to constitutional phrases, originalism, its proponents believe, has two major virtues. It suggests that there is one, and only one, answer to an interpretive question (an answer related to the original linguistic meaning of the words of a phrase). And, it will thereby limit misuse of judicial power, for it will inhibit judges who would otherwise interpret a constitutional phrase in terms of what they believe is "good."[12]

New York State Rifle and Pistol Ass'n v. Bruen (2022)[13]

In *Bruen* (2022), which considered the constitutionality of a New York law requiring a license to carry firearms in public, the Court had to interpret the Second Amendment.[14] That amendment provides:

> A well regulated Militia, being necessary to the security of a free State, the right of the people to keep and bear Arms, shall not be infringed.[15]

In an earlier case, in 2008, *District of Columbia v. Heller*,[16] the Court, in a 5–4 decision, had held that this amendment protects the right of law-abiding citizens to possess a handgun *in the home* for purposes of self-defense.[17] In *Bruen*, decided in 2022, the Court considered the amendment's application to handgun possession *outside the home*—specifically the right to "carry a handgun for self-defense outside the home."[18] It held, 6–3, that New York's law requiring a citizen to have a license to carry a gun outside the home violated the Second Amendment.[19]

Under the New York law, to obtain a license permitting carrying a handgun in public, an individual generally had to be twenty-one years old and "of good moral character." He could not previously have been convicted of a felony, been dishonorably discharged from the military, or have been involuntarily committed to a psychiatric facility. Unless he or she worked in certain (say, law enforcement–related) professions, that person also had to show that "proper cause exist[ed]" for the issuance of a license.[20] "Proper cause" meant that a person who seeks a license for target practice or hunting must show "a sincere desire to participate in target shooting or hunting." An applicant seeking a license for self-defense had to show "a special need for self-protection distinguishable from that of the general community."[21]

For present purposes, we should focus on the standards, rules, or theories that the majority said that courts must use when deciding whether a gun law or regulation violates the Second Amendment. As the majority acknowledged, virtually all the lower courts had applied a "two-step test." First, they would determine whether "the challenged law regulates activity falling outside the scope of the [Second Amendment] right as originally understood." If so, the law did not run afoul of the Second Amendment. If the law did regulate activity falling within the scope of the Second Amendment, the courts would proceed to the second step of the test. They would ask "how close the law comes to the core of the Second Amendment right and the severity of the law's burden on that right." If the law burdened a core Second Amendment right, courts would analyze whether "the Government c[ould] prove that the law [was] 'narrowly tailored to achieve a compelling governmental interest.'"[22]

The Court majority referred to this second step as "means-end scrutiny." It then held that the second step should not, and did not, constitute part of the constitutional analysis. It thought that a "means-end" analysis would give judges "the power to decide on a case-by-case basis whether the [Second Amendment] right is *really worth* insisting upon." It said that a "constitutional guarantee subject to future judges' assessments of its usefulness is no constitutional guarantee at all."[23]

Instead, the Court wrote, the constitutional "test" must be "rooted in the Second Amendment's text as informed by history."[24] Indeed, to show that the law is constitutional its proponents must "identify an American tradition justifying" the law's requirements.[25] They must prove that the law or regulation "is part of the historical tradition that delimits the outer bounds of the right to keep and bear arms."[26] The Court added that to determine the meaning of the Second Amendment's text, one must find "the *public understanding* of [the] legal text in the period after its enactment or ratification."[27]

Here is originalism, pure and simple. When determining the scope or meaning of a constitutional provision, do not look to the consequences of an interpretation, do not look to purposes, do not even look to current linguistic usage. Instead, look to (and perhaps only to) the "public understanding" of the text at about the time the provision was originally enacted.

There are at least three basic problems with the "originalist" approach.

The first two are highlighted in my dissent in *Bruen* (an opinion in which I was joined by Justices Sotomayor and Kagan). First, too often originalism is simply impractical, because judges are not historians. I do not say "never" look to history. Often it is a useful tool. But to tell judges they must rely exclusively upon history imposes upon them a task that they cannot accomplish. They understand how to weigh a law's objectives (its "ends") against the methods used to achieve those objectives (its "means"). But they are less accustomed to resolving difficult historical issues. And they have little experience answering contested historical questions or applying those answers to resolve contemporary problems.[28]

Consider a few of the problems that exclusive reliance upon history can raise. Do lower courts have the research resources necessary to conduct exhaustive historical analyses in many, perhaps every, Second Amendment case? What happens when and if new historical evidence becomes available? To what extent can a judge use historical debate or "law office history" to cloak a personal preference?[29]

What historical regulations and decisions qualify as analogues to modern regulatory laws? The majority in *Bruen* looked to history that long preceded the writing of our Constitution. They likely believed that earlier laws and cases from Britain, for example, shed light on what the term "arms" meant at the time the Constitution was written. But to what extent can, for example, fourteenth-century laws or regulations or rules addressing repeating crossbows, launcegays, dirks, daggers, skeins, stilladers,[30] and even Greek fire (tossed over the top of a besieged city's walls[31]), determine the meaning of "arms" in the eighteenth century?

The majority did not explain precisely what an "analogue" is. It discussed an example when swords, not guns, were commonly used weapons. One might ask, are swords "analogous to" guns?[32] Do we not have to look to the purposes of old and new regulations to answer these questions? And, if so, are we not considering the very "means" and "ends" that the Court told us not to consider? Indeed, when considering whether old regulatory laws are analogous to New York's law, the Court did not "provide an exhaustive survey of the features that render regulations relevantly similar" for Second Amendment purposes.[33] Rather, it considered just "how and why" a gun control regulation "burden[s] a law-abiding citizen's right to armed self-defense,"[34] i.e., it considered the regulation's "means" ("how") and "ends" ("why").[35]

The majority, in arguing for originalism, suggested that the interpretation of no other constitutional right depends on an interest-balancing approach.[36] But is that so? What about the Fourth Amendment, which asks courts to determine whether a search and seizure is "unreasonable"?[37] What about the First Amendment, which looks to history to decide whether the kind of speech at issue (e.g., political speech, child pornography) falls within a "protected" category (akin to the first step that the circuit courts had been using in the Second Amendment context), and then looks to "means-ends" analysis to determine whether the First Amendment protects the particular speech at issue? Courts use what they call "strict scrutiny," "intermediate scrutiny," and other "interest-balancing" concepts to weigh harms, justifications, and potentially less restrictive alternatives.[38] Did the Court mean to erase these commonly used forms of analysis from the Court's First Amendment case law?

Consider the Court's use of history in the gun cases themselves. In the foundational case, *Heller*, the Court examined the text of the Second Amendment. Recall it: "A well regulated Militia, being necessary to the security of a free State, the right of the people to keep and bear Arms, shall not be infringed."[39] The majority opinion, written by Justice Scalia, held that the right to "keep and bear arms" historically encompassed an "individual right to possess and carry weapons in case of confrontation."[40] And it held that the amendment gave individuals the right to keep a handgun in the home for self-defense.[41] Justice Stevens, in a dissent, which I joined, concluded that the term "bear arms" was an idiom that protected only the right "to use and possess arms in conjunction with service in a well-regulated militia."[42]

The historical debate in the two opinions accounts for about eighty pages.[43] The dissent argued that the Second Amendment was designed to show skeptical state opponents of the Constitution that Congress lacked the power (under Article I) to call state militias up for duty and disband them.[44] The majority disagreed. And in doing so, it relied heavily upon an eighteenth-century analysis by Blackstone of the seventeenth-century English Bill of Rights, which, the majority said, permitted "having and using arms for self-preservation,"[45] and had "nothing whatever to do with serving in a militia."[46]

In *McDonald v. City of Chicago*,[47] the next major Second Amendment case, twenty-one historians specializing in English and Early American history (at leading universities in Britain, the United States, and Australia) said that the majority in *Heller* had gotten its history wrong. The English Declaration of Rights "did not . . . protect an individual's right to possess, own or use arms for private purposes such as to defend a home against burglars." Rather, the English right to "have arms" sought to ensure that the Crown could not deny Parliament (which represented the people) the power to arm the landed gentry and raise a militia—or the right of the people to possess arms in order to take part in that militia—"should the sovereign usurp the laws, liberties, estates, and Protestant religion of the Nation." Blackstone's statement that the English Bill of Rights sought to protect a right of "self-preservation" was correct. But that right was not a right exercised separately by individuals; it was a right to participate in a militia organized by their elected representatives.[48]

Then, in *Bruen*, the Court received another brief, this one written by linguistic experts. They told us that since *Heller* was decided, experts had searched more than 120,000 founding-era texts written between 1760 and 1799. They had also searched 40,000 other texts written as far back as 1475.[49] They found that the phrase "bear arms" was overwhelmingly used to refer to "war, soldiering or other forms of armed action by a group rather than an individual."[50] Scholars seem to have concluded that the Court majority in *Heller* misread the history.[51] I have found little to the contrary.

So, if the scholars are right, what should the Court do? Anything? Perhaps not. After all I was in dissent in these cases. The historians and linguists simply add weight to the opinions of four dissenters. My point here, however, is that judges are not very good historians. And the historians and linguists certainly help build that case. Why advocate a method of deciding cases that is likely in difficult cases (which comprise most of the Court's docket) to produce mistake after mistake after mistake?

What about the Court's use of history in *Bruen* itself? The State of New York (and the dissent) pointed to many laws that, in its view, historically speaking, were analogous. The dissent pointed, for example: a) to thirteenth- and fourteenth-century English laws prohibiting persons from "going armed";[52] b) to the fourteenth-century Statute of Northampton, which forbade going "armed" by day or night in fairs, markets, or other places (perhaps without the king's permission);[53] c) to early colonial laws, such as New Jersey's, which forbade privately wearing "pocket pistol[s], skeines, stilladers, daggers or dirks" within "this Province";[54] d) to founding-era statutes, such as Virginia's, which prohibited any person from going or riding armed "by night nor by day, in fairs markets or in other places, in terror of the Country";[55] e) to nineteenth-century laws, such as Georgia's, which made it unlawful to carry "unless in an open manner and fully exposed to view, any pistol, . . . dirk, [or] sword . . . man-ufactured and sold for purpose of offence and defence";[56] f) to post–Civil War laws in many Western states prohibiting any carriage of firearms with a few limited exceptions;[57] g) to twentieth-century laws, such as New York's law, first enacted in 1911;[58] and h) to many others.[59]

The majority did not deny the existence of these laws. It simply said they were not analogous. Some, such as England's thirteenth-century laws, were too old.[60] Some, such as New York's law, were too recent.[61] Some did not last long enough.[62] Some applied to too few people (such as colonial laws present in only three of the thirteen colonies).[63] Some did not involve licensing and applied only after an armed individual was determined to have threatened the peace.[64] Some resembled New York's law only in re-spect to concealed carrying but did not regulate open carrying.[65]

Moreover, many pages of the majority and dissenting opinions are spent discussing matters where the evidence just does not exist. Did the Statute of Northampton, for example, forbid only carriage of weapons with an intent to terrorize, or was terrorizing a reason for the enactment of the statute, not an element of the crime?[66] I think it is fair to say, "Who knows?" But if these many laws, rules, and regulations forbidding unlicensed carriage of weapons are not analogous to New York's law, then what is? What ever could be? How could judges possibly work their way through heaps of this kind of (often minor) historical evidence? And that is the main point here.

Bruen also highlights a second, and in my view even worse, problem with the originalist approach. Originalism tells judges not to consider the practical consequences of their interpretations or the purposes of, and the values protected by, the constitutional provisions at issue in a case.[67] That perspective threatens the workability of our constitutional system and im-pinges on the ability of democratic legislatures to create modern solutions to modern problems.

As the *Bruen* dissent explains, modern America looks very different from the pre-founding era. In 1790, the country's four million people lived largely in rural settings.[68] Today, our nation's population has grown sig-nificantly, with a large portion living in densely packed cities. Guns, too, have evolved in a way that permits a single shooter to kill a large number of people in a short amount of time, to a degree likely unimaginable to the Founders.[69] Moreover, America is the world's leader in the number of firearms per capita possessed by civilians—nearly 400 million. (Yemen is second.) In part for these reasons, guns today pose a unique threat to American society if not properly regulated. Indeed, in 2020, an average of about 124 people died from gun violence every single day, a figure that reflects a 25 percent increase just compared to 2015.[70]

The lower courts, which had upheld the New York law, had examined these realities and New York's statute with care. The court of appeals had decided that "New York has substantial, indeed compelling, public interests in public safety and crime prevention."[71] The court pointed to numerous "studies and data demonstrating that widespread access to handguns in public increases the likelihood that felonies will result in death and fundamentally alters the safety and character of public spaces."[72]

But originalism says that judges cannot consider these modern developments and practical realities. Nor can judges weigh the resulting interest of federal, state, and local governments in regulating guns to protect the health and welfare of all their citizens.[73]

Think about the number of mass shootings, the number of firearm-assisted suicides,[74] the number of domestic violence homicides committed with guns,[75] and the number of police officers killed by guns in the line of duty.[76] And think, too, about the evidence suggesting that limiting the number of guns and their carriage helps to limit unwarranted firearms deaths.[77] Now go back to Chief Justice Marshall and *McCulloch*. Go back to the need for a "workable" Constitution—a Constitution that will provide an enduring American government and hold together a diverse population for hundreds of years. How can a jurisprudential philosophy grounded in that Constitution ignore these practical realities and the deadly consequences of striking down the efforts of democratically elected bodies to address those realities? I do not think it can.

There is a third problem with originalism illuminated here. To explain it, I shall briefly discuss a case that we will return to in more depth later in this chapter: *Dobbs v. Jackson Women's Health Organization*.[78] In that case, the Court, relying on originalism, overturned long-standing Supreme Court precedent that had recognized that the Fourteenth Amendment protects a woman's right to have an abortion.[79] I will address the implications of originalism for *stare decisis* later on with reference to this case.[80] For now, I will focus on how the case highlights a deeply regressive feature of the originalist approach.

In *Dobbs*, the majority's reasoning boiled down to one basic proposition: Because the people who ratified the original Constitution and the Fourteenth Amendment did not understand the document to protect reproductive rights, the document could not be read, now, as protecting those rights.[81]

The dissent, which Justices Sotomayor, Kagan, and I authored together, pointed out that "people" did not ratify the original Constitution in 1788 or the Fourteenth Amendment in 1868. White men did. Women were not understood as full members of the political community at either of these points in history. Indeed, they would not gain the right to vote until 1920. The recognition of women's rights—from the right to vote to the right to an abortion—flowed from, and contributed to, women's ever-growing role in society, particularly in the workplace and in politics. In the face of this progress, originalism would limit the kinds of liberty interests cognizable under the Fourteenth Amendment to those contemplated by men who existed in a time when women were not considered to have a legal identity separate from their husbands. And so, by saying that "we must read our foundational charter as viewed at the time of ratification," the majority "consign[ed] women to second-class citizenship."[82]

Again, think back to the nature of the Constitution and Chief Justice Marshall's approach to interpreting it. The document contains broad phrases, like the Fourteenth Amendment's guarantee that no state shall "deprive any person of life, liberty, or property, without due process of law" or "deny to any person within its jurisdiction the equal protection of the laws."[83] The framers of the Fourteenth Amendment chose these broad references to "liberty" and "equality," rather than defining rights by reference to specific practices at the time of ratification, because they understood that they were designing a framework intended to endure and adapt to changing circumstances over hundreds of years.[84] This flexible feature of our Constitution has permitted American society, including the courts, to recognize new facets of the rights to liberty and equality that the document protects: the right to contraception,[85] to same-sex intimacy,[86] to interracial marriage,[87] to gay marriage.[88]

An interpretive approach like originalism that tells us that the scope and meaning of these terms are fixed at the time they are ratified and in the manner contemplated by the (predominantly white, heterosexual) men who framed them would sweep away all this—and much more. For instance, consider that, for decades after the Fourteenth Amendment was adopted, the Court interpreted the amendment's equal protection provision to allow for racial segregation, on the view that public accommodations could be "separate but equal."[89]

Perhaps the framers of the Fourteenth Amendment, too, believed that allegedly separate but equal facilities would satisfy the new constitutional right they were enshrining. Scholars debate whether *Brown v. Board of Education*,[90] which overturned the "separate but equal" principle, is consistent with an originalist reading of the Fourteenth Amendment's requirement that states guarantee their citizens equal protection of the laws.[91]

Regardless of which side has the better of the argument with respect to originalism and *Brown*, originalist reasoning can offer no compelling justification of another landmark desegregation case: *Bolling v. Sharpe*,[92] decided the same day as *Brown* in 1954. Whereas *Brown* held that the Fourteenth Amendment's equal protection guarantee (which does not apply to the federal government) prevented state governments from maintaining segregated school systems, *Bolling* relied on the Fifth Amendment's Due Process Clause (which does apply to the federal government) to hold that the federal government could not constitutionally maintain a segregated school system within the District of Columbia. Though the Fifth Amendment does not contain any sort of "equal protection" requirement, the *Bolling* Court held that its due process guarantee was broad enough to encompass the requirement that the federal government refrain from unreasonable discrimination. After all, the Court reasoned, "it would be unthinkable that the same Constitution would impose a lesser duty on the Federal Government" than on the states.[93]

The Court's reasoning in *Bolling* is impossible to reconcile with the original understanding of the Fifth Amendment. The amendment was ratified in 1791, a time when slavery was legal, practiced in a majority of states, and few would have thought its "due process" guarantee to encompass a protection against unequal treatment on the basis of race.[94] *Dobbs's* unwavering insistence on the use of originalist methodologies, then, plainly calls into question decades of precedent requiring the federal government to treat people equally under the law.[95]

But whatever "due process" and "equal protection" were understood to mean in 1791 and 1868, those understandings did not stop the activists of the Civil Rights Movement from campaigning for equal status and treatment under the mantle of the Constitution through nonviolent civil disobedience. Nor did it stop the Court from later recognizing that the Fourteenth and Fifth Amendments did not tolerate racial segregation in schools.[96] Can proponents of originalism intend to unravel all these rules of law if they do not reflect an understanding of the constitutional text that its framers would have held?

In sum, originalism's exclusive focus on the historical meaning of text creates three significant problems. First, it requires judges to be historians— a role for which they may not be qualified—constantly searching historical sources for the "answer" where there often isn't one there. Second, it leaves no room for judges to consider the practical consequences of the constitutional rules they propound. And third, it does not take into account the ways in which our values as a society evolve over time as we learn from the mistakes of our past. The last two problems are very similar to the problems that arise under textualism's other "cousin": a preference for broadly applicable, rigid rules.

A "Law of Rules"

When it comes to constitutional interpretation, judges who favor textualism tend to favor clear-cut, broadly applicable rules.[97] Of course, every case creates a precedent, and that precedent itself can be seen as a rule. But those who advocate a preference for setting forth rules often prefer a fairly broad rule, the scope of which reaches well beyond the facts of the case.[98] Whether a rule is broad or narrow is a matter of degree. But it is fair to say that those who favor textualism and originalism have expressed a preference for broad specific rules at the expense of, say, standards, norms, principles, and approaches—at least where creating a strict rule is possible (and they recognize that sometimes it is not).[99]

To understand this preference for strict rules, it is important to understand that it is commonplace in the law to distinguish between "rules" and "standards." As the Harvard professors Henry Hart and Albert Sacks put it in their description of the legal process, a rule is a clear-cut "legal direction which requires for its application nothing more than a determination of the happening or non-happening of physical or mental events—that is, determinations of *fact*." As an example, they point to a speed limit law that makes it illegal to go over 50 miles per hour. You violate the law if you are going 51 miles per hour, but not if you are going 50 miles per hour.[100] Clear-cut, simple.

By contrast, a standard is a "legal direction which can be applied only by making, in addition to a finding of what happened or is happening in the particular situation, a qualitative appraisal of those happenings in terms of their probable consequences, moral justification, or other aspect of general human experience." Hart and Sacks point to the common law concept that no person should drive "at an unreasonable rate of speed." Whether a given speed is reasonable may depend on a range of factors— the type of road, the weather, the presence of pedestrians, the speed of other cars, the reason for the driver's urgency in reaching his or her destination, and many other factors that may or may not be presented by a particular court case.[101]

Or recall my earlier example of the "functional equivalent" standard in the pollution case. There, again, is a standard—not a rule—and one that captures the common law, incremental approach to establishing the contours of permissible and impermissible action in a legal area, as opposed to the preference for broadly applicable, black-and-white rules.[102] As should be clear, "the standard . . . represents a much looser form of control than the rule,"[103] leaving much to future judicial elaboration and discretion.

That is not to say that standards, as opposed to rules, are infallible. Standards, too, can become rigid over time. This can happen when judges woodenly apply standards without appreciating the important values these standards are meant to represent.[104] But the risk of an overly wooden application is far greater when it comes to clear-cut rules, which leave no room whatsoever for taking into account important values.

Justice Scalia, a proponent of textualism and originalism, reflected his own views and those of many other proponents when he said that the Supreme Court Justices should, as far as possible, set forth their holdings in the form of rules, not standards.[105] They should not take the path I described in the pollution permit case that would leave to agencies, lower courts, or the Supreme Court at a later date the task of expanding the original case-based holding. Justice Scalia wrote that the latter common law–like approach is "ill suited . . . to a legal system in which the supreme court can review only an insignificant proportion of the decided cases."[106] Rules, he believed, produce greater uniformity among the lower courts; they establish "clear, general principle[s] of decision";[107] they leave judges less free to substitute their own policy judgments for those, like members of Congress, whom the Constitution allows to make the law; and they thereby discourage "personal rule" by judges. Justice Scalia added that he agreed with Aristotle that "personal rule, whether it be exercised by a single person or a body of persons, should be sovereign only in those matters on which law is unable, owing to the difficulty of framing general rules for all contingencies, to make an exact pronouncement."[108]

Justice Scalia recognized that sometimes it is difficult to find general rules. But, he said, "it is perhaps easier for me than it is for some judges to develop general rules, because I am more inclined to adhere closely to the plain meaning of a text." He added that just as

textual exegesis facilitates the formulation of general rules, so does, in the constitutional field, adherence to a more or less originalist theory of construction. The raw material for the general rule is readily apparent. If a barn was not considered the curtilage of a house in 1791 or 1868 and the Fourth Amendment did not cover it then, unlawful entry into a barn today may be a trespass but not an unconstitutional search and seizure. It is more difficult, it seems to me, to derive such a categorical rule from evolving notions of personal privacy.[109]

An emphasis on the creation of, and the use of, constitutional rules is related, as Justice Scalia says, to originalism itself. One can find in history examples and practices that will allow a court to flesh out a rule through situations analogous to the case directly before the court. The creation and use of rules, thus, may plausibly serve two of originalism's purported benefits: a) providing definitive answers to constitutional questions and b) inhibiting a judge from substituting what the judge believes is "good" for the law (i.e., the rule) itself.

Justice Scalia and I were good friends. We both loved our Court sing-alongs using Chief Justice Rehnquist's Old Time Songbook. We also liked to debate proper approaches to interpreting the Constitution, often in public. When we spoke before a group of students in Lubbock, Texas, for instance, I felt that the audience saw we were friends. They recognized that Justices who often disagreed about the law could nonetheless do so in a civil manner.

I also thought we sometimes got to the heart of our legal disagreement. I would describe the need, when interpreting the Constitution, to look to several different factors and particularly the need to assure workable consequences, i.e., the need for a workable Constitution. And, as was obvious, I would say, George Washington knew about the First Amendment but not about the internet.

Justice Scalia would then emphasize the need for definite answers that remained true to the Framers' original intent. He said that my approach to interpretation was simply too complicated. He added that he knew that George Washington did not know about the internet and that there were flaws in his approach to constitutional interpretation. But, he said, it is like the two campers, the first of whom sees the second putting on running shoes thinking a bear is about to enter the camp. "But you cannot outrun a bear," says the first. "True," replies the second, "but I can outrun you."

My answer to this was serious. "Looking to several different factors, looking to constitutional values, considering workability, is complicated, I agree. But, I fear that your more originalist approach would produce a Constitution that no one would want."

The obvious difficulties are those that led judges long ago to apply the methods of the common law: Sometimes it is not possible to determine the right rule. Courts may lack the technical expertise to determine whether, or how, for example, the law should deal with instances that are close to, but not identical to, the case then before the Court. The example of a pollution discharge (from a "point source") illustrates the problem as it arises in a statutory context.[110] Even in a statutory age, the methods of the common law are far from dead.

There are special problems with the search for broad and precise rules, rather than standards, in the constitutional area. My experience as a member of the Court, particularly in applying many of the Constitution's more abstract phrases, leads me not to take direct issue with what Justice Scalia said but to put in front of his rule-based approach a large sign saying, "BEWARE." In some areas of law, clear rules have particular value—procedural rules, for example, where clear general rules can save parties litigation costs, even if the rule may not be the best possible way of doing things.[111] But there are other areas of law, particularly parts of constitutional law, where the judge's search for a clear rule courts danger.

Why? Most importantly because many constitutional provisions are best viewed not simply as having purposes but as embodying important values. The First Amendment's Religion Clauses and Free Speech Clause provide examples.[112] Values seek permanence. But as time passes and circumstances, such as living conditions and technology, change, subsidiary rules, when too specific, can undermine those basic values. That general fact suggests that when deciding constitutional value-laden cases, such as First Amendment cases, judges should appeal more directly to those values than a rules-based approach would advise.

Remember Montaigne's warning that a legal code made up of specific rules rather than flexible standards would inevitably complicate, rather than simplify, the law by creating multiple grounds for legal disputes.[113]

Remember also Montaigne's reference to Eastern Roman emperor Justinian. Justinian thought that he could control his judges by having his legislators write many specific rules thereby preventing the judges from gaining power by substituting their own judgment for that of Justinian (and his legislators). But Justinian forgot that, for lawyers, every extra word is a potential platform for disagreement.[114] And more words to interpret can leave the judges with more power not less.

Consider, too, a general problem with rules. Although they can clearly demarcate boundaries, they cannot readily separate by degree those matters that lie close to a boundary, whether on one side or the other. A professor, for instance, who must grade exams relies on the A/B/C grading boundaries. These boundaries have the advantage of clearly separating As from Bs from Cs; but, what about the "almost A" or the "just barely not a C"? How fair is it to treat those alike? Questions like this led the Court in the EPA case that we discussed earlier to take a common law approach, rather than set forth a rule.[115]

Perhaps most important though is the question: Can we preserve, or sensibly apply, a basic constitutional value when judges, isolated from much of the world, write specific rules the scope of which extends well beyond the particular case, and which endure, continuing to determine outcomes over long periods of time?

The First Amendment and Speech

To illustrate the problems with overemphasizing strict rules, I discuss the First Amendment's relationship to government restrictions on speech. To understand these cases, it is important to know something about how the First Amendment works. In particular, it is important to understand what law professor Burt Neuborne described as its "music."[116]

The First Amendment says: "Congress shall make no law respecting an establishment of religion, or prohibiting the free exercise thereof; or abridging the freedom of speech, or of the press; or the right of the people peaceably to assemble, and to petition the Government for a redress of grievances."[117] Is this just a jumble of rights grouped under a single amendment? No. There is a reason for its structure and cadence. A look at history helps illustrate this. It shows that religion in the eighteenth century embodied, at least in part, internal thought. And one can consider guarantees of religious freedom as (among other things) guarantees of free thought. If so, from there the First Amendment passes on to "freedom of speech." Taken so far, the amendment gives a citizen a) freedom to think; and b) the freedom if one wishes to express the thought aloud or in writing. Next, a free press. The thinker, speaker, or others are free to transmit what is thought and said to a larger audience, helping to build (when matched against other thoughts in what Justice Holmes called the "market[place]" of ideas[118]) public opinion. Then we are free to "assemble," i.e., to discuss the thought (and those of others) publicly. Finally, one is free to petition Congress, i.e., to transmit to Congress the public opinion or other opinions so that those political actors can take (or not take) action.[119] So conceived, the First Amendment is in part a transmission belt, assuring the development, through the marketplace of ideas, of public thought that is not simply speech for the sake of speech, but speech for the sake of political action.[120] This is not the only role the First Amendment plays, but it is surely one important role, a necessary role in a free democracy. With that in mind, let us turn to case examples.

McCutcheon v. Federal Election Commission (2014)[121]

McCutcheon concerned free speech and the First Amendment in the context of political campaign contributions. To what extent does that amendment limit Congress's power to regulate and to restrict the amount of money a citizen can contribute to political campaigns?[122] The case assumed the legitimacy of limits that a congressional statute imposed upon an individual's contributions to a candidate for federal office ($5,200 per election cycle), to a national party committee ($32,400 per year), to a state or local party committee ($10,000 per year), and to a political action committee ($5,000 per year). The question in the case concerned overall, i.e., "aggregate," limits (about $125,000) upon the total amount that an individual could donate to entities in all these categories, among others, put together.[123]

By a vote of 5–4, the Court held that this overall, aggregate limit on campaign contributions enacted by Congress violated the First Amendment. Four members joined a plurality opinion;[124] one member joined that result in a separate opinion;[125] and four members, myself included, dissented.[126]

The plurality and dissent disagreed about many relevant matters, but I will focus on one for present purposes: the plurality's eagerness to latch on to a subsidiary First Amendment rule to the detriment of the underlying constitutional interests.

The plurality put significant weight upon a rule that it derived from an earlier case, *Citizens United v. FEC.*[127] In that case, the Court said that preventing corruption or the appearance of corruption was a legitimate constitutional interest justifying imposing campaign contribution limits. But it added that the interest in preventing corruption was "limited to *quid pro quo* corruption," that is, when elected officials accept monetary contributions in exchange for specific favors, or the appearance of such corruption.[128] And it said that *quid pro quo* corruption does not include "influence over or access to elected officials" because "generic favoritism or influence theory . . . is at odds with standard First Amendment analyses."[129]

The plurality in *McCutcheon* picked up and emphasized this isolated statement. It said that earlier cases had established that Congress can limit contributions that "are given to secure a political *quid pro quo*" or the "appearance" of quid pro quo corruption, but Congress cannot set an aggregate limit for the purpose of stopping contributions that may "influence" politicians or give "the appearance of mere influence or access."[130] In a word, the rule the plurality applied is that the government can limit campaign contributions to prevent actual (or the appearance of actual) bribes, or something like bribes. But it cannot do so in order to limit influence. "[D]rawing that line," the plurality conceded, may be difficult, but the "First Amendment requires us to err on the side of protecting political speech."[131]

What did the dissenters say to this? They explained that the plurality's focus on the quid pro quo statement in *Citizens United* was unwarranted. The language was better construed as dicta or an overstatement, for if read as the plurality chose to read it, *Citizens United* would have conflicted with the Court's prior cases in a way that none of the opinions in *Citizens United* contemplated. And by latching on to this supposed "rule," the plurality failed to appreciate the underlying First Amendment interests that animate both sides of this campaign finance equation.[132]

On the one hand, as the plurality observed, the First Amendment "is designed and intended to remove governmental restraints from the arena of public discussion, putting the decision as to what views shall be voiced into the hands of each of us . . . in the belief that no other approach would comport with the premise of individual dignity and choice upon which our political system rests."[133] When individuals contribute money to a candidate, they generally express support for a candidate and they express an "affiliation" with that candidate. In that way, the contribution reflects a First Amendment interest in participating in the political process through "political expression and political association."[134]

On the other hand, there are also First Amendment interests in limiting an individual's campaign contributions. As I have noted, the First Amendment operates as a transmission belt: One of the First Amendment's major purposes (or values) is to assure a nation where the people help, through their elected representatives, to develop laws; and people can produce sensible laws only if they are free to discuss problems, ideas, details, all those elements of a marketplace of ideas. Only then will we have the necessary transmission belt, from thought through speech to law, that is necessary to assure a workable democratic society.[135]

But what if a rich donor can contribute, say $5 million, to Smith, who is running for the House of Representatives? Smith's door in the House of Representatives is likely to be open—particularly wide open—to Rich Donor. And Rich Donor is likely to have more than ordinary influence upon Smith's actions—not through the power of his ideas but simply because of his money. The result is strongly antidemocratic. And, even if what I have just written were not true (though I believe it is), the public is likely to think it so, and, if so, to lose faith in our democratic system and the First Amendment practices that undergird it.[136]

The dissenters pointed out that abandoning the rule limiting aggregate contribution would allow a single Rich Donor to write a check for

$1.2 million ($20,000 to every state party committee over two years) or possibly $3.6 million ($5,200 to each party candidate over a two-year election cycle) or possibly far more. Much (perhaps all) of this money will end up in the hands of the party's candidates who are most vulnerable to challengers. So the doors to those candidates' offices, were they to be elected, would be more open to Rich Donor than others. At the very least, other citizens might perceive that to be so.[137] While the plurality suggested that would not happen, the dissenters disagreed.[138] And they asked why, if the plurality disagreed about these empirical matters, the Court would not send the case back to the lower courts for fuller evidentiary hearings.[139]

Regardless, the dissenters said, if they are even close to being right empirically speaking about the doors being far more open, then how is it possible to claim that these huge donations will not seriously harm the First Amendment's transmission belt objective—a basic purpose or constitutional value underlying the First Amendment?[140]

That is my point here. Where did the plurality's legal view that aggregate limits were unconstitutional come from? From a rule. Indeed, from the highly specific rule that the government can only limit the amounts of bribe-like quid pro quo contributions, i.e., those sorts of contributions that likely produce in reality or appearance something akin to bribery. And where did that rule come from? The rule came from *Citizens United*, which hardly mentioned that rule and did not purport to justify it.[141] What exactly supported the subsidiary rule's bribe-like definition of quid pro quo? Where was the detailed argument in its favor (or against it) in earlier cases? Since the matter did not determine the result in *Citizens United*, there was little argument either way.[142]

In a word, the Court seemed to pick up a statement in an earlier case and treat it as if that statement had set forth an important subsidiary rule. And there is the danger that I see in the Court going too far in its efforts to look for, and to treat, statements as creating absolute rules, rules that lack flexibility, and sometime lack reasoning justifying broad scope. Would it not have been preferable for the two judicial sides in this debate to have uncovered the facts and likelihoods in greater detail and then to have considered those likelihoods directly in terms of the values underlying the First Amendment?

I do not say "no rules." First Amendment case law contains quite a few.[143] I argue only that "rules" come in different shapes and sizes, e.g., limited scope, broad scope, flexible, inflexible, guidelines, approaches, warnings. It is knowledge of law, of the relevant facts, of experience, of precedent, of the judge's own judicial experience, for example, that will lead a judge to make a sound decision in respect to difficult value-laden constitutional questions. And here is my basic point: It is a mistake to urge judges too strongly in this area to take a rules-based approach—extracting rules from simple statements in earlier cases or feeling a need in complex cases to develop precise rules that will have unknown effects in later cases.

Sorrell v. IMS Health (2011)[144]

Virtually all statutes set forth rules. Virtually every appellate case contains a rule—at least the aspect of the case that makes of it a precedent. So, let me repeat, what is wrong with emphasizing the virtue of rules? The danger of doing so lies in the risk that the judge, anxious to create a rule, will overlook or distort (then or in applying the rule to future cases) the basic value that the underlying constitutional phrase reflects.

The greatest constitutional risk in developing general rules is rigidity. The inflexible application of such rules threatens the kind of rigidity that would (as the world changes) leave the values the constitutional phrase seeks to protect lying behind in the dust. Though the risk of rigidity is perhaps most pronounced when it comes to rules, the problem, too, can exist when it comes to standards. While standards are meant to apply with flexibility, over time, judges may begin to treat them too much like rules. That is, courts may begin to apply the standards reflexively, without taking into account the important values underlying them.

Consider what are perhaps the best-known First Amendment standards— those that tell the judge how strictly to scrutinize a governmental restriction imposed upon speech. The toughest anti-government standard, typically called "strict scrutiny," applies when the government regulates or forbids speech with, for example, a particular political or ideological content. The Court has said that, under strict scrutiny, the government must show that there is a "compelling interest" in maintaining the law under attack and that the law is either very "narrowly tailored" or is the least speech restrictive means available to the government.[145] Thus, a government rule that forbids one political party, but not the other, from advertising during prime viewing time would fail this test; but a rule that prevented persons from giving secret war information to an enemy during wartime would not.

The Court applies looser constraints—often called "intermediate scrutiny"—when the government seeks to restrict, for example, commercial speech subject to a traditional regulatory program,[146] say rules limiting or regulating a retailer's use of the words "free offer" or "for a limited time only." Under intermediate scrutiny, government laws and regulations may significantly restrict speech as long as they also directly advance a substantial interest that could not be served as well by a more limited restriction.[147]

The Court has also applied a still more lenient test, known as "rational basis" review,[148] to much ordinary commercial or regulatory legislation that affects speech in indirect ways. The Court has taken account of the need to defer significantly to legislative judgment in these cases.[149] "Our function" in such cases, Justice Brandeis said, "is only to determine the reasonableness of the Legislature's belief in the existence of evils and in the effectiveness of the remedy provided."[150]

Consider more closely the first two standards, "strict" and "intermediate" scrutiny. How do they differ? The first, applicable to, e.g., political speech, insists that the government show a strong or "compelling" interest in maintaining the law and that there is no other way similarly to serve that interest with significantly less harm to speech.[151] The second, applicable to commercial speech (but perhaps not to ordinary regulation or where harm to speech is indirect), requires the government to show that the restriction advances a "substantial interest" that cannot be served "as well by a more limited restriction."[152]

What is the difference? In both instances, the Court looks to the harm to speech interests; in both instances, the Court looks to the need for the restriction; in both instances, the Court determines whether there are alternative, less restrictive ways of serving the government interest. (And, perhaps, if not, the Court will weigh the harms to speech against the need for the restriction.)

But the important difference is in the tone—of the first ("strict"), the second ("intermediate"), and the third ("rational basis") as well. The tone of the first leans toward "NO" (the law probably does not let the government do this); the tone of the second leans toward "MAYBE" (the First Amendment grants the government some leeway in creating regulations of this type); the tone of the third leans toward "YES" (the First Amendment provides the government with lots of leeway in creating regulations of this type). These standards should be treated like flashing traffic lights, not absolute rules. They should not be considered rigid but instead as guidelines that are fuzzy around the edges and open to interpretation and application in a particular case, depending both upon the circumstances and the basic values that underlie the First Amendment. I would prefer to call them "approaches," used in certain areas of the law, but I care not about labels as long as one recognizes that they often carry with them a degree of flexibility tied to the value-laden objectives of the First Amendment.

Now let me turn to an example of what can happen when one of these standards is treated too much like a categorical rule. Our example case involves druggists and pharmacists, who often keep records showing which doctors prescribe which drugs. In *Sorrell v. IMS Health Inc.*, the Court considered a Vermont statute that forbade druggists from selling those records to drug companies for drug "marketing" purposes and forbade drug manufacturers and their marketers from using those records for "promoting a prescription drug" (unless the doctor who prescribed the drug consents).[153]

A major purpose of the statute was to promote public health and reduce health care expenditures by making it more difficult for selling agents of the drug companies (called "detailers") to know which doctors, say in a particular town, tended to prescribe which drugs. If they had this information, the detailers could plan their selling visits or their selling pitches in ways that would prove more appealing to the particular doctor and thereby increase their chance of obtaining a sale.[154] Suppose, for example, Dr. Smith in Brownsville tended to prescribe Drug X for Condition M. Knowing this, the ABC Pharmaceutical Company's detailer could plan on his visit to Dr. Smith to emphasize ABC's new drug WONDERCURE, which, the detailer might say, is very much like Drug X but cures Condition M more quickly (and just happens to be twice the price). If the detailer knew that Dr. Smith tended to prescribe Drug Y, not X, then he would look for ways in which WONDERCURE was superior to Y.

Vermont's new law tended to diminish the use of this selling practice. How did that help the public? Vermont thought (and there was supporting evidence in the state legislative record) that the practice discouraged doctors from prescribing generic drugs instead of the more expensive brandname drugs that did about the same thing.[155]

The Court in 2011 held by a vote of 6–3 that Vermont's law violated the First Amendment. Why? For one thing, it regulated speech. It prevented (and was designed to prevent) the detailers from making certain kinds of arguments in favor of using (ultimately buying) their products. In particular, it would not let them make arguments to the effect that their products were better than the drugs a doctor previously used, for the law prevented the detailers from knowing what drugs a doctor previously used.[156]

More importantly, it regulated some speech and not other speech. It picked out a particular group of people (namely, the detailers) and it prevented them from uttering a particular kind of speech, i.e., speech with a particular content (namely, marketing speech based on prescriber-identifying information). Thus, it "burden[ed] disfavored speech by disfavored speakers."[157] And because the law "impose[d] a specific, content-based burden on protected expression . . . heightened judicial scrutiny [was] warranted."[158] (I shall discuss this "content-based" rule below; for now, let it be.) The Court added that "whenever the government creates 'a regulation of speech because of disagreement with the message it conveys,'" heightened scrutiny is called for. "Commercial speech is no exception."[159]

Very well. I shall assume "intermediate scrutiny" applies. Now what? Is the government's interest in limiting this speech—in order to help bring about lower prescription drug prices—a "substantial interest"? The majority did not argue to the contrary. Rather, the closest it came to denying the legitimacy of this objective was to say that the "State may not seek to remove a popular but disfavored product from the marketplace by prohibiting truthful, non-misleading advertisements that contain impressive endorsements or catchy jingles." It added that the state's "policy goals may be proper," but it "[did] not advance them in a permissible way." Rather, it did so "through the indirect means of restraining certain speech by certain speakers."[160]

Were there "alternative, less restrictive ways" of achieving the state's "substantial objective"? Here, the Court seemed to say "yes." It said that if Vermont sought to promote cheaper generic drug substitutes, it "could supply academic organizations with prescriber-identifying information to use in countering the messages of brand name pharmaceutical manufacturers and in promoting the prescription of generic drugs."[161] For the most part, however, it said and repeated that the Vermont law burdens some speakers and some content without imposing similar restrictions on other speakers and other content with which the state agrees.[162]

The three dissenting Justices (of which I was one) asked how the ordinary "intermediate scrutiny" standard could lead the Court to its result. The statute threatened commercial speech with only modest harm. It withheld from pharmaceutical companies information that would help them create more effective selling messages.[163] The statute served "substantial" legitimate state interests. Vermont said that it sought 1) to help protect the public health, 2) to help protect the privacy of information, and 3) to help "ensure costs are contained in the private health sector . . . through the promotion of less costly drugs."[164] Protecting the public health in these ways falls within traditional state authority. The statute helps to focus sales discussions on the individual drug's safety, effectiveness, and costs, perhaps compared to other drugs (including generics).[165] The legislative record that Vermont compiled indicated that discussion of the individual doctor's prescription habits diverted attention from scientific research about a drug's safety and effectiveness as well as cost.[166]

The legislative record also showed that the "alternatives" that the Court had proposed (such as helping private groups, or universities or others provide doctors with information about generics) had been tried and found wanting.[167]

The dissent questioned the majority's hostility to "content-based" or "speaker-based" restrictions where commercial speech is at issue. Commercial speech and regulation of commercial speech is filled with distinctions based upon content and speaker. The Securities and Exchange Commission requires certain companies, but not others, to file public forms containing certain specified information, but not other content. Why, the dissenters asked, should the First Amendment require special scrutiny of these common features of regulatory regimes?[168]

The key problem for my current discussion is the kind of inquiry that the "intermediate scrutiny," commercial speech test directs. How important is the state's interest? Are there other ways of serving that interest equally well? And what kind of harm does the law at issue impose on speech? Does it disparately burden particular categories of speech or speakers? These questions display a rule-like focus upon arbitrary elements of the intermediate scrutiny test. Based on the answer to these questions, the majority suggested, the Court had to reflexively strike down the law in question, regardless of whether it bore directly upon the values that undergird the First Amendment.

That is an especially fatal flaw in this particular case. Recall that the First Amendment's transmission belt helps to develop public opinion by protecting a marketplace of ideas and allowing the public and its representatives to transform public opinion through democratic action into legislation. In *Sorrell*, Vermont's statute did not impinge on the transmission belt; that is, it did not target expressive activity central to the democratic development of governmental policies. Rather, the statute itself was the *result* of that transmission belt: Vermont's representatives, acting on behalf of their constituents, chose to focus their policy efforts on promoting public health and affordable prescription drugs. That in turn led to legislative hearings and reports that prompted legislative findings concerning the problems of the detailers' marketing practice and the benefit of limiting that practice. And it resulted in a majority of Vermont's representatives determining to limit that practice. For judges to find that result unconstitutional limits, rather than facilitates, the democratic process. I do not say that the First Amendment has no application to laws that fall on this side of the transmission belt, ever; rather, I suggest caution on the part of the judge.[169]

Vermont's statute neither forbids nor requires anyone to say anything, to engage in any form of symbolic speech or to endorse any particular point of view. The statute's requirements form part of a traditional comprehensive regulatory regime. (The drug industry has been regulated at least since 1906.) And the statute is directed toward information that exists only because of government regulation, namely, rules requiring pharmacists to keep doctors' names and related prescriptions.[170]

To apply a heightened standard of First Amendment review to regulation of commercial speech in these circumstances threatens to transfer legislative power to judges. To do so as a matter of course would, in the words of then-Justice Rehnquist, threaten to "retur[n] to the bygone era of *Lochner v. New York*, in which it was common practice for this Court to strike down economic regulations adopted by a State based on the Court's own notions of the most appropriate means for the State to implement its considered policies."[171]

In sum, the *Sorrell* case illustrates what can go wrong when a court treats a standard (intermediate scrutiny) too rigidly, or too much like a rule, and adds additional corollary rules (such as "content"- and "speaker"-based rules), rather than engaging in a discussion of basic constitutional values.

Reed v. Town of Gilbert (2015)[172] and *City of Austin v. Reagan National Advertising, LLC (2022)*[173]

Two final cases, concerning city signs, will illustrate how the Court's cases can, at times, set forth too many rules.

The Court's various opinions in *Reed v. Town of Gilbert* and disagreements in that case illustrate my fear that the search for, and the use of, rules to explicate strong, constitutional value-laden phrases can go too far. *Reed* focused upon a law enacted by the town of Gilbert, Arizona, which provided a comprehensive code governing the way in which people can display outdoor signs. Its "sign code," for example, prohibited the display of outdoor signs without a permit, but it then exempted many different kinds of signs from that requirement. "Ideological Signs"—those that communicated "a message or ideas for noncommercial purposes"—could be placed in all zoning districts;[174] "Political Signs"—those "designed to influence the outcome of an election"—could be placed on residential property;[175] and "Temporary Directional Signs"—those nonpermanent signs "intended to direct pedestrians, motorists, and other passersby" to events—could be placed on private property or on certain public rights of way.[176]

In finding that the Sign Code violated the First Amendment, the Court majority basically used a rule-like syllogism. First, it defined "content-based laws." It said that content-based laws are "those that target speech based on its communicative content"—that is, if it "applies to particular speech because of the topic discussed or the idea or message expressed." Second, it said that content-based laws "are presumptively unconstitutional and may be justified only if the Government proves that they are narrowly tailored to serve compelling state interests."[177] In other words, the strict scrutiny test we discussed above applies. Third, it said that Gilbert's code was content-based. After all, its harsher treatment of, say, directional signs than of political signs depended upon the content of those signs.[178] Finally, it said that the Sign Code could not pass strict scrutiny's requirements. The interest in "beautify[ing]" the town, for example, could not count as a "compelling" governmental interest, for the Sign Code allowed, without full explanation, many signs, such as certain directional signs, without any effort to require that they be placed or designed in ways that would increase beautification.[179]

Justice Ginsburg, Justice Kagan, and I agreed only in the Court's judgment, not its reasoning. We believed that the Sign Code contained many distinctions that made virtually no sense. Why, for example, did the Code allow most signs to reach a size of twenty square feet, while insisting that directional signs measure six square feet or less? If directional signs are more important, Justice Kagan asked, why must they be smaller?[180]

Our basic problem with the majority, however, was the rule the majority used. Where did this "content-based" rule come from? Why did it automatically invoke "strict scrutiny"? Why was the rule not far too broad when measured against basic First Amendment values?[181] Should the Court not have distinguished (as we would have done) between aspects of the code that, in First Amendment terms, were too strict and others that were not—rather than striking down the entire code on the ground that it constituted "content regulation"? After all, much ordinary government regulation is "content-based." Yet few believe the First Amendment would hold *all* that regulation unconstitutional.

I would here ask the reader to go back to the way in which the Court decided the case: It reveals nothing more than a syllogism of rules. The majority asked whether the facts fit within those rules. It nowhere asked how, or even whether, the facts showed significant First Amendment harm as measured against that amendment's values.[182] And if the Court had done so? Well, as Justice Kagan pointed out, "[a]llowing residents, say, to install a light bulb over 'name and address' signs but no others does not distort the marketplace of ideas."[183]

Before *Reed*, our precedent took a more holistic approach to the constitutionality of "content-based" restrictions on speech. The *Reed* majority seemed to believe that the "content-based" rule came from an earlier case called *Boos v. Barry.*[184] In that case we reviewed a D.C. law that outlawed the display of signs "tending to bring a foreign government into . . . public disrepute."[185] We subjected that law to "the most exacting scrutiny," and we did mention the "content-based" categorization.[186] But the majority applied its strict scrutiny test not simply because the D.C. law was content-based but for many other reasons as well. The Court majority pointed out that the D.C. law was a *"content-based* restriction on political speech* in a *public forum."*[187] Justice O'Connor, writing for the majority, understood the D.C. law's main problem to be its stifling of public political speech central to the values of the First Amendment.[188] It is difficult to believe that the majority's discussion of this type creates a rule requiring the Court, in the future, to apply strict scrutiny to virtually every content-based regulation. My colleagues in *Reed* who concurred only in the Court's judgment would have reached the same result as the majority. But we set forth a test that we believed, without emphasizing "content-based," was more faithful to both the Court's precedent and to the values underlying the First Amendment. A further case will help show why I believe we were right.

City signs and the First Amendment returned to the Court several years later in *City of Austin v. Reagan National Advertising, LLC*.[189] There, the City of Austin had enacted a law forbidding new outdoor signs advertising restaurants, markets, and other goods and services when the signs were located in a place other than the business advertised. A grandfather clause allowed presently existing signs to remain. But those old signs (unlike signs located at the place of business) could not use digitized lighting.[190]

A lower court had found this on-premises/off-premises distinction "content-based" because to apply the city's rule (against digitized lighting), a reader had to inquire "who is the speaker and what is the speaker saying," both "hallmarks of a content-based inquiry."[191]

A majority of the Court disagreed. Several members of the majority stuck by the "content-based rule," but found that the city's rule did "not single out any topic or subject matter for differential treatment."[192] Content depends on the "topic discussed or the ideas or message expressed," not simply one's need to read and to understand a sign.[193] Those members also rejected the claim that the fact that the law's application depended upon a sign's "function or purpose" made the law "content-based." The Court said that was so only if a law "swap[s] an obvious subject-matter distinction for a 'function or purpose' proxy that achieves the same result." That was not the case here.[194]

I agreed but wrote separately to express my continued view that the Court should abandon its "content-based" rule. The Constitution is not the Tax Code. Hence the Court should beware of creating too many black-letter rules, for use of those rules can work against, rather than implement, constitutional interests.[195]

As I have explained in reference to the transmission belt metaphor, the First Amendment helps to protect a "market[place]" of ideas,[196] an environment where "the ultimate good . . . is reached by free trade in ideas."[197] Strictly scrutinizing certain kinds of speech-related regulations can help protect that marketplace. And rules that help determine when speech falls into such a category can do the same. The Court has said, for example, that free speech is in danger when the government imposes restrictions on "core political speech," or when it discriminates against particular views taken by a speaker on a particular subject, and sometimes when it removes an entire topic of discussion from public debate.[198]

But not all content-based rules or regulations fall into categories like these. As I have said, much regulation reflects what the public wants by way of government action or inaction, as revealed by the public opinion that free speech helps to shape—the very goal of the transmission of free ideas that the First Amendment seeks to achieve.[199]

The statute books of many states along with the federal government are filled with regulatory laws that turn, often necessarily, on content.[200] Consider the Federal Trade Commission's efforts in the 1970s to regulate advertising. The FTC considered it an "unfair," hence unlawful, "practice to make an affirmative product claim without a reasonable basis for making that claim." It brought a case against Pfizer, claiming that, without "adequate and well-controlled scientific studies or tests," it could not make the following claim in its advertising: "Un-Burn actually anesthetizes *nerves* in sensitive sunburned skin. Un-Burn relieves pain *fast*."[201] The FTC also required advertisers to submit to the commission tests, studies, and data substantiating any claims, statements, or representations made in their advertisements. It required Clearasil, for instance, to submit reports substantiating the claim that it "contains the same kind of medicine many dermatologists use."[202] I would have thought the lawfulness of these FTC decisions was a matter of statutory, regulatory, and administrative law. Does the "content-based" nature of the rule make them primarily matters of First Amendment law, subject to strict scrutiny, as well?

Consider, too, laws that regulate census reporting requirements, securities, energy conservation labeling, commercial airplane safety briefings, copyright infringement, prescription drug labeling, confidential medical records, consumer electronics, tax disclosures, robocalls, workplace safety warnings, panhandling, solicitation on behalf of charities, signs at petting zoos, and on and on and on.[203]

What possible reason is there for courts to apply "strict scrutiny" to these regulations? To do so is, of course, to substitute a standard of review that normally finds government action unconstitutional for the less strict standard found, for example, in the Administrative Procedure Act, which basically insists that a regulatory rule be reasonable.[204] And, of course, it substitutes determination of regulatory law by judges for determination by the people's elected representatives.[205]

If the Court takes its "content-based" First Amendment rule seriously, I would fear the consequences. One possibility is that the courts will strike down entirely reasonable regulations that reflect the will of the people. If so, as I have said, the Court's content-based line-drawing will substitute judicial for democratic decision-making and threaten the people's ability to translate its thoughts and ideas into policy.[206]

A second possibility is that courts instead, in an effort to avoid striking down reasonable regulations, will (consciously or unconsciously) dilute the stringent strict scrutiny standard. Doing so would weaken the First Amendment's protections in areas, such as political speech, where it should apply.[207]

A third possibility is that courts will develop a matrix of subsidiary rules and exceptions that seek to distinguish between reasonable and unreasonable content-based regulations. Such a patchwork could easily prove unwieldy or unworkable.[208] Consider the efforts in this case to define content in terms of reader-based or function-or-purpose-based tests.[209] At a minimum such an effort will make it more difficult for ordinary Americans to understand the importance of First Amendment values and to live their lives in accordance with those values.

How might the Court's inquiry have proceeded if it reduced its fixation on the "content-based" test? One might have asked instead: 1) How did Austin's law harm free speech interests? The answer, as set forth in this case, was that it stopped some owners of outdoor billboards from lighting the boards in the way they wished, namely with digital lighting.[210] 2) How serious was that harm to speech interests? I would say very little;[211] and I find it difficult to believe that anyone could conclude that the harm to First Amendment interests is serious. 3) What was the reason that Austin wanted to enact a law that caused this harm? The reason was aesthetic: Fewer flashing billboard lights meant a more beautiful city. The law was part of an effort to minimize the negative aesthetic effects of outdoor advertising. In my own view, minimizing outdoor clutter would seem a significant, perhaps important, though perhaps not a compelling, objective.[212] 4) Were there other, less restrictive, ways of producing this result? Perhaps. Though it is reasonable to believe that other approaches would prove complicated, would likely involve exceptions, and would apply differing standards, a less-restrictive ordinance was probably possible.

This approach that I have just engaged in focuses on the First Amendment values at stake and the government's underlying interest in the law; while it bears resemblance to tiers of scrutiny analysis, it treats the tiers as guidelines, or as rules of thumb, rather than as rigid rules divorced from the constitutional values and democratic laws at issue. Understanding many First Amendment rules as rough standards or rules of thumb can, of course, lead judges to balance harms to certain constitutional values against the goals of democratically enacted laws. And, balancing runs the risk of a judge substituting his or her own policy preferences for "the law." But is the creation of a First Amendment "tax code" preferable? Is there not a similar risk when a judge tries to apply "content-based" or other subsidiary rule concepts to a particular case? And aren't there benefits to the rule of thumb approach? Consider the many different ways in which governments can regulate the time, place, or manner used by a speaker. They may differ only to some extent one from the other. And courts may have to draw fine lines between constitutionally permitted, and constitutionally forbidden regulations of this type. Careful balancing, and seeing standards not as inevitably determinative but as guidance, keeps a court closely in touch with the First Amendment's underlying values. The effort to create and apply subsidiary rules does not.

The content-based rule embraced in *Reed* and *City of Austin* does not seem to have helped further to any great extent the values underlying the First Amendment. It has done little, for example, to help assure the American people that they will be able freely to debate and to discuss general and specific ideas, hopes, and experiences, develop and participate in a marketplace of ideas, which, when transmitted to their elected representatives, can help assure a democratic government based upon thoughtful opinions. Rather, it risks creating an obstacle to regulation that those elected representatives have chosen to create.

In sum, where important constitutional values are at issue, too many rules—or even standards applied too rigidly—can prove dangerous, diminishing in some instances the furtherance of those values and creating obstacles that are not germane to the underlying constitutional values at issue. I agree with Justice Scalia that those who advocate textualism in respect to statutes and originalism in respect to constitutional provisions may also find it natural to depend upon clear-cut rules.[213] They may tend to apply them literally. And they will, unfortunately, prove less likely to appeal directly to underlying values in order to interpret constitutional provisions. The discussion here, concerning *McCutcheon, Sorrell, Reed,* and *City of Austin* will, I hope, stand as a warning against that approach.

14.

When the Text Runs Out:
The Limits of Constitutional Textualism

So far, we have discussed problems with constitutional textualism's two cousins—originalism and a preference for clear-cut, broad rules—but what about textualism itself? Might it help in interpreting the Constitution? Hardly at all.

As I noted in my brief summary of the Constitution, many of the Constitution's phrases are very broad and general. Some of its most important text tells us very little about how it should apply to the modern structure of the federal government. In contrast to the fledgling nation of the late eighteenth century, the United States today is a global superpower with an integrated continent-wide economy that must contend with a host of modern phenomena unimaginable two hundred years ago—from technological revolutions to international public health emergencies. The structure of the federal government allows the country to adapt to address changes. But since much of that structure reflects an effort to deal with modern problems of which the Framers knew little or nothing, "originalism" does not help. An effort to develop broadly applicable rules governing structure does not get us much farther. I think it is fair to say that, in this area of constitutional law, textualism and its cousins are not helpful. Turning to what Chief Justice Marshall, in *McCulloch*, considered the critically important constitutional objective of "workability" can, however, help.

The major structural questions that the Court has faced during the past century or so have concerned the scope of the powers the Constitution delegates to the three branches of government. The document itself says: "All legislative Powers herein granted shall be vested in a Congress . . . which shall consist of a Senate and a House of Representatives";[1] the "executive Power shall be vested in a President of the United States";[2] and the "judicial Power of the United States, shall be vested in one Supreme Court, and in such inferior Courts as the Congress shall from time to time . . . establish."[3]

What do these words tell even the most dedicated textualist about the power of Congress to delegate to a commission the authority to set transportation rates, to approve broadcasting applications, to police workplace safety, or to regulate harms to the environment? The answer to this question, I believe, must be "next to nothing." But let us see.

The Legislative Power

The Constitution vests all legislative power in Congress. But Congress, since the founding and especially in the modern era, has delegated substantial authority to create regulations—which look very much like legislation—to executive agencies, such as the FDA, the SEC, and the Occupational Safety and Health Administration.[4] Does the constitutional text mean our modern administrative state is impermissible?

Not under the traditional approach to the Constitution, which has been guided by the workability principle.[5] But in recent years, some, who would probably describe themselves as textualists or originalists, have sought to revive a "non-delegation" theory, which would call much of our modern government structure into question.

I will start by explaining how courts historically understood the permissibility of congressional delegations of rulemaking power through the example of the railroad rate cases. Then, I will turn to the currently hot topic of non-delegation theory. Both will illustrate why workability, not textualism or originalism, must guide constitutional interpretation.

Railroad Rates

At the time of the founding, commercial railroads had not yet begun to spread across America. (The first, the Baltimore and Ohio, incorporated in 1827 and laid its first track in 1830.[6]) But by the end of the nineteenth century, railroads provided the nation's primary commercial transportation system. Between 1865 and 1916, the rail network increased from around 35,000 miles to over 250,000. The industry's annual revenue also increased, from $300 million to $4 billion in that period.[7]

Along with commercial power came the power to set monopoly or discriminatory rates. The public then demanded government regulation of those rates. The states responded by creating commissions with authority to set reasonable railroad rates. And Congress created the Interstate Commerce Commission in 1887, giving it railroad rate–setting authority.[8]

The Interstate Commerce Commission, of course, was not Congress. In 1831, Justice Joseph Story had written that the "general rule of law is, that a delegated authority," i.e., the legislative power that the Constitution delegates to Congress, "cannot be delegated."[9] In 1892, Justice John Marshall Harlan wrote, "That congress cannot delegate legislative power . . . is a principle universally recognized as vital to the integrity and maintenance of the system of government ordained by the constitution."[10] And a few years later the Court warned that Congress could not delegate to the Interstate Commerce Commission the "legislative function of prescribing rates which shall control in the future."[11] In other words, the Court adopted a strict non-delegation requirement, derived from the structure of the Constitution, which separates the legislative, executive, and judicial powers into different departments. In the eyes of the nineteenth-century Court, allowing the ICC, a commission within the executive branch, to set rates looked too much like legislation—and thus risked violating the Constitution's separation-of-powers principle.[12]

But within a decade, in 1906, Congress did just what the Supreme Court warned it not to: It delegated authority to the ICC to set reasonable rates. And the Court, neither then nor later, said a word against it.[13] Why not? Chief Justice William Howard Taft, writing later for the Court, distinguished between the "power to make the law" and "authority or discretion as to its execution. . . . The Congress may not delegate its purely legislative power to a commission, but, having laid down the general rules of action under which a commission shall proceed, it may require of that commission the application of such rules to particular situations and the investigation of facts, with a view to making orders in a particular matter within the rules laid down by the Congress."[14] The Court therefore upheld Congress's delegation to an agency to set railroad rates, finding no separation-of-powers problem. At least one state supreme court, facing a similar delegation question, said, "Whether the charges of a railway in any particular case are or are not equal and reasonable is *a fact*" left for the commission "to determine."[15]

To be sure, we can question whether we should call the issue "factual." Later cases challenging wartime price controls revealed a few of the problems inherent in calling the determination of a "reasonable rate" a determination of "fact."[16] In determining what is "reasonable," shall we compare the railroad's rate with the rate (or price) charged by makers of a comparable product? Which products are comparable? How should the railway spread fixed costs (e.g., cost of the tracks) among the many products it carries? What is a reasonable rate of return? To what extent shall the commission take into account special (or ordinary) risks? What happens if inflation causes some input prices to rise? Shall all (some?) railroad rates rise accordingly? Shall a rate equal costs including some kind of markup for profits? What kind? What about innovation, product improvement, faster speeds, fewer accidents, special customer needs, etc.? These kinds of questions, almost inevitably at issue, force a rate-setting commission to determine answers, likely through generally applicable rules or determinations. And those rules or determinations look not like facts but like laws.

One state court said that the legislature could lawfully delegate to the commission an "authority" to exercise discretion "under and in pursuance of the law."[17] This sentence might remind us of Chief Justice Marshall's statement that a Constitution should not "partake of the prolixity of a legal code" scarcely capable of being "embraced by the human mind."[18] Rather, "only its great outlines should be marked . . . and the minor ingredients which compose those objects . . . deduced from the nature of the objects themselves."[19] The "great powers" the Constitution itself delegates include those that "might be appropriate," given a Constitution meant to "endure for ages to come."[20] The Framers would have thought it unwise "to provide, by immutable rules, for exigencies which, if foreseen at all, must have been foreseen dimly, and which can be best provided for as they occur."[21] Thus, the legislature must have the "capacity to avail itself of experience, to exercise its reason, and to accommodate its legislation to circumstances."[22] This, I think, is what Chief Justice Taft must have ultimately had in mind when he distinguished between *lawmaking* power and *discretionary* power to execute.[23]

Is it not changing circumstances that have brought us railroads, automobiles, highways, airplanes, broadcasting, electricity, and vast interstate commerce, among other advances? And haven't those changing circumstances prompted Congress, taking into account public desire for modern solutions, to create regulatory agencies with the power to enact rules—an authority delegated to the agency through legislation enacted by Congress? As time has passed, the courts, sensitive to the needs of the legislature to adapt to changing times, have upheld the constitutionality of congressional delegation of substantive rulemaking power, finding no violation of the separation-of-powers principle so long as Congress also sets forth an "intelligible principle" to guide (and to limit) the agency.[24] The requirement of a "standard," or a "principle," has not proved particularly onerous.[25] What, after all, is the difference between the power to enact substantive rules and the power to *legislate* substantive laws?

Why would Congress feel a need to delegate rate-making power to an agency, and why have courts permitted it? Why should Congress not set rates itself? Perhaps because legislatures have much to do and limited time to work; perhaps because they lack the specialized knowledge (say, of routes and traffic) often necessary to set rates; perhaps because rates will need revision over time; perhaps because the public believes that rate levels should be based upon economics, not politics. But, note: None of these considerations absolutely requires delegation to an agency. Congress, at least in principle, *could* do the job itself. It could create a special congressional committee, staff it with railroad experts, take account, through staff, of rate-related changes, and modify rates through legislation. Indeed, agency heads have often been former members of Congress.[26] Why then not interpret the word "legislation" in the Constitution as requiring Congress to do the job itself, directly?

The answer to this question, I believe, is that such a committee would be exactly the type of agency now considered part of the executive branch, albeit now, because it has been placed (in our hypothetical) in Congress, some might consider it some kind of legislative body. An interpretation of the Constitution that required Congress to create such committees would transform a portion of the legislative branch into a group of administrative agencies—both rate-making agencies and others. That kind of requirement might well be more *un*constitutional. If so, that arrangement would do *more* damage to the constitutional effort to make of Congress a national legislative body than would the current judicial interpretation of the phrase "vests" all "legislative power"—an interpretation that allows Congress to create a broad range of executive-branch agencies with broad rulemaking powers (though some once long ago referred to some of these agencies as being in a "headless fourth branch of government"[27]).

But why then not delegate rate-making authority to courts? Indeed, courts at one time essentially did regulate common carriers.[28] But there are nearly one thousand federal judges and many more state judges.[29] Would not judicial rate-setting produce a patchwork of rates? Moreover, judges typically decide the legality of a matter *after* the event, not before; would railroads have to guess the rates they should set out initially, and then test them in court? And, of course, judges lack rate-setting (and many other kinds of) expertise.

The upshot is that practical considerations led Congress to create agencies, now thought to be executive branch agencies, to perform somewhat technical regulatory jobs. And that is what history has brought us.

The Non-Delegation Theory

As I have noted, the courts have long held that the delegation of substantive rulemaking authority to executive agencies must be guided by an "intelligible principle" standard. That is, Congress may delegate regulatory authority to the executive branch so long as it supplies an "intelligible principle" to guide the executive's use of regulatory discretion.[30] So long as Congress does so, there is no serious risk that the executive branch will abrogate the authority of the legislative branch.[31]

Traditionally, then, the Supreme Court has not insisted upon an "intelligible principle" standard that is definite or strict. In *Cargo of the Brig Aurora*,[32] for example, the Supreme Court saw "no sufficient reason" to declare unconstitutional Congress's delegation of authority to the president to end trade embargoes against Great Britain and France after determining that they had "ceased to violate the neutral commerce of the United States."[33] And in *J.W. Hampton, Jr., & Co. v. United States*,[34] the Supreme Court upheld a statute giving the president the power to impose tariffs that would "equalize the differences in costs of production" between the United States and other countries.[35] These broad terms gave much leeway to the executive branch in the exercise of rulemaking authority yet still provided enough of an intelligible principle to avoid any constitutional issues.

But in 1935, in *A.L.A. Schechter Poultry Corp. v. United States*,[36] the Supreme Court held that Congress had gone too far in its delegation. The statute created commissions for major industries. The members of those commissions consisted in large part of persons who worked in those industries, as executives, workers, or other private citizens. And it was the job of those commissions to write legally binding codes of "fair competition."[37] What is that? Both Chief Justice Charles Evans Hughes and Justice Cardozo explained why "fair" competition was not the opposite of "unfair competition." They argued that there is no way to give that phrase any definite meaning.[38] Put that fact together with the fact that, not government, but private individuals in an industry will set their own code, and we have what Justice Cardozo called "delegation running riot."[39] The Court struck the statute down.[40] But the Court quickly abandoned *Schechter*'s fairly strict non-delegation rule, returning to a looser and more workable version of the intelligible standard.[41] Indeed, aside from *Schechter* and one other case in 1935,[42] the Court has never found a delegation to an agency of rulemaking power to have gone too far.[43]

Recently some judges have urged the courts to return to the non-delegation theory of *Schechter*—this time giving it teeth.[44] Such an approach might, for instance, require Congress to delegate with such specificity that an agency need only "fill up the details,"[45] or allow Congress to make application of a law "dependent on executive fact-finding,"[46] or assign "non-legislative"[47] responsibilities to other branches. In a recent case, the Fifth Circuit embraced this sort of robust non-delegation theory.[48] But there are multiple problems with such an approach. One is historical—while enthusiasts of a robust non-delegation theory such as that in *Schechter* often justify it on historical grounds, the historical basis of the non-delegation theory is in fact highly contested.[49] Another problem is practical. What counts as "fill[ing] up the details"? Where is the line between permissible "executive fact-finding" and forbidden executive lawmaking? When would these rules apply? How would they apply? And above all, what would the implications be of finding an excess of delegation in one case for the thousands of other statutes, rules, regulations, and decisions that federal agencies and departments make?

Additionally, some Justices have thought that something like *Schechter*'s non-delegation doctrine could be strengthened, applying the doctrine in cases reviewing agency interpretations of congressional statutes. For decades, courts have deferred to agency interpretations of statutes that fall within the agency's domain of expertise.[50] The Supreme Court has deferred to countless agency interpretations, including, for instance, the Environmental Protection Agency's interpretation of the term "stationary source" in the Clean Air Act,[51] the Comptroller of the Currency's interpretation of the word "interest" in the National Bank Act,[52] and the Federal Communication Commission's interpretation of the phrase "reasonable period of time" in the Telecommunications Act.[53]

But in the last few years, the Supreme Court has begun to question the practice of deferring to agency interpretations of law, on the ground that such deference causes a constitutional delegation problem. Some Justices have even gone so far as to imply that interpreting statutes in a manner that supports broad delegations of authority to agencies violates the separation of powers. Consider *National Federation of Independent Businesses v. OSHA*,[54] in which the Supreme Court held that a broadly worded statute delegating broad powers to the Occupational Safety and Health Administration to regulate workplace health and safety likely did *not* delegate the authority to require employees to be vaccinated against or regularly test for COVID-19.[55] In justifying its authority to require vaccinations or testing, OSHA cited the Occupational Safety and Health Act, which empowers the agency to promulgate "emergency temporary standards" to "protect employees" from "grave danger" emanating from "new hazards."[56] OSHA argued that risk of spreading COVID-19 in the workplace presented such a "grave danger" and that its vaccination and testing mandate would "protect employees" from death and hospitalization.[57] The statutory language seemed sufficiently broad (at least in my view) to authorize OSHA's action. But the Court majority by a vote of 6–3 held that it did not.[58] The Court majority believed that OSHA's rule constituted a "general public health measure" and that it was too "broad" for a reader to believe Congress delegated to OSHA the power to issue it.

Justice Gorsuch's concurrence, in which Justices Thomas and Alito joined, explained why the statute's broad language, which authorized OSHA to promulgate "standards" that "protect employees" from "grave danger," was not sufficiently clear to justify the agency's vaccine or testing mandate. Justice Gorsuch referred to what he called the "major questions doctrine," or the rule that courts should not defer to agency interpretations of statutes that give those agencies authority over questions of "vast economic and political significance," absent a clear statement of authorization from Congress.[59] To allow OSHA to make rules requiring "individuals to undertake a medical procedure," for example, would have required Congress to delegate that authority explicitly.[60]

Where did this "major questions doctrine" come from? Before the 2022 term—indeed, reaching back as far as the eighteenth century—a majority of the Court had never used the term in deciding a case.[61] According to Justice Gorsuch, however, the doctrine was a derivative of the non-delegation principle. It protects the Constitution's separation of powers by preventing Congress from delegating too much of its authority to an executive agency that "may seek to exploit some gap, ambiguity, or doubtful expression in Congress's statutes to assume responsibilities far beyond its initial assignment."[62]

The Court again referred to the major questions doctrine a few months later in *West Virginia v. EPA*,[63] when it held that the Environmental Protection Agency lacked the authority to require owners of coal-fired generating plants to switch to low-carbon or carbon-free fuel sources.[64] The EPA claimed authority to do so from Section 111(d) of the Clean Air Act, which directs the agency to adopt standards of performance for existing power plants that reflect the "best system of emission reduction."[65] Exercising its statutory mandate, the EPA determined that the "best system of emission reduction" would be to shift electricity generation from high carbon-emitting sources to lower carbon-emitting ones.[66] But the Court rejected the validity of the EPA's action, holding that an interpretation of the word "system" that allowed the EPA to "forc[e] a shift throughout the power grid from one type of energy source to another" violated the major questions doctrine.[67] According to the majority, such a grant of authority to the EPA would be "unprecedented" and would require a clear statement from Congress not present in Section 111(d) of the Clean Air Act.[68]

In a concurrence, Justice Gorsuch, joined by Justice Alito, again linked the major questions doctrine to the non-delegation principle. He argued that the doctrine "ensure[s] that the government does 'not inadvertently cross constitutional lines'" by delegating broad authority to agencies without "clear congressional authorization."[69] Application of the major questions doctrine thereby helps the judicial branch to police legislative delegations of authority to executive agencies and ensure that such delegations do not violate constitutional boundaries.[70]

I joined dissents in both major questions cases. I believed that the statutes authorized the actions that the agencies had taken or proposed. (Indeed, some, but not all, of those who claim the label "textualist" might agree.[71]) Moreover, a narrow interpretation of these statutes could (if Congress, perhaps for partisan reasons, found it difficult to legislate) leave the nation powerless to deal with new important problems (such as COVID-19). But that is not my point here. Here, I simply point out that these cases concerned the interpretation of *statutes*, not an interpretation of the Constitution. The basic question in both cases is how a court might determine whether Congress had delegated to the agency the power in question. And the Court held that Congress must clearly state that its statute is delegating to the agency the power to take a major action or the Court will assume that it has not done so.[72] While Justice Gorsuch's concurrences characterized the majority's clear statement rule as a constitutional requirement derived from the separation of powers,[73] the majority itself did not go so far in either case.[74]

It is not surprising that the Court avoided the constitutional question whether Congress could permissibly delegate the powers the agencies had exercised. After all, many agency statutes, enacted decades ago, are broadly phrased. To hold one or more of them unconstitutional would work chaos; it would set aside hundreds, perhaps thousands, of agency actions, many taken long ago.[75] And, it might reduce, perhaps come close to eliminating, an agency's basic job. Moreover, the statutory question the Court decided is itself an old variation of a more basic question: How is a court to know whether a particular agency action falls within the scope of an arguably authorizing statute? The Court itself has said that there are many different factors, not just one factor called the "major questions doctrine," that help it answer this question.

For example: Does the agency have special expertise in respect to the matter?[76] Is the matter broad in scope or of great importance to the nation? Is the matter a narrow, interstitial matter, related, say, to administration of the statute?[77] Or, as the dissent in the EPA case pointed out, a court might ask: Is the issue one in respect to which the agency has little or no expertise? What is the nature of the agency's delegated power to regulate? What is the relation between the nature of that power and the claimed delegated authority?[78] The Court has also pointed to more: Did the agency promulgate the regulation after having proceeded through participatory rulemaking proceedings? Does the agency have authority to interpret and to control the exercise of the authority it claims?[79]

One can tie these kinds of questions to a broader question that often helps a court decide the meaning or the scope of a statute: What did Congress intend (here, in respect to the delegation of the power in question)? The familiar tools of statutory interpretation we discussed earlier help resolve this question.[80] The legislative history, for instance, might reveal the extent to which Congress intended to delegate authority to the agency. Or, if the legislative history says little or nothing about it, the judge might examine the agency's basic task and its statutory delegations, asking, "what would a reasonable member of Congress have thought about the particular delegation at issue here?" (Justice Barrett later wrote that the "major questions doctrine . . . serves as an interpretive tool reflecting 'common sense as to the manner in which Congress is likely to delegate policy decision of [large] economic and political magnitude to an administrative agency."[81]) Sometimes, application of the "reasonable legislator" concept (or common sense) might lead a judge to conclude that a reasonable member of Congress would not have intended to delegate broad authority to an agency on certain politically charged issues that should be left under the authority of the democratically elected legislature. But, other times, a judge may conclude that a broad interpretation is necessary to achieve the lofty objectives (consumer protection, environmental protection, safety, etc.) that led the reasonable member of Congress to enact the statute in the first place. But regardless of which tools the judge uses, the main focus of her inquiry should be Congress's *intent*, for it is that intent that reflects the will of the democratically elected branch.

Notably absent from these considerations, which for many years guided the Court's analysis of delegations to agencies, is any notion of strict constitutional limitations on delegation of legislative authority. That is because the Constitution does not require the sort of strict limitation on delegation that some Justices claim. Nowhere does the Constitution explicitly prohibit legislative delegation. The most the Constitution says—indeed the only language proponents of a strict non-delegation principle point to—is that "[a]ll legislative Powers . . . shall be vested in a Congress"[82] and that "[t]he executive Power shall be vested in a President."[83] At most, these words direct courts to be wary of significant encroachment upon one branch by the other. But they do not require a formulaic and categorical rule against delegation whenever Congress has made the reasonable determination that its policy goals are best served by relying on agency expertise. After all, a strict non-delegation rule may pose its own separation-of-powers questions, inviting courts to substitute their own judgments for the will of Congress.[84]

Now, in the twenty-first century, many doubt the strength of agency expertise. Numerous students of the subject criticize agency performance.[85] But we should ask: Compared to what? To Congress, or congressional staff, taking on the task? To judges, or judicial staff, doing the same? To a world in which no governmental effort is made to cure environmental, medical, or safety-related ills? Those who think not must find permission or support in the Constitution. And the Court's twentieth-century interpretations read that document as granting the necessary permissions despite the fact that doing so allows Congress to enact legislation delegating broad powers (including rule-making powers)—similar to legislative powers—to agencies or departments located in the executive branch.

It is this practical interpretation of the Constitution's words, not the Constitution's literal language, which has brought us through the twentieth century and the first quarter of the twenty-first with the federal government operating under legislation that delegates to it those broad powers. In a word, the Constitution, as Chief Justice Marshall said, must be workable; and as the nation changes over time, the scope of the Constitution's delegations of authority, both legislative and judicial, will change with it.

The Judicial Power

The same separation of powers problem that arose in respect to legislation in the early twentieth century also arose in respect to adjudication. The "judicial Power of the United States," the Constitution says, "shall be vested in one supreme Court and in such inferior courts as the Congress may . . . establish."[86] In 1916, however, Congress enacted a law that created the Federal Employees' Compensation Commission, a commission outside the judicial branch. And it gave that commission the power to adjudicate certain disputes between private persons. In particular, the commission had the authority to award compensation, paid by an employer, to a harbor worker injured in a workplace.[87]

The commission was not a federal court. Thus, Congress's creation of the commission raised an important constitutional question: Did the Constitution grant Congress the power to delegate to a commission outside the judicial branch the authority to decide this kind of matter—whether one private person must pay money to another? Chief Justice Hughes, in *Crowell v. Benson*,[88] wrote a well-known Court opinion that answered the question "yes."[89] Here, I address how the Court, applying traditional interpretive principles guided by workability, reached that conclusion. And

then I address a related issue of recent interest concerning judicial deference to agency interpretations of statutes.

Agency Adjudication

In *Crowell*, the Court reviewed the commission's order requiring an employer to pay a form of workers' compensation to an employee who was injured on the job.[90] In reviewing the validity of the commission's order, the
Court said it first had to decide whether Congress's statute establishing the
commission in the first place took money from a losing party without (in
the words of the Fifth and Fourteenth Amendments) "due process of law."
The answer to this question was "no." The statute did not violate the Due
Process Clause. Why not? The commission, the Court wrote, would decide
only the facts of a case, not the law. If dissatisfied, a losing party could seek
review from the courts, which would interpret the law and would decide
whether the commission's award fell within its scope. The procedures for
determining the facts would be fair. The statute called for notice and a
hearing. Evidence would be placed in a public record. And, the evidence
must support any award that the commission makes.[91]

Nevertheless, the opinion went on to address the separation-of-powers
question—specifically, whether the statute creating the commission unconstitutionally assigned "the judicial power" to an agency within the executive
branch. In answering this question, the opinion stressed the limited nature
of the commission's adjudication under the statute and the availability of
robust review by the courts. While courts were to defer to the commission
on findings of fact, they retained the power to determine legal questions *de
novo*.[92] How did that help answer the separation-of-powers question? The
Court thought that the limited nature of the commission's adjudicatory
scheme, along with the existence of fair procedures, ensured that there was
"no attempt to interfere with" courts' exercise of the judicial power.[93]

Like the delegation to agencies of rulemaking authority, the delegation
of adjudicatory power has become fairly noncontroversial and normally
has been upheld. *Crowell* has been taken as setting standards for successful
delegation to executive branch agencies of adjudicatory power.[94]

The constitutional delegation of "all legislative" power to Congress and of "judicial Power" to Article III courts has not imposed a serious constraint. Professor Richard Pierce, the author of the leading treatise on administrative law, has pointed out that since 1935, "the Court has upheld scores of statutes that delegate extraordinarily broad power to agencies. Decision-making standards like 'just,' 'reasonable,' and 'public interest' dominate the U.S. Code. Thus, for instance, 'just' appears 2,457 times, 'reasonable' appears 9,189 times, and 'public interest' appears 2,715 times."[95] Very recently, the Court has decided to hear a case that presents a question about the limits of Congress's ability to delegate "adjudicative" power to an agency. Unless the Court departs from the path trodden by earlier cases, however, Congress will remain free to broadly delegate adjudicative power to the executive branch.[96]

Typically, then, Congress delegates adjudicative power to the agency under a standard that can be broad and general. In principle, the courts can set aside agency action if the standard offers inadequate guidance to the decision-maker,[97] but they have rarely done so.[98] The courts can also set aside an agency action if, for example, the agency incorrectly decides a question of law, if the agency's decision is "arbitrary, capricious, [or] an abuse of discretion," if the agency has used improper procedures, or if its fact-finding is not supported by substantial evidence.[99]

For present purposes, I shall not argue the pros and cons of these "classic" rules and approaches, typically found in the Administrative Procedure Act[100] and generally taking the form of basic principles of administrative law.[101] My point is only that "textualism" has little or nothing to do with the matter; nor does "originalism." Rather, here once again, one can find key words in a Court opinion similar to those that Chief Justice Marshall wrote a century before. Chief Justice Hughes said that to apply a strict nondelegation rule "would be to defeat the obvious purpose of the legislation to furnish a prompt, continuous, expert, and inexpensive method for dealing with a class of questions of fact which are peculiarly suited to examination and determination by an administrative agency specially assigned to that task."[102] Instead of applying an inflexible rule, Hughes emphasized that "where constitutional limits are invoked," "regard must be had . . . not to mere matters of form, but to the substance of what is required." And delegating fact-finding authority to a commission, with the guarantee of judicial review in the courts, presented no "constitutional obstacle."[103] Like Chief Justice Marshall, Hughes understood the importance of flexible constitutional rules that allow our system of governance to remain workable over time.

Deference

The issues of congressional delegation of rulemaking and adjudicative authority to agencies are implicated by the Court's practice of upholding reasonable agency interpretations of the statute that agency is tasked with implementing, most famously set forth in the Court's *Chevron*[104] case from 1984. Some members of the Court, along with many other judges, lawyers, and academics, have recently urged the Court to reconsider *Chevron*. What is that case about? An environmental statute required companies, whenever they intended to build a new major "source" of pollution, to go through an elaborate review procedure. Initially the government considered a "source" to include any significant change or addition to any plant or factory. But it later changed that definition so that a "source" amounted to a plant or factory in its entirety. The question was whether the statute (which did not define "source") could be considered to grant the agency the power to adopt its whole plant system.

From an administrative law point of view, the case concerned the degree to which the courts should "defer to," or "give leeway to," an agency's understanding about the scope of its governing statutes.[105] Some textualists and originalists in recent times have thought this principle of deference poses separation-of-powers problems, criticizing *Chevron* for permitting agencies to usurp (as discussed above) the judicial role of interpreting the law or the legislative role of creating law.[106] As I will explain, I think that *Chevron* has everything to do with statutory interpretation and permitting a workable government, and that it presents no serious constitutional issue.

Under *Chevron*, the Court has sometimes held that it would defer to an agency's reasonable interpretation of a statute (particularly when set forth in a "legislative rule"[107]). Thus, in *Chevron* itself, the EPA interpreted the statutory words giving it authority to regulate "new or modified stationary sources" as not insisting that it regulate smokestack-by-smokestack but allowing it to measure the amount of pollution a multi-smokestack plant emits by placing an imaginary bubble over the plant area and measuring the total amount.[108]

On other occasions the Court has rejected an agency's interpretation of a statute. It held, for example, that the statute giving the EPA authority to regulate "any air pollutant" allowed it to regulate carbon dioxide—even though the EPA itself had thought the contrary.[109]

The *Chevron* case purported to create a framework, an approach, or perhaps a rule, for courts to apply in answering the question whether to defer. It said that, if the answer to a statutory question is "clear," the courts should not defer to a contrary agency interpretation. But if the answer is not "clear," i.e., if the statute is "silent or ambiguous,"[110] then the courts should assume that Congress intended to delegate to the agency the power to determine a "reasonable" interpretation of the statute.[111]

Judges and scholars have debated whether *Chevron* upended existing law or merely restated it, with critics of *Chevron* arguing that its framework radically departed from long-standing interpretive practices.[112] But as Professor Thomas Merrill has pointed out, "[t]here is no evidence that Justice Stevens," the author of *Chevron*, "understood his handiwork . . . as announcing fundamental changes in the law of judicial review."[113] Prior to *Chevron*, courts often deferred to reasonable agency interpretations of their statutory authority, but did so after considering a mélange of factors that would help show whether a reasonable member of Congress would have intended to delegate a degree of interpretive authority to the agency. These included "whether the agency interpretation was longstanding, consistently held, contemporaneous with the enactment of the statute, thoroughly considered, or involved a technical subject as to which the agency had expertise."[114] Though *Chevron* itself did not appear to permit consideration of these factors within its neat two-step framework, the Court continued to give them weight in the course of discerning whether an agency was eligible for deference at all—that is, in considering whether *Chevron* applied to a given case.

My opinion for the Court in *Barnhart v. Walton*[115] is a good example. In that case, the Court considered the meaning of the term "disability" in the Social Security Act. The act defines "disability" as "[i]nability to engage in any substantial gainful activities," and the Social Security Administration interpreted "inability" to include "for twelve months." In concluding that *Chevron* was the "appropriate legal lens through which to view the legality of the [agency's] interpretation," the Court considered "the interstitial nature of the legal question, the related expertise of the [a]gency, the importance of the question to administration of the statute, the complexity of that administration, and the careful consideration the [a]gency has given the question over a long period of time."[116] As Professor Louis Jaffe wrote in 1955, these are the sorts of factors courts have employed for decades in considering whether deference is appropriate.[117]

Barnhart is not the only case where the Court imposed limits on *Chevron's* domain. In *Immigration & Naturalization Service v. Cardoza-Fonseca* in 1987,[118] the Court said that "clear" at Step One of *Chevron* meant clear after applying "ordinary" methods of statutory interpretation.[119] And in *United States v. Mead Corp.* in 2001,[120] the Court considered a statute that allowed the federal Customs Service to "fix" according to Treasury Department regulations the "final classification and rate of duty applicable" for imported goods.[121] The Court held that the courts, reviewing a challenged customs duty, should *not* defer to a customs officer's interpretation of the treasury regulations due to the interpretation's informal and non-precedential nature.

It is true that judges have debated the proper scope of *Chevron*, with some (including myself) calling it a "rule of thumb."[122] But such an approach is in fact more aligned with historical understandings of deference, as well as Justice Stevens's belief that *Chevron* simply restated existing law. Nevertheless, the legitimacy of deference continues to be hotly debated—a topic I have written about elsewhere.[123] Here, I simply want to repeat what that dispute is *not* about. It is not about constitutional language. At least I cannot find any constitutional language that argues strongly for one side or the other. And I would add more specifically that I do not see how constitutional textualism or constitutional originalism could help. Presumably, the textualist and originalist judge would say that the Constitution assigns the "judicial Power" to the courts, not executive agencies.[124] And it falls within the judicial, not executive, power to say what the law is.[125] Yet the Constitution does not define with particularity what the "judicial Power" is. Interpretation of that term, just like any vague or ambiguous term in the Constitution, should be guided by the principles of flexibility and workability. And a flexible and workable understanding of the "judicial Power" includes the ability to defer to the reasonable interpretations of agencies on matters that Congress intended to assign to their domain of expertise.

In my view, then, the question whether to defer turns on statutory interpretation. The adverse parties are the judges on the one hand and the agency administrators on the other. Depending on the cases, a judge might lean somewhat in favor of the administrators where the statutes are more technical and concern the agency's area of expertise. The judge might lean somewhat against the administrators where the statutes are not.

But the constitutional value that supports either position consists of the need for a "workable" relationship among agencies, Congress, and the courts. As I have said, this kind of arrangement allows agencies greater leeway to handle matters within their competence while subjecting them to appropriate constraints. Congress can be thought to approve of this arrangement for the simple reason that this arrangement can help its statutes work better. In doing so, it helps the tripartite system work somewhat better in practice. And that fact in turn should help to maintain public confidence in the courts' decisions.

The Executive Power: Appointment of Officers

I turn now to an important question of modern governmental structure and the executive power. The Court has recently found unconstitutional legislation that limited the president's power to dismiss certain moderately high-ranking individuals in the executive branch. In doing so, it has pointed to Article II and, once again, the separation-of-powers principle. The relevant part of Article II says that the "executive Power shall be vested in" the "President"[126] and that the president "shall nominate, and by and with the . . . Consent of the Senate, shall appoint" all "Officers of the United States," but also that "Congress may . . . vest the Appointment" of "inferior Officers" in the "President alone, in the Courts of Law, or in the Heads of Departments."[127]

Notice that this language addresses only the *appointment* and not the *removal* of executive officers. Notice also that this language does not provide clear instruction for distinguishing between "inferior Officers" and their counterparts, known as "principal officers." But the Court, interpreting these phrases, has held that Congress unconstitutionally encroached on the president's removal power in passing legislation requiring (1) that members of the Public Company Accounting Oversight Board be removable only for cause by the Securities and Exchange Commission, the members of which are removable by the president only for cause;[128] (2) that the head of the Consumer Financial Protection Bureau be removable only for cause by the president;[129] and (3) that several hundred administrative patent judges in the Patent Office be removable by the secretary of commerce only for cause.[130]

The majority of the Court thought, in the first and second instances, that the Constitution forbade imposing certain restrictions on the president's authority to remove executive branch officers. Specifically, in the first instance, the Court took issue with "dual for-cause" limitations—that is, the restriction that board members be removable only for cause by commissioners who were themselves removable only for cause by the president.[131] And in the second instance, the Court held that the Constitution forbids giving the head of the agency any kind of tenure, i.e., restricting the power of the president to remove the officer at will.[132] Finally, in the third instance, the Court held that the administrative patent judges' insulation from the president's removal power made them *principal*, not *inferior*, officers, required to go through a senatorial confirmation process.[133]

I disagreed with the majority in each of these cases primarily because I believed the majority's holdings threatened the workability of portions of the federal government, particularly if its reasoning was generalized to apply to all comparable federal employees, including the 1,500 Social Security Administration administrative law judges and numerous others.[134] Rather, I would have agreed with Justice Frankfurter, writing for the Court in *Wiener v. United States*,[135] that whether Congress can impose limitations upon the president's power to remove employees depends upon the nature of the employee's duties.[136] The officers in *Wiener* exercised adjudicative responsibilities. Adjudication benefits from a degree of decision-maker independence; and that fact may justify congressional limitations on the president's power to remove.[137] Consider the unfairness that can result if the president can, at will, remove adjudicative officers such as administrative law judges, who resolve disputes between parties much like judges do, perhaps on the request of a lower-ranking politically appointed official seeking revenge for an administrative law judge decision that he disagrees with.

But, again, I see no need to develop these arguments at length.[138] For present purposes, I need only point to the language of the Constitution itself. I can find nothing in the language I have set forth above that says, within broad limits, just who is a principal "officer" of the United States as contrasted with an "inferior officer." I can find nothing that says whether, or when, Congress can impose a "for cause" removal limitation. And, at least in my view, a constitutional textualist or a constitutional originalist will not have significantly more luck in finding answers in the text or in the history to the constitutional questions posed.[139]

I can, however, find some help in the constitutional notion of "workability." Imagine a government in which administrative law judges lack protection from politically motivated retaliation. Imagine a world where an expansive definition of "principal officer" prevents agencies, government departments, and perhaps even the armed forces, from appointing lower-level officials. Imagine a world in which Congress's ability itself to confirm large numbers of appointments is compromised by political disagreements within Congress. The unworkability of these possibilities suggests that the Constitution grants Congress leeway in deciding just who is a "principal," and who is an "inferior" officer as well as whether, and what forms of, tenure is desirable. The words "executive Power" do not answer these kinds of questions any more than the words "legislative Power" or "judicial Power" answered the questions I discussed earlier.

15.

Legal Stability: *Stare Decisis*

More than three hundred years ago Blackstone, the renowned legal scholar, referred to the principle of *stare decisis* as the "established rule to abide by former precedents."[1] Literally, the term means to "stand by things decided."[2] That is to say, *stare decisis* leads judges to follow earlier precedent, not because the earlier case was necessarily decided correctly but simply because, having been decided, it has become part of the law.

Chief Justice Rehnquist stated that the principle "promotes the even-handed, predictable, and consistent development of legal principles."[3] Blackstone said that it keeps "the scale of justice even and steady, and not liable to waver with every new judge's opinion."[4] Alexander Hamilton contended that the principle "avoid[s] an arbitrary discretion in the courts."[5] And, the Court has said that *stare decisis* "contributes to the integrity of our constitutional system of government" by ensuring that legal decisions "are founded in the law, rather than in the proclivities of individuals."[6] In these ways *stare decisis* maintains a stability in the law; and that stability allows people to order their lives under the law.[7]

Stare decisis means that courts will normally follow legal precedent. But it does not mean that they will *never* overrule an earlier case.[8] And therein lies a serious problem: Just when can a court justifiably overrule precedent? Again, we need not here provide a comprehensive answer to that question. We need only ask: Which approach is likely more helpful? How helpful will textualism (or originalism) prove likely to be? How does it compare with other approaches, those, for example, that put greater weight on constitutional values, particularly upon the need to maintain a Constitution that proves workable over long periods of time? In the recent *Dobbs*[9] case, the Court took both a strong originalist approach and also overruled two earlier cases protecting the abortion rights of women, *Roe v. Wade*[10] and *Planned Parenthood v. Casey*.[11] For that reason, the case serves as a good example.

Dobbs v. Jackson Women's Health Organization (2022)

In *Roe v. Wade*, decided in 1973, the Court by a vote of 7–2 held that the Constitution protects a woman's right to obtain an abortion. The Court believed that this right constituted part of a person's right to personal privacy, a right that itself constituted part of the Constitution's protection of personal "liberty." The Court limited government's ability to regulate or to prohibit an abortion, the extent of the limitation depending upon how many weeks a woman had been pregnant. Governments had less power to interfere with a woman's right to choose an abortion early in her pregnancy than later in her pregnancy.[12]

Nearly twenty years later, in 1992, in *Planned Parenthood v. Casey*, the Court considered whether to overrule *Roe*. It decided not to do so. Instead, it affirmed that the right to choose an abortion constituted a part of a constitutionally protected right to "liberty";[13] that government could not impose an "undue burden" upon that right prior to the time the fetus was viable[14] (usually after about twenty-four weeks of pregnancy[15]); and after that time, the government could regulate the right (or even forbid the abortion) except where, for example, a woman's health or life was at risk.[16]

During the next three decades the Court reaffirmed its basic *Casey* holding.[17] But in *Dobbs*, in 2022 the Court overruled both *Roe* and *Casey*. By a vote of 5–4, it held that the Constitution did not provide a woman with the right to choose an abortion[18] (though state or federal governments, through legislation, could provide that right if they chose to do so[19]). Of the four Justices who did not vote to overrule *Roe* and *Casey* entirely, one would have limited the basic "no undue interference" right to fifteen weeks,[20] and the other three Justices (of which I was one) would not have overruled *Roe* or *Casey* at all.[21]

The dissenting Justices presented many reasons why they believed that the majority was wrong. But here I should like to focus upon one aspect of the argument, namely *stare decisis*. The Court's opinions had long recognized that abortion was a subject about which many Americans disagreed. Many thought that an abortion amounts to a morally unjustified killing of an innocent person—the unborn fetus. Many thought that to deny a woman the right to choose an abortion threatened some with death (for some will choose dangerous methods to carry out an abortion regardless), threatened many with serious illness or disability, and threatened to impose intolerable burdens upon countless lives. The earlier cases did not try to resolve these differences; they simply argued that the constitutional rule they adopted was appropriate, indeed necessary, in a nation where millions of individuals held these opposite opinions.[22]

Irrespective of differences of opinion among both judges and laypersons, by the time the Court considered *Dobbs*, constitutional law, as the Court understood it, had for many years provided women with a right to choose an abortion. *Roe v. Wade* had stood for that legal proposition for nearly fifty years. *Planned Parenthood v. Casey* had stood for that proposition for thirty years.[23] So *Dobbs* required the Court to decide whether to overrule precedents that had set forth the law for an unusually long period of time. *Stare decisis* means that the Court will *normally* not overrule precedent. But sometimes it does so. And it did so in *Dobbs*. What can the different approaches to constitutional law that I have discussed tell us about the appropriateness of this overruling?

The *Stare Decisis* Problem for Originalism and Textualism

Neither originalism nor textualism can tell us much about *stare decisis*. They can, of course, tell us that the textualist or the originalist believes that the substantive constitutional rule that *Roe* set forth (and which *Casey* affirmed) is wrong. The majority in *Dobbs*, for example, argued at some length that the cases setting forth the abortion right were "egregiously" wrong.[24] Why? Because *Roe* rested its argument in significant part upon a constitutional right of privacy, but the word "privacy" appears nowhere in the Constitution. Neither did those who wrote the Bill of Rights or those who wrote the post–Civil War constitutional amendments believe that any constitutional phrase in those amendments protected a woman's right to an abortion.[25] As evidence, the majority cited traditional common law rules making abortion a crime.[26] The dissenters argued that the majority was wrong. Rather, the law permitted abortions prior to what the law called the fetus's "quickening," an old term for the period of time when a fetus could be felt moving in the womb.[27]

But put this argument (purely for argument's sake) to the side. Assume (again purely for argument's sake) that the majority was right about *Roe* and *Casey*. Assume that, for the textualist or the originalist, the earlier Court had made a mistake in both cases. Assume that, from their perspective, the Court was wrong to hold in *Roe* and *Casey* that the Constitution protected a woman's right to an abortion.

The obvious next question is: So what? *Stare decisis* does not exist simply to protect precedent that is right; it keeps the law stable by preventing continuous reexamination of precedent that may well be wrong. Perhaps early-nineteenth-century cases that included corporations within the scope of the constitutional term "persons" were wrongly decided; perhaps cases restricting the kinds of persons able to sue for antitrust damages were wrongly decided; perhaps common law cases setting forth a "reasonable person" standard for determining negligence were wrongly decided. Should we now reexamine those cases, decide whether they are right or wrong, and then overrule or reaffirm them on that basis? That approach, even were it practically possible, would reduce law to a shambles. Who would know what to do next?

Stare decisis has not prevented the Court from sometimes overruling earlier cases. Sometimes the Court will overrule a case only recently decided;[28] sometimes, because the case has only recently been decided or for other reasons, the relevant public has not come to rely upon the holding in the earlier case;[29] sometimes other related law has changed, outdating the overruled case;[30] sometimes living conditions, technological conditions, or other relevant conditions have significantly changed.[31] But the key word here is "sometimes," not too often, and the reasons for abandoning *stare decisis* must be strong ones.

The fact that judges think an earlier case was incorrectly decided cannot be, and never has been, a strong basis, by itself anyway, for overruling an earlier case.[32] Nor does the Constitution contain any text about that matter. Nor did the Founders, to my knowledge, go into the matter in useful detail. Indeed, insofar as we look to historical sources, we find Blackstone, Hamilton, and others who apparently believed that *stare decisis* constituted an important principle of law.[33] So, I repeat, what do textualism and originalism tell us about its application? So far, nothing.

It is, of course, possible that a textualist or originalist might believe that the Court should overturn any case that seems "wrongly" decided when applying textualist or originalist principles.[34] But that path would seem to lead directly to chaos. There are too many cases. Scholars have pointed to cases involving standing, non–Article III judicial tribunals, free speech, equality, enforcement of the Civil War Amendments, search and seizure, the Takings Clause, and numerous others that might not survive an attack based upon originalist principles.[35] So far, very few cases have been overturned solely on grounds of inconsistency with originalism.[36] That in part reflects the fact that there is too much disagreement, even among textualists and originalists, as to which earlier cases were correctly, and which incorrectly, decided.[37] But it is also because there may be no good way of separating earlier nonoriginalist sheep from nonoriginalist goats. Originalism sets out no guideposts for how, or when, to carry out any major program of revision. And so, adhering to unadulterated originalism, we would be left with a program that would overturn those precedents that a judge believes are important enough *and* egregious enough in their legal rationales to warrant overturning. That program is a purely subjective one, precisely the opposite of one of the supposed benefits of textualism and originalism—providing a method that constrains judges from imposing their own policy preferences. And that program would put at risk, through uncertainty, the virtues of the law that Blackstone and the others discussed, and, in all these ways, risk undermining the public's confidence in the Court.

The upshot: Textualism, originalism, and the like tell us nothing, or next to nothing, about when to make an exception to the basic rules of *stare decisis*.

Does the weakness of originalism and textualism in this respect matter? Is it important? I believe it matters very much indeed. Different judges approach the task of interpreting the Constitution in somewhat different ways. And that has been true ever since the Court has undertaken that task. Harvard professor Cass Sunstein has categorized and explained some of those ways,[38] which include:

- Semantic Originalism (looking to what the words of the Constitution mean linguistically);[39]

- Original Public Meaning Originalism (looking to what the general public would have taken the words to mean at the time they were written);[40]

- Protecting Democracy (interpreting the Constitution to assure first and foremost that all Americans have the right to participate in democratic self-governance);[41]

- Traditionalists (like Edmund Burke, looking primarily to history and tradition to determine the values that the Constitution protects);[42]

- Moral readings (interpreting the Constitution to reach results most consistent with morality);[43]

- Thayerism (named for the nineteenth-century law professor James Bradley Thayer; severely limiting the role of courts in overturning on constitutional grounds laws that the legislature has enacted);[44]

- Common Good Constitutionalism (interpreting the Constitution in ways that are consistent with the "common good" as that term has been understood over time).[45]

And many others.[46]

Professor Sunstein has been able to identify at least twelve approaches to constitutional interpretation, many of which resemble others, but all of which differ, at least to some degree, one from the other. A look back into history will make clear that differences in approach have long existed, some between Justices serving at the same time;[47] others between Justices and perhaps entire courts, serving at different times.[48]

What has this to do with *stare decisis*? With so many different approaches to constitutional interpretation, one would have expected those firmly committed to one (or a handful) of them to emphasize the importance of *stare decisis*. If not—if textualists or originalists, for example, feel free, not bound by *stare decisis*, to overturn precedent, the results of which reflect other approaches—then what precedent is safe? Which of these "differently decided" cases is not, for an originalist, "egregiously wrong"? If all, then, as I said, virtually no previously decided case is safe. If only some, then which are those "some," and what is the principle that distinguishes the "egregiously wrong" nonoriginalist case from others? The textualist-originalist has not answered, and likely cannot answer, the latter question; nor has he or she explained why the "originalist" is not free to overturn prior cases decided based on different methodological approaches.[49]

That way lies chaos. The Constitution's principle of workability is not consistent with numerous decisions that overrule earlier decisions on a basis that (as far as *stare decisis* is concerned) is unprincipled.

Principled Departures from *Stare Decisis*

If, as I have explained, a disagreement with the methodological approach used in a prior case cannot be a basis for making an exception to *stare decisis*, what can? And were any such exceptions present in *Dobbs*?

A commonly found reason for departing from *stare decisis* and overruling an earlier decided case is that facts underlying the reasoning in that case have changed. One of the best-known and important cases in which the Supreme Court overturned an earlier case is *Mapp v. Ohio*.[50] In that case, the Court held that evidence obtained against criminal defendants in violation of the Fourth Amendment cannot be introduced against them in state court.[51] The Court overruled an earlier decision in the process. It reasoned that the "factual grounds" upon which that earlier case had been decided were no longer valid.[52] It meant that experience had demonstrated that remedies for Fourth Amendment violations besides the exclusion of evidence from criminal trials had proved "worthless and futile."[53] This factual change in surrounding circumstances justified the change in the law. Virtually every law student knows of this case and the underlying justification for the change.

Returning to our example of *Dobbs*, it is difficult, perhaps impossible, to find any such factual changes that might justify overruling *Casey* or *Roe*. Indeed, factual changes argue to the contrary. Laws forbidding abortions do not normally help protect a woman's life or health. Advances in medical science mean that abortions are normally safe. In fact, an American woman is fourteen times more likely to die carrying a pregnancy to term than by having an abortion.[54] Medical advances may also mean that a fetus has a better chance of living outside the womb. But this kind of change could, at most, justify drawing an earlier line defining viability (some European countries draw the line at fifteen weeks, not twenty-four). It cannot justify laws that impose an undue burden on a woman's right to choose an abortion pre-viability.[55]

What about values? Sometimes a change in values may justify a departure from precedent. Many Americans believe that an abortion is in most circumstances morally wrong. But this has long been true.[56] I am aware of no significant change in this respect since *Roe* was decided in 1973 or *Casey* was decided in 1992.

Those cases themselves reflected a development in values—values that have only grown more deeply embedded in our society over time. When the Fourteenth Amendment became law in 1868, women "were seen only 'as the center of home and family life,' without 'full and independent legal status under the Constitution.'"[57] A woman then "had no legal existence separate from her husband."[58] But that is no longer true. Today, women can and do determine how they live their own lives and contribute to the society around them.[59]

Similarly, since *Roe*, the Court itself has protected the individual's choice about whom to live with, whom to marry, how to raise children, and so forth. And, as the dissenters pointed out, those choices "reflect fundamental aspects of personal identity" and "inevitably shape the nature and future course of a person's life (and often the lives of those closest to her)."[60] Ensuring that these choices "belong to the individual, not to the government" is thus "the essence of what liberty requires."[61]

My point is simply this: One cannot claim that facts or values have changed since the Court decided *Roe* and *Casey*. At the least, they have not changed in any way that might justify departing from *stare decisis* and overruling those earlier cases. Even if the majority's account of abortion's history were right—which it is not—that could not justify overruling those two earlier cases unless, of course, the Court is free to overrule *every* earlier case that a textualist or originalist approach might claim is wrongly decided. But that claim, as I have said, means an end to *stare decisis*. And that way points to chaos.

In an effort to couch their extraordinary overruling of *Roe* and *Casey* as routine, the majority in *Dobbs* listed twenty-eight cases in which, despite *stare decisis*, the Court had overruled an earlier case.[62] The dissenters considered each of those cases and concluded that none of them was comparable to *Dobbs*.[63] They included cases that set forth, or implemented, a broad legal doctrine where later cases had already departed from, or modified that earlier doctrine so that the overruled case no longer was consistent with the law (as the law had come to be).[64] In *Ramos v. Louisiana*,[65] for example, the Court held that the Sixth Amendment requires a unanimous jury verdict for conviction of a serious state crime.[66] The *Ramos* Court overruled *Apodaca v. Oregon*,[67] which held to the contrary,[68] because "in the years since *Apodaca*, this Court ha[d] spoken inconsistently about its meaning" and had undercut its validity "on at least eight occasions."[69] Twelve cases met this criterion. *Dobbs* did not.[70]

The majority also referred to cases where fundamental factual changes had undermined the basic premise of an earlier decision.[71] In *Citizens United v. FEC*,[72] for example, the Court overruled *Austin v. Michigan Chamber of Commerce*,[73] noting that technological changes had made the earlier legal rules easy to work around and consequently made the earlier legal prec-edent ineffective.[74] Three cases met this criterion. *Dobbs* did not.[75]

In some instances overruling an earlier case reflected what the Court believed were both changes in the structure of earlier law and changes in the facts.[76] In the 2018 case *Janus v. American Federation of State, County, and Municipal Employees, Council 31,*[77] for example, the Court by a vote of 5–4 held that the First Amendment forbids laws that would require a govern-ment employer to withhold from an employee's wages union dues (and pay them to the union) if the employee objects.[78] In *Janus* the Court overruled an earlier case, *Abood v. Detroit Board of Education,*[79] which had unanimously held the opposite.[80] The Court wrote that it was warranted in overruling *Abood* because "both factual and legal" developments had "eroded the de-cision's underpinnings and left it an outlier among our First Amendment cases."[81] Six cases fell into this category. *Dobbs* was not among them.[82] The *Dobbs* majority could not, and did not, claim that *Roe* and *Casey* were "outli-ers" or that later pre-*Dobbs* cases had "undermined" them.

Some overrulings took place very close to the time of the original deci-sion. Thus, the case overruled could not yet have created substantial re-liance or have become "embedded" within our "national culture."[83] In *Garcia v. San Antonio Metropolitan Transit Authority,*[84] for instance, the Court in 1985 held that local governments are not constitutionally immune from federal employment laws.[85] In doing so the Court overruled *National League of Cities v. Usery.*[86] But the Court had decided the latter case only nine years earlier, in 1976; and, in the Court's view, its holding had proved unwork-able.[87] Three cases fell into this category. *Roe* and *Casey,* while generat-ing considerable controversy, had not proved unworkable. And women throughout the country had relied upon the rights they guaranteed when planning their education, careers, marriages, and families. The majority did not claim that *Dobbs,* overruling cases decided forty-nine and thirty years earlier, was critically similar to these cases.[88]

The remaining cases on the majority's list (with two exceptions, which I will discuss next) were minor cases having minor effects and modifying part of, or an application of, a prior precedent's test or analysis.[89]

The upshot is that the cases listed, with two exceptions, could not have constituted precedent for the overruling of cases such as *Roe* or *Casey*, which were major cases, decided long ago, that had engendered major reliance interests, where there had been no significant changes in law or fact. So what was the Court's basis for abandoning *stare decisis*—other than the fact that the Court, applying something like originalist principles, thought they had been wrongly decided? That, as I have previously explained, cannot by itself provide a legitimate basis for departing from *stare decisis* without damaging the structure of the law.

What about the two cases that I have just referred to as "exceptions"? I have done so because the majority directly compared *Dobbs* to *West Coast Hotel Co. v. Parrish*[90] and *Brown v. Board of Education*,[91] and it found them similar.[92]

In 1937, *West Coast Hotel* overruled *Adkins v. Children's Hospital of the District of Columbia*[93] and a line of cases that included *Lochner v. New York*.[94] Those earlier cases had found unconstitutional, as violations of the Due Process Clause, laws that imposed minimum wages and maximum hours.[95] But the facts and attitudes that led to the Court's overruling of those cases had changed enormously. Economic historians have pointed out that between, say the end of the Civil War and the beginning of World War I, the American economy had grown exponentially. Inventions such as electric power, automobiles, and radios, along with new financing methods meant that overwhelming numbers of Americans enjoyed a higher standard of living.[96] Many thought that laissez-faire free enterprise was in significant part responsible and that government interference threatened to kill the goose that was laying golden eggs.[97] That the Court emphasized constitutional protections of contract and property should not have been surprising.

By the 1930s, however, most could feel that laissez-faire did not work well—certainly not for everyone. Unemployment was high. The economy was shrinking, and many blamed laissez-faire for low wages and long hours.[98] The *West Coast Hotel* Court noted that the havoc the Great Depression had brought to ordinary Americans was "common knowledge through the length and breadth of the land."[99] Thus, the majority in *Casey*, when upholding *Roe*, distinguished *West Coast Hotel*: it was a case where the "facts of economic life" had proved different "from those previously assumed" when *Adkins* was decided.[100]

There was no such change, in assumed facts or related values, in the years between *Roe* and *Dobbs*.

What about *Brown*? *Brown v. Board of Education* (in 1954) overruled *Plessy v. Ferguson*,[101] decided almost sixty years previously (in 1896). *Plessy* originated the phrase "separate but equal" and it held that separate but equal was what the Constitution's Equal Protection Clause required—little more. In other words, the Court held that state-sanctioned segregation did not violate the guarantee of equal protection under the law.[102] By 1954, however, it had become clear that the facts in reality differed from those assumed in *Plessy* and that the nation's understanding of the relevant constitutionally related values had changed as well. It required only brief exposure to the South of Jim Crow to see that, years later, *Brown*'s "unequal," not *Plessy*'s "equal," was the better word to describe the status quo of de jure segregation. By the time of *Brown*, the experience of the Jim Crow era had shown that segregation reflected inequality and was thus inherently unequal. *Brown* thus reflected the Court's changed understanding of the facts: that "modern authority" showed the "detrimental effect[s]" of state-sanctioned segregation.[103] It "affect[ed]" children's "hearts and minds in a way never likely to be undone."[104]

The law, too, had changed. The practice of Jim Crow ran directly counter to the Fourteenth Amendment's basic purpose: namely providing formerly enslaved people and their descendants with full American citizenship.[105] And the Court in a set of cases had held that public graduate schools could not exclude black students.[106] The reasoning in those cases applied *a fortiori* to children in grade schools and in high schools.[107] Indeed, in *Casey*, thirty years before *Dobbs*, the judges, in their controlling opinion, wrote that, even though *Plessy* was "wrong the day it was decided," the passage of time had made that more clear to ever more citizens: "Society's understanding of the facts" in 1954 was "fundamentally different" than in 1896. "In constitutional adjudication as elsewhere in life, changed circumstances may impose new obligations."[108]

The result: None of the traditional considerations that had led the

Court to overrule prior precedent, despite *stare decisis*, could justify its decision in *Dobbs*. Changes in the facts supported, rather than undermined, *Roe* and *Casey*. Those cases had not proved unworkable. The law had not later produced other cases inconsistent with *Roe* or *Casey*. None of the reasons offered in other cases to justify overruling a precedent applied in *Dobbs*.

But the majority in *Dobbs* provided one reason (and as far as I can tell only one reason) in support of their decision to overrule *Roe* and *Casey*. They believed those two cases were wrongly decided—indeed that they were "egregiously wrong."[109] Yet, as I have said, how can that fact alone justify departing from *stare decisis*? The *Dobbs* majority, in reaching its "egregiously wrong" conclusion, relied primarily upon its own judgment, its own view of legal history, and particularly upon its version of "originalism."[110] As I have pointed out, different judges had used many different approaches when they have decided constitutional cases. And, if the *only* basis for overruling an earlier case is that an originalist judge, applying originalism to the earlier case, concludes that it was wrongly decided, then many, many earlier cases will be candidates for overruling (at least in the mind of that judge). So which of those earlier cases will that judge vote to overrule? All of them? Some of them? Which ones? (One of the Justices in the *Dobbs* majority listed some.[111]) And how are they to be chosen? What happened to Blackstone's and Hamilton's emphasis on the values of stability in the law? Many believe that the judge's black robe symbolizes that judges are engaged in objectively upholding the Constitution and the rule of law.[112] What happens to that symbol, what happens to the law that it symbolizes, when there is no objective way to apply *stare decisis*—when the only criterion for determining which precedent counts as law is a contemporary judge's possibly subjective view?

To summarize, I have shown six reasons, which I believe are important reasons, why constitutional textualism and its cousins, such as originalism and an overapplication of bright-line rules, do not work well in practice. First, the Constitution itself contains many highly general words, representing general values subject to a degree of change over time, as they apply to factual circumstances that themselves change. Originalism would have a hard time finding and applying, in useful detail, their "original" meaning.[113]

Second, the Founders themselves, as *McCulloch* well illustrates, believed that the Constitution must prove workable and designed it to last for centuries. They used many different approaches when interpreting that document, workability proving one of several important considerations. Chief Justice Marshall's opinion in *McCulloch* well illustrates that approach. Textualism and originalism cannot prove similarly adaptive—a fact that many of their proponents will consider a virtue, though I do not.[114]

Third, to place determinative weight on the way in which eighteenth-century speakers used particular words is to ask judges to perform a task they are not well qualified to perform, and quite likely will not perform well. And the approach is regressive: It will not permit modern solutions to modern problems, and it consigns us to a set of views and values that predominated during a period when many groups of people today were not equal citizens.[115]

Fourth, originalism will at least sometimes lead judges to avoid common law case-centered methods and instead try to decide cases through the creation of specific, rigid, perhaps dogmatic, broad rules. This method, on at least some occasions, and particularly where important general values (such as free speech) are at issue, can lead the law away from, not toward, protecting the constitutional phrase's underlying values.[116]

Fifth, textualism and originalism alone cannot interpret some, perhaps many, of the Constitution's critical structural phrases. These include terms such as "legislative," "executive," and "judicial" powers, key to the structural articles that lie at the heart of the Constitution.[117]

Sixth, as practiced so far, originalism does not, perhaps cannot, provide clear methods for applying key concepts, critical to a stable, indeed a workable, legal system—such as *stare decisis*. That fact at worst threatens the law's stability and, at best, permits judges to decide constitutional cases subjectively, i.e., according to what they think is "good."[118]

These examples show why I believe that textualism and its related approaches do not help judges interpret the Constitution's phrases any more than they help the judge interpret statutes. What, then, is the alternative? In the next portion of this book, I will turn to examples that I believe illustrate how best to approach the judicial problem of interpreting the Constitution—a method that considers constitutional values, purposes, and workability, not just text.

IV

WHY VALUES, PURPOSES, AND WORKABILITY PROVIDE A BETTER WAY TO INTERPRET THE CONSTITUTION

So far, I have focused upon weaknesses that arise when judges try to answer difficult statutory and constitutional questions by overemphasizing text, using originalism, and trying too hard to create rigid, broadly applicable rules rather than applying standards or principles. Use of those methods gives the impression that most difficult legal questions have clear answers, that use of those methods points the judge toward the right answers, and that those methods prevent judges from substituting their own views of what is good for what the law demands. By now it should be clear that I do not agree with that approach.

Law, as I have said, is not a hard science. Most truly difficult interpretive questions may have better or worse answers, but they do not have clear "right or wrong" answers. Judges use different legal tools depending upon what they believe the circumstances call for. And judicial instinct, too, plays a role as the judge tries to find the "better" (perhaps the more "sound") answer to the problem raised.

The most serious defect that I find in the use of textualism or originalism lies in what they force the judge to leave out. While original meaning (as well as text) will sometimes prove useful where the Constitution is at issue, there are more often other matters for the judge to consider (especially when the case is difficult), such as history, tradition, precedent, purposes, and consequences. In particular, there is an overarching, practical need to maintain the values that lie at the heart of a document meant to last; in other words, to maintain a workable Constitution.

Three constitutional cases show how the judge can use these tools. These examples will, I believe, also show why it is important to continue to use them and wrong to abandon their use.

16.

Workability: History and Practical Experience

NLRB v. Noel Canning (2014)[1]

As I discussed in Part III, the body of the Constitution itself (along with some of its amendments) concerns the structural relationship among the different branches of the federal government. Those provisions seek to produce a Constitution that is functionally workable by preserving the separation and balance of power among the different branches, as well as the individual liberty underlying our democratic system of government. Over long periods of time, the circumstances under which our government works, the specific objectives that it seeks, and the methods it uses to achieve those objectives change. When the Court interprets governmental methods arguably subject to a constitutional provision, it must do more than simply read the text of the provision to discover precisely what its words meant centuries ago. It must consider, and give considerable weight to, the purposes of the provision as well as related governmental practices that have developed over time.

Noel Canning, a case from 2014, offers a good example of how and why we must apply these tools when interpreting the Constitution's structural provisions. The case concerned the president's authority to make "recess appointments," that is, appointments of executive branch officials made when the Senate is not in session. Article II of the Constitution says that the president *"by and with the Advice and Consent of the Senate,"* shall nominate and appoint "Ambassadors, other public Ministers and Consuls, Judges of the supreme Court, and all other [superior] Officers of the United States."[2] The next clause, however, contains an exception. That clause, known as the Recess Appointments Clause, gives the president alone the "Power to fill up all Vacancies that may happen during the Recess of the Senate, by granting Commissions which shall expire at the End of their next Session."[3]

In this case, the five-member National Labor Relations Board had held (by a vote of 3–2) that a Pepsi-Cola distributor, Noel Canning, had acted unlawfully when it refused to put into writing and to execute a collective bargaining agreement with a labor union. Noel Canning contested the board's holding in court. It claimed, among other things, that the NLRB's holding was unlawful because the appointments of the three board members who had voted against it were invalid. The president had appointed all three on January 4, 2012. The Second Session of the 112th Congress had begun the day before (namely, on January 3), but the Senate then immediately adjourned for a few days. Thus, the appointments, which the president considered to be "recess appointments," were *intra*-session appointments (within a session) and not *inter*-session appointments (between sessions). Noel Canning also pointed out that the vacancies to which the president had appointed the three NLRB members had occurred before the Senate took a recess. Thus, Noel Canning argued that the vacancies did not "*happen* during the recess" under the words of the Recess Appointments Clause.[4]

As it came to the Court, the *Noel Canning* case presented three questions. The first concerned Congress's two-year life. A Congress's First Session normally takes place during the first year after elections, while its Second Session normally takes place during the second year after elections. To illustrate: the 100th Congress existed for two years from January 3, 1987, to January 3, 1989. That Congress held its first one-year session from January 6, 1987, until December 22, 1987; and it held its second one-year session from January 25, 1988, until October 22, 1988.[5]

Congress's setup creates both inter-session and intra-session recesses. The period between the two sessions is known as an *"inter*-session recess." The two houses begin an inter-session recess by enacting a resolution that says something like, "beginning December 27, the house will be in recess *sine die*."

"*Sine die*" refers to the fact that the resolution contains no date for reconvening. Each house may also take "*intra*-session" recesses during the period they are in session. A house, for example, may take a summer break of several weeks. The house would enact a resolution saying something like, "beginning August 2, 1987, the house will be in recess until September 12, 1987."[6]

Noel Canning asked first whether the Recess Appointments Clause applies to *intra*-session recesses as well as to *inter*-session recesses. That is to say, can the president make recess appointments when the Senate is in recess in the midst of a session? (No one doubted that the president could do so between two sessions.)

If so, a second question arose. Does the clause apply to vacancies that arose before the Senate begins its recess? That is to say, if the Senate begins a recess on October 15, 1987, can the president make recess appointments to vacancies that occurred earlier, say on September 20, 1987?[7]

Because the Court in *Noel Canning* answered both these questions "yes" by a vote of 5–4, it proceeded to a third question: What counts as a recess? Suppose the Senate, as here, enacted a resolution stating that it would take, over a period of several weeks, a series of short (three-day) intra-session recesses. Those recesses would be punctuated by *pro forma* sessions at which no business would be (but according to Senate rules might be) conducted. The Court (without dissent) held that the *pro forma* sessions did not count as "recesses," primarily because Senate rules permitted certain kinds of business to be conducted. No recess had lasted longer than three days, and three days was too brief a time to count as a "recess" for Recess Clause purposes. Thus, the three NLRB appointments—all made during that short recess period—were invalid.[8]

Because the Court's opinions on the first two questions differ considerably in methodology, I discuss only those two questions here.[9]

Intra-Session Appointments

Start, then, with the first question: Does the president have the power to make a recess appointment during an *intra*-session recess (e.g., a summer recess during a session)? The five-member majority (in an opinion that I wrote) and the four-member concurrence in the Court's judgment, which here functioned as a dissent (in an opinion that Justice Scalia wrote), all considered the constitutional text, its purpose, its history, and how the government has applied the Recess Appointments Clause in practice in the past. What, then, are the methodological differences?

The differences, I believe, primarily boil down to emphasis, perhaps here driven by judicial instinct. But emphasis can (and here does) certainly matter. Justice Scalia normally tried to emphasize the text, particularly as understood by those who wrote the Constitution in 1787, as well as by the public during the first decades of our nation's history. I normally try to emphasize the need to read the text as informed by the provision's purposes, even if doing so points toward a different result.

As I said, all the judges considered the Recess Appointments Clause's purposes, though the majority thought that those purposes should carry more interpretive weight than did the dissenters.[10] Similarly, all the judges considered the Clause's history and, in particular, historical practice.[11] Again, the majority placed more weight upon practice, and specifically, practice that took place during the past eighty years. The dissenters placed more weight upon practice that took place during approximately the first eighty years of the Constitution's existence. The majority's opinion in answering the first question, will, I hope, show how and why I emphasized more current practice, for I thought that by doing so, our interpretation would better maintain a workable government.

Purpose

I begin with the clause's general purpose because the majority opinion began with purpose, and because the dissent seemed to agree at least with part of what the majority said. The majority offered, as background, that the "Recess Appointments Clause sets forth a subsidiary, not a primary, method for appointing officers of the United States."[12] The Founders intended Senate approval to be the norm, at least for principal officers.[13] As Alexander Hamilton wrote, they placed the power of nomination in the president alone because "one man of discernment is better fitted to analise [*sic*] and estimate the peculiar qualities adapted to particular offices, than a body of men."[14] But the need to secure Senate approval provides an excellent check upon a spirit of favoritism in the president.[15] Thus, "ordinary power of appointment is confided to the President and Senate *jointly*." But, since "it would have been improper to oblige [the Senate] to be continually in session for the appointment of officers; and as vacancies might happen *in their recess* which it might be necessary . . . to fill without delay," the Recess Appointments Clause "is evidently intended to authorise the President *singly* to make temporary appointments."[16]

The majority added that it tried to interpret the clause "as granting the President the power to make appointments during a recess but not offering the President the authority routinely to avoid the need for Senate confirmation."[17]

The dissent did not directly disagree with this statement of the purpose of the clause. It added, however, that the clause formed part of the Constitution's "separation of powers" structure and that structure was designed to protect "liberty" and not simply an efficient government.[18] (The majority did not disagree.[19])

Text

The text relevant to the first question says that the president has the power to make a recess appointment "during the Recess of the Senate."[20] The majority points out that at the time of the founding, as today, the word "recess" can simply refer to "a period of cessation from usual work."[21] As so defined, it can apply as easily to an intra- as to an inter-session break. The word "the" added to "recess" (i.e., *the* recess) might suggest that the phrase refers to only *one* recess for each Congress. But it need not do so.[22] The term "the recess" can refer generically to the kind of thing that a recess is, as when the Constitution directs the Senate to choose a president *pro tempore* "in *the* absence of the Vice-President."[23] It is not poor grammar to use this phrase if there are many absences during a Congress, and it is not poor grammar to use the same kind of phrase in respect to "recess." At worst, the word "the" creates an indeterminacy.

The majority turned back to *purpose* to help resolve that indeterminacy. It noted that the clause gives the president a recess-appointment power "so that the President can ensure the continued functioning of the Federal government when the Senate is away."[24] It added that the "Senate is equally away during both an inter-session and an intra-session recess," and its capacity to participate in the appointments process has nothing to do with the words (such as *sine die*) that it uses in its recess resolution to signal its departure.[25] Thus, the text, read in light of its purpose, pointed strongly toward an affirmative answer to the first question.

The dissent observed that the clause refers to commissions that shall be granted during *"the Recess of the Senate"* and then adds that the commissions shall expire at the end of the Senate's *"next Session."*[26] The word "Session," it added, had a formal meaning at the time of the founding; it referred formally to one of the two "sessions" of which a single two-year Congress was composed.[27] And if "next Session" denoted a *formal* session, then "the Recess" had to mean the break between formal sessions. In the early years of the Republic, many commentators used the term in that way. To use the word "session" formally while using the word "recess" informally was therefore "linguistically implausible" in the eyes of the dissent.

The dissent and supporting commentators also pointed out that the Founders likely thought that "recess" referred to the inter-session recess because, at that time, there was no other kind of recess (at least none during which the president made recess appointments).[28] Now there are many, but that fact did not change the meaning of the constitutional phrase as understood by the dissent.

Besides, the dissent added, if we now include intra-session recesses within the scope of the word "Recess," the Senate might decide to give the president too much power by, say, having tens or hundreds of intra-session recesses, lasting for ten minutes each.[29] Further, since the appointment lasts until the end of the "next Session" (and "session" likely means "formal session"), a president could make a recess appointment during a recess in January of Year One, and that person would stay in office until December of Year Two.[30] That, the dissent said, was too long.

The majority replied to each of these points. It said the question was not what kind of "recess" the Founders expected at the time of the founding; rather, it was whether the Founders intended "to restrict the scope of the Clause to the form of congressional recess then prevalent" or whether they intended "a broader scope" permitting the clause to apply, where appropriate, to somewhat changed circumstances.[31] Referring to *McCulloch*, the majority thought that "the Framers likely did intend the Clause to apply to a new circumstance that so clearly falls within its essential purposes, where doing so is consistent with the Clause's language."[32]

The majority dealt with the problem of the "ten-minute recess" by accepting the solicitor general's suggestion that a recess shorter than ten days was presumptively too short—and a recess shorter than three days was *definitely* too short and consequently did not fall within the scope of the clause's word "recess."[33] The majority analogized the latter, three-day limitation to the Adjournments Clause, which says that during a session, neither house "shall, without the Consent of the other, adjourn for more than three days."[34] This clause suggests a break of three days or less is, as far as doing business is concerned, *de minimis*. The majority also based the ten-day period on the fact that there had never been a recess appointment made during an intra-session recess (and only a handful during an inter-session recess) of less than ten days.[35]

In respect to the hypothetical long (nearly two-year) recess appointment, the majority agreed with the dissent about its possibility, but did not believe that it was a particularly serious problem.[36]

History and Practice

Both *Noel Canning* opinions also refer to history and practice. The majority said that when "interpreting the Constitution, we put significant weight upon historical practice."[37] It referred directly to Chief Justice Marshall's statement in *McCulloch* that "doubtful question[s]" where "the great principles of liberty are not concerned, but the respective powers of those who are equally the representatives of the people, are to be adjusted . . . ought to receive a considerable impression" from "the practice of the government."[38] And, it referred to language in an earlier case stating that "long settled and established practice is a consideration of great weight in a proper interpretation of constitutional provisions."[39]

The Justices debated which side historical practice supported. The majority said that pre–Civil War history was "not helpful."[40] Congress took long breaks between sessions but took virtually no significant intra-session breaks during that period. Hence, the lack of intra-session recess appointments during that time period is not surprising. In 1867 and 1868, Congress first took substantial nonholiday intra-session breaks; during those breaks, the president made dozens of recess appointments.[41] Between the Civil War and the Great Depression, Congress took substantial intra-session breaks (other than holiday breaks) in only four years, but in each of those breaks the president made intra-session recess appointments.[42] Since 1929, Congress has shortened its inter-session breaks and taken more intra-session breaks; and presidents have correspondingly made more intra-session recess appointments. Indeed, if we include military officers, presidents have made thousands of intra-session recess appointments, including, for example, Dwight Eisenhower to the rank of major general, Dean Acheson to the position of undersecretary of state, and Alan Greenspan to the position of chairman of the Federal Reserve Board.[43]

With one exception, the president's legal advisors found intra-session recess appointments to be legal. Some did so expressly because of the need to keep the government functioning during lengthier recesses.[44] Some senators objected (for example, when President Theodore Roosevelt made multiple recess appointments during a recess that lasted just a few minutes). But their objections were primarily upon functional grounds (i.e., too short a recess), and those grounds could apply to both kinds of recess.[45] Neither the Senate nor any Senate committee formally noted opposition. In short, presidents since 1929 have made frequent intra-session recess appointments.

The dissenters minimized the importance of this latter-day history. They highlighted that the first intra-session recess appointments were not made until after the Civil War, when President Andrew Johnson made about twenty during 1867 and 1868.[46] Later, many in Congress opposed President Roosevelt's 1903 effort, which I just mentioned, to make many such appointments during a break that lasted only a few minutes.[47] And the one attorney general—Philander Knox—who took the view in 1902 that the clause applied only to inter-session recesses, wrote (in the dissent's view) a more convincing opinion than did all the others combined.[48] The dissenters added that, even though presidents had made many more intra-session recess appointments since 1921, if one subtracted military appointments, these amounted perhaps to many hundreds of appointments but not to many thousands.[49]

The upshot of the dissenters' position was that presidents had made hardly any intra-session recess appointments during the first 130 years of the Republic's existence; but they had made many (indeed, large numbers of) such appointments during the last eighty years. Permitting this practice to continue, the dissent argued, would aggrandize the president's power at the expense of that of the Senate.[50] And neither the president nor the majority, by departing from the formal language of the Recess Appointments Clause as originally understood, should have been able to do so.

Vacancies That "May Happen"

Turning to the second question in the case, recall that the Recess Appointments Clause gives the president the power to fill "vacancies *that may happen during the recess of the Senate*."[51] Do the words "may happen" refer (1) only to vacancies that first occur during the recess, or (2) do they include vacancies that first occurred before the recess but have not at the time of the recess yet been filled? The Court accepted the second meaning by the same 5–4 vote.

The majority conceded that the most natural meaning of "happen," as applied to a vacancy, was that the vacancy "happens" when it first occurs. But that was not, the majority argued, the only possible meaning.[52] Thomas Jefferson wrote that it may also mean that a vacancy "may happen to be" or "may happen to fall" during a recess.[53] Or, as William Wirt, President James Monroe's attorney general, wrote, "[The phrase] may mean 'happen to take place': that is, '*to originate*,' or it 'may mean, also, without violence to the sense, 'happen to exist.'"[54] In other words, neither interpretation of the phrase is so beyond reason that it does violence to the text. The majority added that, since a broader reading here is at least a permissible reading of what *McCulloch* counsels is a "doubtful" phrase, the majority would go on to consider the clause's purpose and historical practice.[55]

Turning to purposes, the majority found ample support for a broad reading of the clause. The clause's purpose is "to permit the President to obtain the assistance of subordinate officers when the Senate, due to its recess, cannot confirm them."[56] "[I]f," wrote Wirt in 1823, "the President's power is to be limited to such vacancies only as happen to occur during the recess of the Senate, the vacancy in the case [which first occurred before the recess] must continue, however ruinous the consequences may be to the public."[57] To avoid this kind of result, the majority thought, the words "may happen" must be given their broader meaning.

The majority noted a problem: Its interpretation meant that the clause applied to many, perhaps nearly all, vacancies. A president might then avoid Senate confirmations by waiting for the next recess before transforming all his appointments into "recess appointments," and then appointing officers once again to recess appointments at the next recess after the "next session" expired.[58] But, the majority pointed out, the third (and close-to-unanimous) part of its opinion made clear that the Senate could prevent this by providing for only brief, less than three-day recesses, punctuated by *pro forma* sessions.[59]

In canvassing the historical data, the majority found it strongly suggested that many historical intra-session appointments were made to fill vacancies that "initially arose prior to the recess."[60] The majority then used sampling, statistics, and other empirical methods to buttress its conclusion that, in all probability, presidents have used recess appointments to fill vacancies that occurred before, but continued during, a recess.[61]

The dissent did not dispute that many presidents had made such appointments over the last few decades.[62] But it also noted that many senators, attorneys general, and others had argued that the word "happen" nonetheless must be narrowly interpreted.[63] Consequently, the dissent said, neither text nor a "clear historical practice" supported the majority.

Rather, according to the dissent, the majority had a text that it was neither clearly in its favor nor even ambiguously so. And the "historical practice" is "at-best[] ambiguous." That, the dissent concluded, was insufficient to support the majority's interpretation of the clause.[64]

The heart of the dissenters' approach, I believe, is this sentence: "The majority replaces the Constitution's text with a new set of judge-made rules to govern recess appointments," namely the majority's discussions of *pro forma* sessions and three-day limitations.[65] The Senate confirmation requirement limiting the president's power, the dissent continued, "is there not for the benefit of the Senate, but for the protection of the people."[66]

As the details of this case illustrate, I disagree with the methodology that this statement, and the dissenters' most important arguments, reflect. First, in a case concerning the Constitution's provisions setting forth the details of government structure, I would emphasize the purpose of the constitutional provision in question. Then, after determining that purpose, I would examine the Constitution's language to see if it would *support* an interpretation that furthers (and does not undercut) the carrying out of that purpose. If the enacted language says "rabbit," a judge cannot say it means "giraffe." But if the language says "may happen," it is not so far-fetched for a judge to say that phrase means "first happens before . . . and then continues to happen during," as such an interpretation is both linguistically permissible and serves the underlying purpose of the provision. I instinctively favor that more practical approach.

Second, long-standing practice matters. As Chief Justice Marshall pointed out, the Constitution is written in general terms in part because it must last through "ever-changing circumstances over centuries."[67] During those centuries, technological, social, political, economic, and other conditions change. The public's methods for managing their affairs will need to change with the circumstances. *The judge's job is not to read literally those constitutional provisions written 250 years ago without regard to such changes.* Rather, it is to try to assure that the changes made as the nation evolves are consistent with the values that underlie those provisions. In that way, the Constitution and the values it contains will, as Chief Justice Marshall pointed out in *McCulloch*, more likely last.

Noel Canning shows how judges can—and why they should—follow Chief Justice Marshall's approach. The reason I have discussed this case at length and in detail is that by doing so, I can show why I believe Justice Scalia was wrong when he said that the judges in the majority were substituting their own views or their own "novel framework" for those of the Constitution. To the contrary, the need in *Noel Canning* for detailed reasoning, the thorough examination of history, and the weighing of relevant practice all indicate that the judges in the majority believed they were writing not what they themselves wished but what the Constitution demands. They were trying to write an opinion that would maintain that document's "recess appointments" objectives. Doing so with an eye toward past practice and constitutional purposes, as well as text and historical context, does not amount to judicial fiat but rather judicial service to the Constitution's purposes and endurance over time.

17.

Workability:
Deciding Where Values Conflict

District of Columbia v. Heller (2008)[1]

Different constitutional provisions seek, at least in part, to protect basic democratic values. Judges have often used different forms of interest-balancing to interpret and to apply those provisions in circumstances where values conflict. For example, courts use "rational basis" analysis when they are determining the lawfulness of economic or social regulation. Application of a rational basis standard will normally lead a court to uphold a regulation as constitutional so long as it bears "a rational relationship" to a "legitimate governmental purpose." By contrast, courts apply "strict scrutiny" when the government seeks to regulate, say, political speech. In doing so, they are likely to strike down the regulation as a violation of the First Amendment unless it is "narrowly tailored to achieve a compelling governmental interest." Courts also apply "intermediate scrutiny" to other types of laws, such as those regulating commercial speech. When applying intermediate scrutiny, a court will ask whether a government regulation "burdens a protected interest in a way that is out of proportion to the statute's salutary effects upon other important governmental interests."[2] In many other countries, courts term this approach "proportionality."[3] All three approaches require interest-balancing.

Previously, I argued in the context of the First Amendment that these three tests are useful as long as the judge considers them to be standards, or approaches, rather than absolute rules. Here, I want to show in more detail how, in a difficult case, interest-balancing works, and how it can help maintain a workable Constitution. To do so, I return to a subject that I discussed earlier: gun control and the Second Amendment.[4] I consider interest-balancing, which the Court disavowed in its 2022 *Bruen* decision as "means-end" scrutiny.[5] A reminder to the reader: I shall accept (for argument's sake and contrary to what I actually believe) that the Second Amendment provides an individual with a right to keep, say, loaded handguns in his home. Even so, there still must be a way to determine which "arms" that person can keep, and where, when, and in what conditions. Interest-balancing provides a practical way to maintain the constitutional interest that the *Heller* majority found in the Second Amendment—namely, a constitutional right to carry a handgun—without abandoning the governmental interest in preserving the lives and safety of American citizens.

Heller concerned the constitutionality, under the Second Amendment, of a District of Columbia gun control law that prohibited (in most cases) the registration and keeping of a firearm in the District.[6] That law generally prevented people in the District from possessing handguns. The Second Amendment says, in its entirety, that "A well regulated Militia, being necessary to the security of a free State, the right of the people to keep and bear Arms, shall not be infringed."[7] The Court held in *Heller* by a vote of 5–4 that the District's law violated the constitutional right "to keep and bear Arms."[8] Justice Scalia wrote the majority opinion, and there were two dissents. Justice Stevens wrote one,[9] and I wrote the other.[10] (Justices Stevens, Souter, Ginsburg, and I joined both.)

The main disagreement in the case concerned the scope of the words "keep and bear Arms." The majority held that those words protected a personal right of self-defense.[11] It added that "the right secured by the Second Amendment is not unlimited."[12] It did not "cast doubt" on laws prohibiting "the possession of firearms by felons and the mentally ill, or laws forbidding the carrying of firearms in sensitive places such as schools and government buildings, or laws imposing conditions and qualifications on the commercial sale of arms."[13] The problem with the District's "handgun" ban, however, was in the majority's view that it extended to the "home, where the need for defense of self, family and property is most acute."[14] And "banning from the home 'the most preferred firearm in the nation to "keep" and use for protection of one's home and family' . . . fail[s] constitutional muster."[15]

In his dissent, Justice Stevens thoroughly examined the history of the Second Amendment. He concluded the following: 1) A significant number of those who opposed adopting the Constitution argued, in 1787, that Congress might use its Article I powers to weaken the power of the state militias. In particular, Article I seemed to give Congress the power to call up state militias and then disband them.[16] 2) Madison and other Founders thought they could destroy the force of this argument by adding what became the Second Amendment to the Bill of Rights, which said Congress could not destroy state militias.[17] 3) That is why the Second Amendment refers directly to the militia; its words "the right of the people to keep and bear Arms" refer to the right of the people to maintain those militias.[18] Thus, the Second Amendment does not provide a personal, non-militia-related right allowing persons to keep handguns in their homes.[19]

My dissent took a different tack. I assumed, purely for argument's sake, that the majority was correct about the existence of a personal right.[20] Still, I thought that the District's law was valid. Why? Because:

> [A] legislature could reasonably conclude that the law will advance goals of great public importance, namely, saving lives, preventing injury, and reducing crime. The law is tailored to the urban crime problem in that it is local in scope and thus affects a geographic area both limited in size and entirely urban; the law concerns handguns, which are specially linked to urban gun deaths and injuries, and which are the overwhelmingly favorite weapon for armed criminals; and, at the same time, the law imposes a burden upon gun owners that seems proportionately no greater than restrictions in existence at the time the Second Amendment was adopted.[21]

It seemed fairly clear to me that, at the time the Founders adopted the Second Amendment, cities such as New York, Philadelphia, and Boston all regulated the storage and use of firearms, including handguns.[22] There was no suggestion in the historical record that anyone thought the Second Amendment made illegal those regulations or other reasonable regulations like them. Thus, "[t]he historical evidence demonstrate[d] that a self-defense assumption [was] the *beginning*, rather than the *end*, of any constitutional inquiry."[23] And that inquiry had to be practical and detail-oriented, including examining "the statute's rationale, the problems that called it into being" and "its relation to those objectives."[24] That is to say, once one decides that the Second Amendment provides a personal right to "keep and bear" handguns, one must go on to decide whether a law or regulation that limits that right falls within the zone the amendment leaves open to regulation by legislatures.

In answering that question, what standard should we apply?

A Proportionality Standard

To apply a "rational basis" standard would likely have produced a different result in this case. It is at least rational to forbid the possession of handguns within a highly urban area. But it seemed unlikely that a majority of the *Heller* Court would have adopted that standard.

On the other hand, a "strict scrutiny" standard could risk rendering unconstitutional all sorts of gun regulations, such as keeping guns out of the hands of felons.

That left a form of "intermediate scrutiny" that fits most gun regulations where important interests lie on both sides of the constitutional equation. The question then is: Does the statute burden a protected interest in a way that, or to an extent that, is out of proportion to the statute's salutary effect upon other important governmental interests? This is how I, in dissent, thought through that question.

The first question to consider was whether the District's law helped achieve the compelling governmental goal of saving lives and preventing injuries. Two subquestions were embedded here: First, whether the government's goal was compelling, and second, whether the law helped address that goal. The relevant legislative body, the District of Columbia Council, adopted reports in the 1970s (when the law was passed) strongly indicating the answer to the first subquestion was "yes." For example, a 1976 congressional House committee report said that the "easy availability of firearms . . . has been a major factor contributing to the drastic increase in gun-related violence and crime over the past 40 years."[25] The committee provided statistics suggesting that guns were responsible nationally for approximately 25,000 deaths and 200,000 injuries each year.[26] It said that a crime committed with a pistol "is seven times more likely to be lethal than a crime committed with any other weapon."[27] And, after reciting many similar statistics, it recommended a "restriction" on handgun registration to make clear that "pistols . . . are no longer justified in this . . . purely urban environment."[28]

Did the D.C. law help address that compelling interest? Why, then, did the District's restrictive mid-1970s laws not bring deaths and injuries down? Those opposing the gun law pointed out, for example, that in 2008, when *Heller* was decided, the District's homicide rate was substantially *higher* when compared to other cities than it was before D.C.'s gun law took effect.[29] Some statistical studies, which looked at European countries, suggested that strict gun laws there were correlated with *more*, not *fewer*, murders.[30] And other studies indicated that those who owned firearms and used them for self-defense often scared away intruders.[31]

The conflicting studies, however, did not show that the D.C. Council's conclusion was unreasonable. Though crime was up, was that *because* of D.C.'s gun laws or despite them? That is to say, would the crime rate, without laws restricting guns, not have been still higher? Foreign nations with more gun laws had a higher crime rate. But was that because high crime means more (legal or illegal) guns and a greater need for governments to regulate them through laws? Unless one believed that strict gun laws *caused* crime—a proposition for which there is no evidence—what would have happened to crime without the gun laws?

I could find no completely satisfactory answer to those counterfactual questions.

In my view, the second subquestion required the Court to address sets of studies and counter studies that would likely leave most judges uncertain about the proper policy conclusion. If so, that uncertainty favors the constitutionality of the law, for it is legislators (and not judges) who have primary responsibility for drawing policy conclusions from empirical facts.[32] Courts, the Supreme Court has said, in reviewing a legislature's "predictive judgments," typically (though not always) seek to assure that, in formulating its judgments, the legislature "has drawn reasonable inferences based on substantial evidence."[33] In the dissenters' view, based on considerably more evidence than I have listed here, the D.C. Council's conclusions justified its efforts to further the sort of life-preserving and public safety interests that the Court has called "compelling."

Insofar as the Second Amendment interest is militia-related, the District's law burdened it very little. None of those affiliated directly with the case belonged, or argued they wanted to belong, to a militia.[34] In any event, citizens could train to serve in a militia by taking the metro to gun clubs a few miles outside the District.[35] Similarly, the District's law did not prevent anyone from hunting in nearby states.[36]

But there was no doubt that the law did burden those who wished to keep a loaded handgun in their home for purposes of self-defense. And the majority believed that the Second Amendment protects an individual's right to do just that. Taking that right as a given, again, just for argument's sake, the District's law imposed a serious burden upon an individual's ability to exercise that right.[37] But, in my view, the fact that the District's law burdened the exercise of Second Amendment rights as formulated by the majority, standing alone, was not dispositive. Rather, at that point, it became necessary to weigh that burden against the need for D.C.'s gun law, taking account of what reasonable alternative measures the District might have had to safeguard public safety.[38]

D.C.'s specific object was to reduce the number of handguns in homes. That objective may, because of its lifesaving potential, have had a compelling justification. But there was no way to avoid noticing that, to the extent D.C. achieved that objective, it also interfered with the right to keep a loaded handgun in the home.[39] And, if D.C. was right about the association between handguns, injury, and death, then any measure less restrictive in respect to the use of handguns for self-defense would, to that same extent, have likely proven less effective in preventing the use of handguns for illicit purposes.[40] If an individual had a handgun in the home that he could use for self-defense, then he had a handgun in the home he could also use to kill himself or engage in acts of domestic violence.[41] And that, I suspect, is more often the case than protecting the handgun owner against burglars. The upshot is that there was no readily apparent less restrictive, but similarly effective, alternative.[42]

The dissent found it persuasive that the District's law was not an outlier when compared to laws passed by other municipalities and states. Outright prohibitions on firearms were not unique to D.C., but had been passed by a wide variety of cities and states for similar reasons as the D.C. law.[43] A licensing restriction, though certainly "less restrictive" on the right to carry a firearm for self-defense inside the home, is not a meaningful "alternative" in the sense that it "would not similarly reduce the handgun population."[44]

What are the consequences of these three considerations? The gun law's objective—reducing life-threatening risks—is a compelling government interest. There was no less restrictive way to achieve it. But in doing so, the claimed Second Amendment interest, as understood by the majority, was seriously harmed. These three considerations thus seemed to approach equipoise in this case.[45]

In weighing these features of the law in our effort to determine whether the law violates the Second Amendment, I would have made a judgment: Did the law treat the harms—both to the individuals at physical risk and to the amendment's protective interests—proportionately? Because the law in part rested upon factual inferences, and because policy-related fact-finding was more of a job for legislative bodies than for the Supreme Court, I would have phrased the question in a way that gave the District the benefit of the doubt: Did the District's law *disproportionately* burden Second Amendment–protected interests?[46]

I answered "no." The law did not disproportionately burden the interests protected by the amendment. Consequently, in my view, the law was constitutional.

Why was the burden not disproportionate? For one thing, the self-defense interest in maintaining loaded handguns in the home to shoot intruders was not the primary interest that the Second Amendment sought to serve but was rather, at most, a subsidiary interest.[47] The amendment's reference to state "militias," along with the fact (as found by Justice Stevens) that the Founders' fear of seeing those militias destroyed "was *the reason*" they enacted the Second Amendment, and the fact that armed intrusion in urban settings was not the major threat to life in the eighteenth century all suggested that loaded handgun protection in the home was not the amendment's *primary* objective.[48] Nor was there evidence that a need for *handguns* lay at the center of the Founders' concerns. Indeed, Samuel Adams, while advocating for a strong gun protection law, likely knew of, but did not object to, a contemporary Boston law that would have normally prevented Bostonians from keeping loaded handguns in the home.[49]

For another thing, I explained that the majority's contrary view would likely have serious adverse consequences.[50] I predicted that it would encourage legal challenges to gun laws throughout the nation. At the same time, because the majority opinion said little about how to evaluate legislative judgments in this area, I thought it would leave the nation without clear standards for evaluating those gun law challenges. That uncertainty as to results would leave cities without effective protection against gun violence for long periods of time. (Unfortunately, I tend to think many of my predictions have been borne out.)

Finally, a decision striking down D.C.'s gun law—without clear and limiting standards for evaluating future gun law challenges—would take from the hands of the elected branches of government (and turn over to unelected judges) the right to decide whether to insist upon a handgun-free urban population in a city facing a serious crime problem.[51]

In my view, these considerations—the importance of the handgun possession question; the fact that the interest in possessing a handgun in the home is, at most, a subsidiary and not primary Second Amendment goal; the Court's inability to set forth standards or explain how its conclusions in this case would apply to the possession of other weapons in other circumstances; and the unusual importance of having those explanations, given the problem of gun possession in the nation—when taken together, tipped the balance. They indicated that the D.C. law was a proportionate, not a *disproportionate*, response to the compelling concerns that led the District to adopt it.

I hope the reader will note the following methodological points: The balancing test I have used does not give judges too much power to decide important constitutional cases.[52] To the contrary, my approach requires the judge to examine the details of the case; it orders the requisite decision-related factors into separate parts; and it requires the judge to examine the arguably compelling interests, the burden imposed on the relevant constitutional interest, and the possibility of less restrictive alternatives. The judge must provide explanations for each conclusion. Most importantly, where, as here, these factors approach equipoise, the judge must explain in detail why, in the judge's view, the law at issue either does, or does not, disproportionately injure a constitutionally protected interest. The reader may disagree with the judge's reasoning or conclusion. But the reader will know just what that reasoning is. And it is the obligation to set forth that reasoning that protects the public from an abuse of power by an unelected judge. For these reasons, my approach tends to leave the legislative process in the hands of elected legislators.

By way of contrast, consider the majority's methodology in *Heller*. It relied upon disputed, centuries-old history. It did not explain how that history should be extrapolated. It rejected the considered views of "every Court of Appeals to consider the question [prior to 2001]."[53] In my view,

Heller's reliance on originalism suffers from a lack of transparency, particularly compared to an approach, such as the one I follow, that takes account of conflicting constitutional values and seeks to find a workable balance. That lack of transparency makes it easier, not harder, for a judge to substitute views about what is "good" for the law itself.[54]

18.

Workability:
Direct Application of Basic Values

McCreary County v. American Civil Liberties Union of Kentucky (2005)[1]
and *Van Orden v. Perry* (2005)[2]

Of the many different tools that judges can use in a difficult case to interpret or to apply a constitutional provision, the basic values that underlie the provision are important. Reference to, and an understanding of, those values is particularly important when there is little but an ambiguous text and perhaps conflicting precedent to which the judge can otherwise turn. Two cases arising out of the First Amendment's Religion Clauses illustrate the point.

The Bill of Rights begins, "Congress shall make no law respecting an establishment of religion, or prohibiting the free exercise thereof."[3] Alexis de Tocqueville, among others, pointed out in the nineteenth century that these clauses seek to maintain that "separation of church and state" that is critical to the "peaceful dominion of religion" in this country.[4] In America, he said, the "spirit of religion" and the "spirit of freedom" are productively "united"; they "reigned in common" but in separate spheres "over the same country."[5]

Why are the Religion Clauses featured so prominently in our Constitution? There are those who believe the main reason these clauses come first stems from the seventeenth-century religious wars in England.[6] After Henry VIII beheaded Sir Thomas More, after Catholics burned the Protestant bishops Latimer and Ridley—and Archbishop Cranmer—at the stake in downtown Oxford, after a Protestant Queen Elizabeth ordered her Catholic cousin executed, after James II was deposed for religious reasons, and after Parliament passed the Test Act of 1673 (which imposed civil disabilities on Catholics, among others), many in England thought, *enough is enough.* Liberty and social stability demanded a religious tolerance that respected the religious views of all citizens, permitted those citizens to worship God in their own way, and allowed all families to teach their children and to form their characters as they wished. And if some of them were wrong and their views led them to eternal damnation, then so be it. The First Amendment's Religion Clauses, then, reflect the Framers' vision of an American nation free of the religious strife that had long plagued the nations of Europe.[7]

The religious liberty protected by the Religion Clauses gives rise to other kinds of liberties, too. In 1960, Lord Radcliffe, a United Kingdom Supreme Court Justice, pointed to a "complex of liberties which are needed to preserve the freedom of the human spirit."[8] They include "marital and parental relationships, freedom of religious worship, freedom of association, freedom of labor, and freedom of artistic and productive expression."[9] Once the law protected the religious rights of individuals, it also began to protect other basic liberties, many of which were designed to create a tolerant society, a society in which each would "[l]ive and let live," and a society that respects the right of each individual "to discern what is good and to choose it for himself."[10] In this sense, "political liberty is a product, almost a byproduct, of religious liberty."[11] Going further, Radcliffe quotes the German philosopher Friedrich Schiller: The law helps the individual to fulfill the "aim of humanity," namely the development of "powers of man."[12] It is "God's will," adds Schiller, "that man, free and independent, should find his natural aim in the communal life and communal work of the State and his earthly happiness in self-reliance and free activity."[13]

Thus, philosophers, legal and otherwise, can find much, including the basic aims of law itself, in those few initial words of the Bill of Rights.

In 1962, the Court held that the Establishment Clause forbids school-sponsored prayer in public schools.[14] It did so in part because it recognized the "anguish, hardship and bitter strife that could come when zealous religious groups struggled with one another to obtain the Government's stamp of approval."[15] When government has allied itself with one particular religion, the Court added, "the inevitable result had been that it has incurred the hatred, disrespect, and even contempt of those who held contrary beliefs."[16] In other cases, the Court added that the "potential for political divisiveness"[17] rooted in religion has "particular relevance" in a school environment,[18] that "political division along religious lines was one of the principal evils" against which the Religion Clauses were intended to protect,[19] and that public assistance to religious schools risks "continuing political strife over aid to religion."[20]

In deciding these cases, the Court did not deny that early American society would have found a less clear-cut separation between church and state compatible with social tranquility.[21] After all, the nation's first public schools were Protestant. Those students recited Protestant prayers, read the King James version of the Bible, and learned Protestant religious ideals. But given the small number of members of minority religions at the time, these practices did not threaten serious social conflict. (Consider that Catholics accounted for less than 2 percent of the church-affiliated population at the time of the founding and Jews even less.[22])

By the end of the nineteenth century, however, the number of religions and the number of members of minority religions had multiplied. Conflict over matters such as Bible reading intensified. Catholics, for example, were victims of prejudice that sometimes included physical beatings. That potential for conflict has only grown today: America currently is home to members belonging to many dozens of different religious denominations,[23] not to mention a growing number of atheists.

How could courts in the twentieth century apply the Establishment Clause in these changed circumstances? To give each religion an "equal opportunity" to secure, say, government aid or the right to pray in the public square seemed unworkable. The Court instead emphasized *separation*. It tried to draw fairly clear lines of separation between church and state—at least where the heartland of religious belief, such as primary religious education, was at issue.

Applying the "separation" principle, however, was easier said than done. The Court's Establishment Clause jurisprudence appeared indecisive and vacillating to outside observers. Consider some of the cases in which the Court had to decide whether a government's action violated the Establishment Clause:

- A daily period of silence at public schools for meditation or prayer *did* violate the Establishment Clause,[24] but,

- Opening a state legislature's day with prayer did *not* violate the Establishment Clause.[25]

- A state statute giving "maintenance and repair grants" to religious schools *did* violate the Establishment Clause,[26] but,

- Paying bus fares for parochial school students did *not* violate Establishment Clause.[27]

- Reimbursing parents for part of the cost of parochial school education *did* violate the Establishment Clause,[28] but,

- Paying for an interpreter for a disabled child's education at a parochial school did *not* violate the Establishment Clause.[29]

- Tax exemption favoring religious publishers *did* violate the Establishment Clause,[30] but,

- Tax exemption for real property owned by a church or synagogue did *not* violate the Establishment Clause.[31]

Now consider a few of the Court's holdings concerning the Free Exercise Clause:

- Refusals to pay unemployment compensation to those who for religious reasons will not work at an armaments factory *did* violate the Free Exercise Clause,[32] but,

- Insistence that those with religious objections to paying taxes used to finance a war must pay phone taxes did *not* violate the Free Exercise Clause.[33]

- A state's refusal to pay unemployment benefits to otherwise qualified individuals who used state-banned peyote at religious services did *not* violate the Free Exercise Clause,[34] but,

- An animal cruelty law forbidding religious sacrifice of poultry *did* violate the Free Exercise Clause.[35]

- A state's refusal to pay unemployment compensation to otherwise qualified individuals who refuse to work on their Sabbath *did* violate the Free Exercise Clause,[36] but,

- Prohibition of wearing religious garb (a Jewish yarmulke) while on military duty did *not* violate the Free Exercise Clause.[37]

These individual cases are difficult to square with each other without close reference to the details and facts of specific circumstances. The Court has routinely balanced interests in dealing with the Religion Clauses, and has taken a close look at the contexts, motivations, purposes, and consequences of laws and practices to decide whether they meet constitutional requirements.

It is unusually difficult to find intermediate principles that will help courts apply the Religion Clauses. And the uncertainty and difficulty of finding intermediate principles in this context have led me to believe that, when deciding related, difficult cases in this domain, we must often refer back to (and depend upon) the basic purposes of the clauses themselves. The application of the Religion Clauses, therefore, further lends support to my suggestion throughout this book that a search for clear-cut, broad rules is not only futile in respect to particular constitutional questions but also counterproductive to honoring the objectives of the constitutional provisions in question.

How, then, can judges discern and apply the animating purposes behind constitutional provisions in a way that is workable in the long run? Two related cases from 2005 provide examples of how I believe this can be done. In the first case, *McCreary County v. ACLU*, executives of two Kentucky judicial districts posted large copies of the Ten Commandments on the walls of their courthouse hallways.[38] In response to a lawsuit brought by the American Civil Liberties Union of Kentucky, the state legislature doubled down, adopting a resolution suggesting that the Ten Commandments were the state's "precedent legal code" and expanding upon the display.[39] In one district, the Commandments were hung by the county judge-executive, who called them "good rules to live by" and who recounted the story of an astronaut who became convinced "there must be a divine God" after viewing the earth from the moon.[40] Pursuant to the state legislature's resolution, state officials subsequently posted other documents around the Ten Commandments, such as the Declaration of Independence and the constitution of Kentucky, which in places use the term "God."[41] The lower court found that, in each courthouse, the display was hung in a "very high traffic area" and was "readily visible to . . . county citizens who use the courthouse to conduct their civic business, to obtain or renew drivers' licenses and permits, to register cars, to pay local taxes, and to register to vote."[42]

The primary question before the Court concerned the purpose of the display. The lower courts had held that the hallway display in question "'lack[ed] any secular purpose' because the Commandments 'are a distinctly religious document, believed by many Christians and Jews to be the direct and revealed word of God.'"[43] The display was not "educational" because "a single religious text unaccompanied by any interpretation explaining its role as a foundational document" can "hardly be said to present meaningfully the story of this country's religious traditions."[44]

The 5–4 Supreme Court majority (which I joined) agreed. The five members of the majority wrote that the primary question was whether the county had a secular purpose in creating a public display of a document the primary significance of which was religious.[45] The majority said, "[m]anifesting a purpose to favor one faith over another or adherence to religion generally clashes with the 'understanding reached . . . after decades of religious war that liberty and social stability demand a religious tolerance that respects the religious views of all citizens.'"[46] The fact that initially the Ten Commandments alone made up the display; the fact that the courts had previously found that the revised display violated the Establishment Clause; the fact that the portions of the additional documents put next to it did not significantly change the appearance of the state's religious objectives; the fact that the state seemed to be looking for a way to avoid the holdings of the previous cases while maintaining its display; and various other facts related to the case[47] convinced the majority that the state's purpose was to create a display that was primarily religious in nature and favored some religions over others.

Justice Sandra Day O'Connor joined the majority, which besides myself included Justices Stevens, Souter, and Ginsburg, and wrote separately to express her views in greater detail.[48] She reiterated the basic values underlying the Religion Clauses. She said that:

> [T]he goal of the Clauses is clear: to carry out the Founders' plan of preserving religious liberty to the fullest extent possible in a pluralistic society. . . . Our guiding principle has been James Madison's— that "the Religion . . . of every man must be left to the conviction and conscience of every man." . . . [Government] may not prefer one religion over another or promote religion over nonbelief.[49]

She added that "given the history of this particular display of the Ten Commandments, the Court correctly finds an Establishment Clause violation."[50] "The purpose behind the counties' display . . . conveys an unmistakable message of endorsement" of religion to the reasonable observer.[51]

I found the second case, *Van Orden v. Perry*, more difficult. That case concerned a large granite monument bearing the text of the Ten Commandments on the grounds of the Texas State Capitol.[52] The case, I thought, was a "borderline" one. Indeed, if the relation between government and religion is one of separation but not one of mutual hostility and suspicion, judges will inevitably have to decide difficult borderline cases.[53] And in those cases, no exact formula can dictate a resolution. That fact— the absence of a bright-line, decision-determining rule, as I discussed earlier—means that the decision may well turn on the details of the case; and the judge must examine those details with care in light of the underlying values inherent within the Religion Clauses. I was the only Justice in the majority in both *Van Orden* and *McCreary*; in *Van Orden*, I voted with Chief Justice Rehnquist and Justices Scalia, Anthony Kennedy, and Thomas in upholding the Texas Ten Commandments display. How could I come to these two different conclusions?

Begin with the published text at issue, which here involved the same Ten Commandments as promulgated in *McCreary County*. The text of course carried a religious message. But, in my view, we also had to examine how the text was used. Was its display used (as the Kentucky display was used) to carry a primarily religious message? After all, the Ten Commandments also carry a *moral* message. It can also sometimes be used to carry a historical message about law. That is why it is displayed in dozens of courthouses throughout the nation (including the Supreme Court) without objection or suit.

Many features of the display in *Van Orden* suggested that it was being used to convey a primarily secular message.[54] For one, the tablets were donated by the Fraternal Order of Eagles, a civic and secular organization, as part of that group's efforts to help shape civic morality, and, in particular, its efforts to combat juvenile delinquency. A tablet on the display notes that the Eagles were the donors.[55] Compare those facts to the circumstances surrounding the display at issue in *McCreary County*, which was put up by the judiciary and not donated by a nongovernmental entity.

The Texas display also sat in a large park surrounding the Texas State Capitol. The park contained "17 monuments and 21 historical markers" commemorating sundry people, ideals, and events that compose Texan identity.[56] Those surroundings thus suggested a "moral" message reflecting the general "ideals" of Texans. Moreover, the display had remained in that place for forty years without challenge.[57] That fact suggested that few individuals, whatever their beliefs, understood the display as amounting in any significantly detrimental way to a government effort to favor or to disfavor any particular religious sect, or to work deterrence of any kind to religious or nonreligious belief. The Texas display was thus unlike the display in *McCreary County*, where a short (and stormy) history demonstrated the substantially religious objectives of those who mounted the Ten Commandments marker there. History in *McCreary County* indicated a governmental effort substantially to *promote religion*, not simply an effort primarily to *reflect* the *secular* impact of a religiously inspired document on history and culture.

Moreover, to reach the same conclusion in *Van Orden* as in *McCreary County* that the Ten Commandments display was unconstitutional, based solely upon the religious nature of the text, might well have encouraged disputes concerning the removal of long-standing depictions of the Ten Commandments from public buildings across the nation.[58] Such a result would have tended to create the very kind of religiously based divisiveness that the Establishment Clause seeks to avoid.[59] These circumstances led me to conclude that the Texas display served a mixed but primarily nonreligious purpose. It did not primarily advance or inhibit religion or excessively entangle the government with religion.

In reaching this conclusion, putting the Ten Commandments in *McCreary County* on one side of the constitutional line and the *Van Orden* display on the other, I relied less upon the literal application of any particular constitutional text or court-fashioned test than upon consideration of the basic purposes of the Religion Clauses themselves. The fact that the Texas display had stood uncontested for nearly two generations suggested to me that, as a practical matter of *degree*, the Texas display was unlikely to prove divisive, unlike the display in *McCreary County*. In my view, this matter of degree is critical in a borderline case.

In short, the values underlying the Religion Clauses reflect an effort to prevent social hostility based upon religion. In borderline cases like the two I have just discussed, judges can often find a workable way to implement that value over time by referring back to the constitutional provision's basic purpose, rather than relying on intermediate rules or broadly applicable, clear-cut tests.

With all three of these examples—*Noel Canning, Heller,* and *McCreary/Van Orden*—I have sought to illustrate how reliance on the traditional, broad range of interpretive tools can help judges maintain a workable Constitution. Only by doing so can we preserve a society in which people with diverse backgrounds and views can live peacefully among each other, supported by a democratic government that is empowered to promote the safety and welfare of all.

V

PARADIGM SHIFTS ON THE COURT

Philosophers of science have sometimes referred to major changes in the way scientists think about their fields as "paradigm shifts."[1] Copernicus's work, for example, eventually convinced astronomers to think of the sun—and not the earth—as the center of the solar system. Newton's views of particles and mechanics radically changed physicists' views of the nature of the universe. And Einstein again changed basic thinking about the scientific laws that govern that universe.

I do not think it is far-fetched to view major changes in the way the legal community thinks about the role of judges through a similar lens. Over its history, the nation has seen, from time to time, analogous changes in the way in which Supreme Court Justices have interpreted the law. In the latter nineteenth century and the early twentieth century, the Court emphasized the importance of the Constitution's protections of "property" and of freedom to "contract," and interpreted the Due Process Clause as imposing strong constraints upon the government's power to enact certain legislation, particularly legislation that would protect workers and the workplace. The Court at that time believed that the Constitution favored the protection of laissez-faire economic decision-making. During the late 1930s and the 1940s, the Court reversed course and tended to permit Congress and state legislatures to regulate the economy in this and many other ways. The Court believed that it ought not interfere with legislative efforts to enact social and economic regulation. During the 1950s and 1960s, the Court instead emphasized and read broadly many of the Constitution's protections of privacy, personal liberty, and other basic human rights. The Court ordered legal desegregation; it forbade physical maltreatment of those arrested for criminal behavior; and it held that most of the provisions of the federal Bill of Rights protected individuals from actions by state, as well as by federal, governments.

Are we now in the midst of another shift in "paradigm"—a shift in the direction of textualism, originalism, and the like? No one, I believe, should be certain about the answer to this question. Before explaining why, let me briefly describe the three paradigmatic changes I have just mentioned. This historical context will demonstrate that the Court's paradigm shifts throughout its history have always been guided by the exigencies and circumstances of the real world inhabited by the Justices.

19.

Three Paradigm Shifts

The *Lochner* Court

In 1905, the Court decided *Lochner v. New York*.[1] The case focused upon a New York statute that made it a crime to employ an individual in a bakery more than ten hours a day or sixty hours a week.[2] The question before the Court was whether this statute violated the Fourteenth Amendment's protection of "life, liberty, or property."[3] By a vote of 5–4, the Court held that it did.

The majority wrote that the "right to make a contract" in relation to an individual's business and the right to "purchase or to sell labor" were parts of the "liberty" that the Fourteenth Amendment protected.[4] Although states may, in the exercise of their "police powers," enact legislation designed to secure "the morals, the health, or the safety of the people," the legislation had to be "a fair, reasonable, and appropriate exercise of the police power" and not "an unreasonable, unnecessary, and arbitrary interference with the right of the individual . . . to enter into those contracts in relation to labor which may seem to him appropriate or necessary for the support of himself and his family."[5] The Court reasoned that bakers were "not wards of the State"; rather they were "equal in intelligence to men in other trades or manual occupations," and they were "able to assert their rights and care for themselves without the protecting arm of the State."[6] It was not necessary, the Court decided, to curtail their working hours in order to prevent "material danger to the public health, or to the health of the employees."[7] Hence, the Court concluded that New York's law was not justified and that it violated the Fourteenth Amendment.

The opinion drew two strong dissents. The first, from Justice Harlan, referred to numerous articles showing that bakers *did* run special health risks and *did* need the state's protection.[8] The second, by Justice Holmes, has become a famous opinion. There, Justice Holmes explained why democratically elected state legislatures should generally have broad discretion to enact these kinds of measures.[9] "[S]tate constitutions and state laws may regulate life in many ways which" a court "might think as injudicious or . . . tyrannical . . . and which, equally with this, interfere with the liberty to contract."[10] But "the Fourteenth Amendment does not enact Mr. Herbert Spencer's Social Statics. . . . [A] constitution is not intended to embody a particular economic theory, whether of paternalism . . . or of laissez faire."[11]

In 1923, the Court decided *Adkins v. Children's Hospital*,[12] another case emblematic of the *Lochner* era. There, the Court struck down a District of Columbia statute fixing minimum wages for women and children. Justice George Sutherland, writing for a five-member majority, reaffirmed that "freedom of contract" was part of the liberty that the Constitution granted the individual.[13] Freedom of contract was subject to restraint, he wrote, but restraint was the exception. Here, he reasoned, the restraint did not fit into a category of restraint previously blessed by the Court: It was not limited to a business "impressed with a public interest"; it was not necessary to preserve the health of employees; there was no special emergency justifying the restraint; and there was no special gender-based problem.[14] The Court reasoned that it could not "accept the doctrine that women of mature age . . . require or may be subjected to restrictions upon their liberty of contract which could not lawfully be imposed in the case of men under similar circumstances. . . . [A]dult women . . . are legally as capable of contracting for themselves as men."[15] And so the Court held that the D.C. minimum wage statute violated the Fourteenth Amendment.

Chief Justice Taft (joined by Justice Edward Sanford) dissented.[16] He suggested that women workers may not have "a full level of equality of choice with their employer" and must accept "pretty much anything that is offered."[17] Like Justice Holmes in *Lochner*, Taft thought that the matter was up to the legislature, not the Court, protesting that "it is not the function of this Court to hold congressional acts invalid simply because they are passed to carry out economic views which the Court believes are unwise or unsound."[18]

Between the beginning of the twentieth century and the mid-1930s, the Court also struck down laws making it easier to organize labor unions[19] and laws regulating prices[20]—cases that further illustrate the mindset of the *Lochner* Court. For example, in *Ribnik v. McBride*,[21] the Court agreed that a legislature could limit prices where a business "is affected with a public interest," but that that category did not include "prices for food or clothing, of house rental or of wages."[22] Justice Harlan Fiske Stone, dissenting, thought that "regulation is within a state's power whenever any combination of circumstances seriously curtails the regulative force of competition, so that buyers or sellers are placed at such a disadvantage in the bargaining struggle that a legislature might reasonably anticipate serious consequences to the community as a whole."[23] Justice Holmes, in an earlier case,[24] held to his view that the powers the Constitution granted to Congress (and the state legislatures) were broad. He added that judges were not always well suited to determine what kind of product constituted a public necessity. In respect to theater tickets—which the Court held were "superfluous" and not a "necessity"—Holmes wrote, "We have not that respect for art that is one of the glories of France. But to many people, the superfluous is the necessary, and it seems to me that Government does not go beyond its sphere in attempting to make life livable for them."[25]

Now, here is the important point: Consider what was happening economically to the nation between the end of the Civil War and the First World War.[26] When *Lochner* and *Adkins* were decided, the nation had emerged from the nineteenth century with enormous economic strength. Before the Civil War, this nation was a poor country, with few rich and many so poor they could not easily find schooling, build churches, or rest assured of adequate food and clothing. After the Civil War, the Union created a strong manufacturing base and a rapidly industrializing set of urban centers. Westward expansion—fueled by the 1869 construction of the Transcontinental Railroad—prompted a limitless conception of

American growth and potential. A pre–Civil War country that had been one of the poorest in the world became one of the richest.

Factories, farms, ranches, and mines proliferated as the race to develop and refine raw material carried the nation through the Gilded Age. Americans lured west by the promise of land through the 1862 Homestead Act rapidly and often forcefully displaced Native American populations in the hunt for economic prosperity. Tremendous wealth mixed with tremendous inequality, resulting in both aggregate increases in national wealth and the rise of a new class of "robber barons." Though the Panics of 1873 and 1893 caused deep depressions throughout the country, they were ultimately short disruptions in a half century of almost unparalleled growth in the American economy.

Americans were learning to live in a world that looked and felt incredibly different from the Civil War era that they had recently left behind. From inventions such as motorcars and electricity, to methods of production such as assembly lines and all sorts of mechanical devices, to methods of finance and business organization such as the limited liability company, Americans were graced with developments that many credited with making the United States the richest country in the world.[27] By 1914, Americans enjoyed a per capita income of $346, compared with $244 in Britain, $184 in Germany, and $153 in France.[28] The extraordinary economic growth between the end of the Civil War and 1914 benefited the working class as well as business owners: There was steady real wage growth from 1860 to 1918 among unskilled workers.[29] In vaulting ahead of traditional Great Powers in manufacturing, energy consumption, population growth, and aggregate growth, Americans justifiably admired their economic progress.

Not surprisingly, many thought that the growth in income and wealth was in large part due to the security of property and contract guaranteed by the Constitution and its laissez-faire underpinnings. The laissez-faire zeitgeist was reflected in the views of prominent thought leaders of the era, who fervently believed that free markets were indispensable to American growth. Historian and political scientist Robert McCloskey cites, for instance, William Graham Sumner, a prominent Yale professor, Stephen J. Field, a long-tenured Justice on the Supreme Court, and Andrew Carnegie, the Scottish steel titan, as exemplars of the public figures who carried forth the banner of laissez-faire through the Gilded Age and beyond.[30] Across academia, law, and industry, prominent members of the informed public were wholly supportive of laissez-faire, and believed that the Constitution affirmed their economic views.

Is it surprising, then, that many Supreme Court Justices who had seen this growth believed in 1905, when *Lochner* was decided, that the Constitution emphasized the protection of property and contract, and that courts were better suited to protect those rights than legislatures? The Court was certainly not against all governmental regulation. Congress successfully enacted laws establishing the Interstate Commerce Act of 1887 (regulating railroads) and the Sherman Antitrust Act of 1890 (protecting competition), for example. But a majority of the Justices likely believed that the American economy would develop better with less government intervention.[31]

Historians and legal academics have long criticized the *Lochner* Court's reasoning and the subsequent refinement of its laissez-faire principles in cases like *Adkins*.[32] The Justices in *Lochner*, however, may have viewed themselves as maintaining a system that they believed was working well for the most part for most Americans. Some of the Justices may have believed that legislative regulation, if allowed, would kill the goose that was laying golden eggs. The Court's paradigm in *Lochner* can be seen as an effort to minimize disruption of a system that had generated significant national prosperity.[33]

The America of 1923, when *Adkins* was decided, was similar in many respects to the America of 1905. Though two decades of Progressive-inspired reforms had brought additional government regulation to bear on the national economy, many Americans remained adherents of laissez-faire. Electrification and motorization had turned sleepy towns into well-lit, motorcar-heavy cities. Frederick Taylor's 1911 *Principles of Scientific Management* gave birth to a renewed focus on industrial efficiency. Ford Motor Company had separately pioneered the assembly line for over a decade, with tremendous increases in manufacturing output.[34] Though the immediate aftermath of World War I had brought about a temporary economic depression, the economy had come back to life and was about to enter into the "Roaring Twenties" with renewed vigor. By campaigning on a "return to normalcy" after World War I and the Spanish flu outbreak, Warren Harding won the popular vote in the 1920 presidential election by a landslide.[35] "Property," "contract," and "laissez-faire" remained the watchwords of American economic development.

The Justices in 1923 were eager to preserve those laissez-faire principles. Robert Post, writing about the Court during the tenure of Chief Justice Taft in the 1920s, describes its members as seeking to "restor[e] economic liberty to the center of the American constitutional order" by protecting "a core realm of economic and moral freedom that it believed lay at the foundation of the American republic."[36] Chief Justice Taft himself—a former U.S. president—had harsh words for much legislation, calling it a production of "gusty and unthinking passions of temporary majorities."[37] Taft, a "man filled with practical common sense,"[38] sought to harmonize both public sentiment and what he viewed as property's necessary role in sustaining material growth by re-centering laissez-faire and reviving *Lochner*. The Court may not have needed to try to preserve the proverbial goose that had been laying golden eggs. But the Court found in the Constitution encouragement to make that effort.

The Court's decision in *Adkins* shows its commitment to what then-president Warren G. Harding called a "return to normalcy." Minimum wage laws were cropping up throughout the country in the wake of World War I, and many in the public viewed *Adkins* as providing a litmus test for the new Justices appointed by President Harding.[39] And though Justice Sutherland did not make moral arguments about perceived policy problems with the minimum wage law, a good portion of the general public at the time still believed that laissez-faire in this context was preferable to government regulation.[40] The *Adkins* opinion captured the spirit of the 1920s in a way that was later echoed by President Calvin Coolidge: "Government price fixing, once started, has alike no justice and no end. It is an economic folly from which this country has every right to be spared."[41]

I have summarized some of the history of the laissez-faire era not to suggest that this view of the history is incontrovertibly true, or that the Justices did not decide these cases based on their good-faith views of what the law commanded. Justices in the majority may well have believed that they were merely articulating what the law is, not what it ought to be. But, as I discuss below, the approach taken in cases like *Lochner* and *Adkins* has been long abandoned and discredited. I relate this history to show that these doctrines that we now consider antiquated did not spring out of thin air. Rather they evolved in response to what the Justices viewed as pressing, contemporary problems of national significance. And it may well have seemed appropriate to emphasize the Constitution's words "contract" and "property," and other constitutional doctrines that would in their view help to preserve the nation's prosperity. But as times changed, that enthusiasm did not last.

The New Deal Court

By the mid-1930s, the Court had begun to change—and to change radically. The country was in the midst of a depression.[42] President Franklin Roosevelt proposed legislation that he hoped would bring the economy back to life, but the Court struck down many of those measures as unconstitutional. For example, the Court found unconstitutional, as an excessive delegation of power to the president, legislation that would have restricted oil production and thereby raised the price of oil.[43] It held that Congress could not provide a compulsory pension scheme for railroad workers.[44] It invalidated a statute regulating prices and wages in the coal industry.[45] As it had done in *Adkins*, it again struck down a statute setting minimum wages for women.[46] And it struck down, as a misuse of the taxing power, the New Deal's Agricultural Adjustment Act, which was designed to give farmers more purchasing power and to raise agricultural prices.[47]

Faced with an intransigent Court, President Roosevelt then introduced his "court packing" plan in February 1937.[48] That plan, if enacted by Congress, would have given the president the power to appoint one new Justice for every Justice over the age of seventy years and six months who had not retired.[49] New appointments, the president hoped, would switch the direction of the Court toward validating New Deal legislation.

Though Congress did not enact the "court packing" plan, the Court nevertheless did change direction. In 1937, the Court upheld as constitutional a Washington State statute fixing minimum wages for women.[50] In the process, it overruled *Adkins*. A few weeks later, in *NLRB v. Jones & Laughlin Steel Corp.*,[51] it upheld the National Labor Relations Act, which allowed, and strongly supported through regulation, employee unionization. Soon thereafter, several of the older, more conservative Justices retired, President Roosevelt appointed new members, and New Deal legislation (as well as social and economic regulatory legislation) was upheld as constitutional.

For present purposes, the most important change was in the Court's basic approach to interpreting the Constitution. Unlike the *Lochner* Court, the New Deal Court did not find in the Constitution special protection for contract, property, and laissez-faire. Rather, it took a view that many have called "judicial restraint": The view that the legislatures, not the courts, should decide policy matters. As explicated in a famous footnote in the 1938 case of *United States v. Carolene Products Co.*,[52] members of that Court believed that the judiciary should only rarely hold that a statute was unconstitutional.

Oliver Wendell Holmes had foreseen this view in his *Lochner* dissent when he wrote: "I think that the word 'liberty' in the Fourteenth Amendment is perverted when it is held to prevent the natural outcome of a dominant opinion, unless it can be said that a rational and fair man necessarily would admit that the statute proposed would infringe fundamental principles as they have been understood by the traditions of our people and our law."[53] Over a quarter century later, Justice Owen Roberts wrote along the same lines in upholding a New York price-fixing statute, saying: "If the laws passed are seen to have a reasonable relation to a proper legislative purpose . . . the requirements of due process are satisfied."[54]

As generally understood by the public, judicial restraint urges judges considering constitutional questions to grant substantial deference to the views of the elected branches and invalidate their actions only when constitutional limits have clearly been violated.[55] It is strongly associated with the views of Justices Holmes, Brandeis, and Frankfurter. The "conservatives" of the early twentieth century strongly objected to this approach, but by the late 1930s, they were in dissent. Justice Sutherland, dissenting in *West Coast Hotel Co. v. Parrish*,[56] the case that overruled *Adkins* and upheld a minimum wage law, wrote: "What a court is to do . . . is to *declare the law as written*, leaving it to the people themselves to make such changes as new circumstances may require. The meaning of the constitution is fixed when it is adopted, and it is not different at any subsequent time when a court has occasion to pass upon it."[57]

Here is a paradigm shift indeed. How did it come to pass? Perhaps in part because new Justices replaced old ones. Perhaps because the new ones thought that economic conditions played an important role in constitutional interpretation. Perhaps in part because the political left had long seen a "conservative Court" as posing an obstacle to social legislation. Perhaps in part because a president and Congress from the political left had replaced those from the political right. But in significant part because times had changed. A legal approach that might have worked reasonably well when the country experienced phenomenal growth did not work well when the country faced economic disaster.

By the 1930s, few thought that laissez-faire was flawless; many were now willing to embrace laws once derided as "economic folly" by President Coolidge and the *Lochner* Court. After a sixfold increase in the Dow Jones Industrial Average from 1921 to September 1929, the New York Stock Exchange declined dramatically in value over the next few years. By the middle of 1932, the Dow Jones had dropped almost 90 percent from its historic peak.[58] Economic calamity was not limited to the financial sector; the unemployment rate reached over 24 percent in 1932, and the gross national product fell by 30 percent from 1929 to 1933. The Great Depression was officially in full swing.[59]

The causes of the Great Depression were myriad, but popular blame at the time focused on financial greed, agricultural collapse in the American heartland, and protectionist tariffs. President Roosevelt's first inaugural address blamed the "[p]ractices of the unscrupulous money changers," or bankers, for the perils of the Depression.[60] A severe drought in 1930 devastated the prairies and led to enormous human displacement and agricultural desolation—events dramatized in John Steinbeck's *The*

Grapes of Wrath.[61] Congress's attempt to implement protectionist policies through the Smoot-Hawley Tariff of 1930 only prompted retaliatory tariffs from other countries, leading to a collapse in consumer spending.[62] Shantytowns—labeled by Democrats as "Hoovervilles" for the embattled president—sprang up throughout the nation as visual reminders of economic failure.

Whatever the causes of the Great Depression, society was ready for an alternative to the *Lochner*-era status quo. Who could believe in that moment that it was critical to maintain deregulation and laissez-faire as constitutional principles? Indeed, if those policies had resulted in economic collapse, some thought that perhaps increased government oversight and control over the economy would provide a way out of economic stagnation. Franklin Roosevelt, the decisive winner of the 1932 presidential election, campaigned on an expansive role for the federal government and collective action supplementing individual initiative.[63]

The support for this view was sufficient for Chief Justice Hughes to write this striking passage for the Court in *West Coast Hotel*:

> There is an additional and compelling consideration which recent economic experience has brought into a strong light. The exploitation of a class of workers who are in an unequal position with respect to bargaining power and are thus relatively defenseless against the denial of a living wage is not only detrimental to their health and well being, but casts a direct burden for their support upon the community. . . . We may take judicial notice of the unparalleled demands for relief which arose during the recent period of depression and still continue to an alarming extent.[64]

In *Dobbs*, the opinion of Chief Justice Roberts concurring in the judgment recognized *West Coast Hotel* as "part of a sea change in this Court's interpretation of the Constitution," one that was "issued against a backdrop of unprecedented economic despair that focused attention on the fundamental flaws of existing precedent."[65]

In a word, the Supreme Court—faced with these exceptionally challenging economic circumstances and a public newly hostile to laissez-faire—adapted its methodology to allow the Roosevelt administration to experiment with solutions to the Great Depression. The Justices might well have thought that there was sufficient support among the public for the change. Some might have thought that the public needs a Constitution that it believes will work.

The Warren Court

By the 1950s, the Court again changed methodological direction. Under the leadership of Chief Justice Earl Warren, it abandoned "judicial restraint" in part, and instead emphasized those parts of the Constitution that protected human rights, including the right of every person to be treated with equal dignity before the law. Justice Brandeis, though writing before the Warren Court era, expressed its methodology well when he compared, on the one hand, the "general limitations . . . embodied in the due process clauses of the Fifth and Fourteenth Amendments," which do not forbid governments "from meeting modern conditions by regulations which '[in the past] probably would have been rejected as arbitrary and oppressive,'" with, on the other hand, those "[c]lauses guaranteeing to the individual protection against specific abuses of power, [which] must have a similar capacity of adaptation to a changing world."[66] Thus, the Warren Court's fervent protection of individual rights nevertheless left government free to experiment on economic and social legislation.

The Warren Court's major decisions are well known. It held racial segregation unconstitutional by overruling *Plessy v. Ferguson*,[67] which had held that the Constitution's Equal Protection Clause meant that government could maintain separate but "equal" access for the races to transportation and other government facilities. Instead, the Warren Court replaced *Plessy* with *Brown v. Board of Education*,[68] which held that racial segregation violated the Constitution's Equal Protection Clause.

It held that most of the limitations contained in the Bill of Rights applied to the states as well as to the federal government.[69]

It held that government could not draw electoral boundaries in ways that gave one person more voting power than another. The Constitution required "one person" to have "one vote," not more.[70]

It held that the Fifth Amendment requires police and prosecutors to inform arrested persons that they have a right not to answer questions but to remain silent.[71] And that they have a right to a lawyer.[72]

Together with its successor, the Burger Court, it held that the Constitution protected an individual's privacy, that government could not prevent the sale of contraceptives,[73] and that the Constitution protected a woman's right to have an abortion.[74]

These holdings do not reflect "judicial restraint." Indeed, in light of these cases, one might consider the Warren Court's basic approach—at least in the area of civil rights—as a paradigm shift. For present purposes, I would again ask about the relationship between that shift and informed public opinion. Certainly, many of the Warren Court's holdings were unpopular. Some who study the Court have criticized it as "activist."[75] Still, the main shift in outlook came at the beginning. For decades before *Brown*, the South had practiced Jim Crow segregation, and the Court had done nothing about it. Did new appointments, new Justices, make all the difference? I think not.

For one thing, ever since the 1930s, foreign affairs and then war had begun to make clear to Americans the evils of segregation in the South. Hitler would ask his audiences: How can America criticize our treatment of the Jews? Do you know how the American South treats Black men and women?[76] During World War II, many Americans became aware of the heroic fighting by "Black" brigades—segregated units made up of African American soldiers.[77]

And after the war, the Allied nations emphasized the fact that they had fought for freedom (and won). President Harry Truman, Dean Acheson, George Marshall, and others (including from those nations that had been defeated) were determined to follow policies that emphasized 1) democracy, 2) basic human rights, 3) equality before the law, 4) increased free trade, and 5) collaboration through international agreements and organizations such as the United Nations.[78] And they signed agreements to this effect.[79]

At the same time, Communist nations and organizations criticized the United States for not living up to its fine words. And American organizations active at the time of the Cold War made a similar point. The NAACP, for example, filed at the United Nations in 1947 a document (supervised by W.E.B. Du Bois) called "An Appeal to the World."[80] It argued that it "is not Russia that threatens the United States so much as Mississippi."[81] Criticisms of this kind spread throughout the world, leading some historians to describe postwar America as highly interested in "defining and defending democratic principles."[82]

Is it surprising that, in this environment, the Warren Court emphasized the protection of individual rights? In *Brown*, it explicitly declined to "turn the clock back to 1868 when the [Fourteenth] Amendment was adopted or even to 1896 when *Plessy v. Ferguson* was written" in interpreting the scope of the Constitution.[83]

To be sure, *Brown* was unpopular in the South, where "Impeach Earl Warren" signs were ubiquitous. The South resisted integrated education.[84] Some school districts closed their schoolhouse doors, rather than follow court orders to integrate. Congress did not help the Court. In 1957, President Dwight Eisenhower sent one thousand paratroopers from Fort Bragg to assure integration of Little Rock's schools. But the troops could not stay forever. And, when they left, Governor Orval Faubus closed the schools.

But it was too late. This was the era of Martin Luther King Jr., the Montgomery Bus Boycott, the Freedom Riders, and the Selma-to-Montgomery marches. The nation had become aware of what segregation meant. And the nation insisted upon change. It is in this environment that the Court initially decided, and then repeatedly did its best to enforce, *Brown*.

I saw the Court trying to abolish segregation when I was a law clerk at the Court, working for Justice Arthur Goldberg. That Court in 1964 decided *Heart of Atlanta Motel, Inc. v. United States*,[85] upholding the constitutionality of Title II of the Civil Rights Act of 1964, which forbade segregation in restaurants, hotels, and other places of public accommodation.[86] The desegregation efforts, and their support among much of the general public, may have influenced both the Court's approach to that case as well as its drive to enforce the Constitution's criminal procedural rights and other basic human rights.

Contemporaneous observers saw a connection between the Court's criminal justice rulings and the Civil Rights Movement. That connection may have influenced the Court in its efforts to expand the Constitution's human rights protections, extending them to encompass state as well as federal actions. Its redistricting cases and other human rights cases headed off more radical critiques of American democracy and reflected American ideals of the rule of law. So did their increased protections for domestic privacy.

In discussing the *Lochner* Court, the New Deal Court, and the Warren Court periods, I do not mean to suggest that external political circumstances directly motivated the Court or that the Court should function as nothing more than a glorified public opinion pollster. The Justices no doubt believed that they were correctly interpreting the law. In writing their opinions they would consider the text, history, and the structure of the law. They would seek workable solutions. But, robes aside, the Supreme Court is not a monastery. The Justices are not computer scientists. And legal questions are not mathematical problems capable of being worked out with exactitude. The Court is a coordinate branch of our federal government, and the Justices are human beings with limited time, resources, and perspectives. The Constitution contains phrases written at high levels of abstraction. Cases interpreting those phrases raise complex issues. Precisely how the public will understand or characterize a case result is often difficult to predict. And a decision will often have broader ramifications than even the most diligent Justice can foresee. Justices bring with them different backgrounds, different experiences, and, on occasion, somewhat different general moral understandings. All these factors, and likely others, can play a role in how a judge approaches an interpretive question. Here I have simply pointed out that the "times"—the nation's prevailing attitudes—also have an effect on the Court, as they do on all other aspects of American life. No one can say precisely how public views and understandings, the nation's problems, or current notions about solutions affect the basic attitude of the Court. But I do believe that slowly, over time, they have an effect. The great constitutional scholar Paul Freund said that the Court "should never be influenced by the weather of the day but inevitably . . . will be influenced by the climate of the era."[87]

The Court needs public support. And in the three eras that I have discussed, the Court received sufficient public support that it was able to bring about a basic paradigm shift.

20.

Are We Undergoing the Next Paradigm Shift?

Yes

In addition to *Bruen*, *Dobbs*, and other recent cases described in this book, the Court leaned heavily in a textualist direction in the opinions written in a 2023 environmental law case, *Sackett v. EPA*,[1] and heavily in an originalist direction in opinions written in a 2023 affirmative action case, *Students for Fair Admissions, Inc. v. President and Fellows of Harvard College*.[2] That begs the question: Are we undergoing another paradigm shift, similar to those I have just discussed, but toward textualism and originalism? There are some reasons for believing so. Many of the cases and examples I have discussed move the Court in that direction—often leaving me (along with a few other Justices) in dissent. Majority opinions these days argue strongly in favor of adopting textualist and originalist methodologies. Three of the four newest appointments to the Court have argued strongly in their favor.[3] And these methods were likely necessary to the result in cases such as *Bruen* and *Dobbs*. Judges, as I have stressed, do not think of themselves as deciding cases because they "like" the result or just think it "good." They believe that they are deciding on the basis of reason, as applied to facts and lower court findings, and as deriving strength from reasoned approaches to questions of law. They need an approach based on reason; and textualism and originalism at first blush appear to provide such an approach.

Moreover, textualism and originalism come in various shapes and sizes.

I have tended to assume absolute versions (i.e., exclusive reliance upon language) when I have criticized those approaches here. But judges could emphasize language and history, as those approaches suggest, while being willing to embrace purposes, consequences, and other interpretive tools as well, balancing them together with language and history.

In *Sackett*, the Court interpreted a provision of the Clean Water Act prohibiting the "discharge of any pollutant"[4] into "navigable waters"[5] without a permit from the Environmental Protection Agency or the Army Corps of Engineers.[6] The act defines "navigable waters" as "waters of the United States."[7] The question in front of the Court was how to define "waters of the United States."

That question is trickier than it might at first appear. The Mississippi River is clearly part of the "waters of the United States," while a small puddle clearly is not. But what about something in between, like a stream that trickles into a big river or a wetland that is adjacent to a large lake? The text of the Clean Water Act will not get you very far. It makes clear that "waters of the United States"[8] includes "navigable waters." But it does not go much further.

Yet all nine of the Justices on the Court purported to find an answer in the text. The majority emphasized the statute's use of the plural term "waters." Relying on several dictionaries, the majority noted that the plural form of the word "waters" typically signifies "relatively permanent, standing or continuously flowing bodies of water" such as "streams, oceans, rivers, and lakes."[9] That understanding of "waters of the United States" would seem to exclude wetlands, which are neither continuously flowing nor navigable. But the majority clarified that "at least some wetlands must qualify" as "waters of the United States."[10] One might have said that that is because dumping pollutants into some wetlands will end up polluting flowing waters as well. Or, one might have said that because the statute has long and near universally been thought to regulate at least some wetlands.[11] But the majority did not emphasize these purposive and historical points.

Rather the majority turned to the text of a minor amendment to the Clean Water Act. That 1977 amendment allows states to administer permitting programs on behalf of the Army Corps of Engineers for discharges of materials like sand and dirt into the "waters of the United States"— *except* when those discharges are made into traditional navigable waters, *"including wetlands adjacent thereto."*[12] That provision, the majority concluded, made sense only if "waters of the United States" includes wetlands that are adjacent to "navigable waters."[13] But what, then, constitutes an "adjacent wetland"?

Again relying on dictionaries, the majority adopted a narrow interpretation of the word "adjacent." While dictionaries defined the word to mean either "contiguous" or "near," the majority settled on the former definition.[14] In other words, a wetland is "adjacent" when it "has a continuous surface connection" with a traditional navigable body of water. It is not sufficient that a wetland is merely *near* a navigable body of water, separated, say, by a sand dune or a ditch or a berm.[15]

Four Justices disagreed with that analysis. But they, too, made primarily a textual argument. They would have relied on the dictionary's broader meaning of "adjacent," defining it as synonymous with "near."[16] Under that definition, wetlands that are close to, but not necessarily touching, navigable waters are part of the "waters of the United States."[17]

Those four Justices, then, did not take issue with the majority's interpretive approach. They instead wrote primarily about the ancillary 1977 amendment to the act. They referred to dictionaries to determine the meaning of "waters of the United States."[18] And to the extent they pointed to the EPA's and Army Corps of Engineers' long-standing interpretations of the statute, they did so only to debate the "ordinary meaning" of the phrase "waters of the United States."[19] But, of course, they might have emphasized other matters. They might have thought that neither the text of the statute nor dictionaries do much to illuminate the meaning of the ambiguous, broadly worded phrase "waters of the United States." They might have then emphasized the Clean Water Act's basic objective of "restor[ing] and maintain[ing] the chemical, physical, and biological integrity of the Nation's waters."[20] They might have emphasized the fact that, in 1972, when Congress passed the act, the nation's waters were in crisis: Americans watched on television as the Cuyahoga River burned and a massive oil spill spread in the Santa Barbara Channel.[21] There was an overwhelming sense among lawmakers that something had to be done.[22] It was against this backdrop that Congress made it illegal to discharge pollutants into the "waters of the United States," with the ultimate objective of restoring and maintaining the integrity of those waters.

They might also have emphasized the fact that reading "waters of the United States" to encompass wetlands that are close to, but not necessarily touching, navigable waters is consistent with the Clean Water Act's objective. As the Court had previously recognized, wetlands "filter and purify water draining into adjacent bodies of water" and "prevent flooding and erosion."[23] That filtering and purification process happens even when wetlands do not have a continuous surface connection with nearby bodies of water.[24] Oftentimes, all it takes to block a continuous surface connection between a wetland and a waterway is the presence of man-made dikes and levees or natural berms and dunes that build up gradually over time. And while these barriers prevent a continuous *surface* connection, they do not prevent subsurface connections around the barriers under the ground. Protecting the "waters of the United States" from pollution, then, requires protecting nearby wetlands.

They might have emphasized that precedent, along with decades of EPA and Army Corps practice, confirm that the "waters of the United States" include nearby wetlands. In 1985, the Supreme Court decided *United States v. Riverside Bayview Homes, Inc.*,[25] wherein it recognized that determining where water ends and wetlands begin "is often no easy task."[26] The Court explained that "between open waters and dry land may lie . . . a huge array of areas that are not wholly aquatic but nevertheless fall short of being dry land."[27] Given the EPA's and the Army Corps' "technical expertise" on the matter, the Court opted to defer to their reasoned conclusion that they had jurisdiction over wetlands that "may affect the water quality of adjacent lakes, rivers, and streams even when the waters of those bodies do not actually inundate the wetlands."[28] And so, for forty-five years, the agencies continued to read the Clean Water Act as giving them authority over wetlands that are near navigable waters but are separated only by a dike, levee, berm, or dune.[29] Like the Court in *Riverside Bayview*, the four Justices concurring only in the Court's judgment in *Sackett* might have simply deferred to the agencies' long-standing and reasonable reading of the Clean Water Act,[30] which aligns with the statute's purpose.

In *Students for Fair Admissions*, the Court considered whether the race-conscious admissions policies of Harvard College and the University of North Carolina violated Title VI and the Equal Protection Clause, respectively. Since 1995, the Court has evaluated all racial classifications (whether they intend to burden or benefit a particular group) under strict scrutiny, requiring any race-conscious admissions policy to be narrowly tailored and used to further "compelling governmental interests."[31] In *Regents of the University of California v. Bakke*,[32] Justice Lewis Powell had argued that achieving diversity in education was a compelling interest for the purposes of strict scrutiny.[33] A majority of the Court adopted this position in 2003 but emphasized that racial quotas or automatic "bumps" for underrepresented minorities were impermissible ways of pursuing that interest.[34] In the years that followed, the Court maintained this approach, permitting college admissions programs that used race as a plus in the course of holistically considering an individual applicant.[35]

Students for Fair Admissions applied a more stringent version of strict scrutiny. It held that Harvard's and UNC's admissions policies were unlawful. The Equal Protection Clause, on its face, does not seem to furnish a clear answer as to whether race-conscious admissions policies are constitutional. For one thing, the clause does not mention race. For another, the clause was enacted in part to ensure that formerly enslaved African Americans were treated equivalently to white people under the law, suggesting the appropriateness of at least some race-conscious remedies to historic discrimination.[36] Nevertheless, Chief Justice Roberts's opinion for a Court majority, Justice Thomas's concurrence, and the two dissenting opinions in *Students for Fair Admissions* all relied heavily on text and history to find their answer to the legality of the universities' affirmative action policies at issue.

Citing the enactment debates over the Fourteenth Amendment, Chief Justice Roberts's majority opinion observed that the Equal Protection Clause was intended to hold "over every American citizen, without regard to color, the protecting shield of law" and stood for the principle that "any law which operates upon one man [should] operate *equally* upon all."[37] While the Court "failed to live up to the Clause's core commitments" in *Plessy v. Ferguson*,[38] it corrected course in *Brown v. Board of Education*[39] and "set firmly on the path of invalidating all *de jure* racial discrimination by the States and Federal Government."[40] The majority explained that in light of this historical context, any racial classifications in higher education—even if intended to help minority applicants and promote diversity—had to survive a scrutiny that was so strict that few, if any, could survive it. Because the policies at issue in *Students for Fair Admissions* did not further "interests" that could be "subjected to meaningful judicial review," and because the schools "fail[ed] to articulate a meaningful connection between the means they employ[ed] and the goals they pursue[d]," they were unlawful.[41]

Justice Thomas's concurrence began with the observation that the Fourteenth Amendment "ensures racial equality *with no textual reference to race whatsoever.*"[42] It is true, said Justice Thomas, that some legislation passed in the wake of the Civil War might have "targeted race" in an effort to assist formerly enslaved people with the transition to freedom, but unlike affirmative action programs, those laws sought to "remedy a race-based injury that [the government] ha[d] inflicted" through slavery.[43] "Most notably," continued Justice Thomas, early civil rights laws "stated that the basic civil rights of citizenship shall be secured 'without respect to race or color,'" strongly supporting a color-blind vision of the Equal Protection Clause.[44]

Justice Sotomayor's and Justice Ketanji Brown Jackson's dissents reached a different conclusion. But in doing so, they relied, to a considerable extent, upon text and upon related history. As Justice Sotomayor explained, "[t]he text and history of the Fourteenth Amendment makes clear that the Equal Protection Clause permits race-conscious measures" because affirmative action "helps equalize opportunity and advances [diversity] objectives by increasing the number of underrepresented racial minorities on college campuses."[45] Justice Jackson, too, extensively canvassed nineteenth- and twentieth-century American history in observing the persistence of "race-linked obstacles that the law (and private parties) laid down to hinder the progress and prosperity of Black people."[46] To "say that anyone is now victimized if a college considers whether [this] legacy of discrimination has unequally advantaged its applicants," wrote Justice Jackson, "fails to acknowledge the well-documented 'intergenerational transmission of inequality' that still plagues our citizenry."[47]

As in *Sackett*, the dissenters in *Students for Fair Admissions* did not take serious issue with the majority's (or Justice Thomas's) methodological approach. Instead, they deployed similar techniques to reach a different conclusion about what the Equal Protection Clause meant. Perhaps they could have focused more heavily upon other considerations, such as purpose. As I wrote in my dissent in *Parents Involved in Community Schools v. Seattle School District No. 1*,[48] a case about a race-conscious primary school assignment policy, the "basic objective of those who wrote the Equal Protection Clause" was to "forbid[] practices that lead to racial exclusion."[49] Interpreting the clause with this anti-exclusionary purpose in mind permits a distinction between "the use of race-conscious criteria in defiance of that purpose, namely to keep the races apart, and the use of race-conscious criteria to further that purpose, namely to bring the races together."[50] As to the latter, the clause might be read to allow race-conscious policies—not only to remedy past discrimination against racial minorities but also to facilitate the myriad "educational and democratic" objectives that flow from a diverse student body.[51] In *Gratz v. Bollinger*,[52] an affirmative action case involving the University of Michigan's undergraduate admissions policy, Justice Ginsburg made the same point.[53]

As Alexis de Tocqueville observed almost two centuries ago, "[t]he most formidable of all the ills which threaten the future of the Union" is that the Black and white races "are fastened to each other without intermingling," and are "alike unable to separate entirely or to combine."[54] These concerns remain salient: at the "peak of desegregation in 1988," 37 percent of

Black students attended majority-white schools, but by 2018, that number had declined to 19 percent.[55] Similarly, in 1988, only 63 percent of Black students attended predominantly nonwhite schools, whereas by 2018, that number had grown to 81 percent.[56] Reading the Equal Protection Clause with an eye toward cultivating diversity in education—from preschool to college admissions—provides an antidote to the myriad threats posed by racial separation.

There is adequate precedential authority for this purposive approach. Writing in 1961, Justice John Marshall Harlan II observed that "[t]he regime of a free society needs room for vast experimentation."[57] He cautioned against "stop[ping] experimentation and the testing of new decrees and controls," which he feared would "deprive society of a needed versatility."[58] He thus argued that the Fourteenth Amendment should be interpreted in a "living" way, such that "it guarantees basic rights, not because they have become petrified as of any one time, but because [the Constitution] follows the advancing standards of a free society as to what is deemed reasonable and right."[59] A "new decision," he explained, "must take 'its place in relation to what went before and further [cut] a channel for what is to come.'"[60] Considered under Justice Harlan's framework, the policies at issue in *Students for Fair Admissions* were lawful—indeed commendable—experiments that sought to pursue the Fourteenth Amendment's promise of racial integration and all the benefits that flow from it.

The dissenting Justices in *Sackett* and *Students for Fair Admissions* noticed and touched upon the matters I have just described. But they did not *emphasize* them. Why not? Likely because they wanted to convince their colleagues in the majority. And that is the methodological point. Emphasizing statutory objectives, agency practices, and precedent (in *Sackett*) and purpose (in *Students for Fair Admissions*) would have done little to convince members of a text-and-history-oriented majority to change their minds. Thus, once a majority of the Court sticks strongly to text and history, it becomes more difficult for other members of the Court to emphasize other interpretive tools—at least where they hope to change the majority's direction. For that reason, both *Sackett* and *Students for Fair Admissions* provide some evidence that we are in the midst of a paradigm shift that is moving in a textualist and originalist direction.

No

On the other hand, I doubt that the shift has yet fully occurred; or, at the least, it seems far from permanent. In *Allen v. Milligan*,[61] for example, an important case released in June 2023, the Court set aside, as contrary to a federal statute, an Alabama congressional districting law that created only one district with a majority Black population (out of seven state districts) even though the Black population accounted for about two-sevenths, not one-seventh, of Alabama's population.[62] The statute—Section 2 of the Voting Rights Act—forbids a state from imposing a "standard, practice or procedure" that "*results in* a denial or abridgment of the right . . . to vote on account of race or color."[63] The statute further adds that the foregoing protection does not establish "a right to have members of a protected class elected in numbers equal to their proportion in the population."[64]

Members of the Court wrote opinions totaling more than one hundred pages in length and, to be sure, many of those pages referred to text. But, although textualism did not completely disappear in this case, other critical factors also played an important role, including history, purposes, and precedent. For instance, the Court recounted in detail the Reconstruction and Jim Crow history that led to the passage of the Voting Rights Act and which illustrates its purpose, and it further discussed the legislative process that led Congress to expand the act to include discriminatory impacts—procedures "resulting in" discrimination—rather than just intentional discrimination.[65] These elements of legislative history and purpose, and not simply textual or linguistic factors, led the Court to its result. Of course, one swallow does not make a summer, but a close reading of this case suggests that a text-oriented paradigm shift is not yet a done deal.

The reader might also examine a recent 2023 case, *Twitter, Inc. v. Taamneh*,[66] in which a unanimous Court held that social media companies were not liable for terrorist acts committed by organizations that used their social media outlets to transmit information.[67] The Court's opinion, in explaining its reasoning, did not resort to dictionary definitions or the "ordinary meaning" of the statute under consideration but rather looked to common law applications and understandings and considered how the Court's interpretation would affect the digital world.[68] Similarly, in 2023's *Coinbase, Inc. v. Bielski*,[69] despite the Federal Arbitration Act's textual silence as to whether district court proceedings should be paused pending appeal of the district court's decision not to compel parties to arbitrate a dispute, a 5–4 majority composed of textualist Justices concluded that the statute *required* district courts to pause proceedings.[70]

Why will the Court not soon give itself over entirely to textualism? First, and perhaps foremost, *time* from my perspective is an ally. Time will work against changing the dominant, traditional methodology. And much time remains.

It takes time to adjust to working as a Supreme Court Justice. How long? Justice Souter thought three years, while Justice William Douglas thought five. Whatever impression one gives to the outside world, a new Justice is internally uncertain: "Can I do the job reasonably well? A mistake here is likely to prove major. Can I really learn to avoid mistakes?" After, say, five years, one may still be uncertain about freedom from error, but once-new Justices do know how to do their best, and they have learned that every case—and not just those that receive publicity—requires that effort.

At the same time, no Justice wants to bear responsibility for a serious decline in the public's willingness to accept the Court's decisions. Acceptance of those decisions is too closely linked to the rule of law itself. Where text and original meaning are vague, ambiguous, or otherwise indeterminate, methodological purity may take a back seat to doing the job using all of the tools traditionally available to a Justice.

It also takes time to adjust to the mores of the Court, including its unwritten rules: The basic job is one of making decisions. You can change your mind, but do not do so too often (to keep the workload manageable for yourself and your colleagues). If you give colleagues one impression, do not depart too often from what you have said or written, or they will not be able to maintain a steady view of your approach or your answer to the questions presented. Each case is a new day; we two may have been on opposite sides in a particular case, but that does not prevent us from being the closest of allies in the next (legally unrelated) case. Justices speak in order of seniority during conferences; and no one speaks twice until everyone who wishes to speak has spoken once. Lunch is not the right time to talk about cases, nor for that matter to bring up subjects likely to make your colleagues ill at ease. Personal relations are typically good; keep them that way.

All this matters, and it makes a difference. It helps to keep personal relations among colleagues strong. It encourages Justices to listen to each other. And it keeps in the mind of each Justice that the Supreme Court is a major institution of government, helping continuously to forge and maintain a nation that is "out of many, one."

Recently, major cases have come before the Court while several new Justices have spent only two or three years at the Court. Major changes take time, and there are many years left for the newly appointed Justices to decide whether they want to build the law using only textualism and originalism or instead taking advantage of all of the methods I have described here. But in planning how they would like to change the interpretive system, they must think about what will work best for the Court and for the country. They may well be concerned about the decline in trust in the Court—as shown by public opinion polls. The law is not just something that people read for pleasure (though some might); it changes the social reality of those who must live within its bounds and understand its developments. The passage of time will allow the newer Justices to see whether a textual or an originalist approach, when applied consistently, will help or hinder Americans as they seek to live together justly, peacefully, and prosperously.

Along with the fact that any paradigm change will take time, I also bear in mind that each Justice must work together with eight others. One of my colleagues described an appointment to the Supreme Court as a kind of forced marriage with no possibility of divorce. In general, life is more pleasant when one gets along well with others. And in the closely confined atmosphere of the Court, getting along well includes listening to others and trying to understand how they think about a case, as well as how they think about the law in general. The members of the current Court, I believe, do get along well personally. And that fact will inevitably help to bring them together—at least, to a degree—as they develop approaches or methods over the years for reaching decisions in difficult cases.

Furthermore, the need to maintain the Court's strength among the public—i.e., the need to keep the Court as an effective instrument for furthering the rule of law—means that often the Court's members will try to compromise. One cannot help, while sitting in conference, hearing others; and when the conference works well, it consists not of sets of conflicting arguments but in Justices listening to one another. There is often search for compromise. Sometimes, but not always, it is found. And the more compromise the Court achieves, the less likely it will be that the Court consistently substitutes a rigid version of textualism or originalism for more traditional concerns about purposes, consequences, and workability.

Additionally, if my criticisms of textualism and originalism are even somewhat correct, and if my efforts to follow Chief Justice Marshall's focus on the workability of the law describe an important part of the legal world, then, over time, it should become apparent that strict versions of textualism and originalism simply will not work. Those theories will not bring about the advantages that their advocates hope to achieve. They will not bring certainty to the law. They will not significantly change the ability of a judge to substitute the "good" for the "law." They will not simplify the task of interpreting indeterminate statutory or constitutional phrases. They will not reduce the interpretation-related judicial workload.

The *Dobbs* majority's hope that legislatures and not courts will decide the abortion question[71] will not be realized. After all, different states will enact different laws and enforce them differently. Whether the Constitution assures a woman an abortion needed to save her life, her physical health, or her mental health; whether the Constitution guarantees abortion rights to victims of rape or incest; whether states can forbid sending medical methods of abortion through the mail; whether states can prosecute those in-state persons who aid or abet out-of-state abortions; and other abortion-related questions may well lead to further Court cases, not solely legislative determinations (many of which may also be subject to judicial review). One can—with ease—think of similar issues involving the Second Amendment and affirmative action; those questions may also prove complex and reappear in the Court, requiring answers, which may in turn lead to further cases.

And which of the pre-textualism cases would a textualist Court seek to overturn? Neither *Dobbs* nor any other source convinces me that there is a clear answer to this question—an answer that will not threaten subjective judicial decision-making, undermine the law's stability, or perhaps produce legal chaos. At some point, some of the Justices who currently favor textualism, originalism, or related approaches may decide that the application of their methods creates far too much complexity or uncertainty. They may then reevaluate the value of these methods.[72]

Finally, what about the informed public's acceptance of a major change in approach? Time may lead some of the Justices who favor a change to believe that the Supreme Court's role as a major governmental institution requires it to put other tasks ahead of methodology. I think here of the need to assure that the nation as a whole accepts a "rule of law." It has taken many years to develop that acceptance. Like *stare decisis*, the rule of law does not demand rigid adherence to prior law. But too much change too quickly in the laws that the public believes important can weaken that acceptance.[73] Much here depends upon how many cases arise in which methodology makes a difference, just what those cases concern, and how different Justices weigh the Court's institutional role against a commitment to methodology. But Professor Freund's observation, which I have mentioned before, still rings true: The Court should "never be influenced by the weather of the day but inevitably . . . will be influenced by the climate of the era."[74]

What will create that climate? Will a major paradigm shift in the direction of textualism find sufficient acceptance by an informed public? In asking this question, I still recognize that the Court must decide cases according to law, not according to public popularity. But reread the examples that I have given that reflect paradigm shifts: The *Lochner* Court, the New Deal Court, the Warren Court. In each of those instances, public concerns, desires, beliefs, and observations of social and economic facts played a role in producing a large number of persons who considered, and then accepted, the Court's basic approach to interpretation.

How did those prevailing public attitudes play a role? I think it goes something like this. The "informed public," of course, includes judges. They interpret statutes and the Constitution. And they write opinions embodying and explaining those interpretations. Legal scholars then read those opinions. They draw upon their study of particular areas of law. They use their knowledge to help evaluate the opinions, praising or criticizing them, and suggesting modifications. And then the lawyers who actually practice before the courts read the judges' opinions and the scholars' work. And they use those materials to further their own arguments. The judges become aware of the evaluations and suggestions. They proceed to write new opinions, tweaking their prior views as they find necessary. The circle will be repeated, with each repetition filtering judicial rules and pronouncements through sieves of public commentary, criticism, and experimentation.

The upshot is that those who hold informed opinions, including the judges, cannot escape discovering flaws in their theories. And, if I am right in criticizing textualism and originalism as I have done, the judges will find it difficult to maintain informed support for abandoning traditional, purpose-based methods of interpretation and substituting newer, textualist-based methods instead.

How long will they be able to resist criticisms based on an inability to explain which earlier, nontextual cases they intend to overrule and which they intend to maintain?

How will they be able to explain how their methods protect the law against a judge's desire to substitute what the judge subjectively believes is "good"?

How will they prevent at least some text-based decisions from leading to harmful consequences?

How will they maintain the Founders' (and Chief Justice Marshall's) belief in a workable Constitution, designed for the centuries?

How can they maintain the importance of looking at a statute's purpose, at a constitutional phrase's underlying values, as judges such as Holmes, Brandeis, Cardozo, Frankfurter, and others have done over the centuries since the nation's beginnings?

How will those advocating textualism and originalism find the public acceptance needed for the Court to do its job, as the *Federalist Papers* described it in the eighteenth century, namely, to keep the other branches' actions within constitutional limits?

In a word, will the Court find the necessary general support from the American public? That support may well have been needed to establish the *Lochner* Court, the New Deal Court, and the Warren Court. In my view, it is necessary if we are to maintain public support for Rule of Law itself.[75]

CONCLUSION

As I said at the beginning, my object in writing this book is to provide examples of how I conceive of constitutional and statutory interpretation and why I believe that textualism or originalism will not work. Methods that go by those labels may initially seem attractive, for they suggest that there is a right answer to virtually every interpretive question. If we look at the text long enough; if we work with it hard enough; if we examine what the Framers (or their contemporaries) really thought a phrase's words mean; then, the promise is that we can find that answer. At the very least, supporters say, use of these methods will prevent judges from substituting their own views about what is "good" or "helpful" for the "true" result that application of the law demands. The judge's job is the neutral application of the law, not implementing the judge's own social values.

I hope that the examples given in this book will help the reader see that textualist or originalist methods of interpretation do not carry out these promises. More than that, at the beginning of this book, I pointed out that 450 years ago Montaigne very much doubted the ability of thousands, or hundreds of thousands of laws, to capture "the infinite diversity of human actions," particularly given the ever-changing nature of human life.[1] To insist upon a static, unchanging reading of legal texts, including a Constitution written for the ages, could only make these matters worse, or could only make it more difficult to fit the law to human life. For the reasons explained in this book, I believe that interpretive methodologies that rely on text to the exclusion of purpose, practice, consequences, and workability simply cannot account for that variety and complexity. Truly difficult interpretive questions may have better or worse answers, but trying to find "THE TRUE ANSWER," particularly through the exclusive use of those methods, is a hopeless task. Law, as I have said, is not a hard science. To use text alone (or original meaning alone) is likely to drive a judge farther from, and not closer to, an enduring, workable interpretation. The answers textualists and originalists find will not better reflect what Congress likely intended, nor will they better articulate the values that the Founders hoped to embody in a workable, long-lasting Constitution. A judge who wishes a statute (or the Constitution) to embody his or her own idea of what is "good" can misinterpret the law at least as easily by using textualism (or originalism) as by looking to the traditional interpretive considerations that I have discussed.

I hope the examples in this book further illustrate what should be instinctively unsurprising: that a judge is *more* likely, not less, to discover what legislators intended an obscure phrase to mean by reading (rather than ignoring) the relevant legislative history; considering statutory purposes and constitutional values; and confronting likely consequences with reference to those purposes or values.

These examples also suggest that there are many different and valid tools a judge might use in a difficult case. Which should the judge use? Text? Purpose? History? Tradition? Precedent? Consequences? Values? What a reasonable legislator likely would have thought? Which tools the judge will use, and how much weight she will put upon related results, depends not so much upon the judge as upon the *case*. It is judicial instinct, created and honed by experience, that will typically tell the judge what considerations to use and emphasize in a particular case.

A judge's instinct may be especially well developed given the sheer number of cases she considers. But there is nothing mystical about that instinct; it is the same instinct that helps seasoned lawyers decide what parts of a case to focus on and what to say in their briefs. It is the same instinct that helps any of us navigate a world chock-full of ambiguity, that helps us decide whether a train fare charged for "animals" requires us to pay not only to bring our dogs and cats along with us but also our snails. I probably emphasize purposes, values, and consequences more than do many others. But I also believe that text, history, and tradition are typically relevant. Once a judge looks at and considers these different factors, it is informed instinct that will lead to a result. And ultimately, an informed critic will have to determine whether that judge's choice of results is sound.

I did not create this method of judging. I find it, or something like it, in *McCulloch*, in Holmes, in Brandeis, in Cardozo, and in the work of many other judges whom I admire. I find it in the work of Professors Hart and Sacks, who taught in the mid-twentieth century and who made clear that the ultimate object of law is to allow human beings to live peacefully and prosperously together in communities.

Alexis de Tocqueville remarked that "[s]carcely any political question arises in the United States which is not resolved, sooner or later, into a judicial question."[2] Courts are not well suited to resolve political questions. But even today, it is hard to argue with Tocqueville's observation. For that reason, the message of this book is important for nonlawyers and lawyers alike. Indeed, it is vital for all who care about maintaining a workable democracy.

ACKNOWLEDGMENTS

The many persons who have helped me with ideas for this book, who have suggested appropriate cases, who have corrected errors, and who have helped in many other ways include:

Dean John Manning, former Deans Robert Post and Martha Minow, Professor Cass Sunstein, Professor Paul Gewirtz, Alan Morrison, Sundeep Iyer, Dan Richardson, Sara Solow, Kyle Edwards, Sierra Polston, Eric Xu, Thomas Nielsen, Cody Kahoe, Amy Vargo, Emma Reilly, and members of my own family. My special gratitude to Peter Matson and thanks to Pat Haas as well. Thanks to Fred Chase, Lisa Healy, Larry Hughes, and Johanna Li at Simon & Schuster. I am particularly grateful for the editing of Bob Bender. The book is far better for that editing and for the help of the others. Mistakes, whether of general description or of detail, are my own.

AUTHOR'S NOTE

T his book contains no revelations of private discussions within the Court, at conference or otherwise, or other private information. Its descriptions and analyses refer to cases, to legal opinions, to articles, and to books that are publicly available or to thoughts and analyses that are my own.

NOTES

Citations follow the Harvard Law Review *Bluebook* (a rulebook) format for legal citations. Citations to court cases include the name of the case as well as citations for the "reporter" of the decision—the books in which all opinions and other actions of the Court are contained. The citation "U.S." designates the official United States Reports, while the citation "S. Ct." designates the Supreme Court reporter, a source that publishes new cases more quickly than the U.S. Reports. Before the abbreviation for the reporter (e.g., "U.S."), a number will indicate the volume in which a particular case resides. After the abbreviation for the reporter, another number indicates the first page in that volume on which the cited opinion can be found. And after that number, a third will indicate the particular pages containing the quoted or cited material. Thus, the citation "372 U.S. 335, 344," for example, would refer to volume 372 of the United States Reports, a decision beginning on page number 335, and material appearing on page number 344.

Reports setting forth the opinions of the federal appeals courts and district courts follow a similar format. Federal appeals court decisions appear in the Federal Reporter (e.g., 643 F.2d 863). Federal trial court cases appear in the Federal Supplement (e.g., 4 F. Supp. 2d 927). Other reports, often reporting cases in state courts, for example, will appear in books containing abbreviations for the state at issue.

Citations to the titles of journal articles appear in italics, while citations to the journal itself appear in small and large capitals. The names of journals are abbreviated according to the abbreviation tables at the end of *The Bluebook*. Citations to books appear in small and large capitals. Citations to federal statutes include the abbreviation "U.S.C." for United States Code.

Preface: My Way

1. Harvard Law School, *The Scalia Lecture: A Dialogue with Justice Elena Kagan on the Reading of Statutes*, YouTube at 8:29 (Nov. 17, 2015), https://www.youtube.com /watch?v=dp EtszFT0Tg&source_ve_path=MjM4NTE&feature=emb_title.
2. Van Orden v. Perry, 545 U.S. 677 (2005).
3. Holland v. Florida, 560 U.S. 631 (2010).
4. Brown v. Payton, 544 U.S. 133, 148 (2005) (Breyer, J., concurring); Woodford v. Ngo, 548 U.S. 81, 103 (2006) (Breyer, J., concurring).
5. *Payton*, 544 U.S. at 149 (Breyer, J., concurring) (citing 28 U.S.C. § 2254(d)(1)).
6. WILLIAM SHAKESPEARE, HENRY IV, PART I, act 5, sc. 2, ll. 81–84.
7. *See infra* Chapter 12.
8. *See generally* John C. P. Goldberg, *Rediscovering* The Nature of the Judicial Process: *A Comment on Professors Abraham's and White's* Doctrinal Forks in the Road, 34 YALE J. L. & HUMANS. 99 (2023).
9. *See id.* at 111–12.
10. Felix Frankfurter, *Some Reflections on the Reading of Statutes*, 47 COLUM. L. REV. 527, 538 (1947).
11. United States v. Whitridge, 197 U.S. 135, 143 (1905).
12. *See, e.g.*, Antonin Scalia, *Common-Law Courts in a Civil-Law System: The Role of the United States Federal Courts in Interpreting the Constitution and Laws*, in A MATTER OF INTERPRETATION 3, 23–27 (1997).
13. *See, e.g.*, Antonin Scalia, *Originalism: The Lesser Evil*, 57 U. CINCINNATI L. REV. 849, 856–57 (1989).
14. *See, e.g.*, Scalia, *supra* note 12, at 22–23; Amy Coney Barrett, *Congressional Insiders and Outsiders*, 84 U. CHI. L. REV. 2193, 2203 (2017).
15. *See, e.g.*, Scalia, *supra* note 12 at 38.
16. *See* Frankfurter, *supra* note 10, at 528.
17. *See* J.L. AUSTIN, HOW TO DO THINGS WITH WORDS 4 n.2 (1962).
18. SEC v. Robert Collier & Co., 76 F.2d 939, 941 (2d Cir. 1935) (Hand, J.): ("[W]hile members [of Congress] deliberately express their personal position upon the general purposes of the legislation, as to the details of its articulation they accept the work of the committees; so much they delegate because legislation could not go on in any other way.").
19. *See* Kevin Tobia, Brian Slocum & Victoria F. Nourse, *Ordinary Meaning and Ordinary People*, 171 U. PA. L. REV. 365, 385–88 (2023).
20. John F. Manning, *What Divides Textualists from Purposivists*, 106 COLUM. L. REV. 70, 71–72 (2006).
21. *Compare, e.g.*, Lawrence B. Solum, *The Fixation Thesis: The Role of Historical Fact in Original Meaning*, 91 NOTRE DAME L. REV. 1 (2015) (endorsing textual approach to constitutional interpretation); John F. Manning, *Textualism as a Nondelegation Doctrine*, 97 HARV. L. REV. 673 (1997) (critiquing use of legislative history) *with* Nikolas Bowie, *Why the Constitution Was Written Down*, 71 STAN. L. REV. 1397, 1406–08 (2019) (critiquing historical assumptions underlying textual approaches to constitutional interpretation); William N. Eskridge, Jr., *The New Textualism*, 37 UCLA L. REV. 621 (1990) (critiquing textual approach to statutory interpretation); Cary Franklin, *Living Textualism*, 2020 SUP. CT. REV. 119 (2021) (critiquing textual approach to statutory and constitutional interpretation); Richard H. Fallon, Jr., *The Meaning of Legal "Meaning" and Its Implications for Theories of*

Legal Interpretation, 82 U. Chi. L. Rev. 1235 (2015) (same); Daniel A. Farber, *Legal Pragmatism and the Constitution*, 72 Minn. L. Rev. 1331 (1988) (endorsing pragmatic approach to constitutional interpretation); Abbe R. Gluck & Lisa Schultz Bressman, *Statutory Interpretation from the Inside—An Empirical Study of Congressional Drafting, Delegation, and the Canons: Part I*, 65 Stan. L. Rev. 901, 988–90 (2013) (defending use of legislative history, a statutory interpretation tool associated with purposivism); Robert A. Katzmann, Madison Lecture, *Statutes*, 82 N.Y.U. L. Rev. 637 (2012) (endorsing purpose-oriented approach to statutory interpretation); Victoria F. Nourse, *Elementary Statutory Interpretation: Rethinking Legislative Intent and History*, 55 B.C. L. Rev. 1613 (2014) (defending use of legislative history); Farah Peterson, *Constitutionalism in Unexpected Places*, 106 Va. L. Rev. 559 (critiquing textualist approach to constitutional interpretation). *See also* Tara Leigh Grove, *Which Textualism?*, 134 Harv. L. Rev. 265 (2020) (outlining the strengths and weaknesses of various text-based approaches to statutory interpretation).

22. Mahanoy Area Sch. Dist. v. B.L., 141 S. Ct. 2038, 2043 (2021).

23. *Id.* at 2046.

24. For an example of what I believe is a well-phrased "message," see Justice Robert H. Jackson's statement in *West Virginia State Board of Education v. Barnette*, 319 U.S. 624, 642 (1943): "If there is any fixed star in our constitutional constellation, it is that no official, high or petty, can prescribe what shall be orthodox in politics, nationalism, religion, or other matters of opinion or force citizens to confess by word or act their faith therein."

25. Michel de Montaigne, Of Experience (1588), *reprinted in* 3 Essays of Michel de Montaigne 375 (William Carew Hazlitt ed., Charles Cotton trans., 1877).

26. Lozman v. City of Riviera Beach, 568 U.S. 115, 130–31 (2013). Indeed, who could have guessed that that same litigant would sue Riviera Beach a few years later, this time alleging that the City Council engineered his arrest after he repeatedly criticized the city's leadership? (He won again.) *See* Lozman v. City of Riviera Beach, 138 S. Ct. 1945, 1955 (2018).

27. Boumediene v. Bush, 553 U.S. 723 (2008); *see also* Hamdan v. Rumsfeld, 548 U.S. 557 (2006); Hamdi v. Rumsfeld, 542 U.S. 507 (2004).

28. Piper v. Supreme Ct. of New Hampshire, 723 F.2d 110, 118 (1st Cir. 1983) (Campbell, C.J., and Breyer, J., dissenting).

29. Jerome Frank, Law and the Modern Mind 100 (Stevens & Sons ed. 1949) (1930).

30. Timothy J. Capurso, *How Judges Judge: Theories on Judicial Decision*, 29 U. Balt. L. F. 5, 6 (1998) (citing Frank, *supra* note 29, at 103).

31. Frank, *supra* note 29, at 104.

32. Edward Coke, The First Part of the Institutes of the Lawes of England. Or, A Commentarie Upon Littleton 97b (1628).

33. Oliver Wendell Holmes, *The Path of the Law*, 10 Harv. L. Rev. 457, 465–66 (1897) (emphasis added).

34. Michael Boudin, *Common Sense in Law Practice (or, Was John Brown a Man of Sound Judgment?)*, 34 Harv. L. Sch. Bull., Spring 1983, at 22, 26.

35. *Id.* at 23.

36. *Id.* at 27.

37. Letter from Thomas Jefferson to Walter Jones (Jan. 2, 1814), in 7 The Papers of Thomas Jefferson, Retirement Series (J. Jefferson Looney ed. 2010).

38. Helvering v. Gregory, 69 F.2d 809, 810–11 (2d Cir. 1934) (Hand, J.).

39. Frankfurter, *supra* note 10, at 529.

40. *See* Paul M. Bator, *The Constitution as Architecture: Legislative and Administrative Courts Under Article III*, 65 IND. L. J. 233, 265 (1990) (contending that a "rigid," formalistic approach to interpreting the Constitution "misunderstands" that the Constitution's "content is a product of history and custom distilled in light of experience and expediency").

41. United States v. Butler, 297 U.S. 1, 62 (1936); *see also* Robert Post, *Theories of Constitutional Interpretation*, REPRESENTATIONS, Spring 1990, at 13, 14 ("[S]trictly speaking, [Justice Roberts's] approach is not a theory at all; it is instead a description of what happens when constitutional meaning is not problematic.").

42. For a foundational text on understanding the role of law in regulating communities and institutions, see HENRY M. HART, JR. & ALBERT M. SACKS, THE LEGAL PROCESS: BASIC PROBLEMS IN THE MAKING AND APPLICATION OF LAW (William N. Eskridge, Jr. & Phillip P. Frickey eds. 1994) (1958).

43. *See, e.g.*, Manning, *supra* note 20, at 71–72.

44. *See* THOMAS CAHILL, HOW THE IRISH SAVED CIVILIZATION 3–4 (2010).

Part I: Purpose vs. Textualism

1. *See, e.g.*, Robert A. Katzmann, Madison Lecture, *Statutes*, 82 N.Y.U. L. REV. 637, 668 (2012) ("In approaching the interpretative task, I have, as a judge, several tools I can use, including: text, statutory structure, history, word usage in other relevant statutes, common law usages, agency interpretations, dictionary definitions, technical and scientific usages, lay usages, canons, common practices, and purpose.").

2. United States v. Fisher, 6 U.S. (2 Cranch) 358, 386 (1805).

3. *See, e.g.*, Antonin Scalia, *Common-Law Courts in a Civil-Law System: The Role of the United States Federal Courts in Interpreting the Constitution and Laws*, in A MATTER OF INTERPRETATION 3, 22 (1997). ("The text is the law, and it is the text that must be observed.").

4. *See, e.g.*, Guiseppi v. Walling, 144 F.2d 608, 624 (1944) (Hand, J., concurring) ("As nearly as we can, we must put ourselves in the place of those who uttered the words, and try to define how they would have dealt with the unforeseen situation; and, although their words are by far the most decisive evidence of what they would have done, they are by no means final.").

5. *See* Amy Coney Barrett, *Congressional Insiders and Outsiders*, 84 U. CHI. L. REV. 2193, 2195 (2017).

6. *See* RICHARD A. POSNER, LAW, PRAGMATISM, AND DEMOCRACY 67 (2003) ("Judicial interpretation generally proceeds in two steps. The first is to infer a purpose from the language and context of the contractual or statutory text in issue, or from a body of pertinent judicial decisions that have established a rule. The second step is to decide what outcome in the case at hand would serve that purpose best.").

1: Purpose-Based Approaches

1. Felix Frankfurter, *Some Reflections on the Reading of Statutes*, 47 COLUM. L. REV. 527, 533 (1947).

2. *Id.* at 538–39.

3. United States v. Whitridge, 197 U.S. 135, 143 (1905).

4. BENJAMIN N. CARDOZO, THE NATURE OF THE JUDICIAL PROCESS 23 (1921).

5. *See* Guido Calabresi, A Common Law for the Age of Statutes 2–7 (1982).

6. E. Allan Farnsworth et al., Contracts 7 (9th ed. 2019).

7. *See* Anita Krishnakumar, *The Common Law as Statutory Backdrop*, 136 Harv. L. Rev. 608, 610 (2022).

8. Cardozo, *supra* note 4, at 23 (quoting Munroe Smith, Jurisprudence 21 (1909)).

9. *See, e.g.*, MacPherson v. Buick Motor Co., 111 N.E. 1050, 1053 (N.Y. 1916) (Cardozo, J.) (eliminating the requirement of privity of contract for negligence actions but leaving open questions about the scope of future negligence actions "to deal with . . . when [they] arise[]," as such "difficult[ies]" were "not present in this case"). For an academic discussion of the value of common law incrementalism, see generally Shyamkrishna Balganesh & Gideon Parchomovsky, *Structure and Value in the Common Law*, 163 U. Pa. L. Rev. 1241 (2015).

10. *See* County of Maui v. Haw. Wildlife Fund, 140 S. Ct. 1462 (2020).

11. 33 U.S.C. § 1251(a).

12. *Id.* § 1362(6).

13. *Id.* § 1362(12) (emphasis added).

14. *Id.* § 1362(14).

15. *Id.* § 1311(a).

16. *See* County of Maui v. Haw. Wildlife Fund, 140 S. Ct. 1462, 1469 (2020).

17. *Id.* at 1477.

18. *See id.* at 1471.

19. *Id.* at 1476.

20. *Id.* at 1476–77.

21. *Id.* at 1476.

22. *Id.* at 1477.

23. *Id.* at 1483 (Alito, J., dissenting).

24. *Id.* at 1479 (Thomas, J., dissenting).

25. 33 U.S.C. § 1362(12).

26. *County of Maui*, 140 S. Ct. at 1479 (Thomas, J., dissenting).

27. *See* 33 U.S.C. § 1362(14).

28. *County of Maui*, 140 S. Ct. at 1479–80 (Thomas, J., dissenting).

29. *Id.* at 1475–76 (majority opinion).

30. Balganesh & Parchomovsky, *supra* note 9, at 1267.

31. *See, e.g.*, David Lat, *Judge Posner, Uncensored: "I Don't Really Care What People Think,"* Above the Law (Sept. 14, 2017, 7:41 PM), https://abovethelaw.com/2017/09/judge-posner-uncensored-i-I-really-care-what-people-think (questioning whether there is a "difference between 'pragmatism' and 'legislating from the bench,' or just deciding cases based on your own policy preferences").

32. In this context, the term "pragmatism" is more akin to the brand of pragmatism practiced by American philosophers like Charles Sanders Peirce, William James, and William Van Orman Quine. These philosophers sometimes emphasized the fact that many of our beliefs about the world, perhaps particularly scientific beliefs, are related, one to the other—to the point where, at least sometimes, we could believe, say X, only if we are willing to give up sufficient other beliefs, say in field Y. *See generally* Charles Sanders Peirce, *The Fixation of Belief*, 12 Popular Sci. Monthly 1, 3 (1877); William James, Pragmatism (1907); W.V. Quine & J.S. Ullian, The Web of Belief (1970). For example, I may believe that (a) I have just seen a summer tanager (a lovely

bird) in a rosebush, but I will give up that belief when (b) I learn that it is winter, for I also believe that (c) summer tanagers are not to be seen in this neighborhood in the winter. Here is where I see an analogy with "pragmatism" in the law. Judges must decide cases that balance competing beliefs, values, and practices. A pragmatic judge will strive for the outcome that works "best" in light of these competing factors, even though another outcome could possibly accommodate them.

33. *See* Felix S. Cohen, *The Problems of a Functional Jurisprudence*, 1 MODERN L. REV. 5, 8 (1937) ("If you want to understand something, observe it in action. . . . Applied to the larger field of general human behaviour, this same approach leads to an appraisal of law in terms of conduct of human beings who are affected by law.").

34. *See* Ronald Dworkin, *Hard Cases*, 88 HARV. L. REV. 1057, 1066 (1975) ("Suppose that some line of precedents is in fact unjust. . . . Even though a judge deciding some hard case disapproves of these precedents for that reason, the doctrine of articulate consistency nevertheless requires that he allow his argument to be affected by them."); *see also id.* at 1090 ("The gravitational force of a precedent may be explained by appeal . . . to the fairness of treating like cases alike. A precedent is the report of an earlier political decision; the very fact of that decision, as a piece of political history, provides some reason for deciding other cases in a similar way in the future.").

35. *See* RICHARD A. POSNER, LAW, PRAGMATISM, AND DEMOCRACY 12 (2003) ("The pragmatic judge does not deny the standard rule-of-law virtues of generality, predictability, and impartiality, which generally favor a stand-pat approach to novel legal disputes. He just refuses to reify or sacralize those virtues. He dares to balance them against the adaptationist virtues of deciding the case at hand in a way that produces the best consequences for the parties and those similarly circumstanced.").

36. *See* HENRY M. HART, JR. & ALBERT M. SACKS, THE LEGAL PROCESS: BASIC PROBLEMS IN THE MAKING AND APPLICATION OF LAW 1125 (William N. Eskridge, Jr. & Phillip P. Frickey eds. 1994) (1958).

37. *See* William N. Eskridge, *Spinning Legislative Supremacy*, 78 GEO. L. J. 319, 324 (1989).

38. *See* Victoria F. Nourse & Jane S. Schacter, *The Politics of Legislative Drafting: A Congressional Case Study*, 77 N.Y.U. L. REV. 575, 596 (2002).

39. *See* HART & SACKS, *supra* note 36, at 1125; Abbe R. Gluck & Lisa Schultz Bressman, *Statutory Interpretation from the Inside—An Empirical Study of Congressional Drafting, Delegation, and the Canons: Part I*, 65 STAN. L. REV. 901, 915 (2013).

40. Farah Peterson, *Expounding the Constitution*, 130 YALE L. J. 2, 24 (2020).

41. *See, e.g.*, King v. Burwell, 576 U.S. 473, 498 (2015) ("[I]n every case we must respect the role of the Legislature, and take care not to undo what it has done. A fair reading of legislation demands a fair understanding of the legislative plan. Congress passed the Affordable Care Act to improve health insurance markets, not to destroy them. If at all possible, we must interpret the Act in a way that is consistent with the former, and avoids the latter.").

42. Arlington Cent. Sch. Dist. Bd. of Educ. v. Murphy, 548 U.S. 291 (2006).

43. Recent empirical findings indicate that ordinary people interpret legal rules in light of their purposes. *See* Kevin Tobia, Brian G. Slocum & Victoria Nourse, *Statutory Interpretation from the Outside*, 122 COLUM. L. REV. 213, 286 (2022); Noel Struchiner, Ivar R. Hannikainen & Guilherme da F.C.F. de Almeida, *An Experimental Guide to Vehicles in the Park*, 15 JUDGMENT & DECISION MAKING 312, 325 (2020). These findings suggest that an overly mechanical interpretation of a statute can widen the gap between how ordinary

voters understand the statute and the objectives the statute, as interpreted by a court, can achieve.

44. *See* Richard A. Posner, *Justice Breyer Throws Down the Gauntlet*, 115 Yale L. J. 1699, 1711 (2006).

45. Peterson, *supra* note 40, at 24; Farah Peterson, *Interpretation as Statecraft: Chancellor Kent and the Collaborative Era of American Statutory Interpretation*, 77 Md. L. Rev. 712, 738 (2018); John F. Manning, *Textualism and the Equity of the Statute*, 101 Colum. L. Rev. 1, 91 (2005); William N. Eskridge, *All About Words: Early Understandings of the "Judicial Power" in Statutory Interpretation, 1776–1806*, 101 Colum. L. Rev. 990, 1002 (2001).

46. *See, e.g.*, John F. Manning, Chevron *and the Reasonable Legislator*, 128 Harv. L. Rev. 457, 457 (2014).

47. *See, e.g.*, Bostock v. Clayton County, 140 S. Ct. 1731, 1738 (2020) (noting that the Supreme Court granted *certiorari* to resolve a circuit split on the meaning of Title VII's prohibition on "discrimination on the basis of sex").

48. See Amy Coney Barrett, *Congressional Insiders and Outsiders*, 84 U. Chi. L. Rev. 2193, 2200 (2017).

49. *Id.* at 2203.

50. Tobia et al., *supra* note 43, at 285.

51. *Id.*

2: The Textualist Approach

1. Antonin Scalia & Bryan A. Garner, Reading Law 16 (2012).

2. Bostock v. Clayton County, 140 S. Ct. 1731, 1755 (2020) (Alito, J., dissenting) (quoting Scalia & Garner, *supra* note 1, at 16) (emphasis omitted).

3. Kisor v. Wilkie, 139 S. Ct. 2400, 2442 (2019) (Gorsuch, J., concurring in the judgment) (arguing that the proper approach to legal interpretation is "elucidate[ing] the law's original public meaning").

4. *See* Amy Coney Barrett, *Congressional Insiders and Outsiders*, 84 U. Chi. L. Rev. 2193, 2203 (2017).

5. *See* Antonin Scalia, *Common-Law Courts in a Civil-Law System: The Role of the United States Federal Courts in Interpreting the Constitution and Laws*, in A Matter of Interpretation 3, 23–24 (1997).

6. *See, e.g.*, Antonin Scalia, *Originalism: The Lesser Evil*, 57 U. Cincinnati L. Rev. 849, 863–64 (1989).

7. Scalia & Garner, *supra* note 1, at xxvii (emphasis added).

8. John F. Manning, *Textualism and Legislative Intent*, 91 Va. L. Rev. 419, 431 (2005).

9. *See id.* at 431–32.

10. *See* Scalia, *supra* note 5, at 17–18; John F. Manning, *The Absurdity Doctrine*, 116 Harv. L. Rev. 2387, 2409–10 (2003).

11. Frank H. Easterbrook, *Text, History, and Structure in Statutory Interpretation*, 17 Harv. J. L. & Pub. Pol'y 61, 62 (1994).

12. *See* NLRB v. Robbins Tire & Rubber Co., 437 U.S. 214, 242 (1978).

13. 5 U.S.C. §§ 552(b)(5), (7).

14. Milner v. Dep't of the Navy, 562 U.S. 562 (2011).

15. *See* Scalia, *supra* note 5, at 17–18.

16. Manning, *supra* note 8, at 444–45 n.84.

17. *See* King v. Burwell, 576 U.S. 473, 515–16 (2015) (Scalia, J., dissenting).

18. John F. Manning, *What Divides Textualists from Purposivists?*, 106 COLUM. L. REV. 70, 92 (2006).

19. Scalia, *supra* note 5, at 25–27.

20. *See generally* Barrett, *supra* note 4, at 2199–207 (describing how "[t]extualists use dictionaries and canons as a way of signifying the linguistic expectations of the regulated," *id.* at 2203).

21. SCALIA & GARNER, *supra* note 1, at 174 (describing the surplusage canon).

22. *Id.*

23. *Id.* at 170.

24. *See id.* at 195.

25. Abbe R. Gluck & Lisa Schultz Bressman, *Statutory Interpretation from the Inside—An Empirical Study of Congressional Drafting, Delegation, and the Canons: Part I*, 65 STAN. L. REV. 901, 942 (2013) (describing the federalism canon).

26. *Id.* at 933–37, 945–47; *see also* Lisa Schultz Bressman & Abbe R. Gluck, *Statutory Interpretation from the Inside—An Empirical Study of Congressional Drafting, Delegation, and the Canons: Part II*, 66 STAN. L. REV. 725 (2014).

27. *See, e.g.*, SCALIA & GARNER, *supra* note 1, at 281 (describing the presumption against waiver of sovereign immunity); *see also* Gluck & Bressman, *supra* note 25, at 945 n.141 (reporting that most drafters of legislation are unaware of such a presumption).

28. Gluck & Bressman, *supra* note 25, at 968–69.

29. 18 U.S.C. § 229(a)(1).

30. *Id.* § 229F(8)(A).

31. Bond v. United States, 572 U.S. 844, 886 (2014).

32. *Id.* at 862–64.

33. *See* Barrett, *supra* note 4, at 2193 ("There is a general consensus that the text constrains.").

34. 42 U.S.C. § 2000e-2.

35. 140 S. Ct. 1731 (2020).

36. *Id.* at 1737.

37. *Id.*

38. Manning, *supra* note 18, at 92–93.

39. Scalia, *supra* note 5, at 10; *see also* Amy Coney Barrett, *Substantive Canons and Faithful Agency*, 90 B.U. L. REV. 109, 113–16 (2010).

40. Scalia, *supra* note 5, at 13.

41. *See* John F. Manning, *Textualism as a Nondelegation Doctrine*, 97 COLUM. L. REV. 673, 697–99 (1997).

42. Manning, *supra* note 18, at 99.

43. SCALIA & GARNER, *supra* note 1, at 61.

44. Scalia, *supra* note 5, at 14–18.

45. Finely v. United States, 490 U.S. 545, 556 (1989).

46. See Gluck & Bressman, *supra* note 25, at 924–60.

47. Scalia, *supra* note 5, at 17; *see also* Manning, *supra* note 8, at 450 ("[E]fforts to augment or vary the text in the name of serving a genuine but unexpressed legislative intent risks displacing whatever bargain was actually reached through the complex and path-dependant legislative process.").

48. *See* Barrett, *supra* note 4, at 2209.
49. Niz-Chavez v. Garland, 141 S. Ct. 1474, 1486 (2021).
50. *See* Scalia, *supra* note 5, at 23–29.
51. *Id.* at 38 ("What I look for in the Constitution is precisely what I look for in a statute: the original meaning of the text, not what the original draftsmen intended.").
52. *See* Lawrence B. Solum, *The Fixation Thesis: The Role of Historical Fact in Original Meaning*, 91 NOTRE DAME L. REV. 1, 27–28 (2015); *see also* New York State Rifle & Pistol Ass'n, Inc. v. Bruen, 142 S. Ct. 2111, 2163 (2022) (Barrett, J., concurring) (identifying "scholarly debate" over "whether courts should primarily rely on the prevailing understanding of an individual right when the Fourteenth Amendment was ratified in 1868" or when the Bill of Rights was ratified in 1791).
53. *See, e.g.*, Seila L. LLC v. Consumer Fin. Prot. Bureau, 140 S. Ct. 2183, 2197–98 (2020) (relying on evidence from the founding to hold that the president's authority to remove executive officers is constitutionally protected, despite the lack of any constitutional text referencing such authority).
54. *See infra* Chapter 13.
55. *See, e.g.*, Finely v. United States, 490 U.S. 545, 556 (1989).
56. *See* Scalia, *supra* note 6, at 861; Amy Coney Barrett, *Originalism and Stare Decisis*, 92 NOTRE DAME L. REV. 1921, 1921 (2017).
57. Dobbs v. Jackson Women's Health Org., 142 S. Ct. 2228 (2022).
58. *See infra* Chapter 15.
59. *See infra* Chapter 5.
60. *See infra* Chapter 6.
61. *See infra* Chapter 7.
62. *See infra* Chapter 8.

Part II: Interpreting Statutory Law

1. *See* PRELIMINARY ADDRESS ON THE FIRST DRAFT OF THE CIVIL CODE PRESENTED IN THE YEAR IX BY MESSRS. PORTALIS, TRONCHET, BIGOT-PRÉAMENEU AND MALEVILLE, MEMBERS OF THE GOVERNMENT-APPOINTED COMM'N (1801), https://www.justice.gc.ca/eng/rp-pr/csj-sjc/ilp-pji/code/index.html (last visited Oct. 21, 2023) (translated).
2. *See id.* ("[W]hen [the law] is unclear, the provisions must be further elaborated.").
3. *See* Jon Moline, *Aristotle, Eubulides and the Sorites*, 78 MIND 393 (1969) (describing the "Sorites paradox").
4. *See* 18 U.S.C. § 2113 (federal bank robbery statute).
5. Alex Woodward, *Coronavirus: Televangelist Kenneth Copeland "Blows Wind of God" at Covid-19 to 'Destroy' Pandemic*, THE INDEPENDENT (Apr. 6, 2020), https://www.independent.co.uk/news/world/americas/kenneth-copeland-blow-coronavirus-pray-sermon-trump-televangelist-a9448561.html ("I blow the wind of God on you. You are destroyed forever, and you'll never be back. Thank you, God. Let it happen. Cause it to happen.").
6. FDA v. Brown & Williamson Tobacco Corp., 529 U.S. 120 (2000).
7. 21 U.S.C. §§ 321(g)–(h), 393.
8. *See Brown & Williamson*, 529 U.S. at 162 (Breyer, J., dissenting) (citing United States v. Article of Drug . . . Bacto-Unidisk . . . , 394 U.S. 784, 798 (1969)).
9. *See, e.g.*, James E. Rogers College of Law, *A Conversation on the Constitution: Principles of*

Constitutional Statutory Interpretation, YouTube (Oct. 26, 2009), https://www.youtube .com/watch?v=jmv5Tz7w5pk&ab.

10. *See, e.g.,* John F. Manning, *The Absurdity Doctrine*, 116 HARV. L. REV. 2387, 2388 (2003).

11. *See infra* Chapter 6 (discussing Azar v. Allina Health Servs., 139 S. Ct. 1804 (2019)).

12. *Cf.* Frank H. Easterbrook, *Statutes' Domains*, 50 U. CHI. L. REV. 533, 546–47 (1983) (arguing that judges should refrain from extrapolating from statutory purposes where the legislature has proscribed both the means and the ends of a given statute).

13. *See, e.g.*, Blanchard v. Bergeron, 489 U.S. 87, 98 (1989) (Scalia, J., concurring in part and concurring in the judgment) (criticizing the majority's use of legislative history).

3: The Traditional Use of Text and Purpose

1. 529 U.S. 120 (2000).

2. Federal Food, Drug, and Cosmetic Act, Pub. L. 75-717, 52 Stat. 1040 (1938) (codified at 21 U.S.C. § 301 *et seq.*).

3. 21 U.S.C. § 321(g)(1)(C).

4. *See generally* U.S. DEP'T HEALTH & HUM. SERVS., THE HEALTH CONSEQUENCES OF SMOKING—NICOTINE ADDICTION: A REPORT OF THE SURGEON GENERAL (1988).

5. Regulations Restricting the Sale and Distribution of Cigarettes and Smokeless Tobacco to Protect Children and Adolescents, 61 Fed. Reg. 44,396 (Aug. 28, 1996).

6. *Id.* at 44,397, 44,402.

7. *Id.* at 44,404–07 (citing 21 U.S.C. § 360j(e)).

8. FDA v. Brown & Williamson Tobacco Corp., 529 U.S. at 120, 161 (2000).

9. *See id.* at 140 (citing United States v. Rutherford, 442 U.S. 544, 555 (1979)).

10. 21 U.S.C. §§ 355(d)(1)–(2), (4)–(5).

11. *Id.* §§ 355(e)(1)–(3).

12. *Id.* §§ 360c(a)(A)(i), (B), (C); Regulations Restricting the Sale and Distribution of Cigarettes and Smokeless Tobacco to Protect Children and Adolescents, 61 Fed. Reg. 44,396, 44,412 (Aug. 28, 1996).

13. *Brown & Williamson*, 529 U.S. at 137.

14. 21 U.S.C. § 360e(d)(2)(A).

15. *See* 7 U.S.C. § 1311(a).

16. *Brown & Williamson*, 529 U.S. at 142 ("Considering the FDCA as a whole, it is clear that Congress intended to exclude tobacco products from the FDA's jurisdiction.").

17. *Id.* at 137–38, 143–45 (citing statutes, congressional reports, and hearings).

18. *Id.* at 146.

19. *Id.* at 155.

20. *Id.* at 151 (citing S. REP. NO. 94-251, at 43 (1975)).

21. *Id.* at 157.

22. 21 U.S.C. § 321(g)(1)(C).

23. *Brown & Williamson*, 529 U.S. at 162 (Breyer, J., dissenting).

24. *See id.* (emphasis omitted) (citing United States v. Article of Drug . . . Bacto-Unidisk . . . , 394 U.S. 784, 798 (1969)).

25. *Id.* at 176.

26. *Id.* at 176–77.

27. *See id.* at 185–86.

28. *Id.* at 188–89.

4: The Text/Purpose Divide

1. 139 S. Ct. 1853 (2019).
2. *See* 35 U.S.C. §§ 154(a)(1)–(2).
3. *See id.* §§ 101–03.
4. *See id.* §§ 271(a), 281–84.
5. *See id.* § 282(b).
6. *See* Microsoft Corp. v. i4i L.P., 564 U.S. 91, 97 (2011).
7. *See* 35 U.S.C. §§ 321.
8. *See id.* § 6(c).
9. *See id.* § 326.
10. *See id.* § 328(b).
11. *See id.* § 329.
12. *See id.* § 321.
13. *See* Return Mail, Inc. v. U.S. Postal Serv., 139 S. Ct. 1853, 1861 (2019).
14. *Id.* at 1867–68.
15. See *id.* at 1861–62 (citing United States v. Cooper Corp., 312 U.S. 600, 604–05 (1941) (interpreting the Sherman Antitrust Act) and Davis v. Pringle, 268 U.S. 315, 317–18 (1925) (interpreting the Bankruptcy Act)).
16. *See* 1 U.S.C. § 1.
17. *Return Mail*, 139 S. Ct. at 1862–63.
18. *See, e.g.*, 35 U.S.C. § 207(a)(1).
19. *Return Mail*, 139 S. Ct. at 1866–67.
20. *Id.* at 1865.
21. *Id.* at 1866.
22. *Id.*
23. *See id.* (comparing 35 U.S.C. § 1498 (restricting private patent owners to only "reasonable and entire compensation" for governmental infringing use) with *id.* § 271(e)(4) (allowing those same patent owners to seek an injunction, jury trial, or punitive damages against nongovernmental infringers)).
24. *Id.* at 1866–67.
25. *Return Mail*, 139 S. Ct. at 1867.
26. *Id.* at 1868 (Breyer, J., dissenting).
27. *Id.* (citing United States v. Cooper Corp., 312 U.S. 600, 604–05 (1941)).
28. *Id.* (quoting Int'l Primate Prot. League v. Admins. of Tulane Ed. Fund, 500 U.S. 72, 83 (1991)).
29. *Id.* at 1869 (citing 35 U.S.C. §§ 6(a), 257(e), 2(b)(11), 100(h)).
30. *Id.* at 1868 (citing 35 U.S.C. §§ 252, 307(b), 318(c), 328(c)).
31. *Id.* at 1870 (internal quotation marks omitted) (citing H.R. Rep. No. 112-98, pt. 1, at 39, 48 (2011); and then citing U.S. Dep't of Commerce, Pat. & Trademark Off., Manual of Patent Examining Procedure §§ 2203, 2212 (4th rev. ed., Sep. 1982)).
32. *Id.*
33. *See id.* at 1871 (citing Hughes Aircraft Co. v. United States, 31 Fed. Cl. 481, 488 (1994) (listing value of infringing technologies as exceeding $3.5 billion)).
34. *Id.* at 1871 (noting that "the situation the Majority attempts to avoid is already baked into the cake").
35. *Id.*

36. *Id.*

37. 533 U.S. 167 (2001).

38. *See* 28 U.S.C. § 2254(a).

39. The prisoner is said to have "procedurally defaulted" on his claim or issue if he has not first presented the claim to state judges in a state proceeding. *See, e.g.*, Wainwright v. Sykes, 433 U.S. 72, 85 (1977); 28 U.S.C. § 2254(b).

40. 28 U.S.C. § 2244(d)(1).

41. *Id.* § 2244(d)(2) (emphasis added).

42. *Duncan*, 533 U.S. at 170.

43. *Id.*

44. *Id.*

45. 28 U.S.C. § 2244(d)(2).

46. *Duncan*, 533 U.S. at 171–72.

47. *Id.* at 172–73 (citing 28 U.S.C. § 2244(d)(2)).

48. *See id.* at 173 (citing 28 U.S.C. § 2254(i)).

49. *Id.* at 174.

50. *See id.*

51. 28 U.S.C. § 2244(d)(2).

52. *Duncan*, 533 U.S. at 185 (Breyer, J., dissenting).

53. *Id.* at 186 (citing statistics showing that 63 percent of all *habeas* petitions are dismissed, and that 57 percent of that subset were dismissed for failure to exhaust state remedies).

54. *Id.* at 189–90.

55. *Id.* at 190 ("Faced with this statutory ambiguity, I would look to statutory purposes in order to reach a proper interpretation.").

56. *See id.* at 191 (showing that 93 percent of all *habeas* petitioners in one study were unrepresented).

57. *Id.*

58. *Id.* at 192–93 (citing the Court's rejection of the notion that complete exhaustion should become a "'trap' for 'the unwary *pro se* prisoner'" (quoting Slack v. McDaniel, 529 U.S. 573, 487 (2000))).

59. *Id.* at 179 (majority opinion).

60. *Id.* at 190–92 (Breyer, J., dissenting).

61. *Id.* at 186 (citing U.S. Dep't of Just., Off. of Just. Programs, Bureau of Just. Stats., Federal Habeas Corpus Review: Challenging State Court Criminal Convictions 19 (1995)).

62. *Id.* at 192 (noting that prisoners have few incentives to delay under the existing statutory scheme).

63. *Id.* at 181 (majority opinion) (emphasis added).

64. *Id.* at 193 (Breyer, J., dissenting) (noting the propriety of judges assuming that, absent a contrary indication, "congressional purpose would mirror that of most reasonable human beings knowledgeable about the area of the law in question").

5: Static or Dynamic?

1. *Cf.* 16 U.S.C. § 1532 (codifying part of the Endangered Species Act).

2. 138 S. Ct. 2067 (2018).

3. This statute was named the Railroad Retirement Act of 1937. *See* Railroad Re-

tirement Act of 1937, Pub. L. No. 75-162, ch. 382, 50 Stat. 307 (1937) (codified as amended at 26 U.S.C. § 3231).

4. *See* 26 U.S.C. §§ 3201(a)–(b), 3221(a)–(b).

5. *Id.* § 3231(e)(1).

6. *See Wisconsin Central*, 138 S. Ct. at 2070.

7. *Id.* at 2075 (Breyer, J., dissenting).

8. *Id.* at 2074–75 (majority opinion).

9. *Id.* at 2070–71 (discussing and citing definitions from Webster's New International Dictionary, the Oxford English Dictionary, and Black's Law Dictionary).

10. *Id.* at 2070 (citing Perrin v. United States, 444 U.S. 37, 42 (1979)).

11. *See id.* at 2071–72.

12. *See id.* at 2071 (citing 26 U.S.C. § 305(b)(1)).

13. *Id.* at 2071–72 (citing 26 U.S.C. § 3121).

14. *Id.* at 2071 (quoting Henson v. Santander Consumer USA, Inc., 582 U.S. 79, 86 (2017)).

15. *Id.* at 2076 (Breyer, J., dissenting).

16. *Id.* at 2075.

17. *Id.* at 2079.

18. *Id.* at 2076 (discussing and citing definitions from the Oxford English Dictionary, Black's Law Dictionary, and the New Century Dictionary of the English Language).

19. *Id.*

20. *Id.*

21. *Id.* at 2076–77.

22. *Id.* at 2077 (quoting S. REP. NO. 697, at 8 (1937)).

23. *Id.*

24. *Id.* at 2078.

25. *Id.* at 2079, 2080.

26. 139 S. Ct. 759 (2019).

27. Pub. L. 79-291, 59 Stat. 669 (1945) (codified at 22 U.S.C. § 288).

28. 22 U.S.C. § 288a(b) (emphasis added).

29. *See Jam*, 139 S. Ct. at 766.

30. *See* Foreign Sovereign Immunities Act of 1976, Pub. L. 94-583, 90 Stat. 2891 (1977) (codified as amended at 28 U.S.C. §§ 1330, 1391(f), 1441(d), 1602–11).

31. *See* 28 U.S.C. § 1605(a)(2) (providing for foreign governmental liability where they engage in commercial activity that has a sufficient nexus with the United States).

32. *See Jam*, 139 S. Ct. at 764.

33. *Id.* at 772 ("The International Organizations Immunities Act grants international organizations the 'same immunity' from suit 'as is enjoyed by foreign governments' at any given time.").

34. *Id.* at 768.

35. *Id.*

36. *See id.* at 760.

37. *See id.* at 769 (citing 2 JABEZ G. SUTHERLAND, STATUTORY CONSTRUCTION §§ 5207–08 (3d ed. 1943)). For a more modern citation to the "reference canon," the Court cited *FTC v. Grolier, Inc.*, 462 U.S. 19, 20, 26–27 (1983)).

38. *Jam*, 139 S. Ct. at 769.

39. *Jam*, 139 S. Ct. at 771–72.

40. *See* 22 U.S.C. § 288.

41. *Jam*, 139 S. Ct. at 770.

42. *Id.* at 770.

43. *Id.* at 769 (quoting American Tobacco Co. v. Patterson, 456 U.S., 63, 68 (1982)).

44. *See id.* at 773–74 (Breyer, J., dissenting).

45. *Id.* at 775.

46. *Id.* at 774.

47. *See id.* (citing Kugler's Appeal, 55 Pa. 123, 123–25 (1867); and then citing Gaston v. Lamkin, 21 S.W. 1100, 1104 (1893); and then citing O'Flynn v. East Rochester, 54 N.E.2d 343, 346 (N.Y. 1944)).

48. *Id.* at 774–75.

49. *Id.* at 775 (citing R.J. Fox, *Effect of Modification or Repeal of Constitutional or Statutory Provision Adopted by Reference in Another Provision*, 168 A.L.R. 627, 628 (1947); and then citing 82 C.J.S. *Statutes* § 485, 637 (2009)).

50. *See id.* at 775–77.

51. *See id.* at 775 (citing S. REP. NO. 861, at 3 (1945)).

52. *Id.* (citing S. REP. NO. 861, at 3 (1945)).

53. *Id.* at 775–76.

54. *Id.* at 776.

55. *See id.* at 777 (detailing the history of UNRRA).

56. *See id.* (emphasis added) (citing 1 GEORGE WOODBRIDGE, UNRRA: THE HISTORY OF THE UNITED NATIONS RELIEF AND REHABILITATION ADMINISTRATION 3 (1950)).

57. *Id.* (describing how UNRRA obtained billions of pounds of food, clothing, and other relief supplies for children freed from concentration camps).

58. *See id.* (citing BEN SHEPHARD, THE LONG ROAD HOME: THE AFTERMATH OF THE SECOND WORLD WAR 54, 57–58 (2012)).

59. *Id.*

60. *See id.* at 766 (majority opinion) (citing the State Department's policy changes in 1952).

61. *See id.* at 777–78 (Breyer, J., dissenting) ("This history makes clear that Congress enacted the Immunities Act as part of an effort to encourage international organizations to locate their headquarters and carry on their missions in the United States.").

62. *Id.* at 778 (citing Atkinson v. Inter-American Dev. Bank, 156 F.3d 1335, 1340–41 (D.C. Cir. 1998)).

63. *Id.*

64. *Id.*

65. *Id.* at 778–79.

66. *Id.* at 779–80.

67. Convention on Privileges & Immunities of the United States, Art. VIII, § 29, 21 U.S.T. 1438, T.I.A.S. No. 6900.

68. *See Jam*, 139 S. Ct. at 780 (Breyer, J., dissenting) (citing Restatement (Third) of Foreign Rel. L. of the U.S. § 467, reporter's note 7 (Am. L. Inst. 1987)).

69. *See id.* (citing 22 U.S.C. § 288)).

70. *Id.*

71. *Id.*

72. *Id.*

73. *Id.*

74. *Id.* at 781.

75. *Id.*

76. *Id.*

6: Consequences

1. 139 S. Ct. 1804 (2019).

2. Pub. L. 79-404, 60 Stat. 237 (1946) (codified as amended at 5 U.S.C. §§ 551, 553–59, 701–06).

3. *See* 5 U.S.C. § 553(b)–(c).

4. *See id.* § 553(b)(3)(A).

5. 42 U.S.C. § 1395hh(a)(2) (emphasis added).

6. *Allina Health*, 139 S. Ct. at 1810 (noting that the phrase "doesn't seem to appear anywhere else in the entire United States Code").

7. *Id.* at 1811 (quoting 42 U.S.C. § 1395hh(a)(2)).

8. *Id.* at 1811–12.

9. *Id.* at 1814.

10. *See id.* at 1817 (Breyer, J., dissenting).

11. *Id.* at 1821–22 (quoting Shalala v. Ill. Council on Long Term Care, Inc., 529 U.S. 1, 13 (2000)).

12. *Id.* at 1822.

13. *Id.* (citing Denise Fantone, U.S. Gov't Accountability Off., GAO-09-205, Federal Rulemaking: Improvements Needed to Monitoring and Evaluation of Rules Development as Well as to the Transparency of OMB Regulatory Reviews 5, 19 (2009)).

14. *Id.*

15. *Id.* at 1822–23.

16. 42 U.S.C. § 1395f(b).

17. Ctrs. for Medicare & Medicaid Servs. Provider Reimbursement Manual 15-1 § 2140; *see also* Visiting Nurse Ass'n Gregoria Auffant, Inc. v. Thompson, 447 F.3d 68, 76–77 (1st Cir. 2006) (holding that the rule regarding retirement benefits was not required to go through a notice-and-comment proceeding).

18. Ctrs. for Medicare & Medicaid Servs. Provider Reimbursement Manual 15-1 § 2134.1(B); *see also* Am. Med. Int'l, Inc. v. Sec'y of Health, Educ. & Welfare, 466 F. Supp. 605, 615–16 (D.D.C. 1979) (holding that the rule regarding reimbursement for costs associated with complying with securities regulations was not required to go through a notice-and-comment proceeding).

19. *Allina Health*, 139 S. Ct. at 1823 (Breyer, J., dissenting); *see also id.* (collecting examples, including the Medicare General Information, Eligibility and Entitlement Manual; the Medicare Claims Processing Manual; the Medicare Benefit Policy Manual; the Medicare Secondary Payer Manual; the Medicare Program Integrity Manual; and the Medicare Prescription Drug Benefit Manual).

20. *Id.*

21. *Id.*

7: Legislative History

1. For empirical studies on the prevalence of legislative history as a tool of judicial interpretation, see David S. Law & David Zaring, *Law Versus Ideology: The Supreme Court*

and the Use of Legislative History, 51 Wm. & Mary L. Rev. 1653, 1665–68 (2010); *see also* Stuart M. Benjamin & Kristen M. Renberg, *The Paradoxical Impact of Scalia's Campaign Against Legislative History*, 105 Cornell L. Rev. 1023, 1025 (2020) ("Until the 1970s, there was a fairly broad consensus in the U.S. Supreme Court (and among scholars) that it is appropriate for courts to utilize legislative history in interpreting statutes.").

2. For discussion on the varying forms that legislative history can take, see John F. Manning & Matthew C. Stephenson, Legislation and Regulation: Cases and Materials 234–48 (4th ed. 2021).

3. *See* Patricia M. Wald, *Some Observations on the Use of Legislative History in the 1981 Supreme Court Term*, 68 Iowa L. Rev. 195, 197–98 (1983).

4. *See* Jonathan R. Siegel, *The Legacy of Justice Scalia and His Textualist Ideal*, 85 Geo. Wash. L. Rev. 857, 861–68 (2017) (chronicling Justice Scalia's evolving opposition to the use of legislative history).

5. *See* Conroy v. Aniskoff, 507 U.S. 511, 519 (1993) (Scalia, J., concurring in the judgment) (referencing Judge Harold Leventhal's quote to that effect from the 1970s).

6. *Cf.* Lewis Carroll, The Hunting of the Snark: An Agony, in Eight Fits (1876).

7. *See, e.g.*, John F. Manning, *Textualism as a Nondelegation Doctrine*, 97 Colum. L. Rev. 673, 731 (1997).

8. Members of the Court continue to use variations on this language when citing to legislative history after my retirement. *See, e.g.*, Delaware v. Pennsylvania, 143 S. Ct. 696, 711 (2023) (Jackson, J.).

9. My arguments in favor of legislative history are long-standing. *See, e.g.*, Stephen G. Breyer, *On the Uses of Legislative History in Interpreting Statutes*, 65 S. Cal. L. Rev. 845 (1992).

10. *See* Lon Fuller, *Positivism and Fidelity to Law—A Reply to Professor Hart*, 71 Harv. L. Rev. 630, 663 (1958).

11. Transcript of Oral Argument at 37, FCC v. NextWave Personal Commc'ns Inc., 537 U.S. 293 (2003) (No. 01-653).

12. *See* Karen Matthews, *RoboCop? No, RoboDog: Robotic Dog Rejoins New York Police*, AP News (Apr. 12, 2023), https://apnews.com/article/robot-dog-nypd-61bd64c94360e30f 110f65626cc1687c (describing the introduction of a robot named "Digidog" for use in hostage standoffs and locating stolen cars).

13. *See, e.g.*, Benjamin & Renberg, *supra* note 1, at 1082 (arguing that judges responded to Justice Scalia's critique by jettisoning unreliable legislative history and continuing to cite more reliable committee reports).

14. *See, e.g.*, Frank H. Easterbrook, *The Absence of Method in Statutory Interpretation*, 84 U. Chi. L. Rev. 81, 91 (2017) ("Like most other textualists, I am willing to consult legislative history as a cue to linguistic usage, even though not as an authoritative guide to meaning.").

15. Green v. Bock Laundry Mach. Co., 490 U.S. 504, 527 (1989) (Scalia, J., concurring in the judgment) (approving of legislative history where its use avoids "an absurd, and perhaps unconstitutional, result").

16. 1 William Blackstone, Commentaries *91.

17. *Id.*

18. *See* Church of the Holy Trinity v. United States, 143 U.S. 457, 461 (1892) (recounting Pufendorf anecdote).

19. For my prior treatment of this example, see Breyer, *supra* note 9, at 849.

20. Fed. R. Evid. 609(a)(1).

21. *See* Green v. Bock Laundry Mach. Co., 490 U.S. 504, 527 (1989) (holding that the rule applied only to criminal cases).

22. *Id.* at 527 (Scalia, J., concurring in the judgment).

23. *Id.*

24. *See* Breyer, *supra* note 9, at 850–51.

25. 18 U.S.C. § 485.

26. *See* United States v. Falvey, 676 F.2d 871 (1st Cir. 1982).

27. *See id.* at 873 ("It was recognized as early as 1832 that this statute did not reach the counterfeiting of foreign coins without limitation.").

28. Breyer, *supra* note 9, at 851.

29. *Id.* at 851–53.

30. Pierce v. Underwood, 487 U.S. 552, 564–65 (1988).

31. *Id.*

32. Consol. Edison Co. v. NLRB, 305 U.S. 197, 229 (1938).

33. Breyer, *supra* note 9, at 852–53 (recounting the legislative history of the APA).

34. 305 U.S. 197 (1938).

35. For criticisms of the use of legislative history on these grounds, see, for example, Kenneth A. Shepsle, *Congress Is a "They," Not an "It": Legislative Intent as Oxymoron*, 12 INT'L REV. L. & ECON. 239 (1992). For a rebuttal of that position, see, for example, Ryan D. Doerfler, *Who Cares How Congress Really Works?*, 66 DUKE L. J. 979, 982 (2017) (arguing that legislative intent remains coherent even assuming that Congress is a "they" and not an "it").

36. *See* Felix Frankfurter, *Some Reflections on the Reading of Statutes*, 47 COLUM. L. REV. 527, 541–43 (1947); *cf.* William Baude & Stephen Sachs, *The Law of Interpretation*, 130 HARV. L. REV. 1079, 1114–15 (2017) (noting that different societies are entitled to craft different laws of interpretation to give weight to varying considerations).

37. Frankfurter, *supra* note 36, at 542–43 (contrasting the Supreme Court's approach with the developed English approach).

38. The following is a high-level summary of the legislative process in the United Kingdom, drawn from 2 JOINT COMM. ON CONVENTIONS, CONVENTIONS OF THE UK PARLIAMENT, ev. 1–3 (2005–06).

39. *See, e.g.*, TOM BINGHAM, THE RULE OF LAW 162–68 (2010).

40. *See* Richard H. Fallon, Jr., *The Statutory Interpretation Muddle*, 114 NW. UNIV. L. REV. 269, 270 (2019) (comparing Antonin Scalia, *Common-Law Courts in a Civil-Law System: The Role of the United States Federal Courts in Interpreting the Constitution and Laws*, in A MATTER OF INTERPRETATION 3, 14 (1997) wit h HENRY M. HART, JR. & ALBERT M. SACKS, THE LEGAL PROCESS: BASIC PROBLEMS IN THE MAKING AND APPLICATION OF LAW (William N. Eskridge, Jr. & Phillip P. Frickey eds. 1994) (1958)).

41. Harvard Law School, *The Scalia Lecture: A Dialogue with Justice Elena Kagan on the Reading of Statutes*, YouTube at 8:29 (Nov. 17, 2015), https://www.youtube .com/watch?v=dpEtszFT0Tg&source_ve_path=MjM4NTE&feature=emb_title.

42. *See, e.g.*, Tara Leigh Grove, *Which Textualism?*, 134 HARV. L. REV. 265, 266–67 (2020) (drawing out tensions between the majority and dissenting opinions in *Bostock v. Clayton County*, 140 S. Ct. 1731 (2020), both of which purported to be employing textualism as a methodology).

43. *See* Nicholas Quinn Rosenkranz, *Federal Rules of Statutory Interpretation*, 115 HARV. L. REV. 2085, 2141–47 (2002).

44. *See supra* Chapter 2, note 26 and accompanying text; Abbe R. Gluck & Lisa Schultz Bressman, *Statutory Interpretation from the Inside—An Empirical Study of Congressional Drafting, Delegation, and the Canons: Part I*, 65 STAN. L. REV. 901 (2013); Lisa Schultz Bressman & Abbe R. Gluck, *Statutory Interpretation from the Inside—An Empirical Study of Congressional Drafting, Delegation, and the Canons: Part II*, 66 STAN. L. REV. 725 (2014).

45. *See* Frankfurter, *supra* note 36, at 542 (citing United States v. Fisher, 6 U.S. (2 Cranch) 358, 386 (1805) (Marshall, C.J.)).

46. 552 U.S. 214 (2008).

47. 28 U.S.C. § 1346(b)(1).

48. *Id.* § 2680(c) (emphasis added).

49. *Ali*, 552 U.S. at 215.

50. *Id.*

51. *Id.* at 228.

52. *Id.* at 218–20.

53. *Id.* at 219–20 (citing United States v. Gonzalez, 520 U.S. 1, 5 (1997); and then citing Harrison v. PPG Inds., Inc., 446 U.S. 578, 588–89 (1980)).

54. *Id.* at 219 (citing *Gonzalez*, 520 U.S. at 4).

55. *Id.* at 220.

56. *Id.* at 221 (citing 28 U.S.C. § 2680(c)(1)-(4)).

57. *Id.* at 221–22 (emphasis added).

58. *Id.* at 222–23.

59. *See id.* at 223–28.

60. *Id.* at 224 (citing the *ejusdem generis* canon).

61. *Id.* at 226–27.

62. *See id.* at 243 (Breyer, J., dissenting).

63. *Id.*

64. *Id.* at 244.

65. *Id.* at 244–45.

66. *Id.* at 245 (citing S. 4377, 71st Cong. (1930)); *see also* 74 CONG. REC. 85 (1930).

67. *Ali*, 552 U.S. at 245–46 (Breyer, J., dissenting).

68. *Id.* at 245 ("Initially, the relevant provision of the bill exempted only claims 'arising in respect of the assessment or collection of any tax or customs duty.'").

69. *Id.* at 245.

70. *Id.*

71. *Id.* at 246.

72. *Id.* at 246–47.

73. *See id.* at 238 (Kennedy, J., dissenting) ("If Congress wanted to say that all law enforcement officers may detain property without liability in tort, including when they perform general law enforcement tasks, it would have done so in more express terms.").

74. Whitman v. Amer. Trucking Ass'ns, Inc., 531 U.S. 457, 468 (2001).

75. 562 U.S. 223 (2011).

76. 42 U.S.C. § 300aa-22(b)(1).

77. *Bruesewitz*, 562 U.S. at 227.

78. *Id.* (citing academic scholarship on the phenomenon).

79. *Id.* at 228.

80. 42 U.S.C. § 300aa-22(b)(1) (emphasis and numbering added).

81. *Bruesewitz*, 562 U.S. at 230–31.

82. *Id.* at 243.

83. *Id.* at 235.

84. *Id.* at 237 (citing 21 C.F.R. § 601.12).

85. *Id.* at 236 (citing 42 U.S.C. § 300aa-22(b)(1)).

86. *Id.*

87. *Id.*

88. *Id.* at 232.

89. *Id.* (citing a tort law treatise).

90. *Id.* at 232.

91. *Id.* at 243 (Breyer, J., concurring).

92. *Id.* at 249.

93. *Id.* at 244 (citing H.R. REP. NO. 99-908, pt. 1, at 26 (1986)).

94. *Id.*

95. *Id.*

96. Garcia v. United States, 469 U.S. 70, 76 (1984).

97. *Bruesewitz*, 562 U.S. at 244–45 (Breyer, J., concurring).

98. *Id.*; *see also id.* at 243 (majority opinion) (rebutting the dissent's reading of the reference to the Restatement of Torts in the legislative history).

99. *Id.* at 245–48 (Breyer, J., concurring).

100. *Id.* at 247.

101. *Id.*

102. *Id.* at 248–49.

103. 548 U.S. 291 (2006).

104. That statute, the Individuals with Disabilities Education Act, is codified in relevant part at 20 U.S.C. § 1400(d)(1)(A).

105. *See generally id.* § 1415.

106. The facts of the case are described by the majority opinion. *See Murphy*, 548 U.S. at 294–95.

107. 20 U.S.C. § 1415(i)(3)(B).

108. *Murphy*, 548 U.S. at 294–95.

109. *Id.* at 297–98.

110. *Id.* at 300–03 (citing Crawford Fitting Co. v. J.T. Gibbons, Inc., 482 U.S. 437, 439 (1987); and then citing W. Va. Univ. Hosps. v. Casey, 499 U.S. 83, 102 (1991)) (interpreting FED. R. CIV. PROC. 54(d) and 42 U.S.C. § 1988).

111. *Id.* at 297 (describing the Murphy family's argument to that effect).

112. *Id.* at 315 (Breyer, J., dissenting).

113. *See id.* at 313–14 (citing the act's language to uncover its stated purposes).

114. *Id.* at 315 ("In a word, the Act's statutory right to a 'free' and 'appropriate' education may mean little to those who must pay hundreds of dollars to obtain it.").

115. H.R. REP. NO. 99-687, at 5 (1986) (Conf. Rep.) (emphasis added).

116. *Murphy*, 548 U.S. at 308–09 (Breyer, J., dissenting).

117. *Id.* at 304 (majority opinion).

118. *Id.*

119. *Id.* at 324 (Breyer, J., dissenting) (criticizing the majority for adopting an approach that "divorces law from life").

120. For examples of these criticisms, see Breyer, *supra* note 9, at 845 n.1 (reviewing literature).

121. Wald, *supra* note 3, at 214.

122. *See Murphy*, 548 U.S. at 308–09 (Breyer, J., dissenting).

123. *See, e.g.*, Kenneth W. Starr, *Observations About the Use of Legislative History*, 1987 DUKE L. J. 371, 375–76 (identifying "democratic theory concerns" with the judicial use of legislative history).

124. For an example of this type of argument, see, e.g., John F. Manning, *Putting Legislative History to a Vote: A Response to Professor Siegel*, 53 VAND. L. REV. 1529, 1530 (2000) ("I have argued that the Court's separation-of-powers case law powerfully undermines any approach to legislative history that generally treats it as authoritative.").

125. For an example of this type of argument, see, e.g., Manning, *supra* note 7, at 739 ("Congress's ability to specify legal norms without formally adopting them reduces the decision costs of lawmaking, but at the expense of disserving the important structural objectives promoted by bicameralism and presentment.").

126. *See* Frank H. Easterbrook, *Statutes' Domains*, 50 U. CHI. L. REV. 533, 547–58 (1983) (arguing that legislative bodies can only have outcomes and not intents).

127. *See generally* Shepsle, *supra* note 35, at 239 (arguing that to claim that legislative history has meaning is to "entertain a myth").

128. The following discussion draws from my previous writing on the subject. *See* Breyer, *supra* note 9, at 864–65.

129. *See* Victoria F. Nourse, *A Decision Theory of Statutory Interpretation: Legislative History by the Rules*, 122 YALE L. J. 70, 82 (2012) ("We talk about collective entities all the time: Harvard thinks this, Yale does that. Positive political theorists are right on this score: the idea that we do not talk about collective entities flies in the face of general linguistic usage and common law practice.").

130. *See id.* at 83–84.

131. Professor Nourse uses the example of corporations to reinforce this point: We often speak (sensibly) about corporate statements and actions despite the corporation's nonexistence as a singular, human entity. *See id.* at 82 & nn.46–47.

132. *Cf.* GILBERT RYLE, THE CONCEPT OF MIND 16 (1949) ("A foreigner visiting Oxford or Cambridge for the first time is shown a number of colleges, libraries, playing fields, museums, scientific departments and administrative offices. He then asks 'But where is the University? I have seen where the members of the Colleges live, where the Registrar works, where the scientists experiment and the rest. But I have not yet seen the University in which reside and work the members of your University.'").

133. For an explication of this criticism, *see, e.g.*, William N. Eskridge, Jr., *Politics Without Romance: Implications of Public Choice Theory for Statutory Interpretation*, 74 VA. L. REV. 275, 316–17 (1988).

134. *See* Breyer, *supra* note 9, at 872–73.

135. *See* Anti-Drug Abuse Act of 1986, Pub. L. 99-570, 100 Stat. 3207 (1986) (codified as amended primarily in scattered sections of 18 and 21 U.S.C.).

136. 21 U.S.C. § 844(a).

137. Breyer, *supra* note 9, at 873–74.

138. *Id.* at 847 (arguing that legislative history is defensible as a judicial tool insofar as it tends "to make the law itself more coherent, workable, or fair").

8: Constitutional Values

1. *See, e.g.*, Ashwander v. Tenn. Valley Auth., 297 U.S. 288, 346 (1936) (Brandeis, J., concurring).

2. Indeed, Justices Thomas and Scalia have both employed the avoidance canon in their opinions. *See, e.g.*, Wash. State Grange v. Wash. State Republican Party, 552 U.S. 442, 450 (2008) (Thomas, J.); Vt. Agency of Nat. Res. v. United States *ex rel.* Stevens, 529 U.S. 765, 787 (2000) (Scalia, J.)).

3. 533 U.S. 678 (2001).

4. 8 U.S.C. § 1231(a)(6).

5. *Id.* § 1231(a)(1)(A).

6. *See, e.g., id.* § 1227(a).

7. *Id.* § 1231(a)(6) (emphasis added).

8. *See Zadvydas*, 533 U.S. at 684–86.

9. *Id.* at 682.

10. *Id.* at 702.

11. *Id.* at 682.

12. Twining v. New Jersey, 211 U.S. 78, 100 (1908).

13. 4 WILLIAM BLACKSTONE, COMMENTARIES *293–97.

14. Ch. 20, 1 Stat. 73 § 33 (1789).

15. *Id.* § 33.

16. *See, e.g.*, United States v. Salerno, 481 U.S. 739, 752–55 (1987) (upholding the constitutionality of the Bail Reform Act of 1984).

17. 138 S. Ct. 830 (2018).

18. *Id.* at 862 (Breyer, J., dissenting).

19. *Id.* at 838–39 (majority opinion).

20. *See id.* at 866–69 (Breyer, J., dissenting) (reviewing case law).

21. *See id.* at 865–66 (comparing bail treatment for confined noncitizens with bail treatment for criminal defendants).

22. Zadvydas v. Davis, 533 U.S. 678, 696 (2001).

23. *Compare id.* ("[W]e believe that an alien's liberty interest is, at the least, strong enough to raise a serious question as to whether . . . the Constitution permits detention that is indefinite and potentially permanent.") *with Jennings*, 138 S. Ct. at 869 (Breyer, J., dissenting) ("The Constitution's language, its basic purposes, the relevant history, our tradition, and many of the relevant cases point in the same interpretive direction. They tell us that an interpretation of the statute before us that would deny bail proceedings where detention is prolonged would likely mean that the statute violates the Constitution.").

24. *Jennings*, 138 S. Ct. at 869 (Breyer, J., dissenting) (citing *Zadvydas*, 533 U.S. at 696).

25. 8 U.S.C. § 1231(a)(6).

26. *Zadvydas*, 533 U.S. at 697.

27. *Id.* at 682.

28. *Id.* at 700.

29. *Id.* at 701.

30. *Id.*

31. *Id.*

32. Jennings v. Rodriguez, 138 S. Ct. 830, 836 (2018).

33. *Id.* at 850–51.

34. *Id.* at 865–66 (Breyer, J., dissenting).

35. *Id.* at 842 (majority opinion) (citing 8 U.S.C. §§ 1225(b)(1)(B)(ii), (b)(2)(A)).

36. *Id.* at 870 (Breyer, J., dissenting) (citing the Oxford English Dictionary's history of the term).

37. *Id.* at 870–71.

38. *Id.* at 871.

39. *Id.* at 871–72 (emphasis added) (citing 8 U.S.C. § 1225(b)(1)(B)(iii)(IV)).

40. *Id.* at 872 ("An interpretation that permits bail—based upon history, tradition, statutory context, and precedent—is consistent, not inconsistent, with what Congress intended the statutory provision to do.").

41. *Id.* at 851 (majority opinion) (remanding the constitutional question to the court of appeals).

9: Resolving the Text/Purpose Tension

1. *Cf.* Joseph C. Hutcheson, Jr., *The Judgment Intuitive: The Function of the "Hunch" in Judicial Decision*, 14 CORNELL L. Q. 274, 285 (1929); JEROME FRANK, LAW AND THE MODERN MIND 111–12 (Stevens & Sons ed. 1949) (1930) (describing the "personality of the judge" as a "pivotal factor in law administration," *id.* at 111).

2. FDA v. Brown & Williamson Tobacco Corp., 529 U.S. 120 (2000).

3. 143 U.S. 457 (1892).

4. Alien Contract Labor Law of 1885, ch. 164, § 1, 23 Stat. 332 (amended 1887, 1888).

5. *Holy Trinity*, 143 U.S. at 458–59.

6. *Id.* at 457–58.

7. *Id.* at 472.

8. *Id.* at 458 ("It must be conceded that the act of the corporation is within the letter of this section.").

9. *Id.* at 459.

10. *Id.* at 461 (quoting United States v. Kirby, 74 U.S. (7 Wall.) 482, 486–87 (1868)).

11. *Id.* at 461–62.

12. *Id.* at 463.

13. *Id.*

14. *Id.*

15. *Id.*

16. *Id.* at 464.

17. *Id.* at 464–65.

18. *Id.* at 465.

19. *Id.* at 465–72.

20. *Id.* at 465.

21. *Id.* at 460–61.

22. For criticisms of *Holy Trinity*, of which there are many, see, for example, John F. Manning, *The Absurdity Doctrine*, 116 HARV. L. REV. 2387, 2462, 2463 n.275 (2003); Adrian Vermeule, *Legislative History and the Limits of Judicial Competence: The Untold Story of* Holy Trinity Church, 50 STAN. L. REV. 1833, 1835, 1837 (1998); Antonin Scalia, *Common-Law Courts in a Civil-Law System: The Role of United States Federal Courts in Interpreting the Constitution and Laws*, in A MATTER OF INTERPRETATION 3, 18–23 (1997).

23. Jam v. Int'l Fin. Corp., 139 S. Ct. 759 (2019).

24. Scalia, *supra* note 22, at 21.
25. For examples of the current-day Court reading ministerial exemptions into otherwise silent statutes by referencing constitutional values, see Hosanna-Tabor Evangelical Lutheran Church & Sch. v. EEOC, 565 U.S. 171, 188 (2012).
26. I might also have been moved by the fact that, in the absence of any dissent, the opinion would have been unanimous. Prior to 1941, the Supreme Court operated with a high degree of consensus and unanimity. *See* Cass R. Sunstein, *Unanimity and Disagreement on the Supreme Court*, 100 CORNELL L. REV. 769, 773–76 (2015) (charting dissent, concurrence, and 5–4 occurrences on the Court from 1800 through 2000 and beyond). The underlying data was compiled in LEE EPSTEIN ET AL., THE SUPREME COURT COMPENDIUM: DATA, DECISIONS & DEVELOPMENTS 246–69 (5th ed. 2012). This is not to say that the pre-1941 Court did not engage in sustained debate and disagreement with one another. Sunstein, *supra*, at 780 (citing famous divisions among members of the Court in the pre-1941 era). But unanimity of opinion is a virtue that a member of the Court often considers.
27. 534 U.S. 438 (2002).
28. *See id.* at 442.
29. *Id.* at 443–45.
30. *Id.* at 444–45 ("[B]y June 1991, the 120,000 individuals who received health benefits from the funds were in danger of losing their benefits.").
31. Pub. L. 102-486, 106 Stat. 2776 (1992) (codified in scattered sections of 12 U.S.C., 16 U.S.C., 25 U.S.C., 26 U.S.C., 30 U.S.C., and 42 U.S.C.).
32. *See Barnhart*, 534 U.S. at 447.
33. 26 U.S.C. § 9706(a).
34. *Id.*
35. *Id.* § 9701(c)(2).
36. *Id.* § 9706(a) ("For purposes of this chapter, the Commissioner of Social Security shall, before October 1, 1993, assign each coal industry retiree who is an eligible beneficiary to a signatory operator.").
37. *See id.* § 9701(c)(2).
38. *Id.* § 9706(a) (emphasis added).
39. *Id.* § 9706(a)(1)(A)–(B).
40. *Id.* § 9706(a)(2)(A)–(B).
41. *Id.* § 9706(a)(3).
42. *Id.* § 9701(c)(2)(A)(i)–(iii).
43. *Id.* (emphasis added).
44. Barnhart v. Sigmon Coal Co., 534 U.S. 438, 447–48 (2002).
45. *Id.*
46. *Id.* at 454. Irdell had changed its name to "Jericol" before the case had reached the Court, so the discussion in the majority opinion references Irdell as "Jericol" throughout.
47. *Id.* at 452.
48. *Id.*
49. *Id.*
50. *Id.*
51. *Id.* at 454.
52. *Id.*

53. *Id.* at 461–62 (quoting Conn. Nat'l Bank v. Germain, 503 U.S. 249, 253–54 (1992)).

54. *Id.* at 465 (Stevens, J., dissenting) ("Two examples illustrate the absurdity of the Court's reading.").

55. *Id.* at 464 n.1 (citing 26 U.S.C. § 9701(c)(2)(A)).

56. *Id.* at 466.

57. *Id.* at 465–66 (citing 138 CONG. REC. 34034, 34033 (1992)).

58. *Id.* at 466 n.2.

59. *Id.* at 468–69.

60. *Cf.* Burwell v. Hobby Lobby Stores, Inc., 573 U.S. 682, 755 (2014) (Ginsburg, J., dissenting) (noting that "[h]ad Congress intended [a statute] to initiate a change so huge, a clarion statement to that effect likely would have been made in the legislation").

61. *Barnhart*, 534 U.S. at 469–70 (Stevens, J., dissenting) (citing 1 U.S.C. § 1).

62. *Id.* at 470.

63. *Id.*

64. *Id.* at 472.

65. As Justice Stevens wrote in dissent, "[t]here are occasions when an exclusive focus on text seems to convey an incoherent message, but other reliable evidence clarifies the statute and avoids the apparent incoherence. In such a case—and this is one—we should never permit a narrow focus on text to obscure a commonsense appraisal of that additional evidence."). *Id.*

10: Why Judges Should Consider Purposes: A Summary

1. These two theories of political accountability are often termed the "delegate" and "trustee" models of representation, respectively. *See, e.g.*, Justin Fox & Kenneth W. Shotts, *Delegates or Trustees? A Theory of Political Accountability*, 71 J. POL. 1225, 1225 & n.1 (2009) (tracing these theories back to Edmund Burke, James Madison, and John Stuart Mill).

2. Ali v. Fed. Bureau of Prisons, 552 U.S. 214 (2008).

3. *See, e.g.*, Bostock v. Clayton County, 140 S. Ct. 1731, 1755 (2020) (Alito, J., dissenting) ("If every single living American had been surveyed in 1964, it would have been hard to find any who thought that discrimination because of sex meant discrimination because of sexual orientation—not to mention gender identity, a concept that was essentially unknown at the time.").

4. For an argument that certain "super-statutes" (that is, laws that "seek[] to establish a new normative or institutional framework" and "stick" in the public culture such that they have a "broad effect on the law") are especially susceptible to pragmatic interpretations, *see* William N. Eskridge, Jr. & John Ferejohn, *Super-Statutes*, 50 DUKE L. J. 1215, 1216 (2001).

5. *See* Charles L. Barzun, *The Forgotten Foundations of Hart and Sacks*, 99 VA. L. REV. 1, 20–21 (2013) (attributing to Professors Henry M. Hart and Albert M. Sacks the notion that the basic function of law is to create the conditions necessary for community life to develop).

6. Jam v. Int'l Fin. Corp., 139 S. Ct. 759 (2019).

7. Duncan v. Walker, 533 U.S. 167 (2001).

8. ST. THOMAS AQUINAS, SUMMA THEOLOGICA, pt. II-II, q. 60, art. 5, ad 2 (Fathers of the English Dominican Province trans., Benzinger Bros. ed. 1947) (c. 1271).

9. 1 William Blackstone, Commentaries *91.

10. Farah Peterson, *Expounding the Constitution*, 130 Yale L. J. 2, 77 (2020).

11. Oliver Wendell Holmes, Jr., *The Theory of Legal Interpretation*, 12 Harv. L. Rev. 417, 417 (1899).

12. Benjamin N. Cardozo, The Nature of the Judicial Process 116 (1921).

13. *Id.*

14. Learned Hand, How Far Is a Judge Free in Rendering a Decision? (1933), *reprinted in* The Spirit of Liberty 103, 107 (Irving Dilliard ed., 3d ed. 1963).

15. The term "imaginative reconstruction" was adopted from Learned Hand's philosophy by Judge Richard Posner, who defended such an approach at the beginning of his career. *See* Thomas W. Merrill, *Learned Hand on Statutory Interpretation: Theory and Practice*, 87 Fordham L. Rev. 1, 4 (2018) (citing Richard A. Posner, *Statutory Interpretation—In the Classroom and in the Courtroom*, 50 U. Chi. L. Rev. 800, 817 (1983)).

16. United States v. Fisher, 6 U.S. (2 Cranch) 358, 386 (1805) (Marshall, C.J.).

17. *See, e.g.*, Delaware v. Pennsylvania, 143 S. Ct. 696, 711–12 (2023) (Jackson, J.) (using legislative history and common sense to reject an unworkable and "ineffectual" reading of the Federal Disposition Act).

18. Stephen G. Breyer, *On the Uses of Legislative History in Interpreting Statutes*, 65 S. Cal. L. Rev. 845, 874 (1992).

Part III: Interpreting the Constitution

1. McCulloch v. Maryland, 17 U.S. (4 Wheat.) 316, 407, 415 (1819).

2. *Id.*

3. *See supra* Chapter 2.

4. Lawrence B. Solum, *The Fixation Thesis: The Role of Historical Fact in Original Meaning*, 91 Notre Dame L. Rev. 1, 27 (2015); *see also* Randy E. Barnett, Restoring the Lost Constitution 92 (2004) ("'[O]riginal meaning' originalism seeks the public or objective meaning that a reasonable listener would place on the words used in the constitutional provision at the time of the enactment."); Antonin Scalia & Bryan A. Garner, Reading Law 16 (2012) ("In their full context, words mean what they conveyed to reasonable people at the time they were written."); Amy Coney Barrett, *Originalism and Stare Decisis*, 92 Notre Dame L. Rev. 1921, 1924 (2017).

5. *See generally* Antonin Scalia, *The Rule of Law as a Law of Rules*, 56 U. Chi. L. Rev. 1175 (1989).

11: The Constitution

1. U.S. Const.; Stephen Gardbaum, *The Myth and the Reality of American Constitutional Exceptionalism*, 107 Mich. L. Rev. 391, 399 (2008); Sol Bloom, *Constitution Questions and Answers*, Nat'l Archives (July 5, 2022), https://www.archives.gov/founding-docs/constitution-q-and-a.

2. Marbury v. Madison, 5 U.S. (1 Cranch) 137, 177–78 (1803).

3. U.S. Const. art. I, § 1.

4. *Id.*

5. *Id.* art. II, § 1.

6. *Id.* art. III, § 1.

7. *Id.* art. IV, § 1.

8. *Id.* § 3.

9. *Id.* art. V.

10. *Id.* art. VI.

11. *Id.* art. VII.

12. *See id.* amends. I–X.

13. *Id.* amend. I.

14. *Id.* amend. IV.

15. *Id.* amend. VI.

16. *Id.* amend. XI.

17. *Id.* amend. XII.

18. *Id.* amend. XIII.

19. *Id.* amend. XIV.

20. *Id.* amend. XV.

21. *Id.* amend. XIX.

22. *Id.* amend. XXVI.

23. *Id.* amend. XXIV.

24. *Id.* amend. XVII.

25. *Id.* amend. XXII.

26. *Id.* amend. XX.

27. *Id.* amend. XXV.

28. *Id.* amend. XXIII.

29. *Id.* amend. XVIII.

30. *Id.* amend. XXI.

31. *Id.* amend. XXVII.

32. *Id.* amend. XVI.

33. *Id.* amend. XIV, § 1; *see also id.* amend. V.

34. *Id.* amend. I.

35. *Id.* art. I, § 8, cl. 3.

36. *Id.* cl. 18.

37. *Id.* § 3.

38. *Id.* amend. XX.

39. *Id.* art. I, § 10.

40. *Id.* art. I, § 8, cl. 4.

41. *Id.* cl. 8.

42. *Id.* art. II, § 2.

43. *Id.* art. I, § 10.

44. *Id.* amend. III.

45. *Id.* amend. I.

46. Schenck v. United States, 249 U.S. 47, 52 (1919) (emphasis added).

12: The Traditional Approach to Constitutional Interpretation

1. 17 U.S. (4 Wheat.) 316 (1819).

2. *Id.* at 317–19.

3. *Id.* at 401.

4. *Id.* at 425.

5. *Id.* at 400–01.

6. *Id.* at 401.

7. *Id.* at 402–03.

8. Farah Peterson, *Expounding the Constitution*, 130 YALE L. J. 2, 29–31 (2020).

9. *McCulloch*, 17 U.S. at 403.

10. U.S. CONST. pmbl.

11. *McCulloch*, 17 U.S. at 403–04.

12. *Id.* at 404–05.

13. *See id.* at 405.

14. *Id.*

15. *Id.* at 406 (quoting U.S. CONST. art. VI).

16. *Id.* at 407.

17. *Id.* at 409.

18. *Id.* at 407–08.

19. *Id.* at 411–12 (quoting U.S. CONST. art. I, § 8, cl. 18).

20. *Id.* at 413–14.

21. *Id.* at 415.

22. *Id.* at 415–16.

23. *Id.* at 418.

24. *Id.* at 419.

25. *Id.* at 419–20.

26. *Id.* at 421.

27. *Id.*

28. *Id.* at 424.

29. *Id.* at 431.

30. U.S. CENSUS BUREAU, A CENTURY OF POPULATION GROWTH: FROM THE FIRST CENSUS OF THE UNITED STATES TO THE TWELFTH 9 (1909).

31. *Id.* at 415; *see also* Cohens v. Virginia, 19 U.S. (6 Wheat.) 264, 387 (1821) (Marshall, C.J.) ("[A] constitution is framed for ages to come, and is designed to approach immortality as nearly as human institutions can approach it.").

32. *McCulloch*, 17 U.S. at 407.

33. Youngstown Sheet & Tube Co. v. Sawyer, 343 U.S. 579, 635 (1952) (Jackson, J., concurring).

34. Nevada v. Hall, 440 U.S. 410, 433 (1979) (Rehnquist, J., dissenting).

35. MICHAEL J. KLARMAN, THE FRAMERS' COUP: THE MAKING OF THE UNITED STATES CONSTITUTION 624 (2016).

36. Vieth v. Jubelirer, 541 U.S. 267, 356 (2004) (Breyer, J., dissenting) (alterations in original) (quoting GORDON S. WOOD, THE CREATION OF THE AMERICAN REPUBLIC: 1776–1787, at 595 (1969)).

37. Saul Cornell, *President Madison's Living Constitution: Fixation, Liquidation, and Constitutional Politics in the Jeffersonian Era*, 89 FORDHAM L. REV. 1761, 1778 (2021) ("The Constitution, [Madison] wrote, ought to be given 'that just construction, which with the aid of time and habit, may put an end to the more dangerous schisms otherwise growing out of it.'" (quoting Randy E. Barnett, *An Originalism for Nonoriginalists*, 45 LOY. L. REV. 611, 628 (1999)))).

38. Letter from Thomas Jefferson to James Madison (Sep. 6, 1789), in 15 THE PAPERS OF THOMAS JEFFERSON 392, 396 (Julian P. Boyd ed., 1958).

NOTES

39. David A. Strauss, The Living Constitution 24 (2010) (citing Letter from Thomas Jefferson to James Madison, *supra* note 38).
40. Parents Involved in Cmty. Schs. v. Seattle Sch. Dist. No. 1, 551 U.S. 701, 858 (2007) (Breyer, J., dissenting).

13: Constitutional Textualism

1. U.S. Const. art. I, § 8, cl. 1.
2. *See* South Dakota v. Dole, 483 U.S. 203, 207 (1987) (affirming Congress's authority to exercise its spending power broadly).
3. *See id.* (upholding Congress's imposition of conditions on state expenditures of federal highway funds).
4. *See, e.g.,* Frank H. Easterbrook, *Statutes' Domains*, 50 U. Chi. L. Rev. 533, 536 (1983).
5. *See* sources cited *supra* Part III, note 4.
6. *See generally* Antonin Scalia, *The Rule of Law as a Law of Rules*, 56 U. Chi. L. Rev. 1175 (1989).
7. Lawrence B. Solum, *The Fixation Thesis: The Role of Historical Fact in Original Meaning*, 91 Notre Dame L. Rev. 1, 26–27 (2015).
8. Antonin Scalia & Bryan A. Garner, Reading Law 435 (2012).
9. Ruth Marcus, Opinion, *Originalism Is Bunk. Liberal Lawyers Shouldn't Fall for It.*, Wash. Post (Dec. 1, 2022, 9:21 AM), https://www.washingtonpost.com/opinions /2022/12/01/originalism-liberal-lawyers-supreme-court-trap/.
10. 142 S. Ct. 2111 (2022).
11. *Id.* at 2127–28 (quoting District of Columbia v. Heller, 554 U.S. 570, 605 (2008)).
12. *See* Scalia & Garner, *supra* note 8, at 87 ("The conclusive argument in favor of originalism is a simple one: It is the only objective standard of interpretation even competing for acceptance. . . . The choice is this: Give text the meaning it bore when it was adopted, or else let every judge decide for himself what it should mean today.").
13. *Bruen*, 142 S. Ct. at 2122.
14. 142 S. Ct. 2111 (2022).
15. U.S. Const. amend. II.
16. 554 U.S. 570 (2008).
17. *Id.* at 635–36.
18. *Bruen*, 142 S. Ct. at 2122.
19. *Id.*
20. *Id.* at 2169 (Breyer, J., dissenting).
21. *Id.* at 2170 (quoting Kachalsky v. County of Westchester, 701 F.3d 81, 86 (2d Cir. 2012)).
22. *Id.* at 2126 (majority opinion) (first quoting Kanter v. Barr, 919 F.3d 437, 441 (7th Cir. 2019); then quoting Kolbe v. Hogan, 849 F.3d 114, 133 (4th Cir. 2017)).
23. *Id.* at 2129 (quoting District of Columbia v. Heller, 554 U.S. 570, 634 (2008)).
24. *Id.* at 2127.
25. *Id.* at 2138.
26. *Id.* at 2127.
27. *Id.* at 2128 (quoting *Heller*, 554 U.S. at 605).
28. *Id.* at 2177 (Breyer, J., dissenting).
29. *See id.* (citing Saul Cornell, Heller, *New Originalism, and Law Office History: "Meet the New Boss, Same as the Old Boss,"* 56 UCLA L. Rev. 1095, 1098 (2009)).

30. *See id.* at 2181; *see also id.* at 2139–42 (majority opinion) (discussing implications of the Statute of Northampton, a fourteenth-century regulation, for New York's present-day regulation).

31. *See* J.R. PARTINGTON, A HISTORY OF GREEK FIRE AND GUNPOWDER 27 (1999 ed.) (1960) (discussing the use of Greek fire in fourteenth-century Europe).

32. *See Bruen*, 142 S. Ct. at 2181 (Breyer, J., dissenting).

33. *Id.* at 2132 (majority opinion).

34. *Id.* at 2133.

35. *See id.* at 2179 (Breyer, J., dissenting).

36. *Id.* at 2130 (majority opinion).

37. U.S. CONST. amend. IV.

38. *See id.* at 2176 (Breyer, J., dissenting) (citing Ariz. Free Enter. Club's Freedom Club PAC v. Bennett, 564 U.S. 721, 734 (2011); then citing Ward v. Rock Against Racism, 491 U.S. 781, 791 (1989); and then citing Cent. Hudson Gas & Elec. Corp. v. Pub. Serv. Comm'n of N.Y., 447 U.S. 557, 564–66 (1980)).

39. U.S. CONST. amend. II.

40. District of Columbia v. Heller, 554 U.S. 570, 592 (2008).

41. *Id.* at 602.

42. *Id.* at 651 (Stevens, J., dissenting).

43. *See id.* at 576–619 (majority opinion); *id.* at 640–679 (Stevens, J., dissenting).

44. *Id.* at 660–61 (Stevens, J., dissenting).

45. *Id.* at 594 (majority opinion) (quoting 1 WILLIAM BLACKSTONE, COMMENTARIES *140).

46. *Id.* at 593.

47. 561 U.S. 742 (2010).

48. Brief for English/Early American Historians as Amici Curiae in Support of Respondents at 2–3, McDonald v. City of Chicago, 561 U.S. 742 (2010) (No. 08-1521), 2010 WL 77316, at *2–3.

49. Brief for Corpus Linguistics Professors and Experts as Amici Curiae Supporting Respondents at 11, N.Y. State Rifle & Pistol Ass'n v. Bruen, 142 S. Ct. 2111 (2022) (No. 20-843), 2021 WL 4353034, at *11.

50. *Id.* at 14.

51. For more scholarly work questioning *Heller*'s historical analysis, see generally Saul Cornell, *The Changing Meaning of the Right to Keep and Bear Arms: 1688–1788: Neglected Common Law Contexts of the Second Amendment Debate*, in GUNS IN LAW 20, 20–47 (Austin Sarat et al. eds., 2019); Paul Finkelman, *The Living Constitution and the Second Amendment: Poor History, False Originalism, and a Very Confused Court*, 37 CARDOZO L. REV. 623 (2015); Douglas Walker, Jr., *Necessary to the Security of Free States: The Second Amendment as the Auxiliary Right of Federalism*, 56 AM. J. LEGAL HIST. 365 (2016); William G. Merkel, Heller *as Hubris, and How* McDonald v. City of Chicago *May Well Change the Constitutional World as We Know It*, 50 SANTA CLARA L. REV. 1221 (2010).

52. *Bruen*, 142 S. Ct. at 2182 (Breyer, J., dissenting) (citing, *inter alia*, 4 CALENDAR OF THE CLOSE ROLLS, EDWARD I, 1296–1302, p. 318 (Sep. 15, 1299) (1906)).

53. *Id.* at 2182–83.

54. *Id.* at 2184 (quoting an Act Against Wearing Swords, &c., ch. 9, in GRANTS, CONCESSIONS, AND ORIGINAL CONSTITUTIONS OF THE PROVINCE OF NEW JERSEY 290 (2d ed. 1881)).

55. *Id.* at 2185 (quoting 1786 VA. ACTS, ch. 21).

56. *Id.* at 2186 (quoting GA. CODE § 4413 (1861)).

57. *Id.* at 2188 (citing, *inter alia*, CONG. GLOBE, 39th Cong., 1st Sess., 908 (1866)).

58. *Id.* at 2189.

59. *See id.* at 2181–89.

60. *See id.* at 2138–40 (majority opinion).

61. *Id.* at 2154 n.28.

62. *Id.* at 2144 (discussing a New Jersey regulation from the early colonial period).

63. *Id.* at 2142–44 (discussing early colonial regulations in Massachusetts, New Hampshire, and New Jersey).

64. *Id.* at 2148 (discussing antebellum surety statutes).

65. *Id.* at 2143–44 (discussing a New Jersey regulation from the early colonial period).

66. *See id.* at 2139–42; *id.* at 2182–84 (Breyer, J., dissenting).

67. *See* Amy Coney Barrett, *Originalism and Stare Decisis*, 92 NOTRE DAME L. REV. 1921, 1924 (2017) ("Nonoriginalists consider the text's historical meaning to be a relevant factor in interpreting the Constitution, but other factors, like value-based judgments, might overcome it. Originalists, by contrast, treat the original meaning as a relatively hard constraint.").

68. *Bruen*, 142 S. Ct. at 2180 (Breyer, J., dissenting) (citing Charles R. McKirdy, *Misreading the Past: The Faulty Historical Basis Behind the Supreme Court's Decision in* District of Columbia v. Heller, 45 CAP. U. L. REV. 107, 151 (2017)).

69. *See* Adeel Hassan, *Dayton Gunman Shot 26 People in 32 Seconds, Police Timeline Reveals*, N.Y. TIMES (Aug. 13, 2019), https://www.nytimes.com/2019/08/13/us/dayton -shooter-video-timeline.html.

70. *Bruen*, 142 S. Ct. at 2164–65 (Breyer, J., dissenting).

71. Kachalsky v. County of Westchester, 701 F.3d 81, 97 (2d Cir. 2012).

72. *Id.* at 99.

73. *See Bruen*, 142 S. Ct. at 2128–29.

74. *See id.* at 2164 (Breyer, J., dissenting) (noting that, in 2015, 22,018 died by firearm-assisted suicide).

75. *See id.* at 2166 (noting that women are five times more likely to be killed by their partners when their partners have access to firearms).

76. *See id.* (noting that most police officers who are killed in the line of duty are killed by firearms).

77. *See id.* at 2173.

78. 142 S. Ct. 2228 (2022).

79. *Id.* at 2242.

80. *See infra* Chapter 15.

81. *Dobbs*, 142 S. Ct. at 2242–43.

82. *Id.* at 2324–25 (Breyer, Sotomayor & Kagan, JJ., dissenting).

83. U.S. CONST. amend. XIV.

84. *See Dobbs*, 142 S. Ct. at 2326 (Breyer, Sotomayor & Kagan, JJ., dissenting).

85. *See* Griswold v. Connecticut, 381 U.S. 479 (1965).

86. *See* Lawrence v. Texas, 539 U.S. 558 (2003).

87. *See* Loving v. Virginia, 388 U.S. 1 (1967).

88. *See* Obergefell v. Hodges, 576 U.S. 644 (2015).

89. *See* Plessy v. Ferguson, 163 U.S. 537, 543–44 (1896).

90. 347 U.S. 483 (1954).

91. *Compare, e.g.*, Michael W. McConnell, *Originalism and Desegregation Decisions*, 81 VA. L. REV. 947, 1140 (1995) ("[S]chool segregation was understood during Reconstruction to violate the principles of equality of the Fourteenth Amendment."); *with* Michael J. Klarman, Brown, *Originalism, and Constitutional Theory: A Response to Professor McConnell*, 81 VA. L. REV. 1881, 1883 (1995) ("[T]he crux of McConnell's claim is unpersuasive: He fails to show either that *Brown* is correct on originalist grounds, or even, as he more modestly claims, that *Brown* is 'within the legitimate range of interpretations' of the Fourteenth Amendment." (quoting McConnell, *supra*, at 1093)).

92. 347 U.S. 497 (1954).

93. *Id.* at 500.

94. *See* Ryan C. Williams, *The One and Only Substantive Due Process Clause*, 120 YALE L. J. 408, 428–54 (2010).

95. *See* Cass R. Sunstein, *Is Living Constitutionalism Dead? The Enigma of* Bolling v. Sharpe 2 (Harv. Pub. L., Working Paper No. 22-30, 2022).

96. Brown v. Bd. of Educ. of Topeka, 347 U.S. 483, 495 (1954); *Bolling*, 347 U.S. at 500.

97. *See generally, e.g.*, Scalia, *supra* note 6.

98. *Id.* at 1179.

99. *Id.* at 1182–83.

100. HENRY M. HART JR. & ALBERT M. SACKS, THE LEGAL PROCESS: BASIC PROBLEMS IN THE MAKING AND APPLICATION OF LAW 139 (1994 ed.).

101. *Id.* at 140–41.

102. *See supra* Chapter 1, note 23.

103. HART & SACKS, *supra* note 100, at 140.

104. *See id.* at 140–41.

105. *See generally* Scalia, *supra* note 6.

106. *Id.* at 1178.

107. *Id.* at 1179.

108. *Id.* at 1182 (quoting 3 THE POLITICS OF ARISTOTLE 127 (Ernest Barker trans., 1946)).

109. *Id.* at 1184.

110. *See supra* Chapter 1, note 25.

111. *See, e.g.*, FED. R. CIV. P. 6(c)(1) (requiring a written motion and notice of a hearing to be served at least fourteen days before the time specified for the hearing).

112. U.S. CONST. amend I.

113. *See supra* Preface, note 24 and accompanying text.

114. *See* Paul D. Carrington, *Meaning and Professionalism in American Law*, 10 CONST. COMMENT. 297, 297 (1993).

115. *See supra* Chapter 1, notes 10–29.

116. BURT NEUBORNE, MADISON'S MUSIC: ON READING THE FIRST AMENDMENT 1 (2015) ("[A] careful study of the order, placement, meaning, and structure of the forty-five words in Madison's First Amendment will trigger a responsive poetic chord in you that will enable us to recapture the music of democracy in our most important political text.").

117. U.S. CONST. amend I.

118. Abrams v. United States, 250 U.S. 616, 630 (1919) (Holmes, J., dissenting).

119. NEUBORNE, *supra* note 116, at 17–18.

120. *See generally* Robert Post, *Participatory Democracy and Free Speech* 97 VA. L. REV. 477 (2011) (arguing that the First Amendment protects speech for the purpose of facilitating a participatory democracy).

121. 572 U.S. 185, 191 (2014).

122. *Id.* at 191 (plurality opinion).

123. *Id.* at 193–94.

124. *Id.* at 191, 199.

125. *Id.* at 227 (Thomas, J., concurring in the judgment).

126. *Id.* at 232 (Breyer, J., dissenting).

127. 558 U.S. 310 (2010).

128. *Id.* at 359.

129. *Id.* (quoting McConnell v. FEC, 540 U.S. 93, 296 (2003) (Kennedy, J., concurring in the judgment in part and dissenting in part)).

130. *McCutcheon*, 572 U.S. at 207–08 (plurality opinion).

131. *Id.* at 209 (quoting FEC v. Wisc. Right to Life, 551 U.S. 449, 457 (2007)).

132. *Id.* at 243–44 (Breyer, J., dissenting).

133. *Id.* at 203 (plurality opinion) (alteration in original) (quoting Cohen v. California, 403 U.S. 15, 24 (1971)).

134. *Id.*

135. *Id.* at 236 (Breyer, J., dissenting).

136. *See id.* at 248.

137. *Id.* at 248–49.

138. *Id.* at 245.

139. *Id.* at 258–61.

140. *See id.* at 236–39.

141. *See id.* at 207–08 (plurality opinion) (citing Citizens United v. FEC, 558 U.S. 310, 359 (2010)).

142. *See id.* at 243 (Breyer, J., dissenting).

143. *See, e.g.*, N.Y. Times Co. v. Sullivan, 376 U.S. 254, 279–80 (1964) ("The constitutional guarantees require, we think, a federal rule that prohibits a public official from recovering damages for a defamatory falsehood relating to his official conduct unless he proves that the statement was made with 'actual malice'—that is, with knowledge that it was false or with reckless disregard of whether it was false or not.").

144. 564 U.S. 552 (2011).

145. United States v. Playboy Ent. Grp., 529 U.S. 803, 813 (2000).

146. *See* Cent. Hudson Gas & Elec. Corp. v. Pub. Serv. Comm'n of N.Y., 447 U.S. 557, 573 (1980) (Blackmun, J., concurring in the judgment).

147. *Id.* at 564 (majority opinion).

148. United States v. Carolene Prods. Co., 304 U.S. 144, 152 (1938).

149. *See, e.g.*, Zauderer v. Off. of Disciplinary Couns. of Sup. Ct. of Ohio, 471 U.S. 626, 651–53 (1985).

150. New State Ice Co. v. Liebman, 285 U.S. 262, 286–87 (1932) (Brandeis, J., dissenting).

151. United States v. Playboy Ent. Grp., 529 U.S. 803, 813 (2000).

152. Cent. Hudson Gas & Elec. Corp. v. Pub. Serv. Comm'n of N.Y., 447 U.S. 557, 564 (1980).

153. Sorrell v. IMS Health Inc., 564 U.S. 552, 558–59 (2011).

154. *Id.* at 557–58.

155. *Id.* at 560–61.

156. *Id.* at 564.

157. *Id.*

158. *Id.* at 565.

159. *Id.* at 566 (quoting Ward v. Rock Against Racism, 491 U.S. 781, 791 (1989)).

160. *Id.* at 577–78.

161. *Id.* at 564.

162. *See id.* at 564–66.

163. *Id.* at 580–81, 593 (Breyer, J., dissenting).

164. *Id.* at 596.

165. *Id.* at 597.

166. *Id.*

167. *Id.* at 600–01.

168. *See id.* at 586–89.

169. *See id.* at 602–03.

170. *Id.* at 586.

171. *Id.* at 585 (citation omitted) (quoting Cent. Hudson Gas & Elec. Corp. v. Pub. Serv. Comm'n of N.Y., 447 U.S. 557, 589 (1980)).

172. 576 U.S. 155 (2015).

173. 142 S. Ct. 1464 (2022).

174. *Id.* at 159–60 (alteration omitted).

175. *Id.* at 160 (alteration omitted).

176. *Id.* at 160–61 (alteration omitted).

177. *Id.* at 163.

178. *Id.* at 164.

179. *Id.* at 172.

180. *Id.* at 184 (Kagan, J., concurring in the judgment).

181. *See id.* at 176–77 (Breyer, J., concurring in the judgment).

182. *See id.* at 163–64 (majority opinion).

183. *Id.* at 182 (Kagan, J., concurring in the judgment).

184. 485 U.S. 312 (1988).

185. *Id.* at 316.

186. *Id.* at 321.

187. *Id.*

188. *Id.* at 334. For arguments that the promotion of democratic self-government is the core value protected by the First Amendment, see generally ALEXANDER MEIKLE-JOHN, FREE SPEECH AND ITS RELATION TO SELF-GOVERNMENT (1948); CASS R. SUNSTEIN, DEMOCRACY AND THE PROBLEM OF FREE SPEECH (1993).

189. 142 S. Ct. 1464 (2022).

190. *Id.* at 1469–70.

191. *Id.* at 1470 (quoting Reagan Nat'l Advert., Inc. v. City of Austin, 972 F.3d 696, 706 (5th Cir. 2020)).

192. *Id.* at 1472.

193. *Id.* at 1471 (quoting Reed v. Town of Gilbert, 576 U.S. 155, 163 (2015)); *see id.* at 1473–74.

194. *Id.* at 1474.

195. *Id.* at 1476 (Breyer, J., concurring).

196. *Id.* (citing Abrams v. United States, 250 U.S. 616, 630 (1919) (Holmes, J., dissenting).

197. *Abrams*, 250 U.S. at 630 (Holmes, J., dissenting).

198. *City of Austin*, 142 S. Ct. at 1477 (quoting Buckley v. Am. Const. L. Found., Inc., 525 U.S. 182, 186–87 (1999)).

199. *Id.*

200. *Id.*

201. *In re* Pfizer, Inc., 81 F.T.C. 23, 26, 29 (1972).

202. John D. Morris, *E.T.C. Orders Data to Back Ad Claims*, N.Y. TIMES (Nov. 3, 1973), https://www.nytimes.com/1973/11/03/archives/ftc-orders-data-to-back-ad-claims -targets-involve-deodorants-and.html.

203. *City of Austin*, 142 S. Ct. at 1477 (Breyer, J., concurring).

204. *See* 5 U.S.C. § 706(2)(A) (directing courts to review agency regulations for arbitrari- ness and capriciousness).

205. *City of Austin*, 142 S. Ct. at 1477–78 (Breyer, J., concurring).

206. *Id.*

207. *Id.* at 1478.

208. *Id.*

209. *Id.* at 1471, 1474 (majority opinion).

210. *Id.* at 1469–70.

211. *Id.* at 1479 (Breyer, J., concurring).

212. *Id.*

213. *See generally* Scalia, *supra* note 6.

14: When the Text Runs Out: The Limits of Constitutional Textualism

1. U.S. CONST. art. I, § 1.

2. *Id.* art. II, § 1.

3. *Id.* art. III, § 1.

4. Julian Davis Mortenson & Nicholas Bagley, *Delegation at the Founding*, 121 COLUM. L. REV. 277, 332–49 (2021).

5. *See* McCulloch v. Maryland, 17 U.S. (4 Wheat.) 316, 406–07 (1819).

6. JAMES D. DILTS, THE GREAT ROAD: THE BUILDING OF THE BALTIMORE AND OHIO, THE NATION'S FIRST RAILROAD, 1828–1853, at xv–xvi (1993).

7. JOHN F. STOVER, AMERICAN RAILROADS 96–97 (2d ed. 1997).

8. ROBERT E. GALLAMORE & JOHN R. MEYER, AMERICAN RAILROADS: DECLINE AND RENAISSANCE IN THE TWENTIETH CENTURY 24–25 (2014).

9. Shankland v. Washington, 30 U.S. (5 Pet.) 390, 395 (1831).

10. Marshall Field & Co. v. Clark, 143 U.S. 649, 692 (1892).

11. Interstate Com. Comm'n v. Cincinnati, N. O. & T. P. R. Co. (*Queen & Crescent*), 167 U.S. 479, 506 (1897).

12. *Id.* at 505–06.

13. *See* Thomas W. Merrill, *Rethinking Article I, Section 1: From Nondelegation to Exclusive Delegation*, 104 COLUM. L. REV. 2097, 2111–12 (2004).

14. J.W. Hampton, Jr. & Co. v. United States, 276 U.S. 394, 407–08 (1928) (first quoting Cincinnati, Wilmington & Zanesville R.R. Co. v. Clinton Cnty. Comm'rs, 1 Ohio St. 77, 88 (1852); and then quoting Interstate Com. Comm'n v. Goodrich Transit Co., 224 U.S. 194, 214 (1912)).

15. State *ex rel.* R.R. & Warehouse Comm'n v. Chi., Milwaukee & St. Paul. Ry. Co., 37 N.W. 782, 788 (Minn. 1888) (emphasis added).

16. *See* Yakus v. United States, 321 U.S. 414, 426 (1944).

17. Cincinnati, Wilmington & Zanesville R.R. Co., 1 Ohio St. at 88–89.

18. McCulloch v. Maryland, 17 U.S. (4 Wheat.) 316, 407 (1819).

19. *Id.*

20. *Id.* at 415.

21. *Id.*

22. *Id.*

23. J.W. Hampton, Jr. & Co. v. United States, 276 U.S. 394, 407–08 (1928).

24. *Id.* at 409.

25. *See, e.g.*, Whitman v. Am. Trucking Ass'ns, 531 U.S. 457, 473–74 (2001) (holding that the Clean Air Act's delegation of authority to the Environmental Protection Agency to promulgate air quality standards "at a level that is requisite to protect the public health" provided enough of an intelligible principle to guide the agency's use of discretionary power).

26. *See, e.g.*, Sheryl Gay Stolberg, *Senate Confirms Xavier Becerra as the Secretary of Health and Human Services*, N.Y. TIMES (Mar. 18, 2021), https://www.nytimes.com/2021/03/18/us/politics/xavier-becerra-health-secretary.html.

27. PRESIDENT'S COMM. ON ADMIN. MGMT., ADMINISTRATIVE MANAGEMENT IN THE GOVERNMENT OF THE UNITED STATES 29 (1937).

28. Paul Stephen Dempsey, *The Rise and Fall of the Interstate Commerce Commission: The Tortuous Path from Regulation to Deregulation of America's Infrastructure*, 95 MARQ. L. REV. 1151, 1162 (2012).

29. U.S. COURTS, AUTHORIZED JUDGESHIPS 8 (2022); QUALITY JUDGES INITIATIVE, FAQs: JUDGES IN THE UNITED STATES 3 (2014).

30. KRISTIN E. HICKMAN & RICHARD J. PIERCE, JR., FEDERAL ADMINISTRATIVE LAW 29 (3d ed. 2020) (quoting J.W. Hampton, Jr. & Co. v. United States, 276 U.S. 394, 409 (1928)).

31. *See* Mistretta v. United States, 488 U.S. 361, 381 (1989) ("In adopting this flexible understanding of separation of powers, we simply have recognized Madison's teaching that the greatest security against tyranny—the accumulation of excessive authority in a single Branch—lies not in a hermetic division among the Branches, but in a carefully crafted system of checked and balanced power within each Branch.").

32. 11 U.S. (7 Cranch) 382 (1813).

33. *Id.* at 384, 388.

34. 276 U.S. 394 (1928).

35. *Id.* at 403.

36. 295 U.S. 495 (1935).

37. *Id.* at 521–22.

38. *Id.* at 531–37; *id.* at 551–52 (Cardozo, J., concurring).

39. *Id.* at 553 (Cardozo, J., concurring).

40. *Id.* at 550 (majority opinion).

41. Lichter v. United States, 334 U.S. 742, 785 (1948).

42. Panama Refin. Co. v. Ryan, 293 U.S. 388 (1935).

43. Gundy v. United States, 139 S. Ct. 2116, 2129 (2019).

44. *Id.* at 2131 (Gorsuch, J., dissenting).

45. *Id.* at 2136 (discussing Wayman v. Southard, 23 U.S. (10 Wheat.) 1 (1825)).

46. *Id.* (discussing Cargo of Brig Aurora v. United States, 11 U.S. (7 Cranch) 382 (1813)).

47. *Id.* at 2137.

48. See Jarkesy v. SEC, 34 F.4th 446 (5th Cir. 2022), *cert. granted*, 143 S. Ct. 2688 (2023) (mem.).

49. Compare, e.g., Mortenson & Bagley, *supra* note 4, at 332–66 (arguing that the Constitution was "not originally understood to contain a nondelegation doctrine," *id.* at 277) with Ilan Wurman, *Nondelegation at the Founding*, 130 YALE L. J. 1288 (2021) (arguing that "there was a nondelegation doctrine at the Founding," *id.* at 1288).

50. *See* Chevron, U.S.A. v. Nat. Res. Def. Council, Inc., 467 U.S. 837 (1984).

51. *Id.* at 866.

52. Smiley v. Citibank (S.D.), N.A., 517 U.S. 735, 743–44 (1996).

53. City of Arlington v. FCC, 569 U.S. 290, 305–07 (2013).

54. 142 S. Ct. 661 (2022) (*per curiam*).

55. *Id.* at 664–66.

56. 29 U.S.C. § 655(c)(1).

57. *Nat'l Fed'n of Indep. Bus.*, 142 S. Ct. at 670 (Breyer, Sotomayor & Kagan, JJ., dissenting).

58. *Id.* at 665 (majority opinion).

59. *Id.* at 667 (Gorsuch, J., concurring) (quoting Ala. Ass'n of Realtors v. Dep't of Health & Human Servs., 141 S. Ct. 2485, 2489 (2021) (*per curiam*)).

60. *Id.* at 668.

61. Mila Sohoni, Comment, *The Major Questions Quartet*, 136 HARV. L. REV. 262, 275 (2022).

62. *Nat'l Fed'n of Indep. Bus.*, 142 S. Ct. at 669 (Gorsuch, J., concurring).

63. 142 S. Ct. 2587 (2022).

64. *Id.* at 2610.

65. 42 U.S.C. § 7411(a)(1); *see also id.* §§ (b)(1), (d).

66. *West Virginia*, 142 S. Ct. at 2627–28 (Kagan, J., dissenting).

67. *Id.* at 2611–12 (majority opinion).

68. *Id.* at 2612–14.

69. *Id.* at 2620 (Gorsuch, J., concurring) (quoting Amy Coney Barrett, *Substantive Canons and Faithful Agency*, 90 B.U. L. REV. 109, 175 (2010)).

70. *Id.* at 2616–17.

71. *See id.* at 2641 (Kagan, J., dissenting) ("Some years ago, I remarked that '[w]e're all textualists now.' It seems I was wrong. The current Court is textualist only when being so suits it. When that method would frustrate broader goals, special canons like the 'major questions doctrine' magically appear as get-out-of-text-free cards." (alteration in original) (citation omitted)). For an academic critique of the major questions doctrine and other canons on textualist grounds, see generally Benjamin Eidelson & Matthew C. Stephenson, *The Incompatibility of Substantive Canons and Textualism* 137 HARV. L. REV. (forthcoming 2023).

72. Nat'l Fed'n of Indep. Bus. v. Dep't of Lab., Occupational Safety & Health Admin., 142 S. Ct. 661, 665 (2022) (*per curiam*); *West Virginia*, 142 S. Ct. at 2614.

73. *Nat'l Fed'n of Indep. Bus.*, 142 S. Ct. at 667 (Gorsuch, J., concurring); *West Virginia*, 142 S. Ct. at 2616–17 (Gorsuch, J., concurring).

74. *See Nat'l Fed'n of Indep. Bus.*, 142 S. Ct. at 665–66; *West Virginia*, 142 S. Ct. at 2610–14.

75. *See* Jody Freeman, Opinion, *Supreme Court's EPA Ruling Goes Far Beyond Climate Change*, BOST. GLOBE (Jul. 1, 2022, 7:17 AM), https://www.bostonglobe.com/2022/06/30 /opinion/supreme-courts-epa-ruling-goes-far-beyond-climate-change; Jody Freeman & Matthew Stephenson, *The Anti-Democratic Major Questions Doctrine*, 2022 SUP. CT. REV. 1, 47 & n.152 (2022) (citing various post–*West Virginia* cases challenging agency actions under the major questions doctrine).

76. *See, e.g.*, Barnhart v. Walton, 535 U.S. 212, 225 (2002).

77. *Id.* at 222.

78. *West Virginia*, 142 S. Ct. at 2633 (Kagan, J., dissenting).

79. United States v. Mead Corp., 533 U.S. 218, 229–31 (2001).

80. *See generally supra* Part II.

81. Biden v. Nebraska, 143 S. Ct. 2355, 2378 (2022) (Barrett, J., concurring) (quoting FDA v. Brown & Williamson Tobacco Corp., 529 U.S. 120, 133 (2000)).

82. U.S. Const. art. I, § 1.

83. *Id.* art. II, § 1.

84. *See West Virginia*, 142 S. Ct. at 2643 (Kagan, J., dissenting).

85. *See, e.g.*, Alfred E. Kahn, *Deregulation: Looking Backward and Looking Forward* 7 Yale J. on Reg. 325, 329–30 (1990).

86. U.S. Const. art. III, § 1.

87. Crowell v. Benson, 285 U.S. 22, 36–37 (1932).

88. 285 U.S. 22 (1932).

89. *Id.* at 48–51.

90. *Id.* at 36–37.

91. *Id.* at 45–48.

92. *Id.* at 49–50.

93. *Id.*

94. *See* Commodity Futures Trading Comm'n v. Schor, 478 U.S. 833, 848–49 (1986).

95. Richard J. Pierce, Jr., *The Remedies for Constitutional Flaws Have Major Flaws*, 18 Duke J. Const. L. & Pub. Pol'y 105, 112 (2023).

96. *See* Jarkesy v. SEC, 34 F.4th 446 (5th Cir. 2022), *cert. granted*, 143 S. Ct. 2688 (2023) (mem.). For an argument in favor of limits on Congress's power to delegate adjudicative questions to agencies, see John Golden & Thomas Lee, *Federalism, Private Rights, and Article III Adjudication*, 108 Va. L. Rev. 1547 (2022). See also John M. Golden & Thomas H. Lee, *Congressional Power, Public Rights, and Non-Article III Adjudciation*, 98 Notre Dame L. Rev. 1113 (2023).

97. *Cf., e.g.*, Stern v. Marshall, 564 U.S. 462, 493 (2011) (finding Congress's delegation of adjudicative authority to a non–Article III bankruptcy court unconstitutional in part because the grant of jurisdiction to adjudicate bankruptcy claims was "not limited to a 'particularized area of the law'" (quoting N. Pipeline Constr. Co. v. Marathon Pipe Line Co., 458 U.S. 50, 85 (1982) (plurality opinion)).

98. *See, e.g.*, Wellness Int'l Network, Ltd. v. Sharif, 575 U.S. 665, 682–83 (cautioning against an expansive reading of *Stern*).

99. 5 U.S.C. §§ 706(2)(A)–(E); *see also* Universal Camera Corp. v. NLRB, 340 U.S. 474 (1951).

100. 5 U.S.C. §§ 551, 553–559, 701–06.

101. *See, e.g.*, Hickman & Pierce, *supra* note 30, at 472–506 (discussing judicial review of agency adjudications).

102. Crowell v. Benson, 285 U.S. 22, 46 (1932).

103. *Id.* at 53–54.

104. Chevron U.S.A., Inc. v. Nat'l Res. Def. Council, 467 U.S. 837 (1984).

105. *See id.* at 842–43, 865–66.

106. *See, e.g.*, Buffington v. McDonough, 143 S. Ct. 14, 16–21 (2022) (Gorsuch, J., dissenting from the denial of *certiorari*) (criticizing *Chevron* on originalist and textualist grounds).

107. *See* Azar v. Allina Health Servs., 139 S. Ct. 1804, 1818–19 (2019) (Breyer, J., dissenting) (describing legislative rules as binding the public and having the force and effect of law).

108. *Chevron*, 467 U.S. at 839–42, 866–66.

109. Massachusetts v. EPA, 549 U.S. 497, 506–07, 510–14, 529 n.26 (2007).

110. *Chevron*, 467 U.S. at 842–43.

111. *Id.* at 843–44.

112. *See, e.g.*, Aditya Bamzai, *The Origins of Judicial Deference to Executive Interpretation*, 126 YALE L. J. 908 (2017).

113. Thomas W. Merrill, *The Story of* Chevron*: The Making of an Accidental Landmark*, 66 ADMIN. L. REV. 253, 276 (2014); *see also* Gary Lawson & Stephen Kam, *Making Law out of Nothing at All: The Origins of the* Chevron *Doctrine*, 65 ADMIN. L. REV. 1, 4 (2013).

114. *Id.* at 256.

115. 535 U.S. 212 (2002).

116. *Id.* at 222.

117. Louis Jaffe, *Judicial Review: Question of Law*, 69 HARV. L. REV. 239, 264 (1955). *See also id.* at 272–74 (providing examples).

118. 480 U.S. 421 (1987).

119. *Id.* at 431–32.

120. 533 U.S. 218 (2001).

121. *Id.* at 222.

122. SAS Inst., Inc. v. Iancu, 138 S. Ct. 1348, 1364 (2018) (Breyer, J., dissenting).

123. *See* STEPHEN BREYER, MAKING OUR DEMOCRACY WORK 116–20 (2010); Stephen Breyer, *Judicial Review of Questions of Law and Policy*, 38 ADMIN. L. REV. 365, 372–82 (1986). *But see* Gutierrez-Brizuela v. Lynch, 834 F.3d 1142, 1158 (10th Cir. 2018) (Gorsuch, J., concurring) (maintaining that courts should review all questions of law de novo rather than deferring to agency interpretations).

124. U.S. CONST. art. III, § 1.

125. *See Gutierrez-Brizuela*, 834 U.S. at 1152 (Gorsuch, J., concurring).

126. U.S. CONST. art. II, § 1.

127. *Id.* § 2.

128. Free Enter. Fund v. Pub. Co. Accounting Oversight Bd., 561 U.S. 477, 492 (2010).

129. Seila L. LLC v. Consumer Fin. Prot. Bureau, 140 S. Ct. 2183, 2197 (2020).

130. United States v. Arthrex, Inc., 141 S. Ct. 1970, 1976, 1982 (2021).

131. *Free Enter. Fund*, 561 U.S. at 492.

132. *Seila L.*, 140 S. Ct. at 2197.

133. *Arthrex*, 141 S. Ct. at 1980–85.

134. *Free Enter. Fund*, 561 U.S. at 542–43 (Breyer, J., dissenting).

135. 357 U.S. 349 (1958).

136. *Free Enter. Fund*, 561 U.S. at 532–33 (Breyer, J., dissenting) (citing *Wiener*, 357 U.S. at 355).

137. *Id.* at 533.

138. See Pierce, *supra* note 96; *see also* Andrea Scoseria Katz & Noah A. Rosenblum, *Removal Rehashed*, 136 HARV. L. REV. F. 404, 406 (2023) ("[T]he Court's separation of powers decisions over the last decade have sparked a boom in research on the history of the early republic, the bulk of which undercuts the Court's rulings.").

139. *See* Katz & Rosenblum, *supra* note 139, at 406.

15: Legal Stability: *Stare Decisis*

1. 1 WILLIAM BLACKSTONE, COMMENTARIES *69.
2. *Stare Decisis*, BLACK'S LAW DICTIONARY (11th ed. 2019).
3. Payne v. Tennessee, 501 U.S. 808, 827 (1991).
4. BLACKSTONE, *supra* note 1, at *69.
5. THE FEDERALIST No. 78 (Alexander Hamilton), at 516 (2009).
6. Vasquez v. Hillery, 474 U.S. 254, 265 (1986).
7. Dobbs v. Jackson Women's Health Org., 142 S. Ct. 2228, 2333 (2022) (Breyer, Sotomayor, & Kagan, JJ., dissenting).
8. BLACKSTONE, *supra* note 1, at *70 ("The doctrine of the law then is this: that precedents and rules must be followed, unless flatly absurd or unjust.").
9. Dobbs v. Jackson Women's Health Org., 142 S. Ct. 2228 (2022).
10. 410 U.S. 113 (1973).
11. 505 U.S. 833 (1992).
12. *Roe*, 410 U.S. at 152–56, 162–66.
13. *Casey*, 505 U.S. at 846.
14. *Id.* at 874 (opinion of O'Connor, Kennedy & Souter, JJ.).
15. *See id.* at 860 (majority opinion).
16. *Id.* at 846.
17. Whole Woman's Health v. Hellerstedt, 136 S. Ct. 2292, 2309 (2016); June Med. Servs. L.L.C. v. Russo, 140 S. Ct. 2103, 2120 (plurality opinion).
18. Dobbs v. Jackson Women's Health Org., 142 S. Ct. 2228, 2242–43 (2022). Although the majority opinion earned only five votes, a sixth Justice, Chief Justice Roberts, also voted to overrule *Casey*'s rule that abortion was protected through the time of the fetus's viability. But unlike the majority, he did not agree to take the further "step of altogether eliminating the abortion right first recognized in *Roe*." *Id.* at 2311–13 (Roberts, C.J., concurring in the judgment).
19. *See id.* at 2305 (Kavanaugh, J., concurring).
20. *Id.* at 2310 (Roberts, C.J., concurring in the judgment).
21. *Id.* at 2317–20 (Breyer, Sotomayor & Kagan, JJ., dissenting).
22. *See id.* at 2320–23.
23. *See id.* at 2323.
24. *Id.* at 2265 (majority opinion); *see id.* at 2244–61.
25. *Id.* at 2244–57.
26. *Id.* at 2249–51.
27. *Id.* at 2324 (Breyer, Sotomayor & Kagan, JJ., dissenting).
28. *See, e.g.*, Pearson v. Callahan, 555 U.S. 223, 233–34 (2009), *overruling* Saucier v. Katz, 533 U.S. 194 (2001).
29. *Pearson*, 555 U.S. at 233.
30. *See, e.g.*, Herrera v. Wyoming, 139 S. Ct. 1686, 1694–97 (2019), *overruling* Ward v. Race Horse, 163 U.S. 504 (1896).
31. *See, e.g.*, Katz v. United States, 389 U.S. 347, 352–53 (1967), *overruling* Olmstead v. United States, 277 U.S. 438 (1928).
32. *See Dobbs*, 142 S. Ct. at 2334 (Breyer, Sotomayor & Kagan, JJ., dissenting); Kimble v. Marvel Ent., LLC, 576 U.S. 446, 455 (2015); Halliburton Co. v. Erica P. John Fund, Inc., 573 U.S. 258, 266 (2014).

33. *See supra* notes 4–7 and accompanying text.

34. *See* Amy Coney Barrett, *Originalism and Stare Decisis*, 92 Notre Dame L. Rev. 1921, 1922 (2017) ("While the debate about stare decisis is old, modern originalism introduced a new issue: the possibility that following precedent might sometimes be unlawful.").

35. *See* Richard H. Fallon, Jr., *Selective Originalism and Judicial Role Morality* 20–30 (Feb. 3, 2023) (unpublished manuscript), https://papers.ssrn.com/sol3/papers.cfm?abstract_id=4347334.

36. *See id.* at 4.

37. *See, e.g.*, TransUnion LLC v. Ramirez, 141 S. Ct. 2190, 2204–05 (2021) (calling into question the validity of standing doctrine precedents on originalist grounds); *id.* at 2218 (Thomas, J., dissenting) (defending those precedents on originalist grounds).

38. *See generally* Cass R. Sunstein, How to Interpret the Constitution (2023).

39. Lawrence B. Solum, *Semantic Originalism* 2 (Ill. Pub. L. & Legal Theory, Rsch. Paper Series No. 07-24, 2008), https://papers.ssrn.com/abstract=1120244.

40. Lawrence B. Solum, *Originalist Theory and Precedent: A Public Meaning Approach*, 33 Const. Comment. 451, 453 (2018).

41. Robert Post & Reva Siegel, Essay, Roe *Rage: Democratic Constitutionalism and Backlash*, 42 Harv. C.R.-C.L. L. Rev. 373, 374–75 (2007).

42. Ernest Young, *Rediscovering Conservatism: Burkean Political Theory and Constitutional Interpretation*, 72 N.C. L. Rev. 619, 622–23, 659–60 (1994).

43. Ronald Dworkin, Freedom's Law: The Moral Reading of the American Constitution 2 (1996).

44. Cass R. Sunstein, *Thayerism* 2–4 (Sept. 10, 2022) (unpublished manuscript), https://papers.ssrn.com/sol3/papers.cfm?abstract_id=4215816.

45. Adrian Vermeule, Common Good Constitutionalism 1–8, 26–27 (2022).

46. These include "original intentions originalism," which looks to what the authors of the constitutional phrase meant by it, see Richard S. Kay, *Adherence to the Original Intentions in Constitutional Adjudication: Three Objections and Responses*, 82 Nw. U. L. Rev. 226, 229–30 (1988); originalism as reflecting "our law," which looks to the positive law in force at the time of the Constitution's ratification, unless it was lawfully changed since then, see William Baude, Essay, *Is Originalism Our Law?*, 115 Colum. L. Rev. 2349, 2363–67 (2015); "original methods originalism," which looks to how the Founders and others during the founding or amending periods would have *interpreted* the Constitution, see John O. McGinnis & Michael B. Rappaport, *Original Methods Originalism: A New Theory of Interpretation and the Case Against Construction*, 103 Nw. U. L. Rev. 751, 751 (2009); "original expectations originalism," which interprets a constitutional phrase to decide specific cases in the way the Founders or amenders expected the cases to be decided, see Jack M. Balkin, *Abortion and Original Meaning*, 24 Const. Comment. 291, 295–97 (2007); and "common-law constitutionalism," which develops constitutional principles on a case-by-case basis, like the common law, see David A. Strauss, *Common Law Constitutional Interpretation*, 63 U. Chi. L. Rev. 877, 886–88 (1996).

47. *See, e.g.*, Jeffrey D. Hockett, *Justices Frankfurter and Black: Social Theory and Constitutional Interpretation*, 107 Pol. Sci. Q. 479, 479 (1992).

48. *Compare, e.g.*, Dobbs v. Jackson Women's Health Org., 142 S. Ct. 2228, 2244 (2022) (interpreting the Fourteenth Amendment with reference to "our Nation's history and tradition"), *with Brown v. Bd. of Educ. of Topeka*, 347 U.S. 483, 492 (1954) (declaring

that, in interpreting the Fourteenth Amendment, "we cannot turn the clock back to 1868 when the Amendment was adopted").

49. *See* Fallon, *supra* note 35, at 42.

50. 367 U.S. 643 (1961).

51. *Id.* at 655.

52. *Id.* at 651.

53. *Id.* at 650–52.

54. *Dobbs*, 142 S. Ct. at 2329 (Breyer, Sotomayor & Kagan, JJ., dissenting).

55. *Id.* at 2340–41.

56. *See id.* at 2320–22.

57. *Id.* at 2330 (quoting Planned Parenthood of Se. Pa. v. Casey, 505 U.S. 833, 852 (1992)).

58. *Id.* at 2329–30 (quoting *Casey*, 505 U.S. at 897).

59. *Id.* at 2330.

60. *Id.* at 2329.

61. *Id.*

62. *Id.* at 2350–54 (appendix to dissent).

63. *Id.* at 2354.

64. *Id.* at 2351.

65. 140 S. Ct. 1390 (2020).

66. *Id.* at 1397.

67. 406 U.S. 404 (1972).

68. *Id.* at 406 (plurality opinion).

69. *Dobbs*, 142 S. Ct. at 2351 (appendix to dissent) (alteration in original) (quoting *Ramos*, 140 S. Ct. at 1406).

70. *See id.* at 2351–52.

71. *Id.* at 2352.

72. 558 U.S. 310 (2010).

73. 494 U.S. 652 (1990).

74. *Citizens United*, 558 U.S. at 364.

75. *See Dobbs*, 142 S. Ct. at 2352 (appendix to dissent).

76. *Id.* at 2352–53.

77. 138 S. Ct. 2448 (2018).

78. *Id.* at 2478.

79. 431 U.S. 209 (1977).

80. *Id.* at 235–36.

81. *Dobbs*, 142 U.S. at 2353 (appendix to dissent) (quoting *Janus*, 138 S. Ct. at 2482–83, 2485–86).

82. *See id.* at 2352–53.

83. *Id.* at 2353 (quoting Dickerson v. United States, 530 U.S. 428, 443 (2000)).

84. 469 U.S. 528 (1985).

85. *Id.* at 531.

86. 426 U.S. 833 (1976).

87. *Dobbs*, 142 S. Ct. at 2354 (appendix to dissent).

88. *See id.* at 2353–54.

89. *See id.* at 2354.

90. 300 U.S. 379 (1937).

91. 347 U.S. 483 (1954).

92. *Dobbs*, 142 S. Ct. at 2262–63 (majority opinion).

93. 261 U.S. at 525 (1923).

94. 198 U.S. 45 (1905).

95. *Adkins*, 261 U.S. at 545–46; *Lochner*, 198 U.S. at 49.

96. *See* ALAN GREENSPAN & ADRIAN WOOLDRIDGE, CAPITALISM IN AMERICA: A HISTORY 91–93 (2018).

97. *Id.* at 144–45.

98. *Id.* at 197, 209.

99. West Coast Hotel Co. v. Parrish, 300 U.S. 379, 399 (1937).

100. Planned Parenthood of Se. Pa. v. Casey, 505 U.S. 833, 862 (1992).

101. 163 U.S. 537 (1896).

102. *Id.* at 552 (Harlan, J., dissenting); *see also id.* at 544–48 (majority opinion).

103. Brown v. Bd. of Educ. of Topeka, 347 U.S. 483, 494 (1954).

104. *Id. See generally* W.E.B. Du Bois's THE SOULS OF BLACK FOLKS (1909).

105. *See* Dobbs v. Jackson Women's Health Org., 142 S. Ct. 2228, 2241–424 (Breyer, Sotomayor & Kagan, JJ., dissenting).

106. *See, e.g.*, Sweatt v. Painter, 339 U.S. 629 (1950); Sipuel v. Bd. of Regents, 332 U.S. 631 (1948) (*per curiam*); Missouri *ex rel.* Gaines v. Canada, 305 U.S. 337 (1938).

107. *Brown*, 347 U.S. at 493–94.

108. *Dobbs*, 142 S. Ct. at 2342 (Breyer, Sotomayor & Kagan, JJ., dissenting) (quoting Planned Parenthood of Se. Pa. v. Casey, 505 U.S. 833, 864 (1992)).

109. *Id.* at 2265 (majority opinion).

110. *See id.* at 2244–56.

111. *See id.* at 2301–02 (Thomas, J., concurring) ("[I]n future cases, we should reconsider all of this Court's substantive due process precedents.").

112. *See, e.g.*, Sandra Day O'Connor, *Why Judges Wear Black Robes*, SMITHSONIAN MAG., Nov. 2013.

113. *See supra* Chapter 13.

114. *See supra* Chapter 12.

115. *See supra* notes 64–66 and accompanying text.

116. *See supra* Chapter 13.

117. *See supra* Chapter 14.

118. *See supra* Chapter 15.

16: Workability: History and Practical Experience

1. 573 U.S. 513 (2014).

2. U.S. CONST. art. II, § 2, cl. 2 (emphasis added).

3. *Id.* cl. 3.

4. *Noel Canning*, 573 U.S. at 519.

5. *See 100th to 109th Congresses (1987–2007)*, HIST., ART & ARCHIVES: U.S. HOUSE OF REPRESENTATIVES, https://history.house.gov/Institution/Session-Dates/100-109/.

6. *Noel Canning*, 573 U.S. at 526–27.

7. *Id.* at 519.

8. *Id.* at 519.

9. And I shall leave the interested reader to consider the Court's answer to the third question by consulting the opinions themselves. *See id.* at 549–56.

10. *Compare id.* at 556 ("The purpose of the Clause is to allow the Executive to continue operating while the Senate is unavailable."), *with id.* at 579 (Scalia, J., concurring in the judgment) (beginning the analysis with the late-eighteenth-century understanding of the terms "recess" and "session").

11. *Compare id.* at 524 (majority opinion) ("[I]n interpreting the Clause, we put significant weight upon historical practice." (emphasis omitted)), *with id.* at 584–93, 602–13 (Scalia, J., concurring in the judgment) (reviewing historical practice).

12. *Id.* at 522 (majority opinion) (emphasis omitted).

13. *Id.* at 523.

14. *Id.* (quoting THE FEDERALIST No. 76, at 510 (Alexander Hamilton) (J. Cooke ed., 1961)).

15. *Id.*

16. *Id.* (quoting THE FEDERALIST No. 67, *supra* note 14, at 455 (Alexander Hamilton)).

17. *Id.* at 524.

18. *Id.* at 571 (Scalia, J., concurring in the judgment).

19. *See id.* at 525.

20. U.S. CONST., art. II, § 2, cl. 3.

21. 573 U.S. at 527–28.

22. *See id.*

23. U.S. CONST. art. I, § 3, cl. 5 (emphasis added).

24. *Noel Canning*, 573 U.S. at 528.

25. *Id.*

26. *See* 573 U.S. at 577–78 (Scalia, J., concurring in the judgment) (emphasis added).

27. *Id.* at 575.

28. *Id.* at 584–85.

29. *Id.* at 582.

30. *See id.* at 577–78.

31. *Id.* at 533–34 (majority opinion).

32. *Id.* at 534.

33. *See id.* at 536–38.

34. U.S. CONST., art. I, § 5, cl. 4.

35. *Noel Canning*, 573 U.S. at 536–38.

36. *Id.* at 534–35.

37. *Id.* at 524.

38. *Id.* (quoting McCulloch v. Maryland, 17 U.S. (4 Wheat.) 316, 401 (1819)).

39. *Id.* (alteration omitted) (quoting the Pocket Veto Case, 279 U.S. 655, 689 (1929)).

40. *Id.* at 528.

41. *Id.* at 528–29 (noting that those appointments were upheld by a federal court and justified contemporaneously by the attorney general in written opinions).

42. *Id.* at 529 (citing the years 1867, 1868, 1921, and 1929).

43. *Id.*

44. *See id.* at 529–30.

45. *Id.* at 531–32.

46. *See id.* at 585–86 (Scalia, J., concurring in the judgment).

47. *Id.* at 587–89.

48. *Id.* at 586–87 (calling Knox "the first Attorney General known to have opined on the question").

49. *Id.* at 590–91.

50. *See id.* at 614–15.

51. U.S. Const. art. II, § 2, cl. 3 (emphasis added).

52. *See Noel Canning*, 573 U.S. at 538.

53. *Id.* at 539 (quoting Letter to Wilson Cary Nicholas (Jan. 26, 1802), in 36 Papers of Thomas Jefferson 433 (Barbara B. Oberg ed., 2009)).

54. *Id.* (quoting Executive Authority to Fill Vacancies, 1 Op. Att'y Gen. 631, 631–32 (1823)).

55. *See id.* at 540.

56. *Id.*

57. *Id.* (quoting 1 Op. Att'y Gen. at 632).

58. *Id.* at 541–42.

59. *Id.* at 549–56.

60. *Id.* at 545.

61. *Id.* at 545–46 (relying on both a Congressional Research Service study and research from the Supreme Court Library).

62. *Id.* at 612–14 (Scalia, J., concurring in the judgment).

63. *See, e.g., id.* at 605–08, 612–13.

64. *Id.* at 613.

65. *Id.* at 614.

66. *Id.*

67. *See id.* at 533–34 (majority opinion) (citing McCulloch v. Maryland, 17 U.S. (4 Wheat.) 316, 415 (1819)).

17: Workability: Deciding Where Values Conflict

1. 554 U.S. 570 (2008).

2. *Id.* at 689–90 (Breyer, J., dissenting) (quoting Nixon v. Shrink Mo. Gov't PAC, 528 U.S. 377, 402 (2000) (Breyer, J., concurring)).

3. *See generally* Vicki C. Jackson, *Constitutional Law in an Age of Proportionality*, 124 Yale L. J. 3094 (2015).

4. *See* U.S. Const. amend. II.

5. *See* N.Y. State Rifle & Pistol Ass'n v. Bruen, 142 S. Ct. 2111, 2127 (2022).

6. *See Heller*, 554 U.S. at 574.

7. U.S. Const. amend. II.

8. *Heller*, 554 U.S. at 635.

9. *See id.* at 636–80 (Stevens, J., dissenting).

10. *See id.* at 681–723 (Breyer, J., dissenting).

11. *Id.* at 584–86 (majority opinion).

12. *Id.* at 626.

13. *Id.* at 626–27.

14. *Id.* at 628.

15. *Id.* at 628–29.

16. *See id.* at 655–59 (Stevens, J., dissenting).

17. *Id.* at 659–61.

18. *Id.* at 661–62.

19. *See id.* at 680.

20. *See id.* at 681–82 (Breyer, J., dissenting).

21. *Id.* at 682.

22. *See id.* at 683–87.

23. *Id.* at 687.

24. *Id.*

25. *See id.* at 694 (quoting *Firearms Control Regulations Act of 1975 (Council Act No. 1-142): Hearing and Disposition Before the House Committee on the District of Columbia*, 94th Cong. 25 (1976) [hereinafter D.C. Rep.]).

26. *Id.* (quoting D.C. Rep. at 25).

27. *Id.* at 695 (quoting D.C. Rep. at 25).

28. *Id.* (quoting D.C. Rep. at 31).

29. *Id.* at 699–700.

30. *Id.* at 700.

31. *Id.* at 700–01.

32. *See id.* at 704–05.

33. *See id.* at 704 (quoting Turner Broad. Sys. v. FCC, 520 U.S. 180, 195 (1997)).

34. *Id.* at 706–07.

35. *Id.* at 708–09 (citing Maryland and Virginia laws).

36. *Id.* at 709–10.

37. *Id.* at 710.

38. *See id.*

39. *See id.* at 711 (noting a "symmetry" between the District's interests and the constitutional rights burdened).

40. *Id.* at 711–12.

41. While it is difficult to measure the exact effect of firearm possession in the home on suicide or domestic violence, studies generally suggest that higher rates of firearm possession correlate with higher rates of harm, both to the gun owner and to others in the home. *See, e.g.*, David M. Studdert et al., *Homicide Deaths Among Adult Cohabitants of Handgun Owners in California, 2004 to 2016*, 175 ANNALS OF INTERNAL MEDICINE 804 (2022), https://www .acpjournals.org/doi/epdf/10.7326/M21-3762 ("Overall rates of homicide were more than twice as high among cohabitants of handgun owners than among cohabitants of nonowners. These elevated rates were driven largely by higher rates of homicide by firearm."); Beth Duff-Brown, *Handgun Ownership Associated with Much Higher Suicide Risk*, STAN. MED. (June 3, 2020), https://med.stanford.edu/news/all-news/2020/06/handgun-own ership-associated-with-much-higher-suicide-risk.html ("Owning a handgun is associated with a dramatically elevated risk of suicide, according to new Stanford research that followed 26 million California residents over a 12-year period."); Jennifer Mascia, *How Often Are Guns Used for Self-Defense?*, TRACE (Jun. 3, 2022), https://www.thetrace.org/2022/06 /defensive-gun-use-data-good-guys-with-guns/ (providing an overview of difficulties in conclusively comparing data regarding defensive gun use versus firearm victimization, but concluding that "having a gun in your house increases suicides, it increases gun accidents, and it increases homicides, at least of women in the house").

42. *Heller*, 554 U.S. at 712 (Breyer, J., dissenting).

43. *See, e.g., id.* at 712–13.

44. *Id.* at 712.

45. *See id.* at 714.

46. *See id.* ("I turn now to the final portion of the 'permissible regulation' question: Does the District's law *disproportionately* burden [Second] Amendment-protected interests?").

47. *Id.* at 714–15.

48. *See id.* at 714–15.

49. *See id.* at 716–17.

50. *Id.* at 718.

51. *See id.* at 719.

52. *See id.*

53. *See id.* at 638 n.2 (Stevens, J., dissenting) (citing United States v. Haney, 264 F.3d 1161, 1164–66 (10th Cir. 2001); United States v. Napier, 233 F.3d 394, 402–404 (6th Cir. 2000); Gillespie v. Indianapolis, 185 F.3d 693, 710–11 (7th Cir. 1999); United States v. Scanio, No. 97–1584, 1998 WL 802060, at *2 (2d Cir. Nov. 12, 1998); United States v. Wright, 117 F.3d 1265, 1271–74 (11th Cir. 1997); United States v. Rybar, 103 F.3d 273, 285–86 (3d Cir. 1996); Hickman v. Block, 81 F.3d 98, 100–03 (9th Cir. 1996); United States v. Hale, 978 F.2d 1016, 1018–20 (8th Cir. 1992); Thomas v. City Council of Portland, 730 F.2d 41, 42 (1st Cir. 1984) (*per curiam*); United States v. Johnson, 497 F.2d 548, 550 (4th Cir. 1974) (*per curiam*); United States v. Johnson, 441 F.2d 1134, 1136 (5th Cir. 1971)

54. *See id.* at 722 (Breyer, J., dissenting) ("One cannot answer those questions by combining inconclusive historical research with judicial *ipse dixit*.").

18: Workability: Direct Application of Basic Values

1. 545 U.S. 844 (2005).

2. 545 U.S. 677 (2005).

3. U.S. CONST. amend. I.

4. 1 ALEXIS DE TOCQUEVILLE, DEMOCRACY IN AMERICA 308 (Phillips Bradley ed., 1945).

5. *Id.*

6. *See, e.g.*, 3 JOSEPH STORY, COMMENTARIES ON THE CONSTITUTION OF THE UNITED STATES § 1841 (1833) (discussing motivations behind Article IV's prohibition of religious tests as a qualification to hold public office).

7. *See* LORD RADCLIFFE, THE LAW & ITS COMPASS 70–74 (1960).

8. *See id.* at 66.

9. *Id.*

10. *Id.* at 76.

11. *Id.* at 70.

12. *Id.* at 91 (quoting INGE SCHOLL, SIX AGAINST TYRANNY 34, 75 (1955).

13. *Id.* (quoting SCHOLL, *supra* note 12, at 82); *accord* BURT NEUBORNE, MADISON'S MUSIC: ON READING THE FIRST AMENDMENT 132 (2015) ("The Bill of Rights opens with a First Amendment structured as a narrative of a free people governing themselves. That story begins where it must begin, with freedom of conscience.").

14. *See* Engel v. Vitale, 370 U.S. 421, 436 (1962).

15. *Id.* at 429.

16. *Id.* at 431.

17. *See* Lemon v. Kurtzman, 403 U.S. 602, 623 (1971).

18. *See* Sch. Dist. of Abington Township v. Schempp, 374 U.S. 203, 307 (Brennan, J., concurring).

19. *See* Comm. for Pub. Educ. & Religious Liberty v. Nyquist, 413 U.S. 756, 796 n.54 (1973).

20. *Id.* at 794.

21. The following paragraphs draw on my dissent in *Zelman v. Simmons-Harris*, 536 U.S. 639, 719–29 (2002) (Breyer, J., dissenting).

22. *Id.* at 719–20.

23. *See id.* at 723; *see also* Pew Rsch. Ctr., America's Changing Religious Landscape 21 (2015) (summarizing the numbers of religious denominations in United States as of 2015).

24. *See* Wallace v. Jaffree, 472 U.S. 38, 40, 60–61 (1985).

25. *See* Marsh v. Chambers, 463 U.S. 783, 795 (1983).

26. *See* Comm. for Pub. Educ. & Religious Liberty v. Nyquist, 413 U.S. 756, 762–63, 774–80 (1973).

27. *See* Everson v. Bd. of Educ., 330 U.S. 1, 17 (1947).

28. *See* Lemon v. Kurtzman, 403 U.S. 602, 625 (1971).

29. *See* Zobrest v. Catalina Foothills Sch. Dist., 509 U.S. 1, 13–14 (1993).

30. *See* Texas Monthly, Inc. v. Bullock, 489 U.S. 1, 25 (1989).

31. *See* Walz v. Tax Comm'n of the City of N.Y., 397 U.S. 664, 680 (1970).

32. *See* Thomas v. Rev. Bd. of the Ind. Empl. Sec. Div., 450 U.S. 707, 719–20 (1981).

33. *See* United States v. Lee, 455 U.S. 252, 260 (1982).

34. *See* Emp. Div., Dep't of Hum. Res. of Or. v. Smith, 494 U.S. 872, 890 (1990).

35. *See* Church of Lukumi Babalu Aye, Inc. v. City of Hialeah, 508 U.S. 520, 523–24 (1993).

36. *See* Sherbert v. Verner, 374 U.S. 398, 399–402, 409–10 (1963).

37. *See* Goldman v. Weinberger, 475 U.S. 503, 504 (1986).

38. McCreary County v. ACLU, 545 U.S. 844, 850 (2005).

39. *Id.* at 852–54.

40. *Id.* at 851.

41. *Id.* at 853–54.

42. *Id.* at 851–52 (quoting ACLU v. McCreary County, 96 F. Supp. 2d 679, 684 (E.D. Ky. 2000)).

43. *Id.* at 854 (alteration in original) (quoting *ACLU*, 96 F. Supp. 2d at 686).

44. *Id.* (quoting *McCreary County*, 96 F. Supp. 2d at 686–87).

45. *See id.* at 859–60.

46. *Id.* at 860 (quoting *Zelman v. Simmons-Harris*, 536 U.S. 639, 718 (2002) (Breyer, J., dissenting)).

47. *See generally id.* at 867–74.

48. *See id.* at 881 (O'Connor, J. concurring).

49. *Id.* at 882–83 (quoting Memorial and Remonstrance Against Religious Assessments, in 2 Writings of James Madison 183, 184 (Gaillard Hunt ed., 1901)).

50. *Id.* at 883.

51. *Id.* at 883–84.

52. Van Orden v. Perry, 545 U.S. 677, 681–82 (2005).

53. *See id.* at 700 (Breyer, J., concurring in the judgment).

54. *Id.* at 701–03.

55. *Id.* at 701–02.

56. *See id.* at 681 (majority opinion).

57. *Id.* at 702 (Breyer, J., concurring in the judgment).

58. *Id.* at 704.

59. *Id.* (citing *Zelman v. Simmons-Harris*, 536 U.S. 639, 717–29 (2002) (Breyer, J., dissenting)).

Part V: Paradigm Shifts on the Court

1. *See generally* THOMAS S. KUHN, THE STRUCTURE OF SCIENTIFIC REVOLUTIONS (2d ed. 1970).

19: Three Paradigm Shifts

1. 198 U.S. 45 (1905).
2. *Id.* at 52.
3. U.S. CONST. amend. XIV, § 1.
4. *Lochner*, 198 U.S. at 53.
5. *Id.* at 56.
6. *Id.* at 57.
7. *Id.* at 61.
8. *See id.* at 70–71 (Harlan, J., dissenting).
9. *See id.* at 75 (Holmes, J., dissenting).
10. *Id.*
11. *Id.*
12. 261 U.S. 525 (1923).
13. *Id.* at 545–46.
14. *See id.* at 546–51.
15. *Id.* at 553–54.
16. *See id.* at 562 (Taft, C.J., dissenting).
17. *Id.*
18. *Id.*
19. *See, e.g.*, Adair v. United States, 208 U.S. 161, 179–80 (1908) (striking down a federal law prohibiting railroad companies from offering employees "yellow-dog contracts," or contracts that forbade union membership as a condition of employment); *see also* Coppage v. Kansas, 236 U.S. 1, 26 (1915) (same for state laws banning such contracts).
20. *See, e.g.*, Tyson & Brother v. Banton, 273 U.S. 418, 426–27, 442–45 (1927) (theater ticket prices); Ribnik v. McBride, 277 U.S. 350, 355–59 (1928) (employment agency fees); Williams v. Standard Oil Co., 278 U.S. 235, 238–40 (1928) (gasoline prices).
21. 277 U.S. 350 (1928).
22. *Id.* at 355, 357.
23. *Id.* at 360 (Stone, J., dissenting).
24. *See* Tyson & Brother v. Banton, 273 U.S. 418 (1927).
25. *Id.* at 447 (Holmes, J., dissenting).
26. For an account of this time period, see generally ALAN GREENSPAN & ADRIAN WOOLDRIDGE, CAPITALISM IN AMERICA: A HISTORY (2018).
27. *See id.* at 98.
28. *See id.* at 92.
29. *See* Suresh Naidu & Noam Yuchtman, *Labor Market Institutions in the Gilded Age of American Economic History*, in 1 THE OXFORD HANDBOOK OF AMERICAN ECONOMIC HISTORY 329, 333 (Louis P. Cain et al. eds., 2018).
30. *See generally* ROBERT GREEN MCCLOSKEY, AMERICAN CONSERVATISM IN THE AGE OF ENTERPRISE: A STUDY OF WILLIAM GRAHAM SUMNER, STEPHEN J. FIELD, AND ANDREW CARNEGIE (1951).

31. *See* James W. Ely, Jr., The Fuller Court: Justices, Rulings, and Legacy 3 (2003) (describing the Court from 1888 to 1910 as "dedicated to economic liberty as the preeminent constitutional value").

32. *See, e.g.*, Morton J. Horwitz, *The Supreme Court, 1992 Term—Foreword: The Constitution of Change: Legal Fundamentality Without Fundamentalism*, 107 Harv. L. Rev. 30, 73–82 (1993); John Hart Ely, *Toward a Representation-Reinforcing Mode of Judicial Review*, 37 Md. L. Rev. 451, 452 (1978); Cass R. Sunstein, Lochner's *Legacy*, 87 Colum. L. Rev. 873, 873–75 (1987).

33. *See* Ely, *supra* note 31, at 3 ("[T]he Fuller Court assumed the desirability of private economic ordering and looked skeptically at measures that infringed upon the workings of the free market.").

34. *See generally* David A. Hounshell, From the American System to Mass Production, 1800–1932: The Development of Manufacturing Technology in the United States (1984).

35. *See generally* William E. Leuchtenburg, The Perils of Prosperity, 1914–1932 (1958).

36. Robert Post, *Preface to* The Taft Court: The Ambivalent Construction of the Modern State, 1921–1930 (forthcoming 2023) (manuscript at 22–23) (on file with author).

37. William H. Taft, *The Right of Private Property*, 3 Mich. L. J. 215, 218 (1894).

38. Post, *supra* note 36, at 29.

39. *See, e.g.*, *The Chief of These Is Property*, 33 New Republic 59, 60 (1922).

40. For example, the court of appeals below freely invoked such policy arguments. *See* Children's Hospital of the District of Columbia v. Adkins, 284 F. 613, 621 (App. D.C. 1922) ("A wage based upon competitive ability is just, and leads to frugality and honest industry . . . while the equal wage paralyzes ambition and promotes prodigality and indolence.").

41. 68 Cong. Rec. S4771, 4771 (Feb. 25, 1927) (statement of Calvin Coolidge to the Senate respecting veto of the McNary-Haugen Farm Relief Bill).

42. *See* Christina D. Romer, *The Nation in Depression*, J. Econ. Persp., Spring 1993, at 19, 30–31.

43. Panama Refin. Co. v. Ryan, 293 U.S. 388, 408–10, 428–33 (1935).

44. R.R. Ret. Bd. v. Alton R.R. Co., 295 U.S. 330, 344, 362 (1935).

45. Carter v. Carter Coal Co., 298 U.S. 238, 278–80, 302–10 (1936).

46. Morehead v. New York *ex rel.* Tipaldo, 298 U.S. 587, 602, 617–18 (1936).

47. United States v. Butler, 297 U.S. 1, 53–54, 63–75 (1936).

48. For accounts of this episode, see generally William E. Leuchtenburg, The Supreme Court Reborn: The Constitutional Revolution in the Age of Roosevelt (1995).

49. *Id.* at 134.

50. West Coast Hotel Co. v. Parrish, 300 U.S. 379, 386, 399–400 (1937).

51. 301 U.S. 1 (1937).

52. *See* 304 U.S. 144, 152 & n. 4 (1938) (identifying circumstances under which judicial review may be more acceptable).

53. Lochner v. New York, 198 U.S. 45, 76 (1905) (Holmes, J., dissenting).

54. Nebbia v. New York, 291 U.S. 502, 537 (1934).

55. *Judicial Restraint*, Britannica Acad., Encyclopaedia Britannica, https://academic .eb.com/levels/collegiate/article/judicial-restraint/488011.

56. 300 U.S. 379 (1937).

57. *Id.* at 404 (Sutherland, J., dissenting).

58. *See* Gary Richardson et al., *Stock Market Crash of 1929*, FED. RSRV. HIST. (Nov. 22, 2013), https://www.federalreservehistory.org/essays/stock-market-crash-of-1929.

59. *See* Romer, *supra* note 42, at 30.

60. *See* President Franklin D. Roosevelt, First Inaugural Address (Mar. 4, 1933).

61. *See generally* DONALD WORSTER, DUST BOWL: THE SOUTHERN PLAINS IN THE 1930s (2d ed. 2004); *cf.* JOHN STEINBECK, THE GRAPES OF WRATH (1939).

62. *See* Robert Whaples, *Where Is There Consensus Among American Economic Historians? The Results of a Survey on Forty Propositions*, 55 J. ECON. HIST. 139, 144, 151 (1995) (showing academic consensus on the Smoot-Hawley Tariff's detrimental effects on the American economy).

63. *See* William E. Leuchtenburg, *Franklin D. Roosevelt: Campaigns and Elections*, MILLER CTR., https://millercenter.org/president/fdroosevelt/campaigns-and-elections; *cf.* President Franklin D. Roosevelt, State of the Union Address (Jan. 11, 1944) (articulating a proposal for economic rights termed the "Second Bill of Rights").

64. West Coast Hotel Co. v. Parrish, 300 U.S. 379, 399 (1937).

65. Dobbs v. Jackson Women's Health Org., 142 S. Ct. 2228, 2316 (2022) (Roberts, C.J., concurring in the judgment).

66. *See* Olmstead v. United States, 277 U.S. 438, 472 (1928) (Brandeis, J., dissenting) (quoting Village of Euclid v. Ambler Realty Co., 272 U.S. 365, 387 (1926)).

67. 163 U.S. 537 (1896).

68. 347 U.S. 483 (1954).

69. This practice of "selective incorporation" of the Bill of Rights included the double jeopardy requirement, *see* Benton v. Maryland, 395 U.S. 784, 795–96 (1969); the right against self-incrimination, *see* Griffin v. California, 380 U.S. 609, 615 (1965); the right to a speedy trial, *see* Klopfer v. North Carolina, 386 U.S. 213, 222–26 (1967); the right to confront adverse witnesses, *see* Pointer v. Texas, 380 U.S. 400, 400 (1965); and various warrant requirements under the Fourth Amendment, *see, e.g.*, Mapp v. Ohio, 367 U.S. 643, 655–56 (1961); Ker v. California, 374 U.S. 23, 30–31, 33 (1963); Aguilar v. Texas, 378 U.S. 108, 110–12 (1964).

70. *See, e.g.*, Baker v. Carr, 369 U.S. 186, 237 (1962); Wesberry v. Sanders, 376 U.S. 1, 7–8 (1964); Reynolds v. Sims, 377 U.S. 533, 568 (1964).

71. *See* Miranda v. Arizona, 384 U.S. 436, 467–73 (1966).

72. *See* Gideon v. Wainwright, 372 U.S. 335, 345 (1963); Escobedo v. Illinois, 378 U.S. 478, 490–91 (1964).

73. Griswold v. Connecticut, 381 U.S. 479, 484–86 (1965).

74. Roe v. Wade, 410 U.S. 113, 152–56 (1973).

75. *See generally, e.g.*, Herbert Wechsler, *Toward Neutral Principles of Constitutional Law*, 73 HARV. L. REV. 1 (1959) (questioning *Brown v. Board of Education* as unjustifiable on "neutral" principles).

76. For an account of the influence that American Jim Crow segregation had on Nazi Germany, see generally JAMES Q. WHITMAN, HITLER'S AMERICAN MODEL (2017).

77. *See generally* MATTHEW F. DELMONT, HALF AMERICAN: THE EPIC STORY OF AFRICAN AMERICANS FIGHTING WORLD WAR II AT HOME AND ABROAD (2022).

78. *Cf.* President Harry S. Truman, Address Before a Joint Session of Congress (Mar. 12, 1947) ("I believe that we must assist free peoples to work out their own destinies in

their own way. I believe that our help should be primarily through economic and financial aid which is essential to economic stability and orderly political processes.").

79. *See, e.g.*, U.N. Charter; Universal Declaration of Human Rights, G.A. Res. 217A (Dec. 12, 1948).

80. *See generally* W.E.B. DU BOIS, AN APPEAL TO THE WORLD (1947).

81. *Id.* at 12.

82. *See* Morton J. Horwitz, *The Warren Court and the Pursuit of Justice*, 50 WASH. & LEE L. REV. 5, 10 (1993).

83. Brown v. Bd. of Educ. of Topeka, 347 U.S. 483, 492 (1954).

84. *See generally* GEORGE LEWIS, MASSIVE RESISTANCE: THE WHITE RESPONSE TO THE CIVIL RIGHTS MOVEMENT (2006).

85. 379 U.S. 241 (1964).

86. *See id.* at 261–62.

87. Marcia Coyle, *The Supreme Court and the "Climate of the Era,"* NAT'L CONST. CTR. (June 29, 2020), https://constitutioncenter.org/blog/the-supreme-court-and-the-climate-of -the-era.

20: Are We Undergoing the Next Paradigm Shift?

1. 143 S. Ct. 1322 (2023).

2. 143 S. Ct. 2141 (2023).

3. *See generally* NEIL M. GORSUCH, A REPUBLIC, IF YOU CAN KEEP IT (2019); Brett M. Kavanaugh, *Fixing Statutory Interpretation*, 129 HARV. L. REV. 2118 (2016) (reviewing ROBERT A. KATZMANN, JUDGING STATUTES (2014)); Amy Coney Barrett, Lecture, *Assorted Canards of Contemporary Legal Analyses: Redux*, 70 CASE W. RES. L. REV. 855 (2020); Amy Coney Barrett, *Originalism and Stare Decisis*, 92 NOTRE DAME L. REV. 1921 (2017).

4. 33 U.S.C. § 1311(a).

5. *Id.* § 1362(12).

6. *Id.* § 1342; *see also Sackett*, 143 S. Ct. at 1330–31.

7. 33 U.S.C. § 1362(7).

8. *Id.*

9. *Sackett*, 143 S. Ct. at 1336 (quoting Rapanos v. United States, 547 U.S. 715, 739 (2005) (plurality opinion)).

10. *Id.* at 1339.

11. *See, e.g., id.* at 1364–65 (Kavanaugh, J., concurring in the judgment).

12. 33 U.S.C. § 1344(g)(1) (emphasis added).

13. *Sackett*, 143 S. Ct. at 1339–40.

14. *Id.* at 1339.

15. *Id.* at 1332–33, 1341.

16. *Id.* at 1363–64 (Kavanaugh, J., concurring in the judgment).

17. *Id.*

18. *Id.*

19. *Id.* at 1364–66.

20. 33 U.S.C. § 1251(a).

21. RICHARD J. LAZARUS, THE MAKING OF ENVIRONMENTAL LAW 59 (2004).

22. *See* N. William Hines, *History of the 1972 Clean Water Act: The Story Behind How the 1972*

Act Became the Capstone on a Decade of Extraordinary Environmental Reform, J. ENERGY & ENV'T L. 80, 81 (Summer 2013).

23. United States v. Riverside Bayview Homes, Inc., 474 U.S. 121, 134 (1985).

24. *Sackett*, 143 S. Ct. at 1368 (Kavanaugh, J., concurring in the judgment).

25. 474 U.S. 121 (1985).

26. *Id.* at 132.

27. *Id.*

28. *Id.* at 134.

29. *Sackett*, 143 S. Ct. at 1369 (Kavanaugh, J., concurring in the judgment).

30. *See* Chevron, U.S.A., Inc. v. Nat'l Res. Def. Council, Inc., 467 U.S. 837 (1984).

31. *See* Adarand Constructors, Inc. v. Peña, 515 U.S. 200, 227 (1995) (overruling Metro Broadcasting, Inc. v. FCC, 497 U.S. 547 (1990)).

32. 438 U.S. 265 (1978).

33. *Id.* at 313 (opinion of Powell, J.).

34. *See* Grutter v. Bollinger, 539 U.S. 306, 337–38 (2003).

35. *See, e.g.*, Fisher v. University of Texas at Austin, 579 U.S. 365 (2016) (*Fisher II*).

36. *See generally* Reva B. Siegel, *Equality Talk: Antisubordination and Anticlassification Values in Constitutional Struggles over* Brown, 117 HARV. L. REV. 1470 (2004).

37. Students for Fair Admissions, Inc. v. President and Fellows of Harvard College, 143 S. Ct. 2141, 2159 (2023).

38. 163 U.S. 537 (1896).

39. 347 U.S. 483 (1954).

40. *Students for Fair Admissions*, 143 S. Ct. at 2160.

41. *Id.* at 2166–67.

42. *Id.* at 2177 (Thomas, J., concurring).

43. *Id.* at 2186.

44. *Id.* at 2187.

45. *Id.* at 2250 (Sotomayor, J., dissenting).

46. *Id.* at 2266 (Jackson, J., dissenting).

47. *Id.* at 2264.

48. 551 U.S. 701 (2007).

49. *Id.* at 829 (Breyer, J., dissenting).

50. *Id.*

51. *Id.* at 820.

52. 539 U.S. 244 (2003).

53. *Id.* at 302 (Ginsburg, J., dissenting) ("To avoid conflict with the equal protection clause, a classification that denies a benefit, causes harm, or imposes a burden must not be based on race. . . . But the Constitution is color conscious to prevent discrimination being perpetuated and to undo the effects of past discrimination.") (quoting United States v. Jefferson Cnty. Bd. of Educ., 372 F.2d 836, 876 (5th Cir. 1966) (Wisdom, J.)).

54. ALEXIS DE TOCQUEVILLE, 1 DEMOCRACY IN AMERICA 457 (Henry Reeve trans., Francis Bowen ed., 1862) (1835).

55. GARY ORFIELD & DANIELLE JARVIE, BLACK SEGREGATION MATTERS: SCHOOL RESEGREGATION AND BLACK EDUCATIONAL OPPORTUNITY 27 (2020).

56. *Id.*

57. Poe v. Ullman, 367 U.S. 497, 518 (1961) (Harlan, J., dissenting).

58. *Id.*

59. *Id.* n.9.

60. *Id.* at 544 (quoting Irvine v. California, 347 U.S. 128, 147 (1954) (Frankfurter, J., dissenting)).

61. 143 S. Ct. 1487 (2023).

62. *Id.* at 1504–06; *see also id.* at 1525 (Thomas, J., dissenting).

63. 52 U.S.C. § 10301(a) (emphasis added).

64. *Id.* § 10301(b).

65. *Id.* at 1498–1501.

66. 143 S. Ct. 1206 (2023).

67. *Id.* at 1230–31.

68. *Id.* at 1219–20, 1226–29.

69. 143 S. Ct. 1915 (2023).

70. *Id.* at 1918, 1919–22 (emphasizing, for instance, the background principles in place when Congress passed the statute, long-standing practice, and whether its decision would be "sensible"). Other recent examples in which the Court—including its textualist and originalist members—considered interpretive factors such as legislative history, past government practice, and consequences include, for instance, *Bittner v. United States*, 143 S. Ct. 713, 722–23 (2023), and *Dubin v. United States*, 143 S. Ct. 1557, 1572–73 (2023) (considering sweeping potential consequences of the government's proposed reading of a criminal statute).

71. *See* Dobbs v. Jackson Women's Health Org., 142 S. Ct. 2228, 2277 (2022) ("Our decision returns the issue of abortion to those legislative bodies.").

72. I have provided many illustrations of the shortcomings that I identify with excessive reliance on textualism and originalism, and the reader may wish to refresh their recollection of those examples in Parts II and III.

73. As I said in my oral dissent in *Parents Involved in Community Schools v. Seattle School District No. 1*, 551 U.S. 701 (2007), "[i]t is not often in the law that so few have so quickly changed so much." *See* Linda Greenhouse, *Justices Limit the Use of Race in School Plans for Integration*, N.Y. TIMES (Jun. 29, 2007), https://www.nytimes.com/2007/06/29 /washington/29scotus.html.

74. Marcia Coyle, The Supreme Court and the "Climate of the Era," NAT'L CONST. CTR. (June 29, 2020), https://constitutioncenter.org/blog/the-supreme-court-and-the -climate-of-the-era.

75. *See, e.g.,* STEPHEN G. BREYER, THE AUTHORITY OF THE COURT AND THE PERIL OF POLITICS 14–15, 25–30 (2021) (discussing the Court's decisions in *Worcester v. Georgia*, 31 U.S. (6 Pet.) 515 (1832), *Cooper v. Aaron*, 358 U.S. 1 (1958), and *Bush v. Gore*, 531 U.S. 98 (2000), and their ramifications for public acceptance of the Court's authority).

Conclusion

1. MICHEL DE MONTAIGNE, OF EXPERIENCE (1588), *reprinted in* 3 ESSAYS OF MICHEL DE MONTAIGNE 375 (William Carew Hazlitt ed., Charles Cotton trans., 1877).

2. ALEXIS DE TOCQUEVILLE, DEMOCRACY IN AMERICA 280 (Phillips Bradley ed., 1945).

INDEX

Page numbers beginning with 269 refer to notes.

Abood v. Detroit Board of Education, 190
abortion rights, 133–34, 182–84, 187–93, 242,
    257–58, 321
Acheson, Dean, 204, 242
Adams, Samuel, 216
"adjacent," definition of, 247–49
Adjournments Clause, 203
Adkins v. Children's Hospital of the District of
    Columbia, 191, 232–33, 235, 236–37, 238,
    239, 317
    Court's overruling of, 238
Administrative Procedure Act (APA), 63–64,
    66, 71, 157
advertising, regulation of, 156
Affordable Care Act, 274
African Americans, in World War II military,
    242
agencies, federal, rules of, *see* rules, formulated
    by federal agencies
agencies, regulatory, 162–72
    congressional intent and, 170–71, 176
    as part of executive branch, 164–65, 173
Agricultural Adjustment Act, 237
A.L.A. Schechter Poultry Corp v. United States,
    166–67
aliens, government detention and deportation
    of, 89–93, 289
Alito, Samuel, 168, 169
    on textualism, 16
Ali v. Federal Bureau of Prisons, 76–79, 107
Allen v. Milligan, 254

Antiterrorism and Effective Death Penalty Act
    (AEDPA), 47
APA, *see* Administrative Procedure Act
Apodaca v. Oregon, 189
"Appeal to the World, An" (NAACP), 243
appellate courts:
    overly specific language in, xxiv–xxv
    role of, xv–xvi, xxii
    see also Supreme Court, U.S.
Aristotle, 138
Arlington Central School District Board of Education
    v. Murphy, 82–83
Army Corps of Engineers, 247, 248, 249
artificial intelligence, 32
assembly, freedom of, 141–42
asylum-seekers, detention of, 91–93
Austin v. Michigan Chamber of Commerce, 189–90
Azar v. Allina Health Services, 63–67

bail, right to seek, 90–93
Baltimore and Ohio Railroad, 161–62
Barnhart v. Sigmon Coal Co., 98–103, 177, 292
Barrett, Amy Coney, 91, 170, 298
"bear arms":
    Heller majority's interpretation of, 210–11
    historical use of phrase, 131
Bill of Rights, 115, 211, 219, 220
    as applicable to states, 230, 241
Bill of Rights, English, 130–31
Blackmun, Harry, xxiii
Blacks, *see* African Americans

Blackstone, William, 20–21, 70, 90, 130–31
  on *stare decisis*, 181, 193
Board of Immigration Appeals, 93
Bolling v. Sharpe, 135–36
Bond, Carol Anne, 21–22
Book of Common Prayer, xxv–xxvi
Book of Kells, xxix
Boos v. Barry, 154
borderline cases, 225, 227
Bostock v. Clayton County, 23–24
Brandeis, Louis, xix, 147, 238, 241, 263
Bressman, Lisa Schultz, 20, 26, 75–76
Breyer, Stephen:
  Ali dissent of, 77–79
  Allina Health dissent of, 65–67
  background and education of, xviii, xix
  Barnhart opinion of, 101–2, 177
  Brown & Williamson dissent of, 39–40
  Bruen dissent of, 128
  Bruesewitz opinion of, 80
  County of Maui opinion of, 7–10
  Duncan dissent of, 46, 49–50, 280
  Heller dissent of, 130, 210, 211–12
  on *Holy Trinity* decision, 97–98
  Jam dissent of, 56, 58, 62
  Jennings dissent of, xviii–xix, xxvii, 91–93, 289
  legal career of, xv, xviii–xix, xxvii; *see also specific cases*
  legislative history used by, 68–69, 284
  in *McCutcheon* dissent of, 143–44
  NFIB v. OSHA and *West Virginia v. EPA* dissents of, 169
  Noel Canning opinion of, 199–201
  purpose-oriented approach of, xvi, xx, 261–63
  Reagan National Advertising, concurrence of, 155
  in *Reed* concurrence of, 153–54
  Scalia's good-natured debate with, 139–40
  as Senate Judiciary Committee Chief Counsel, 22–23, 72
  in *Sorrell* concurrence of, 150
  Wisconsin Central dissent of, 53–54
  Zadvydas opinion of, 90–91
"*Brown*, Originalism, and Constitutional Theory" (Klarman), 299
Brown v. Board of Education of Topeka, 135, 191, 192, 241, 242, 243, 251, 308

Bruesewitz v. Wyeth, 79–82
Burger, Warren, 22–23
Burger Court, 242
Burwell v. Hobby Lobby Stores, Inc., 292

campaign contributions:
  McCutcheon and, 142–46
  quid pro quo, 143–45
canons of interpretation, 19–20, 56, 77, 78
Cardozo, Benjamin, xix, 109, 166, 263
  on common law, 6
Cargo of the Brig Aurora v. United States, 166
ChatGPT, 32
chemical weapons statutes, 21–22
Chevron U.S.A., Inc. v. National Resources Defense Council, Inc., 175–77
children, minimum wage laws for, 232
Church of the Holy Trinity v. United States, 95–98, 102–3
cigarettes, as delivery devices for nicotine, 38
Citizens United v. FEC, 143–46, 189–90
City of Austin v. Reagan National Advertising, LLC, 155, 158
Civil Rights Act (1964), 243
  Title VII of, 23–24
  Title VI of, 250
civil rights era, 242–43
Civil Rights Movement, 136, 244
Clean Air Act, 167, 168–69, 303
Clean Water Act, 7, 247–50
coal industry, retirement plans of, 98–103
Coal Industry Retiree Health Benefit Act, 98
Cohen, Felix S., 274
Coinbase, Inc. v. Bielski, 255
Coke, Lord Edward, xxv
Cold War, 243
colleges and universities, race-conscious admission policies of, 250
Columba, Saint, xxix
common experience, in statutory law, 34
common law, 5, 6, 8, 9, 10, 14, 255
  canons of interpretation in, 19–20
  incremental approach to, 7, 137, 140
Communists, communism, U.S. racist policies criticized by, 243
compromise, in Supreme Court decisions, 257
Congress, U.S.:
  compromise in, 25
  Constitution's delegation of power to, 119

delegation of judicial powers by, 172–78
intent of, *see* intent, congressional
law-drafting process of, 72–73
powers of, *see* powers, legislative
president's power to remove officers limited
   by, 179–80
public right of petition to, 141–42
regulatory agencies created by, 162–72
sessions of, 198–99
spending power of, 124–25
statues of, *see* statutes (laws), interpretation
   of
workability of, fostered by purpose-oriented
   jurisprudence, 106–7
congressional districts, gerrymandering of, 254
consequences:
   in interpretation of Constitution, 108, 128,
      132, 133, 206, 215–16
   in interpretation of statutes, xvi, 35–36,
      60–61, 63–67
   originalists' discounting of, 132–33
   textualists' discounting of, 17, 28, 216–17
Consolidated Edison Co. v. NLRB, 71
Constitution, U.S.:
   Adjournments Clause in, 203
   amendments to, 113; *see also specific*
      amendments
   American people as party to, 118, 123
   Chief Justice John Marshall's view of, xix,
      111–12, 134
   Due Process Clause of, 90, 92, 115, 173
   Equal Protection Clause of, 135–36, 192,
      241, 250–53
   Establishment Clause of, xvi–xvii, 220–21
   Founders' view of, xxix, 123
   Free Speech Clause of, 140
   general vs. specific language in, 115–16,
      160, 207–8
   lawmaking requirements in, 84
   overview of, 114
   power delegated to Congress by, 119
   Privileges and Immunities Clause of, xxiv
   Recess Appointments Clause of, 197–208
   Religion Clauses in, 140
   as silent on use of legislative history, 85
   states' obligations under, 115; *see also*
      McCulloch v. Maryland
   statutes compared to, 111
   as supreme law of land, 119

three branches of government delineated in,
   114, 160, 162, 171, 173–74, 178–79
values expressed in, *see* values, constitutional
workability as value of, *see* workability, of
   law, as constitutional value
Constitution, U.S., interpretation of, 111–219
   Brown and, 135
   Chief Justice John Marshall and, 134
   Chief Justice John Marshall on traditional
      approach to, 117–23
   different approaches to, 186–87
   Dobbs and, 133–34, 136
   interest-balancing standard and, 129–30,
      209–10, 217–18
   language in, 120, 194
   McCulloch and, 117–23
   McCutcheon and, 142–46
   originalist approach to, *see* originalism,
      originalists
   precedent in, 118
   scrutiny and, 129–30, 146
   Sorrell and, 148–52
   Supreme Court as final word on, xxii, 114
   textualist approach to, *see* textualism,
      textualists, in interpretation of
      Constitution
   tools for, 111, 112
   values in, *see* values, in interpretation of
      Constitution
Consumer Financial Protection Bureau, 179
content-based rules, 153–59
context:
   federal policy as, 35
   in language, 31–32
context, historical, and Second Amendment,
   131–32
context, in statutory law, 4, 14, 16, 33–35
   ambiguous language and, 31–32, 69
   in *Holy Trinity*, 96–98
   legislative history and, 71, 77–79
   in purpose-oriented approach, 78, 89,
      96–98
Coolidge, Calvin, 236, 239
Copeland, Kenneth, 32–33
Copernicus, Nicolaus, 229
costs, use of term, 82–83, 84
County of Maui v. Hawaii Wildlife Fund, 7–10
COVID-19 pandemic, 32–33, 167
   OSHA and, 167–68

Cox, Archibald, Breyer's work for, xviii
Cranmer, Archbishop Thomas, 219–20
Crowell v. Benson, 172, 173
Customs Service, 177
Cuyahoga River, burning of, 249

"Decision Theory of Statutory Interpretation,
    A" (Nourse), 288
deference, judicial, 167, 173, 175–77, 238
democracy, 242, 244
    workability of, *see* workability, of democracy
Depression, Great, 191, 237, 239–41
desegregation, 230
Dictionary Act, 102
"disability," meaning of term, 177
District of Columbia handgun ban:
    conflicting standards and, 213
    Heller and, 210–18
    objective of, 214–15
    predictive judgment and, 214
District of Columbia v. Heller, 126, 130–31,
    209–18, 227, 297
Dobbs v. Jackson Women's Health Organization,
    133–34, 136, 182–84, 187–93, 257–58,
    307, 308
    dissent in, 183, 184
    stare decisis and, 183–84
Douglas, William, 255
Dow Jones Industrial Average, 239
drugs, FDCA definition of, 37
Du Bois, W.E.B., 243
Due Process Clause, 90, 92, 115, 135, 173, 191
due process of law, xvi, 90–92, 115, 135–36,
    173
Duncan v. Walker, 46–50, 280
Dworkin, Ronald, 274

Easterbrook, Frank, 18
economy, U.S., 191
    inequality and, 234
    laissez-faire policy and, 191, 229, 234–36,
        240
    post–Civil War strength of, 233–34
Einstein, Albert, 229
Eisenhower, Dwight, 204, 243
electoral districts, gerrymandering of, 241–42
Elizabeth I, Queen of England, 220
England, religious wars in, 219–20
environmental law, 7–10

Environmental Protection Agency (EPA), 8,
    167, 247, 248, 249
    Chevron and, 175–76
    regulatory powers of, 168–69
    Sackett and, 246–47, 250, 252–54
Epictetus, xix
equality before the law, 242
Equal Protection Clause, 135–36, 192, 241,
    250–53
equal protection of the law, 134–35, 192, 250–53
Establishment Clause, xvi–xvii
    school prayer and, 220–21
    Supreme Court holdings on, 222
executive branch, regulatory agencies as part
    of, 164–65

facts, changes in, *stare decisis* and, 8–9, 187–88,
    189–90, 191–92
Faubus, Orval, 243
FDA v. Brown & Williamson Tobacco Corp, 37–41,
    95
Federal Arbitration Act, 255
Federal Communication Commission, 167
Federal Employees' Compensation
    Commission, 172–73
Federal Food, Drug, and Cosmetic Act, drugs
    and devices defined by, 37
federal government, limited powers of, 118–19
Federalist Papers, 260
Federal Tort Claims Act, 76–77
Federal Trade Commission, and regulation of
    advertising, 156
feedback loop, between legislators and judges,
    textualists' vision of, 25–26
Field, Stephen J., 234–35
Fifth Amendment, 242
    Due Process Clause of, 135
financial crisis of 2008, 35
First Amendment, xxii, 97, 129–30, 140,
    141–42, 146
    Abood and, 190
    Citizens United and, 144
    Janus and, 190
    McCutcheon and, 142–46
    Reagan National Advertising and, 155
    Reed and, 153
    Religion Clauses of, *see* Religion Clauses
    scrutiny and, 146
    Sorrell and, 149–52

as transmission belt, 142, 144–45, 151–52, 155–56
Food and Drug Administration, 33, 81, 95
    in *Brown & Williamson*, 37–41
Ford Motor Company, 235
foreign nations, international organizations compared to, 55–56, 57, 60–61
Foreign Sovereign Immunities Act, 108
    commercial activities exception in, 55
Founders:
    Constitution as viewed by, xxix, 123
    meaning of text as understood by, xx
    recess appointments as understood by, 202–3
    Second Amendment and, 216
    workable Constitution as goal of, 28, 193–94, 259
Fourteenth Amendment, 192, 231, 251
    Dobbs and, 133–34, 308
    Lochner and, 231–33
    Oliver Wendell Holmes on, 232, 238
Fourth Amendment, 129
    Mapp and, 187–88
Framers, original intent of, 139
Frank, Jerome, xxv
Frankfurter, Felix, 179, 238
    on interpretation of statues, xxvi
    purpose-oriented approach of, xix, 5
Freedom of Information Act, 18–19
Free Exercise Clause, Supreme Court holdings on, 222–23
free markets, *see* laissez-faire economics
free trade, 242
French Civil Code, 31
Freund, Paul, 245, 258
Fuller, Lon, xix, 69
"functional equivalent" standard, 8–9

Garcia v. San Antonio Metropolitan Transit Authority, 190
Garner, Bryan, 17, 125, 296
    originalism as defined by, 125
Gilbert, Ariz., Sign Code of, 152–55
Ginsburg, Ruth Bader, 153, 225, 292
Gluck, Abbe, 20, 26, 75–76
Goldberg, Arthur, 243
    Breyer as law clerk for, xviii
Gorsuch, Neil, 26, 168
    on textualism, 16
    West Virginia v. EPA concurrence of, 169

Grapes of Wrath, The (Steinbeck), 239–40
Gratz v. Bollinger, 252
Great Depression, 191, 237, 239–41
Greenspan, Alan, 204
Guiseppi v. Walling, 272
gun control, 126–30
gun deaths, gun violence, 133, 213

habeas corpus petitions, xxiv, 46–50, 108
Hamilton, Alexander, 200
    on *stare decisis*, 181, 193
Hand, Learned, xxvi, 109, 272, 293
"happen," meaning of word, 205–7
"Hard Cases" (Dworkin), 274
Harding, Warren, 236
Harlan, John Marshall, 162
    Lochner dissent of, 232
Harlan, John Marshall, II, 253
Hart, Henry, xix, 137, 263
Harvard College, 250
Health and Human Services Department, U.S., 64–65, 66
Heart of Atlanta Motel, Inc. v. United States, 243
Henry VIII, King of England, 219
historical practice, *Noel Canning* and, 203–8
history:
    legislative, *see* legislative history
    originalists' misuse of, 112
Holmes, Oliver Wendell, 108–9, 111, 142, 263
    on broad powers granted by Constitution, 233
    Lochner dissent of, 232, 238
    overreliance on logic in judicial opinions of, xxv
    purpose-oriented approach of, xix–xx, 5
Homestead Act, 234
Hughes, Charles Evans, 166, 172
    West Coast Hotel opinion of, 240
human rights, 242
    Warren Court's emphasis on, 241–44

imaginative reconstruction, 109, 293
immigrants, government detention and deportation of, 89–93, 289
Immigration and Customs Enforcement, U.S., 93
Immigration & Naturalization Service v. Cardoza-Fonseca, 177
Individuals with Disabilities Education Act, 82

industrialization, post–Civil War, 233–35
inequality, economic, 234
"inferior officers," vagueness of term, 178–80
"intelligible principle" standard, 164, 165–66
intent, congressional, 86–87, 93, 96, 105–6,
    127, 170–71, 176, 280, 286, 290, 292
interest-balancing standard, 129–30, 209–10,
    217–18
  Heller and, 210, 212–18
intermediate scrutiny, 129–30, 147, 149–51,
    209, 212
Internal Revenue Code, 53
international agreements, 242
International Finance Corporation, 56–58
International Organization Immunities Act,
    55, 59, 61
international organizations:
  foreign nations compared to, 55–56, 57,
      60–61
  legal immunity of, 55–62
Interstate Commerce Act, 235
Interstate Commerce Commission, U.S., 162
Iona, Island of, xxix

Jackson, Ketanji Brown, *Students for Fair
    Admissions* dissent of, 251–52
Jackson, Robert H., 271
Jaffe, Louis, 177
James II, King of England, 220
Jam v. International Finance Corp., 55–62, 97
*Janus v. American Federation of State, County, and
    Municipal Employees, Council 31*, 190
Jefferson, Thomas, 123, 205
  on Washington, xxvi
Jennings v. Rodriguez, 91–93, 289, 290
Jim Crow, 192
Johnson, Andrew, recess appointments by, 204
judges:
  accused of lawmaking, 97
  accused of policymaking, 105
  interpretive tools available to, 3–4, 17, 62,
      94, 104–5, 111, 112, 209, 227, 246–49,
      255, 262–63, 272, 321
  legislators' job compared to, 21–22, 26
  paradigm shifts in role of, 229–30
  policymaking by, textualist's rejection of, 18,
      24–25
judicial instinct, xxii, xxv, 94, 102–3, 111, 195,
    200, 262–63

judicial opinions, soundness of, xxv
judicial restraint, 238, 241
Judiciary Act of 1789, 90
jurisprudence, xix
  purpose-oriented approach to, *see* purpose-
      oriented approach
  textualist/originalist approach to, *see*
      originalism, originalists; textualism,
      textualists
Justinian, Roman emperor, legal code of, xxiv,
    141
J. W. Hampton, Jr. & Co. v. United States, 166

Kagan, Elena, 128
  Dobbs dissent of, 134
  Reed concurrence of, 153, 154
  on textualism, 304
Katzmann, Robert A., 272
Kennedy, Anthony, 77, 225–26
Kennedy, Ted, 72
  Breyer's work for, xviii–xix
King v. Burwell, 274
Klarman, Michael J., 298
Knox, Philander, 205

labor unions, 233, 238
laissez-faire economics, 191, 229, 234–36, 240
language:
  artificial intelligence (AI) and, 32
  Chief Justice John Marshall on, 120
  of Constitution, 160, 194
  meaning of, at text's time of writing, 16,
      125–26, 128, 194
language, ambiguous or vague, 11–12, 20, 33,
    50, 67, 84, 93
  in *Brown & Williamson*, 40
  context as tool for interpreting, 31–32, 69
  in *Jam*, 58
  in Second Amendment, 126–28, 129,
      210–11
  in *Wisconsin Central*, 53–54
language, in interpretation of Constitution, in
    Noel Canning, 205–7
Latimer, Bishop Hugh, 219
Law, Pragmatism, and Democracy (Posner), 272,
    274
law-drafting process:
  in Congress, 72–73
  in U.K., 75

laws, *see* statutes (laws), drafting of; statutes
  (laws), interpretation of
legal system, U.S., appellate courts in, *see*
  appellate courts
legislative history, 3, 21, 35, 68–93, 98, 284,
  288
  Ali and, 76
  Barnhart and, 101–3
  Bruesewitz and, 79–82
  Constitution as silent on use of, 85
  criticism of judicial use of, 83–88
  as interpretive tool, 84–85, 86–88
  Jam and, 59–60
  Murphy and, 82–83
  purpose-oriented approach and, 72
  Sorrell and, 150–51
  in statutory law, 35
legislators, 21–22, 26
legislatures, predictive judgments of, 214
Leventhal, Harold, 83–84
liberty, right to, 189, 201
linguistic (semantic) tools, 19–21, 27
Little Rock, Ark., school integration in, 243
Lochner Court, 231–37, 239
Lochner v. New York, 191, 231–33, 235–37, 238

Ma, Kim Ho, 90
Madison, James, 123, 211, 225, 295, 303
major questions doctrine, 168–69, 304
Manning, John, 19, 25, 276
Mapp v. Ohio, 187–88
marketplace of ideas, xxiii, 142, 144, 155
Marshall, George, 242
Marshall, John, 28, 109, 203, 207, 208
  Constitution as viewed by, xix, 111–12,
  134
  on interpretive tools available to judges, 3
  on language, 120
  McCulloch opinion of, xix, xxix, 112, 117–23,
  133
  workability of law emphasized by, 119–23,
  163–64, 172, 194, 257, 259
McCloskey, Robert, 234–35
McConnell, Michael W., 299
*McCreary County v. American Civil Liberties Union
  of Kentucky*, 223–27
McCulloch v. Maryland, xix, xxix, 112, 117–23,
  125, 133, 160, 193–94, 203, 206, 207,
  208, 263

McCutcheon v. Federal Elections Commission,
  142–46
McDonald v. City of Chicago, 130
"meaning," use of term, 23
means-end scrutiny, 127–29
Medicare, 64–65
  reimbursement process of, 66–67
Medicare Act, 66
Merrill, Thomas, 176
militia, in Second Amendment, 130–31,
  210–11, 214, 216
minimum wage laws, 236, 239
  for women and children, 232, 238
Mistretta v. United States, 303
"money," meaning of term, 53–54
Montaigne, Michel de, xxiii–xxiv, 26,
  140–41

NAACP, 243
national bank:
  as exempt from taxation by states, 121
  states' opposition to, *see McCulloch v. Maryland*
National Bank Act, 167
National Childhood Vaccine Injury Act,
  79
*National Federation of Independent Businesses v.
  OSHA*, 167–68
National Labor Relations Act, 238
National Labor Relations Board, 198
National League of Cities v. Usery, 190
Native Americans, displacement of, 234
Nature of the Judicial Process, The (Cardozo),
  xix
"navigable waters," use of term, 247
Neuborne, Burt, 141
New Deal Court, 237–41
New Deal legislation, 237–41
Newton, Isaac, 229
New York State Rifle and Pistol Association v. Bruen,
  126–29, 131–32, 210
New York Stock Exchange, 239
nicotine, addictiveness of, 37, 40
NLRB v. Jones & Laughlin Steel Corp, 238
NLRB v. Noel Canning, 197–208, 227
non-delegation theory, 161, 162, 165–72
North Carolina, University of, 250
notice and comment rulemaking, 64–67
Nourse, Victoria, 14, 288
N.Y. Times Co. v. Sullivan, 300

Occupational Safety and Health Act, 167–68
Occupational Safety and Health
    Administration:
  regulation of testing mandated by, 167–68
  regulatory powers of, 167
O'Connor, Sandra Day, 154
  McCreary concurrence of, 225
"On Experience" (Montaigne), xxiii–xxiv
ordinary person, in textualist opinions, 107
ordinary readers:
  in originalism approach, 112
  statutes as understood by, 14
"Originalism and Desegregation Decisions"
    (McConnell), 299
originalism, originalists, xix, xxi, 27–28, 112,
    124–25, 177–78
  Bolling and, 135–36
  Bruen and, 126–29, 131–32
  clear-cut rules emphasized by, 125, 139–40,
    159, 194
  consequence discounted by, 132–33
  Dobbs and, 133–34, 182, 183–87, 189, 191,
    193–94
  Heller and, 125, 130–31
  limitations of, xxviii, 125, 128–35, 257,
    261–62
  meaning of language at time of writing
    emphasized in, 194
  as paradigm shift, 246–60
  principles of, 16, 125–26
  purpose-oriented approach vs., 256
  stare decisis and, 183
  variations of, 308
  see also textualism, textualists
"Originalism and Stare Decisis" (Barrett), 298
Oxford University, 87

paradigm shifts:
  role of public attitudes in, 258–59
  time and, 255–57
  use of term, 229
paradigm shifts, in Supreme Court, *see*
    Supreme Court, U.S., paradigm shifts in
*Parents Involved in Community Schools v. Seattle
    School District No. 1*, 252
Patent and Trademark Office, U.S., 42, 179
patent law, 42–46
"person," use of term in patent cases, 43–46
petition, right of, 141–42

pharmaceutical industry, regulation of,
    148–52
Pierce, Richard, 174
*Planned Parenthood of Southeastern Pennsylvania v.
    Casey*, 182–84, 188–93
Plessy v. Ferguson, 192, 241, 251
policy, as context, 35
Portalis, Jean-Étienne-Marie, 31
Posner, Richard A., 272, 274, 293
Post, Robert, 236
Postal Service, U.S., 43–44
Powell, Lewis, 250
powers, checked and balanced system of, 303
powers, executive, appointment and dismissal
    of officers in, 178–80
powers, judicial, delegation of, 172–78
powers, legislative, delegation of, 160–72
  non-delegation theory and, *see* non-
    delegation theory
powers, separation of, 107, 114, 160–61, 162,
    171, 173–74, 178–79, 288
pragmatism, judicial, xxi, 5, 10–11, 14–15,
    273–74
  see also purpose-oriented approach
prayer, in public schools, 220–21
precedent, 11
  in constitutional cases, 118
  in *Holy Trinity*, 96
  in interpretation of Constitution, 187
  in statutory law, 34
  see also stare decisis
predictive judgments, 214
president, recess appointments by, *see* recess
    appointments
press, freedom of, 141–42
prices, regulation of, 233
Principles of Scientific Management (Taylor), 235
privacy, personal, 139, 150, 182, 183–84, 230,
    242, 244
privacy, right of, 242, 244
Privileges and Immunities Clause, xxiv
"Problems of a Functional Jurisprudence,
    The" (Cohen), 274
pro forma sessions, 199, 206, 207
Progressivism, 235
proportionality, *see* interest-balancing standard
proportionality standard, 209, 211, 212,
    215–16, 217
protected speech, *see* speech, freedom of

public attitudes:
    influence on Supreme Court of, 244–45
    paradigm shifts and, 258–59
Public Company Accounting Oversight Board, 179
public support, Supreme Court's dependency on, 260
Pufendorf, Samuel von, 70, 96
purpose-oriented approach, xvi, 33–36
    in *Ali*, 107
    in *Allina Health*, 65–67
    arguments in favor of, 104–9
    in *Barnhart*, 101–3
    Breyer's adoption of, xvi, xx, 261–63
    conflicting results of textual reading vs., 94–103
    constitutional values and, 89–93
    context and, 78, 89, 96–98
    in *County of Maui*, 7–10
    in *Duncan*, 48–50, 280
    flexible language in, 10
    general principles of, xxvi–xxvii, 5–15
    in *Heller*, 209–18
    in *Holy Trinity*, 96–98
    in interpretation of Religion Clauses, 223–27
    in *Jam*, 56, 58–62
    legislative history and, 72
    longstanding tradition of, 108–9
    in *McCreary County*, 223–27
    in *McCulloch*, 121–22
    as more complex than other methods, xxvii
    more workable Congress promoted by, 106–7
    in *Noel Canning*, 197, 200–202, 206–8
    reasonable legislator and, xvi, 5, 11–15, 19, 27, 36
    in *Return Mail*, 45–46
    role of legislative history in, 86–87
    in *Sackett*, 253–54
    in *Students for Fair Admissions*, 253–54
    textualism/originalism vs., xvi, xx–xxi, xxvii, 3–4, 17–18, 20, 42–50, 54, 256, 259–60, 272
    as traditional method of interpretation, xix–xx, xxi, xxvi–xxvii
    in *Van Orden*, 225–27
    workable democracy fostered by, xxviii, xxix, 62, 88, 97, 105
purposivism, *see* purpose-oriented approach

"Putting Legislative History to a Vote" (Manning), 288

quid pro quo corruption, 143–45

racism, 243
    see also segregation
Radcliffe, Lord Cyril John, 220
railroad rates, regulation of, 161–72
Railroad Retirement Tax Act, 51–52
Ramos v. Louisiana, 189
"rational basis" standard, 147, 148, 209, 212
Reading Law (Scalia & Garner), 17, 125, 296
reasonable legislator, xvi, 5, 11–15, 19, 27, 36, 171, 176
Recess Appointment Clause, 197–208
recess appointments, 197–208
    Founders' interpretation of, 202–3
    inter-session, 198–99, 201, 202, 204–5
    intra-session, 198–206
    meaning of "happen" in, 205–7
Reed v. Town of Gilbert, 152–55, 158
reference canon, 56–57, 58–59
Regents of the University of California v. Bakke, 250
Rehnquist, William, 69, 123, 152, 225–26
    on *stare decisis*, 181
Religion Clauses, 140–42
    historical context of, 219–21
    see also Establishment Clause; Free Exercise Clause
remuneration, money vs. nonmonetary, 52
Return Mail, Inc. v. United States Postal Service, 42–46
    definition of "person" in, 43–45
Ribnik v. McBride, 233
Ridley, Bishop Nicholas, 219
rigidity, of rules, 146
Riviera Beach, Fla., Lozman's lawsuits against, xxiv, 269
Roberts, John:
    Students for Fair Admissions opinion of, 250–51
    on *West Coast Hotel*, 240
Roberts, Owen, xxvii, 238
Rockefeller, Jay, 101
Roe v. Wade, 182, 188–93
Roosevelt, Franklin D., 59, 239, 240
    "court packing" plan of, 237
Roosevelt, Theodore, recess appointments by, 204–5

rule of law, 193, 244, 257, 260
rules:
    Citizens United and, 143–45
    content-based, 153–59
    definition of, 137
    McCutcheon and, 142–46
    Montaigne on dangers of, xxiii, xxiv, 26,
        140–44
    problems with, 140–59, 163–64
    rigidity of, 146
    Sorrell and, 148–52
    standards vs., 137–38, 140–41
    textualism's emphasis on, xxiv, xxviii, 6, 17,
        23–25, 28, 136–59, 193, 195
rules, formulated by federal agencies,
        63–67
    legislative vs. interpretive, 64
    notice and comment process in, 64–67
Ryle, Gilbert, 87, 288

Sackett v. EPA, 246–47, 250, 252–54
Sacks, Albert, xix, 137, 263
Sanford, Edward, 232
Santa Barbara Channel, oil spill in, 249
Scalia, Antonin, 25, 33, 70, 79, 113, 159, 208,
        225–26
    Breyer's good-natured debate with, 139–40
    Heller opinion of, 130, 210
    on *Holy Trinity* decision, 97
    Noel Canning concurrence of, 200
    on originalism, 17, 125, 296
    originalism as defined by, 125
    rules favored over standards in Supreme
        Court opinions of, 138–39
    science of statutory interpretation proposed
        by, 25
    on textualism, 16–17
    on use of legislative history, 35, 68, 71
Schiller, Friedrich, 220
schools, public:
    prayer in, 220–21
    segregation in, 243
scrutiny:
    intermediate, 129–30, 147, 149–51, 209,
        212
    means-end, 127–29
    strict, 129–30, 146–48, 153–54, 155, 156,
        209, 212, 250
search and seizure, unreasonable, 129

Second Amendment:
    ambiguous language in, 126–28, 129,
        210–11
    Bruen and, 126–28, 210
    gun control and, 126–30
    Heller and, 209–18
    historical context of, 131–32, 211–12
Securities and Exchange Commission, 151
segregation, 135, 192, 242, 243
    Tocqueville on, 252
semantic (linguistic) tools, 19–21, 27
Senate, U.S.:
    Judiciary Committee of, xviii, 22–23, 72
    pro forma sessions of, 199, 206, 207
"separate but equal" doctrine, 135, 192, 241
separation of church and state, xvii, 219,
        221–22
separation of powers, 107, 114, 160–61, 162,
        171, 173–74, 178–79, 197, 201, 288, 303,
        306
Sherman Antitrust Act, 235
signatory operators, use of term, 98–102
Sixth Amendment, *Ramos* and, 189
Slocum, Brian, 14
Smoot-Hawley Tariff, 240
Social Security, 52–53
    coal industry retirement plans overseen by,
        98–103
Social Security Act, 66, 177
Social Security Administration, 179
Sorrell v. IMS Health Inc., 148–52
Sotomayor, Sonia, 128
    Dobbs dissent of, 134
    Students for Fair Admissions dissent of, 251–52
Souter, David, 77, 225, 255
sovereign immunity, 55
Spanish flu pandemic, 236
speech, content-based restriction on, 154–59
speech, freedom of, xxii–xxiii, 116, 129, 140,
        149–52, 155–56, 194, 300
    McCutcheon and, 142–46
    restrictions on, 141, 154–59
    Sorrell and, 148–52
    Sullivan and, 300
stability, legal, 11, 181, 193
    as goal of *stare decisis*, 181, 184
    originalism's undermining of, 194
    textualism's undermining of, 113, 125, 185,
        189, 258

standards:
  definition of, 137
  rigidity of, 146
  rules vs., 137–38, 140–41
stare decisis, 11, 28, 134, 181–94
  Dobbs and, 183–84
  legal stability as goal of, 181, 184
  originalism's undermining of, 194
  principled departures from, 187–93
  textualism's undermining of, 258
  textualist/originalist approach to, 181,
    183–94
  see also precedent
Statute of Northampton, 131, 132
statutes (laws), drafting of:
  in Congress, 72–73
  in U.K., 75
statutes (laws), interpretation of, 31–109
  ambiguous language in, *see* language,
    ambiguous or vague
  common experience in, 34
  compromise and, 11–12
  congressional intent and, *see* intent,
    congressional
  consequences in, xvi, 35–36, 60–61, 63–67
  Constitution compared to, 111
  context in, *see* context, in statutory law
  County of Maui and, 7–10
  interpretive conventions and, 75–76
  legislative history and, *see* legislative history
  narrow vs. broad rulings on, 6–7
  ordinary citizens' understanding of, 106
  ordinary reader and, 14
  overly specific, xxiv–xxv
  precedent and, 34
  purpose-oriented approach to, *see* purpose-
    oriented approach
  reasonableness in, 67, 70–71, 72, 108, 147,
    157
  static vs. dynamic, 51–62
  "super," 292
  textualist approach to, *see* textualism,
    textualists, in interpretation of statutes
  traditional use of text and purpose in, 95
  voters and, 12–13
  workability of, 97
Steinbeck, John, 239–40
Stevens, John Paul, 77, 216, 225
  Barnhart dissent of, 101–2, 292

Chevron opinion of, 176
  Heller dissent of, 130, 210, 211
stock options, as employee compensation,
    52–54
Stone, Harlan Fiske, 233
Story, Joseph, 162
strict scrutiny, 129–30, 146–48, 153–54, 155,
    156, 209, 212, 250
*Students for Fair Admissions, Inc. v. President and
    Fellows of Harvard College*, 246, 250–54,
    320
substantive legal standard, use of term, 65
successor in interest, use of term, 99–102
Sumner, William Graham, 234–35
Sunstein, Cass, 186–87
"super-statutes," 292
Supreme Court, U.S.:
  cases taken up by, 31
  compromise in decisions of, 257
  FDR's "court packing" plan for, 237
  as final word on Constitution's meaning,
    xxii, 114
  importance of clearly written decisions in,
    xxiii
  influence of prevailing public attitudes on,
    244–45
  judicial restraint policy and, 238
  need for compromise in, xxiii
  new Justices' adjustment to, 255–56
  public support needed by, 260
  Religion Clauses cases in, 220–27
  as special legal institution, xxii–xxiii
  unanimous decisions of, 291
Supreme Court, U.S., paradigm shifts in,
    229–30
  Lochner Court, 231–37, 239
  New Deal Court, 237–41
  textualist/originalist approach to, 246–60
  Warren Court, 241–45
Sutherland, George, 232, 236
  West Coast Hotel dissent of, 239

Taft, William Howard, 162, 164, 236
  Adkins dissent of, 232
Taylor, Frederick, 235
Telecommunications Act, 167
Ten Commandments, government display of,
    xviii–xix, 223–27
Test Act (English), 220

textualism, textualists, xxviii
clear-cut rules emphasized by, xxiv, xxviii, 6,
17, 23–25, 28, 136–59, 193, 195
consequences discounted by, 17, 28,
216–17
fairer rulings promised by, 26
growth of, xx–xxi, xxvii
limitations of, xx–xxi, xxviii, 27–29, 257,
261
meaning of language at time of writing
emphasized in, 16, 194
ordinary person invoked by, 107
as paradigm shift, 246–60
principles of, 16–29
purpose-oriented approach vs., xvi, xx–xxi,
xxvii, 3–4, 17–18, 20, 42–50, 54, 256,
259–60, 272
"single-right-answer" doctrine of, 23, 24
see also originalism, originalists
textualism, textualists, in interpretation of
Constitution, xvi–xvii, 111, 112–13,
124–59
in *Bruen*, 129, 131–32
in *Coinbase*, 255
and delegation of judicial powers, 172–73,
177–78
in *Dobbs*, 182–84, 187–93, 257
in *Heller*, 210–18
legal stability undermined by, 185
legislative powers and, 160–72, 177–78
in *McCutcheon*, 142–46
in *McDonald*, 130
in *NFIB v. OSHA*, 168
in *Noel Canning*, 201–2
in *Sackett*, 247–48
stare decisis and, 181, 183–87
in *Students for Fair Admissions*, 251, 254
in *West Virginia v. EPA*, 168–69
"wrongly decided" argument in, 183–85,
187, 189, 191, 193
textualism, textualists, in interpretation of
statutes, xvi
in *Allina Health*, 65, 67
in *Barnhart*, 100, 101, 292
in *Bruesewitz*, 80
canons of interpretation in, 19–20
in *Chevron*, 175
conflicting results of purpose-oriented
reading vs., 94–103

in *Duncan*, 48, 50
feedback loop between legislators and judges
envisioned by, 25–26
in *Jam*, 56–58
judges accused of policymaking by,
105
judicial policymaking rejected by, 18,
24–25
linguistic (semantic) tools in, 19–21, 27
as obstacle to more workable democracy,
29, 105–6
in *Return Mail*, 43, 44
and static vs. dynamic interpretation of
statutes, 51
in *Wisconsin Central*, 52–53
Thayer, James Bradley, 186
Thomas, Clarence, 168, 225–26
County of Maui dissent of, 9
Students for Fair Admissions concurrence of,
250
Thomas Aquinas, Saint, 108
Thurmond, Strom, 72
time:
and new Justices' adjustment to Court's
methods and mores, 255–56
paradigm shifts and, 255–57
tobacco industry, 33, 37–41
Tobia, Kevin, 14
Tocqueville, Alexis de, 219
on role of judiciary, 263
on segregation, 252
tools:
interpretive, 3–4, 17, 62, 94, 104–5, 111,
112, 209, 227, 246–49, 255, 262–63, 272,
321
linguistic (semantic), 19–21, 27
Treasury Department, U.S., 177
Truman, Harry S., 242
on foreign aid, 242, 318–19
Twitter, Inc. v. Taamneh, 254–55

unanimity, in Court decisions, 291
unemployment rate, 239
Uniform Commercial Code, 6
United Kingdom, political and judicial systems
of, 74–75, 107
United Nations, 61, 242
United Nations Relief and Rehabilitation
Administration (UNRRA), 59–60

United States:
   gun deaths and gun violence in, 133, 213, 313
   "waters" of, 247–49
United States Code, 43, 102
United States v. Carolene Products Co., 238
United States v. Mead Corp., 177
United States v. Riverside Bayview Homes, Inc., 249, 250

values:
   in interpretation of statutes, xvi, xxv, 93, 104–5
   language and, 26
   purpose-oriented approach and, 29, 104–5
values, constitutional, xvi, xxi, xxv, xxviii, xxix, 36, 89–93, 94, 141, 145–46, 151, 154–55, 158, 159, 194, 208, 209, 227
   in Religion Clauses cases, 219–27
   stare decisis and, 181–82
   workability as, 28–29, 111–12, 113, 122–23, 133, 139, 140, 160, 161, 172, 178, 179, 180, 187, 190, 193, 223
values, in interpretation of Constitution, xxviii, xxix
   in *Heller,* 209–18
   stare decisis in, 188–90, 192
Van Orden v. Perry, 225–27
Vermont, *Sorrell* and, 148–52
voters, federal statutes and, 12–13
Voting Rights Act, 254

Walker, Sherman, 47–50
Wallop, Malcolm, 101
Warren, Earl, 241
Warren, E. Walpole, 95
Warren Court, 241–45
Washington, George, Jefferson on, xxvi
Watergate scandal, xviii
"waters of the United States," 247–49

West Coast Hotel Co. v. Parrish, 191–92, 239, 240
West Virginia Board of Education v. Barnette, 271
West Virginia v. EPA, 168
Westward expansion, 233–34
wetlands, 247–50
"What Divides Textualists from Purposivists?" (Manning), 276
Wiener v. United States, 180
Wilson, Harold, 21
Wirt, William, 205–6
Wisconsin Central Ltd. v. United States, 51–54
   textualist approach to, 52–53
Wisdom, John Minor, xxvii
women:
   abortion rights of, *see* abortion rights
   minimum wage laws for, 232, 238
   rights of, 133, 182–84, 187–93, 242, 257–58
workability, of democracy, 263
   purpose-oriented approach as fostering, xxviii, xxix, 62, 88, 97, 105
   textualism as obstacle to, 29, 105–6
workability, of law, 196, 241
   as central issue in *McCulloch,* 118, 120–22, 193–94
   Chief Justice John Marshall's emphasis on, 119–23, 163–64, 172, 194, 257, 259
   as constitutional value, 28–29, 111–12, 113, 122–23, 133, 139, 140, 160, 161, 172, 178, 179, 180, 187, 190, 193, 223
   as Founders' goal, 28, 193–94, 259
   Heller and, 209–18
   Noel Canning and, 197–208
   Religion Clauses and, 219–27
   stare decisis and, 182
   of statutes, 97
World War I, 235, 236
World War II, 242

Zadvydas v. Davis, 89–91, 92, 289